PHILLIP HESTER

OVERSIGHT™

SHORT STORIES 1990-2005

DESPERADO
PUBLISHING

Joe Pruett
Publisher

April Doster
Creative Director

Nate Pride
Production

Ian Feller
Media Liaison

Marco White
Web Designer

Joe Karg
Production Assistant

51 South Peachtree Street
Suite 8
Norcross, GA 30071

www.desperadopublishing.c

Erik Larsen
Publisher

Eric Stephenson
Executive Director

Allen Hui
Production Artist

Traci Hui
Administrative Assistant

Todd McFarlane
President

Jim Demonakos
PR & Marketing Coordinator

Joe Keatinge
Traffic Manager

Image Comics, Inc.
1942 University Ave.
Suite 305
Berkeley, CA 94704

Marc Silvestri
CEO

Mia MacHatton
Accounts Manager

Jonathan Chan
Production Assistant

Jim Valentino
Vice-President

Laurenn McCubbin
Art Director

Drew Gill
Production Assistant

www.imagecomics.com

image ®

I was wrong.

Many of the stories you are about to read, or at least start to, were done fairly early in my career as a funnybook maker. At the time I felt my destiny was to become a well respected, well paid mainstream super hero artist the likes of Alan Davis or Jim Lee. The fact that I could not draw as well as those gentlemen never pierced my fog of self deception. The stories in this collection were larks, sideshows, passing nods to some dark artistic impulse I needed to purge on my way to the *Wizard* top ten list. My real work was the super hero stuff- the paying gigs!

Well, I was wrong. Really wrong. Looking back objectively, my super hero work from the same era is completely forgettable. This stuff- these short stories more accurately reflected my skills and goals as a storyteller, for better or worse.

I sort of developed a bifurcated career. One track led to fame and fortune with shiny super heroes and the other to critical success with dark, personal, impenetrable tone poems. Simultaneously the sellout superstar and brooding outsider genius, my goal was to be published in *Raw* and *The Avengers* in the same calendar year. The thing is, it's not a put on. My dream comic book really is equal parts Jack Kirby's *Eternals* and Charles Burns' *Black Hole*. Hopefully, the two dozen or so of you out there that share this aesthetic are now holding this collection. I hope you enjoy it.

Nearly twenty years later I'm still straddling those two paths, but when I look ahead now I see them starting to meander towards each other on the horizon.

But I've been wrong before.

Phil Hester,
Iowa

Many thanks to Joe Pruett, not only for putting this together, but for prodding me back on the right path when I needed it.

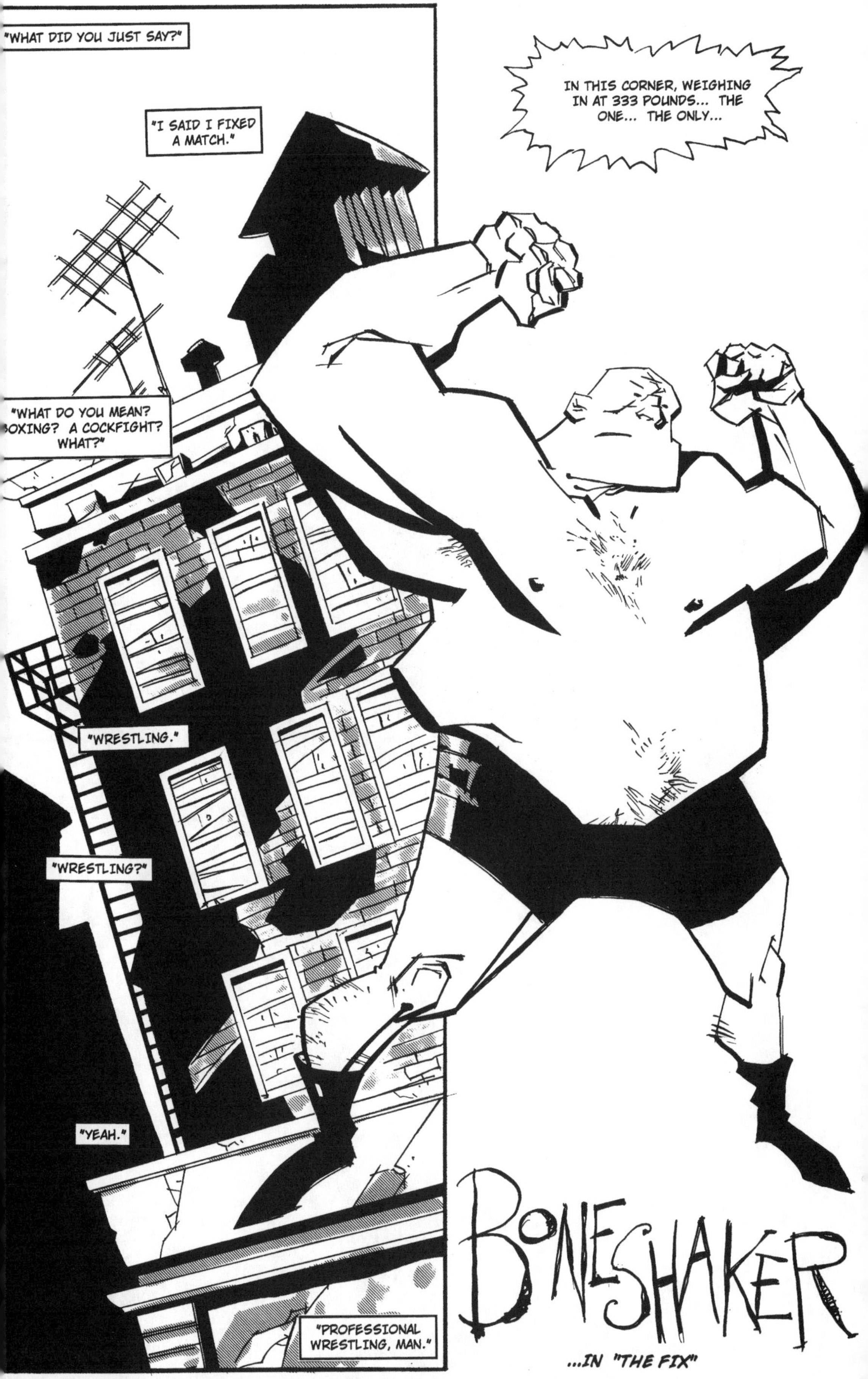
"WHAT DID YOU JUST SAY?"
"I SAID I FIXED A MATCH."
IN THIS CORNER, WEIGHING IN AT 333 POUNDS... THE ONE... THE ONLY...
"WHAT DO YOU MEAN? BOXING? A COCKFIGHT? WHAT?"
"WRESTLING."
"WRESTLING?"
"YEAH."
"PROFESSIONAL WRESTLING, MAN."
BONESHAKER
...IN "THE FIX"

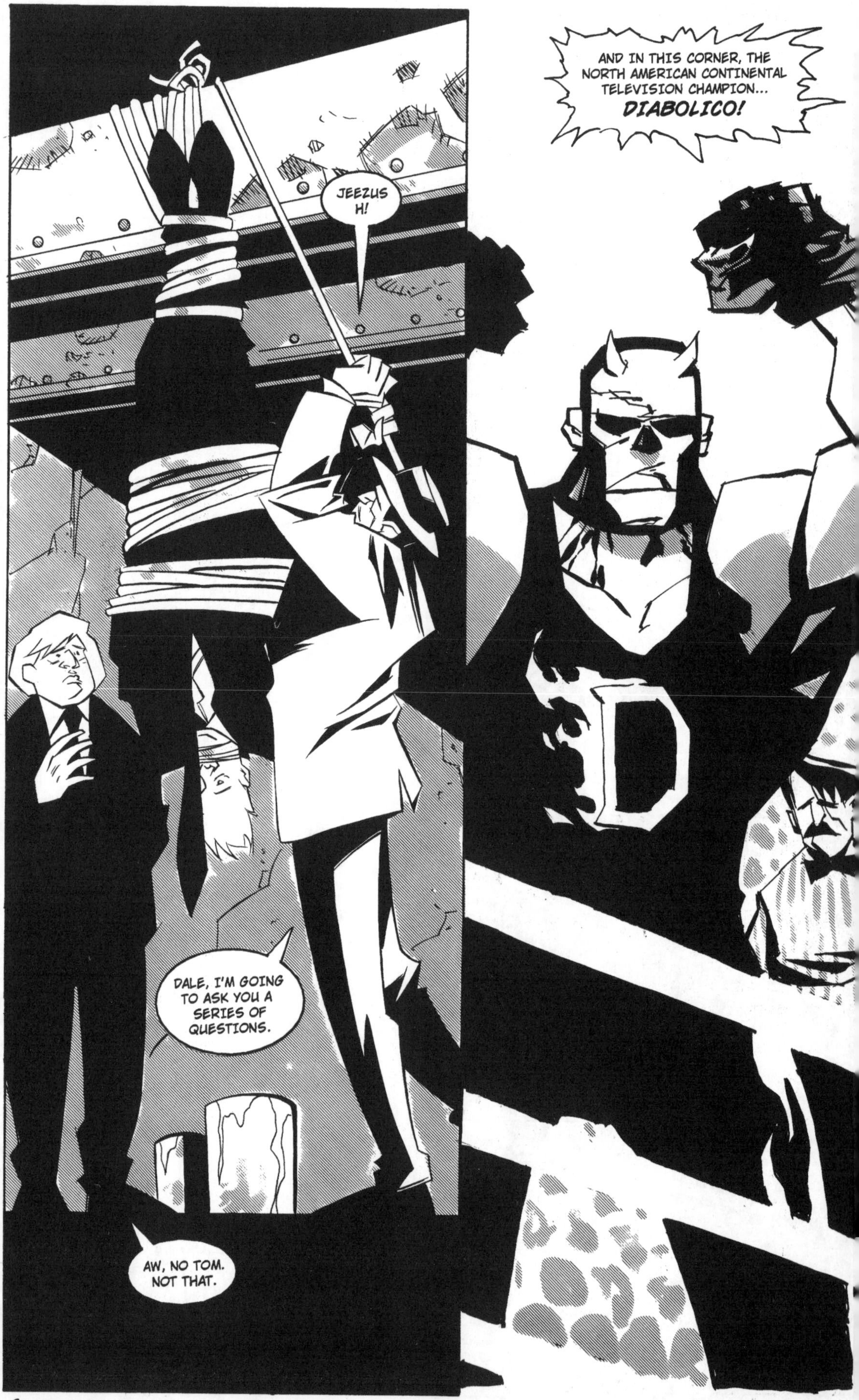
JEEZUS H!
DALE, I'M GOING TO ASK YOU A SERIES OF QUESTIONS.
AW, NO TOM. NOT THAT.
AND IN THIS CORNER, THE NORTH AMERICAN CONTINENTAL TELEVISION CHAMPION... DIABOLICO!

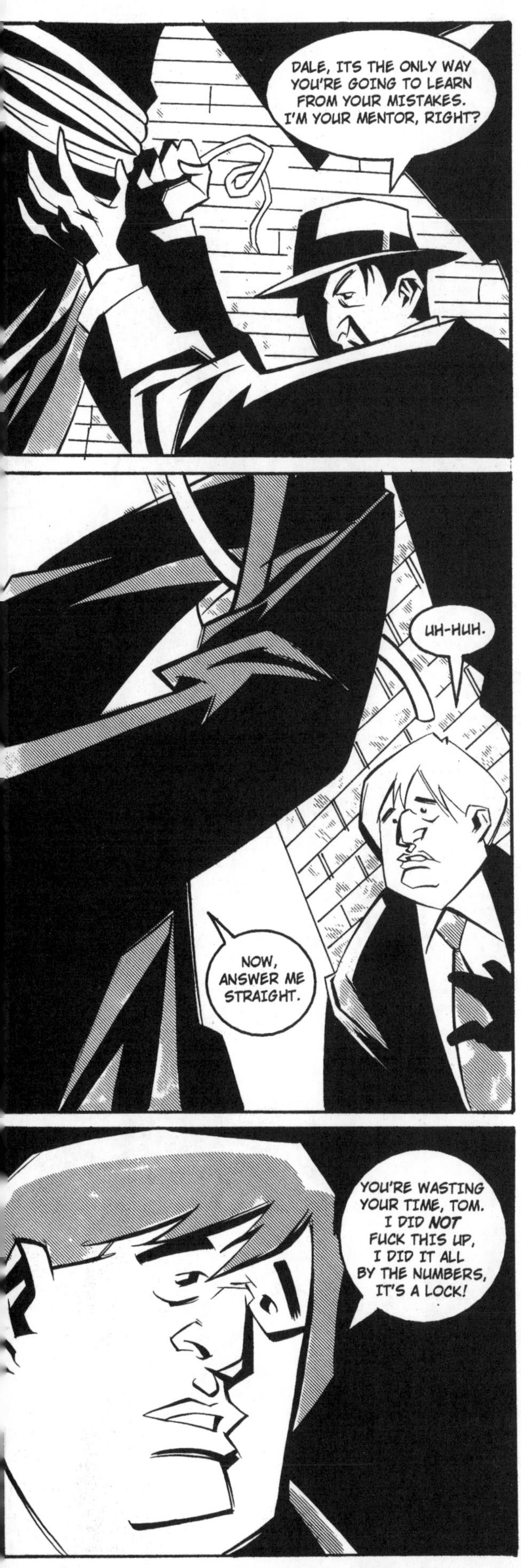
DALE, ITS THE ONLY WAY YOU'RE GOING TO LEARN FROM YOUR MISTAKES. I'M YOUR MENTOR, RIGHT?
UH-HUH.
NOW, ANSWER ME STRAIGHT.
YOU'RE WASTING YOUR TIME, TOM. I DID ***NOT*** FUCK THIS UP, I DID IT ALL BY THE NUMBERS, IT'S A LOCK!

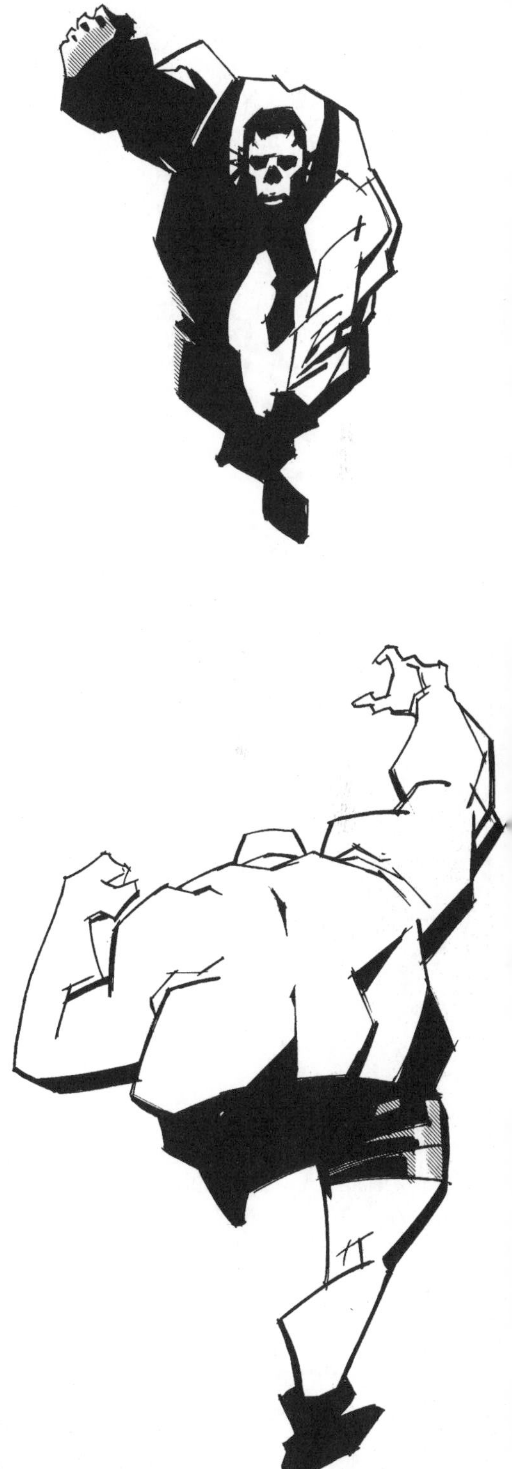

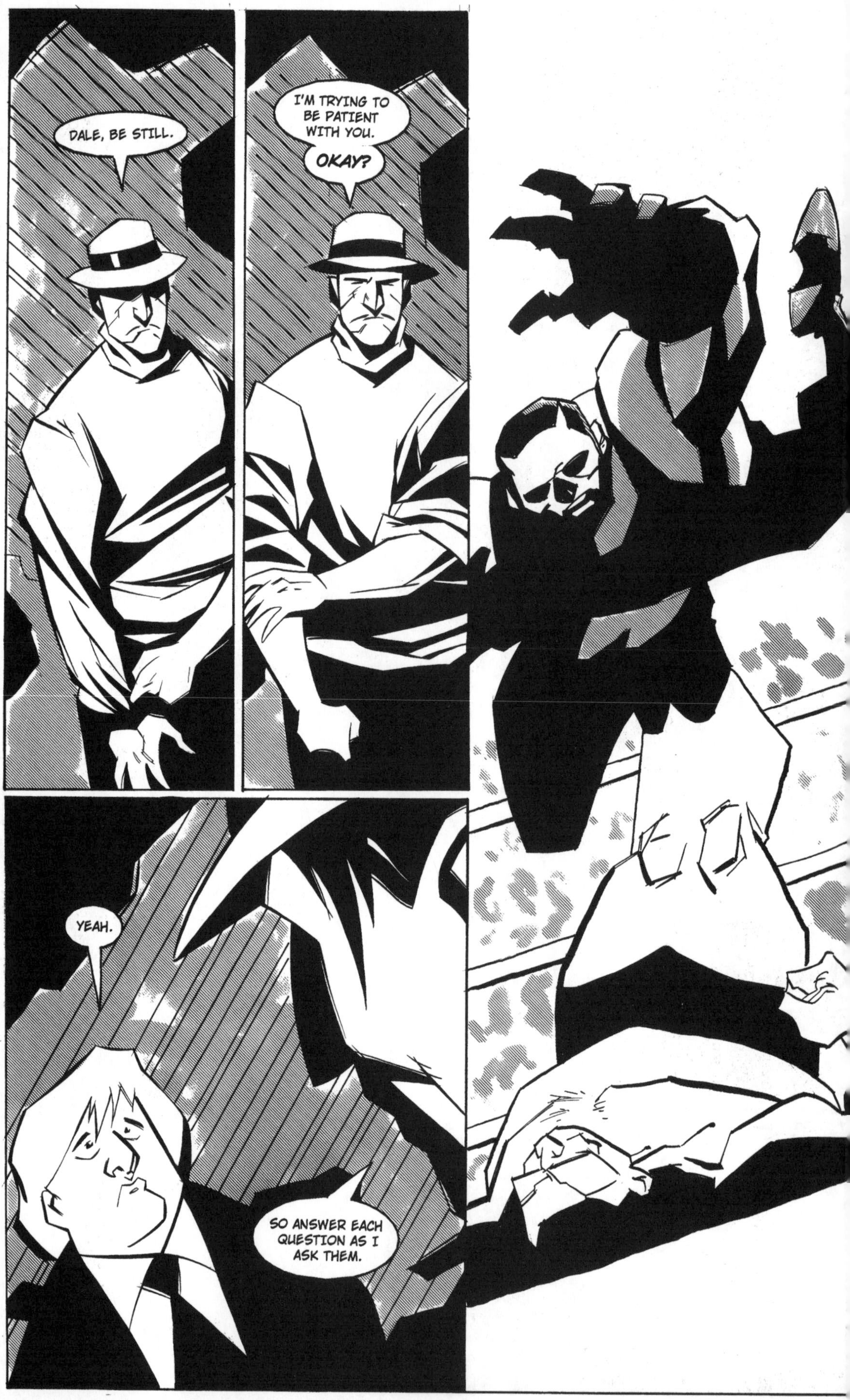
DALE, BE STILL.
I'M TRYING TO BE PATIENT WITH YOU.
OKAY?
YEAH.
SO ANSWER EACH QUESTION AS I ASK THEM.

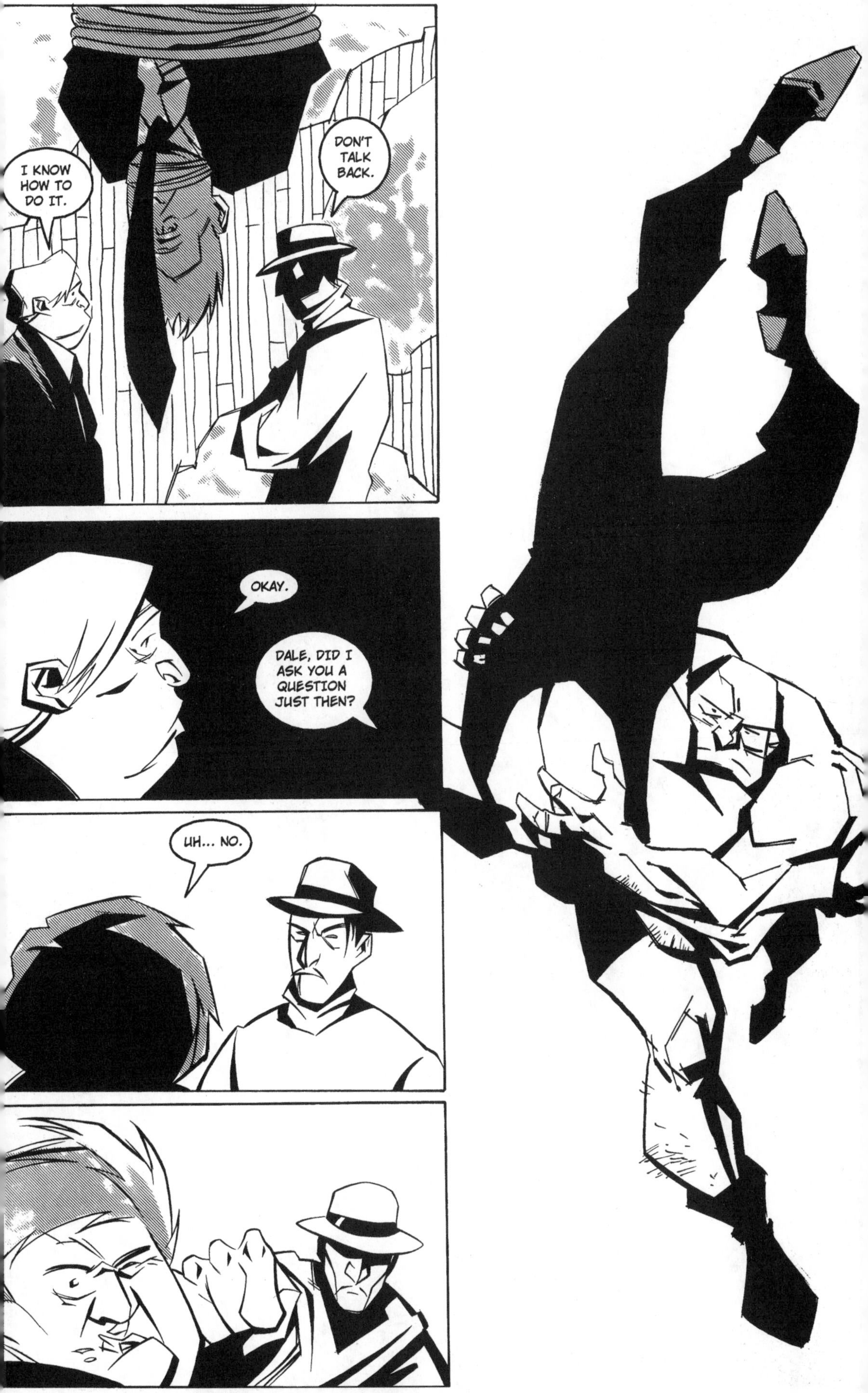
I KNOW HOW TO DO IT.
DON'T TALK BACK.
OKAY.
DALE, DID I ASK YOU A QUESTION JUST THEN?
UH... NO.

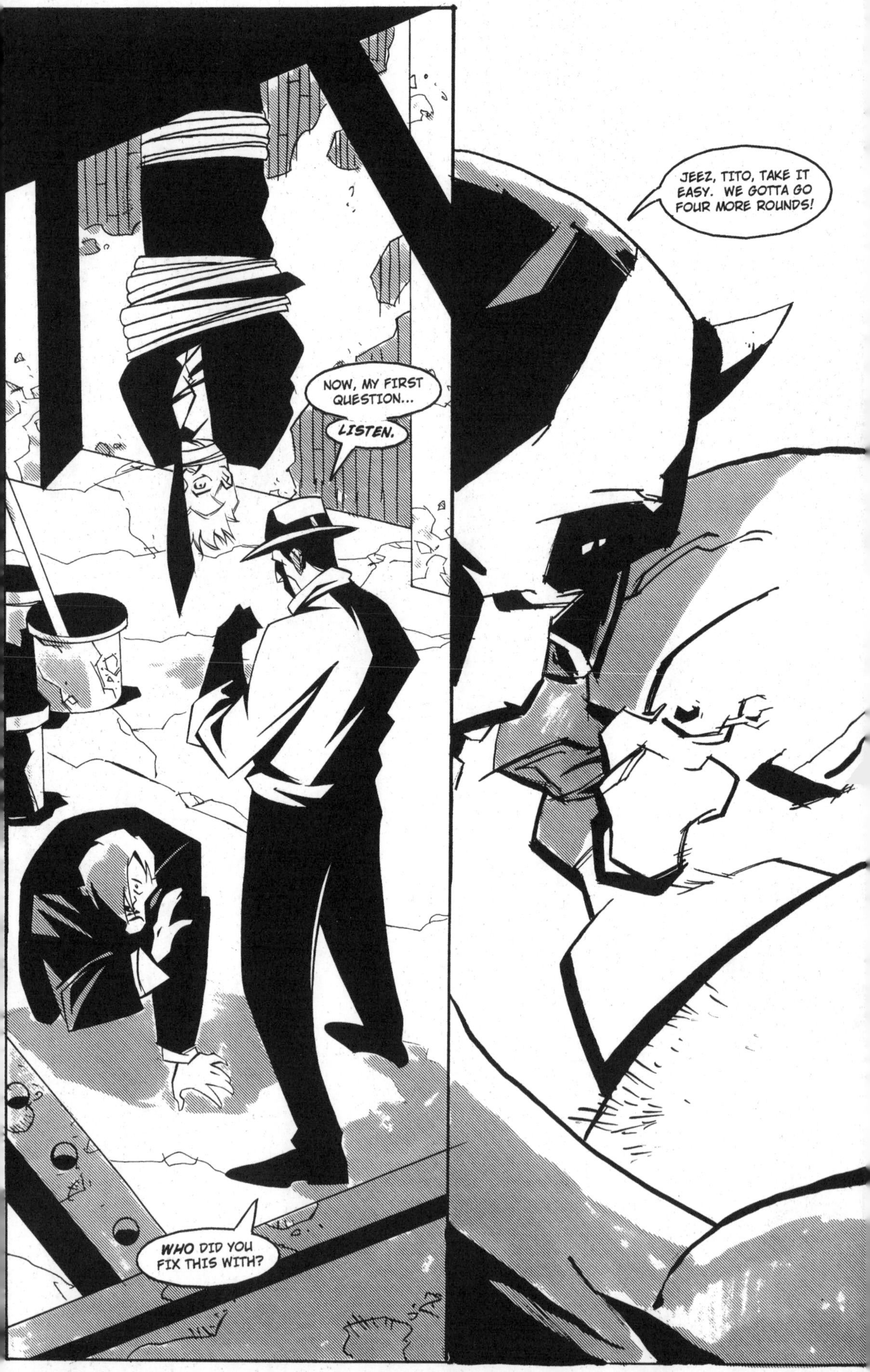
NOW, MY FIRST QUESTION...
LISTEN.
WHO DID YOU FIX THIS WITH?
JEEZ, TITO, TAKE IT EASY. WE GOTTA GO FOUR MORE ROUNDS!

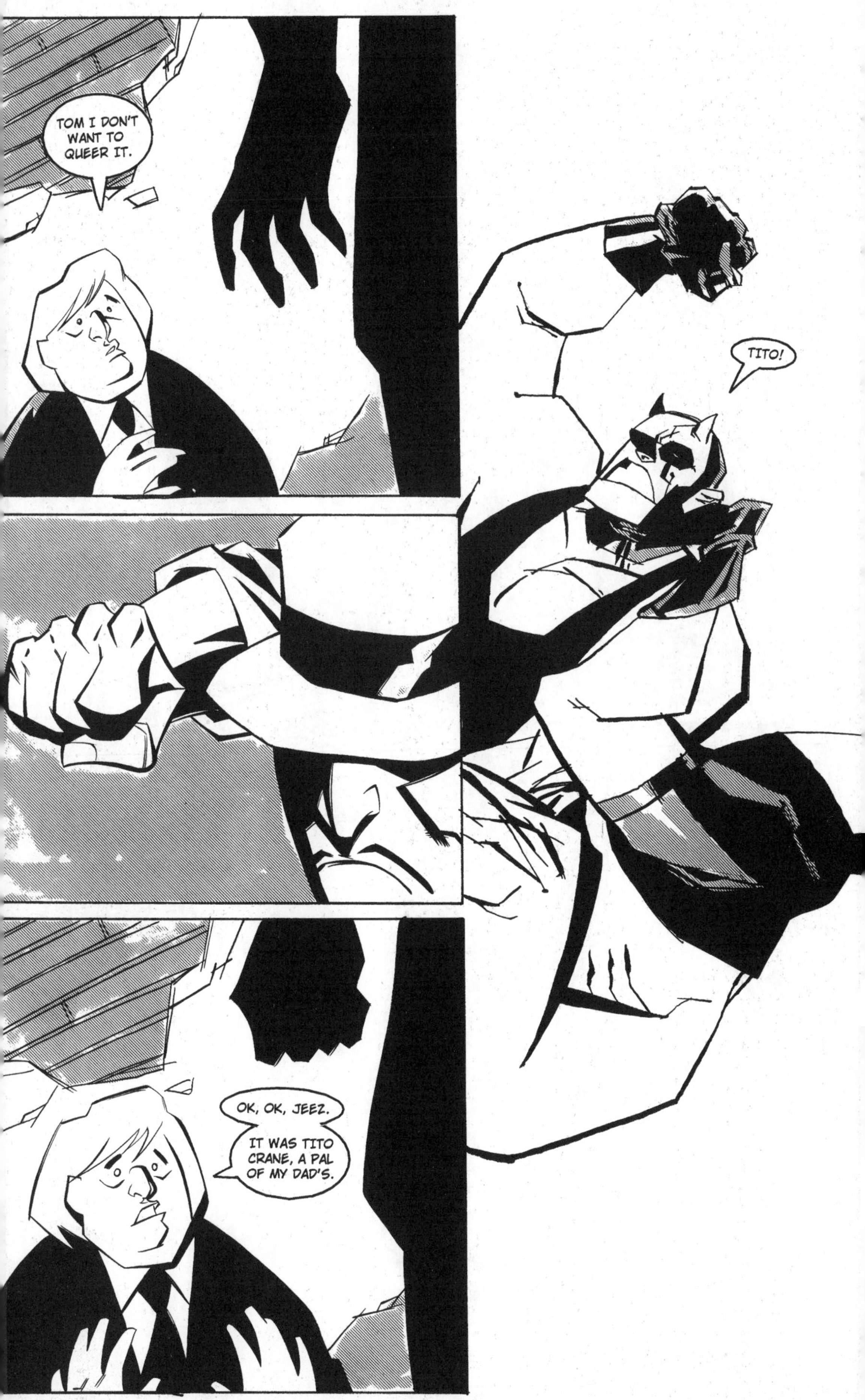
TOM I DON'T WANT TO QUEER IT.
TITO!
OK, OK, JEEZ.
IT WAS TITO CRANE, A PAL OF MY DAD'S.

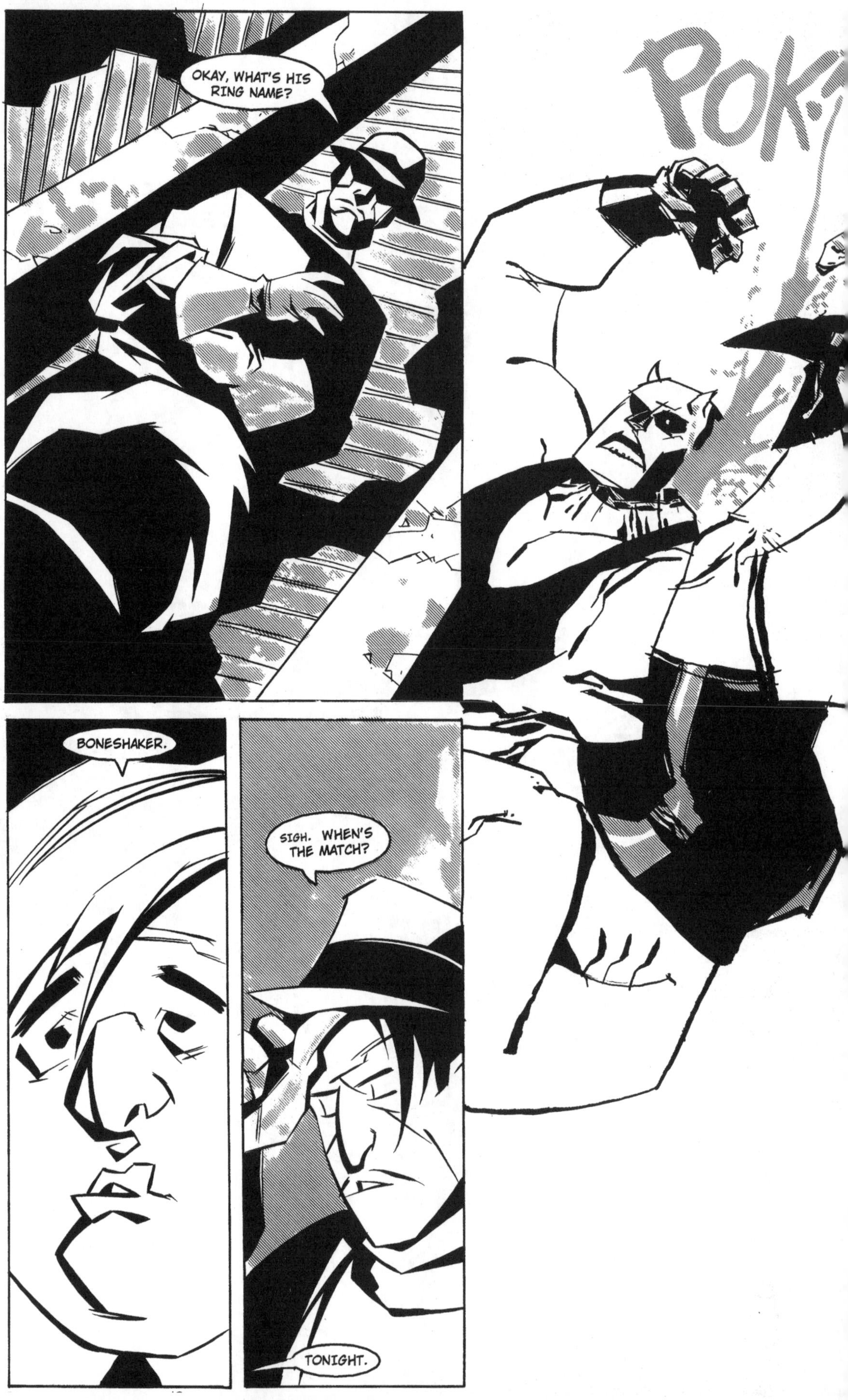
OKAY, WHAT'S HIS RING NAME?
POK-
BONESHAKER.
SIGH. WHEN'S THE MATCH?
TONIGHT.

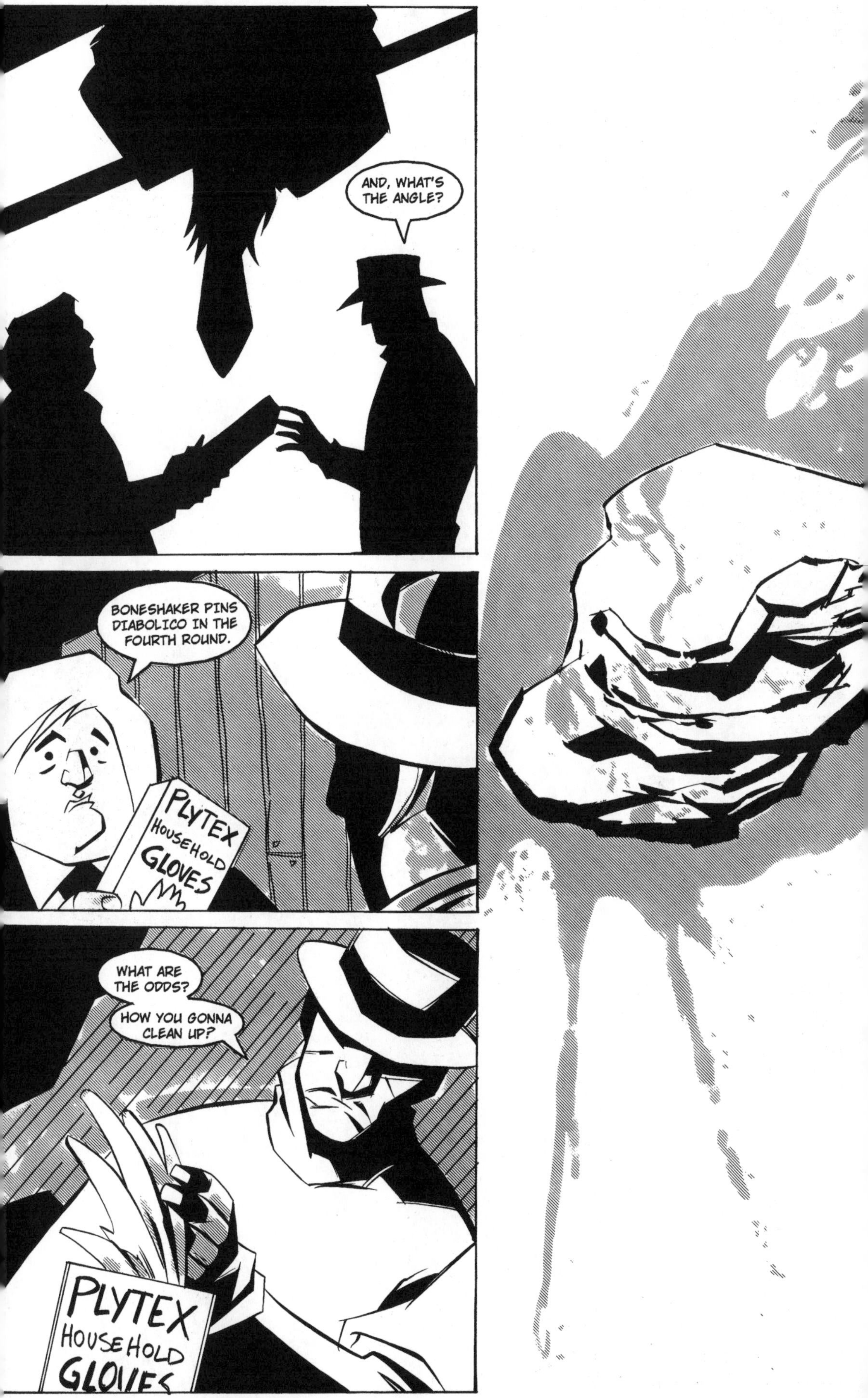
AND, WHAT'S THE ANGLE?
BONESHAKER PINS DIABOLICO IN THE FOURTH ROUND.
PLYTEX HOUSEHOLD GLOVES
WHAT ARE THE ODDS?
HOW YOU GONNA CLEAN UP?
PLYTEX HOUSEHOLD GLOVES

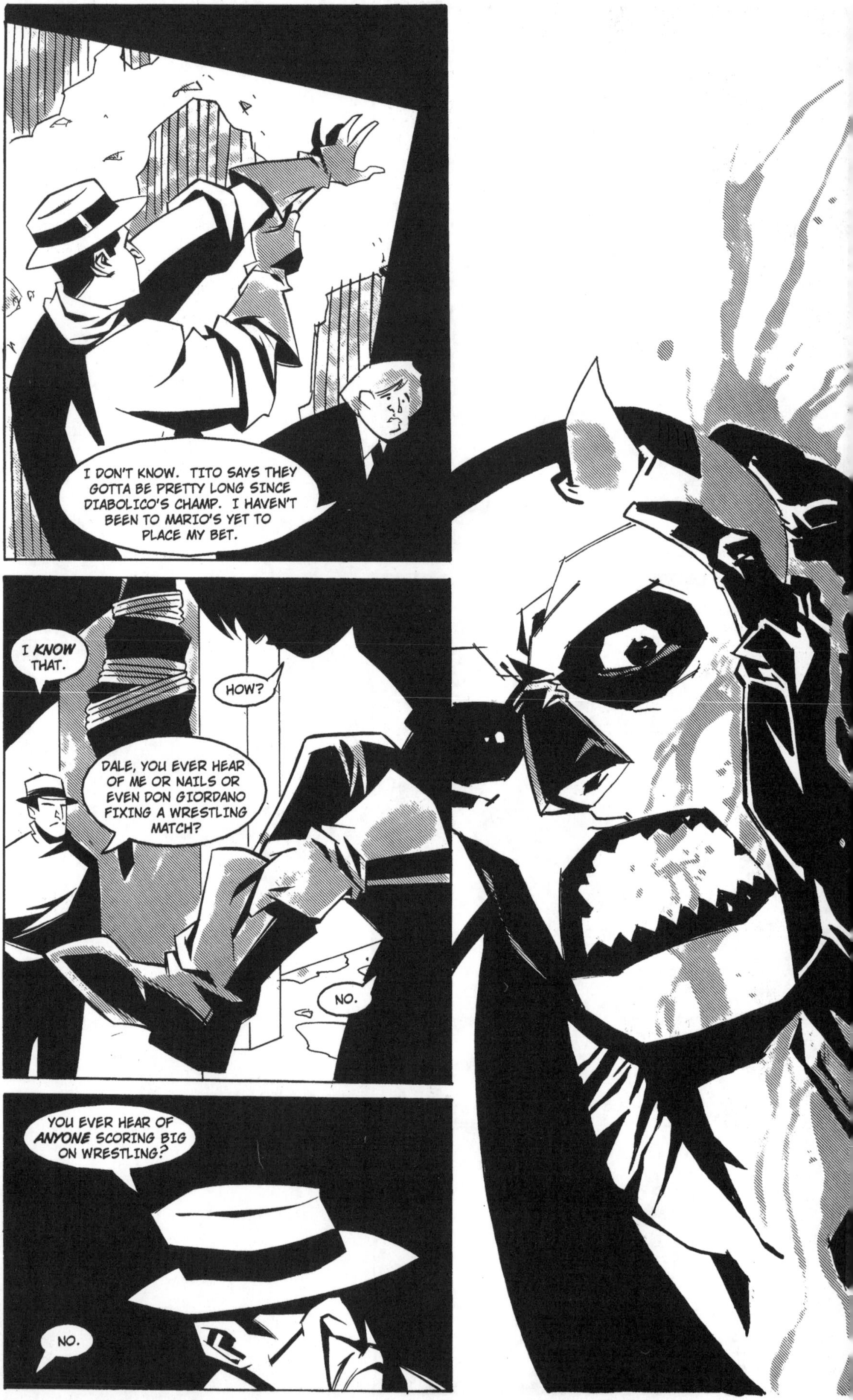
I DON'T KNOW. TITO SAYS THEY GOTTA BE PRETTY LONG SINCE DIABOLICO'S CHAMP. I HAVEN'T BEEN TO MARIO'S YET TO PLACE MY BET.
I *KNOW* THAT.
HOW?
DALE, YOU EVER HEAR OF ME OR NAILS OR EVEN DON GIORDANO FIXING A WRESTLING MATCH?
NO.
YOU EVER HEAR OF *ANYONE* SCORING BIG ON WRESTLING?
NO.

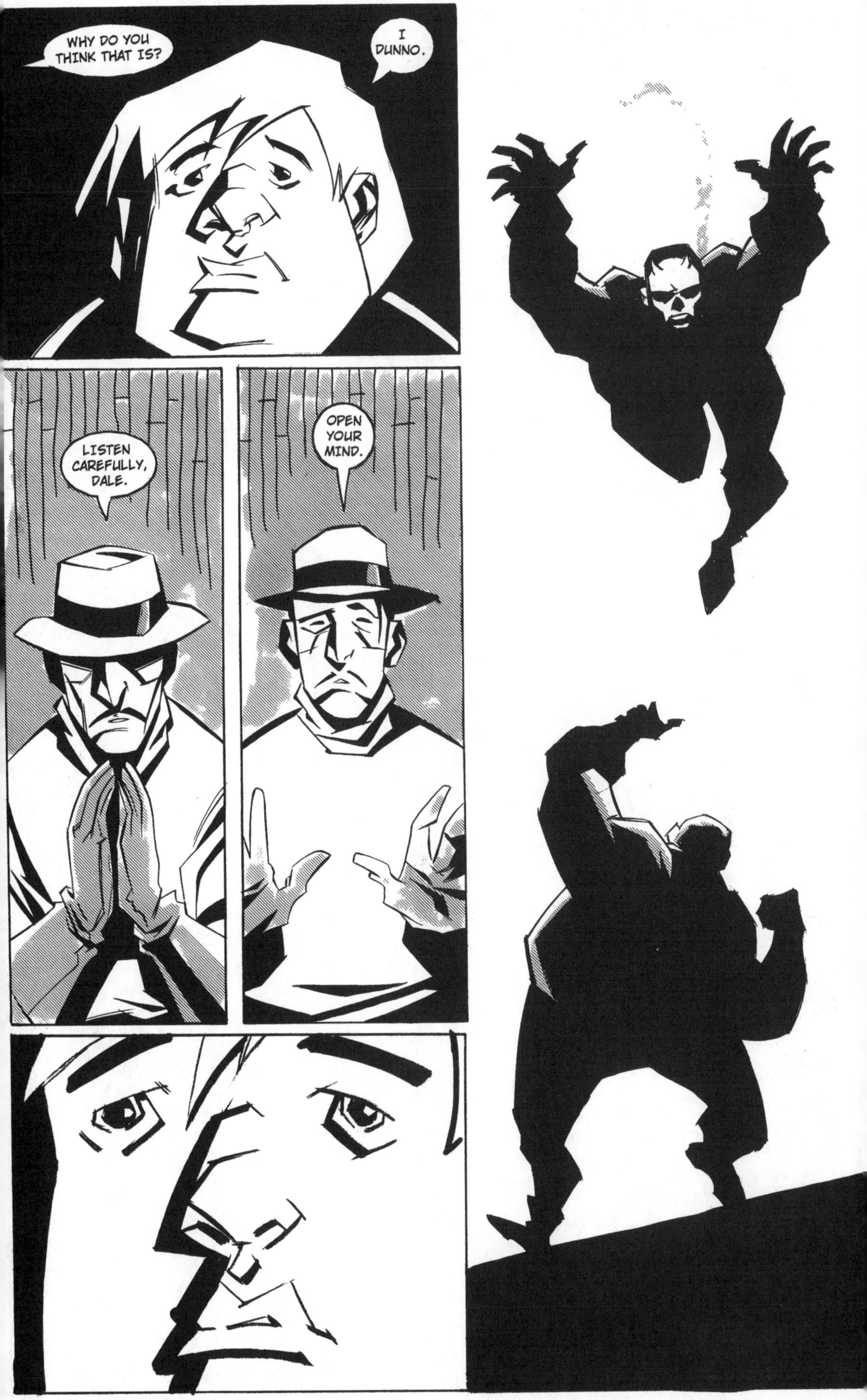
WHY DO YOU THINK THAT IS?
I DUNNO.
LISTEN CAREFULLY, DALE.
OPEN YOUR MIND.

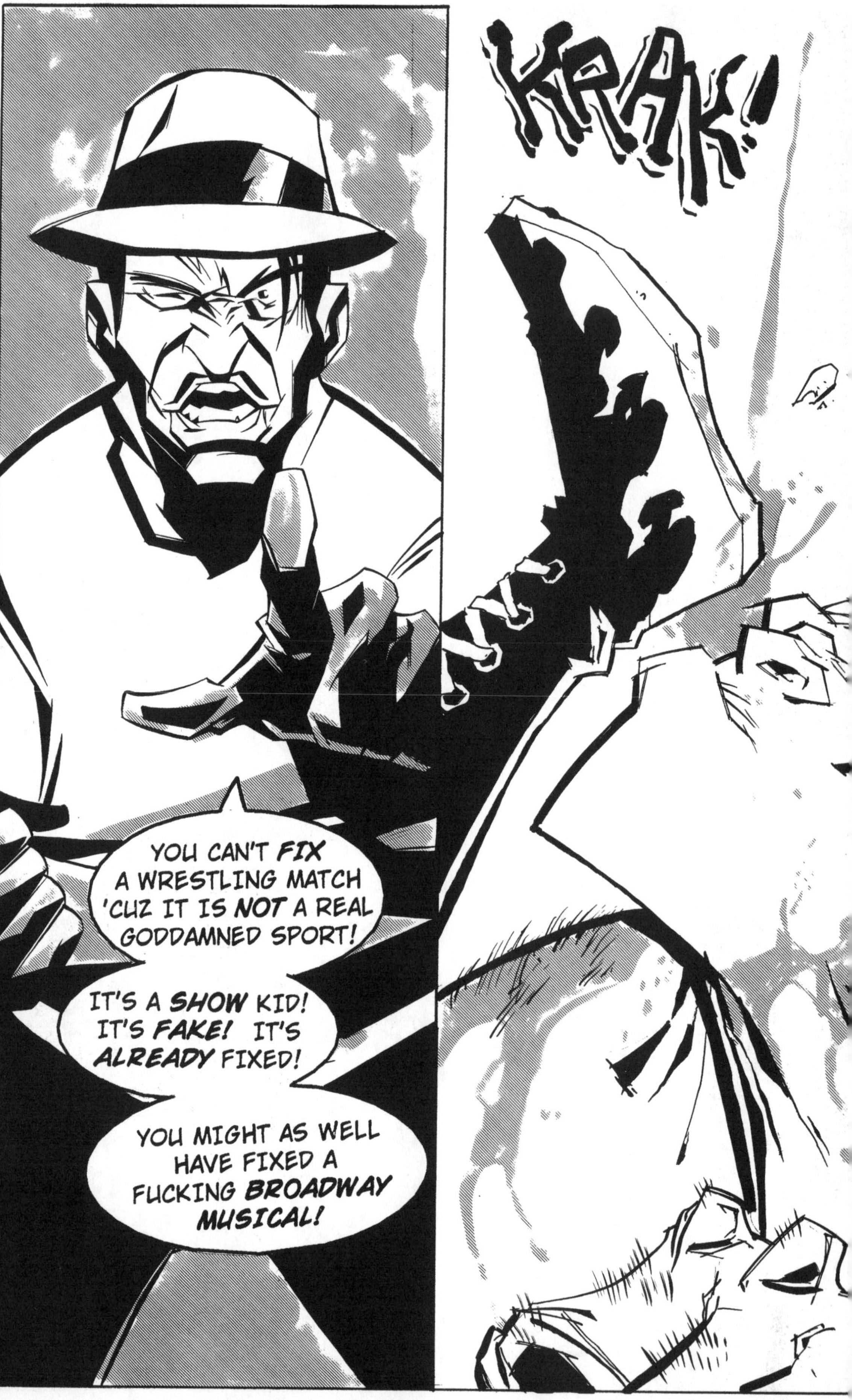
YOU CAN'T FIX A WRESTLING MATCH 'CUZ IT IS NOT A REAL GODDAMNED SPORT!
IT'S A SHOW KID! IT'S FAKE! IT'S ALREADY FIXED!
YOU MIGHT AS WELL HAVE FIXED A FUCKING BROADWAY MUSICAL!
KRAK!

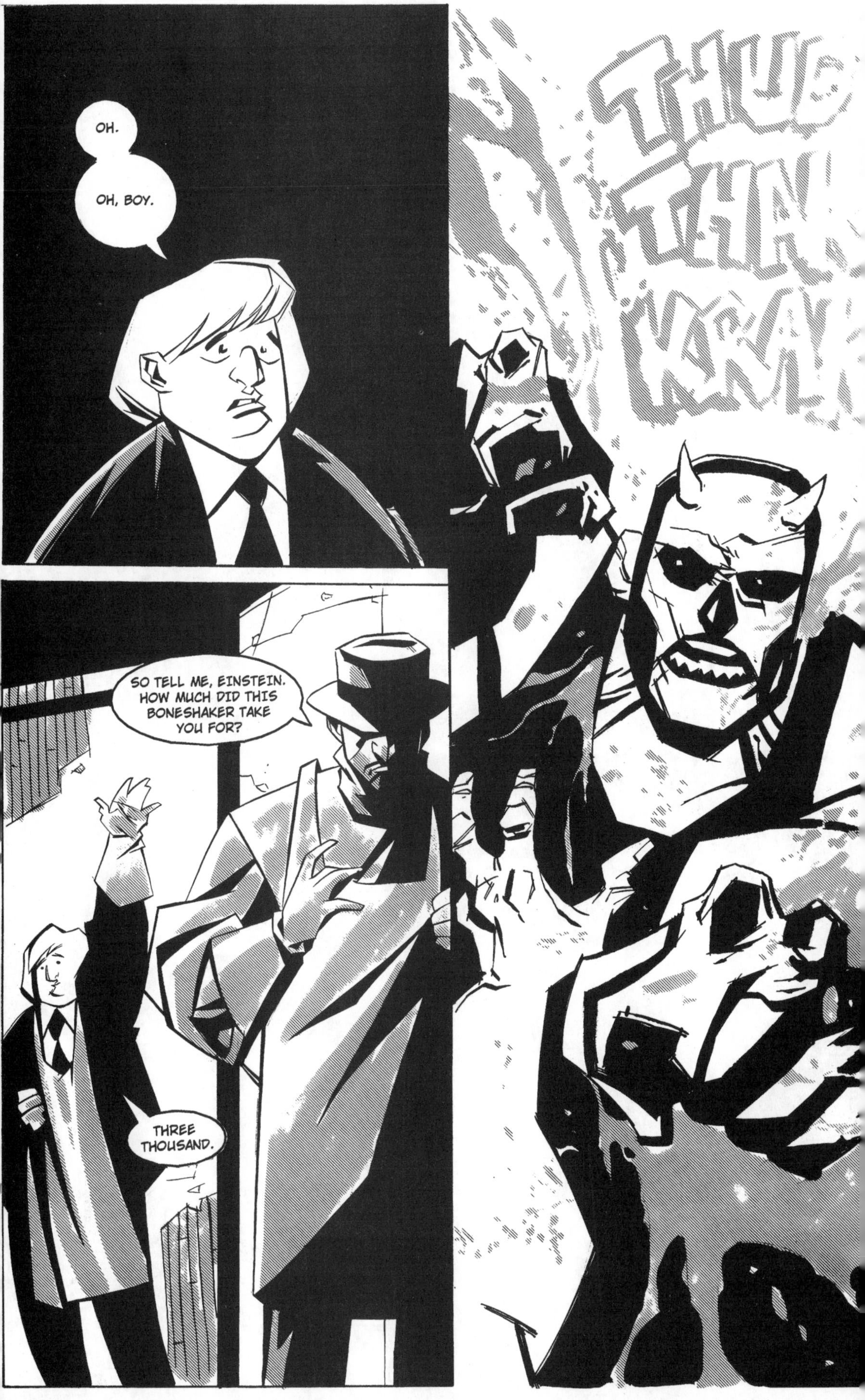
OH.
OH, BOY.
SO TELL ME, EINSTEIN. HOW MUCH DID THIS BONESHAKER TAKE YOU FOR?
THREE THOUSAND.

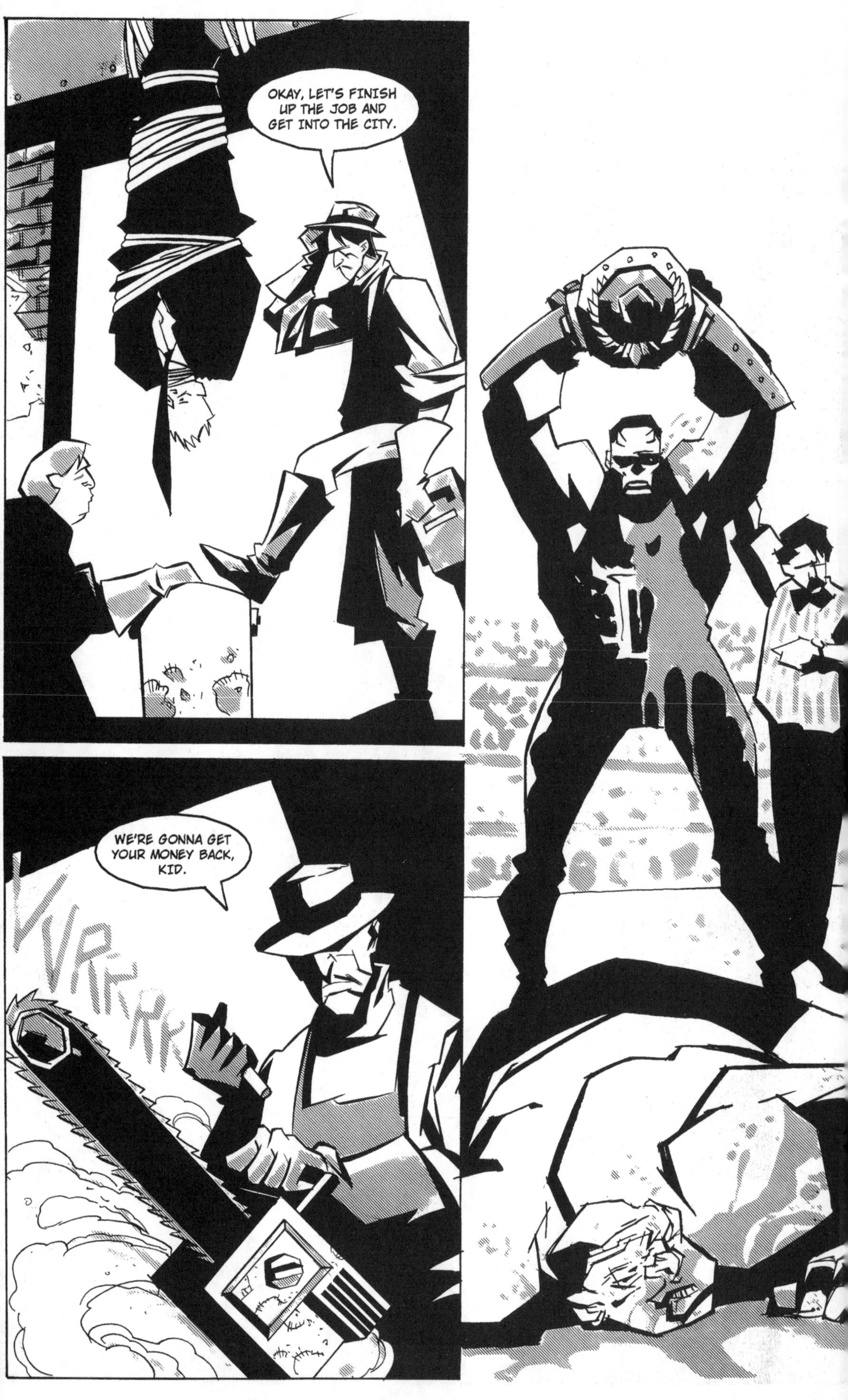
OKAY, LET'S FINISH UP THE JOB AND GET INTO THE CITY.
WE'RE GONNA GET YOUR MONEY BACK, KID.
VRRRRR

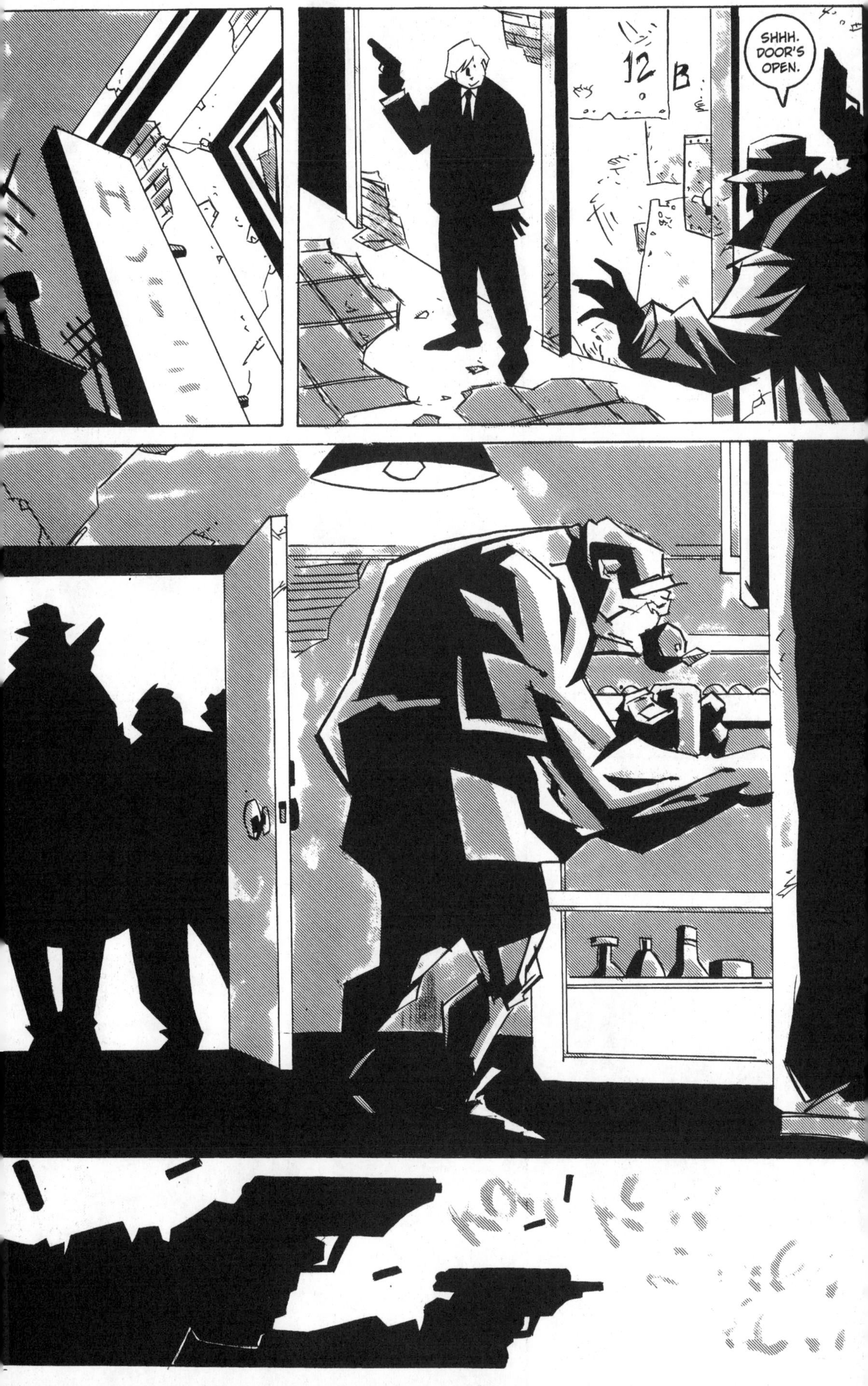
12 B
SHHH. DOOR'S OPEN.

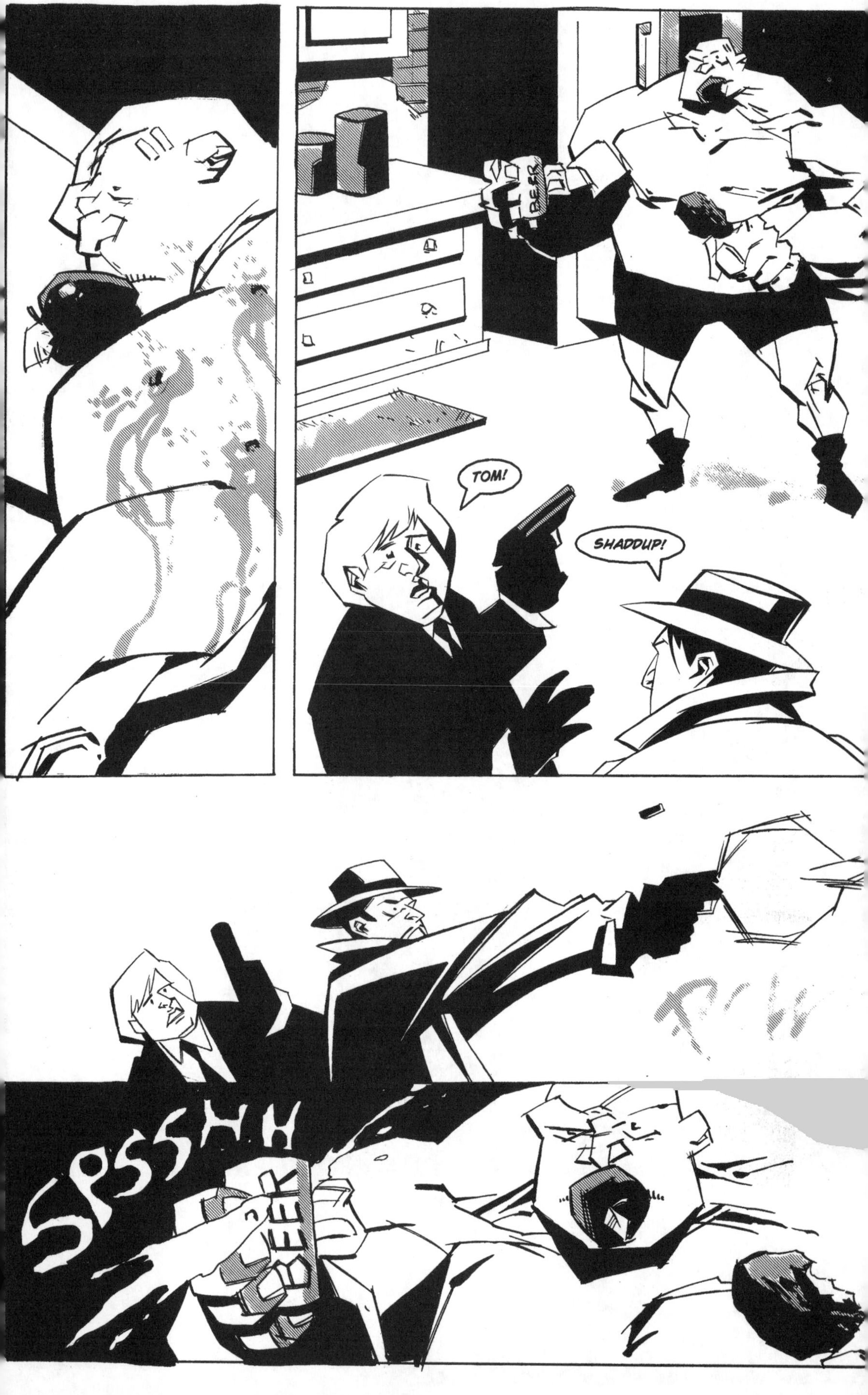
TOM!
SHADDUP!
SPSSHH

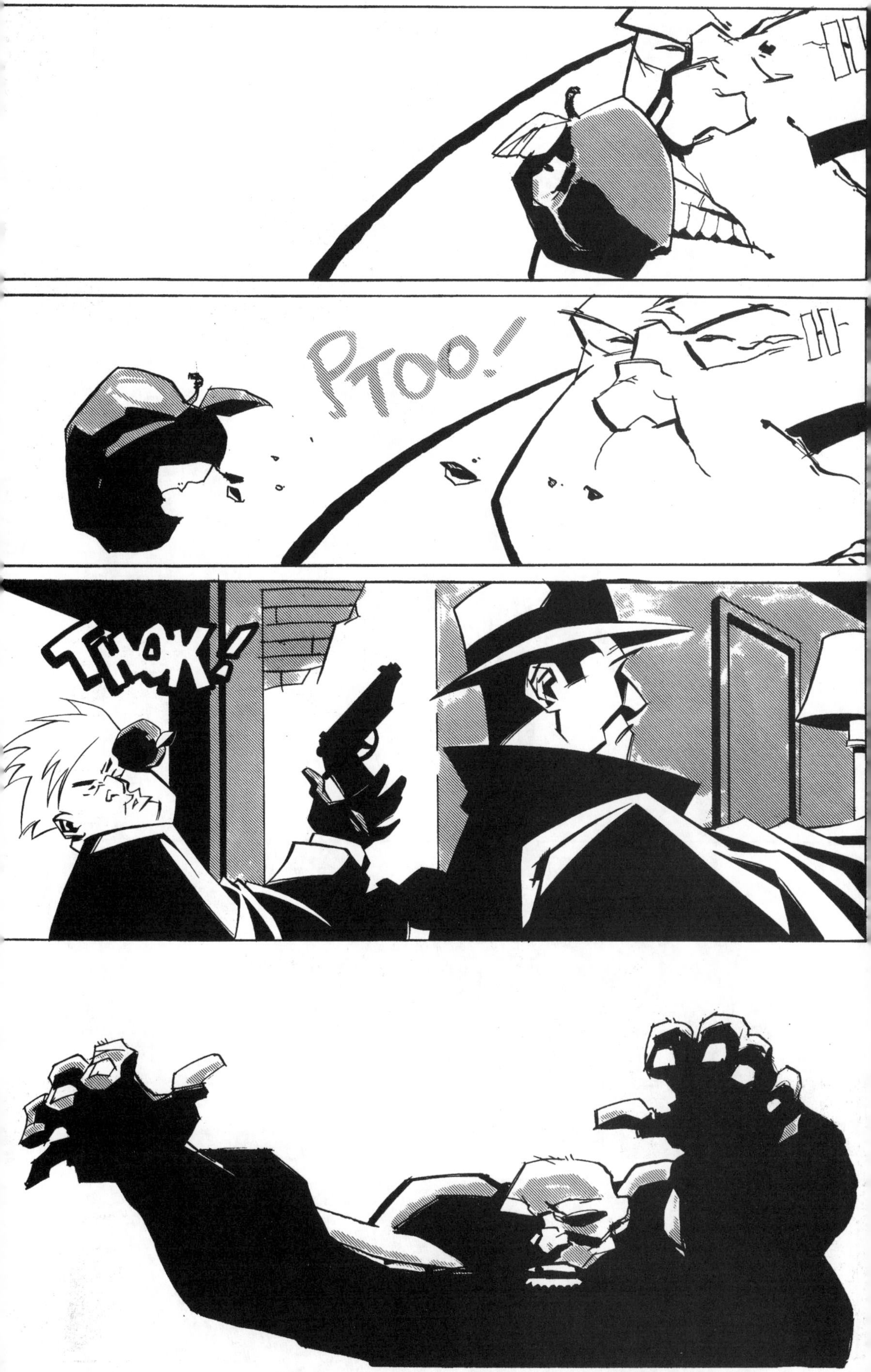
PTOO!
THOK!

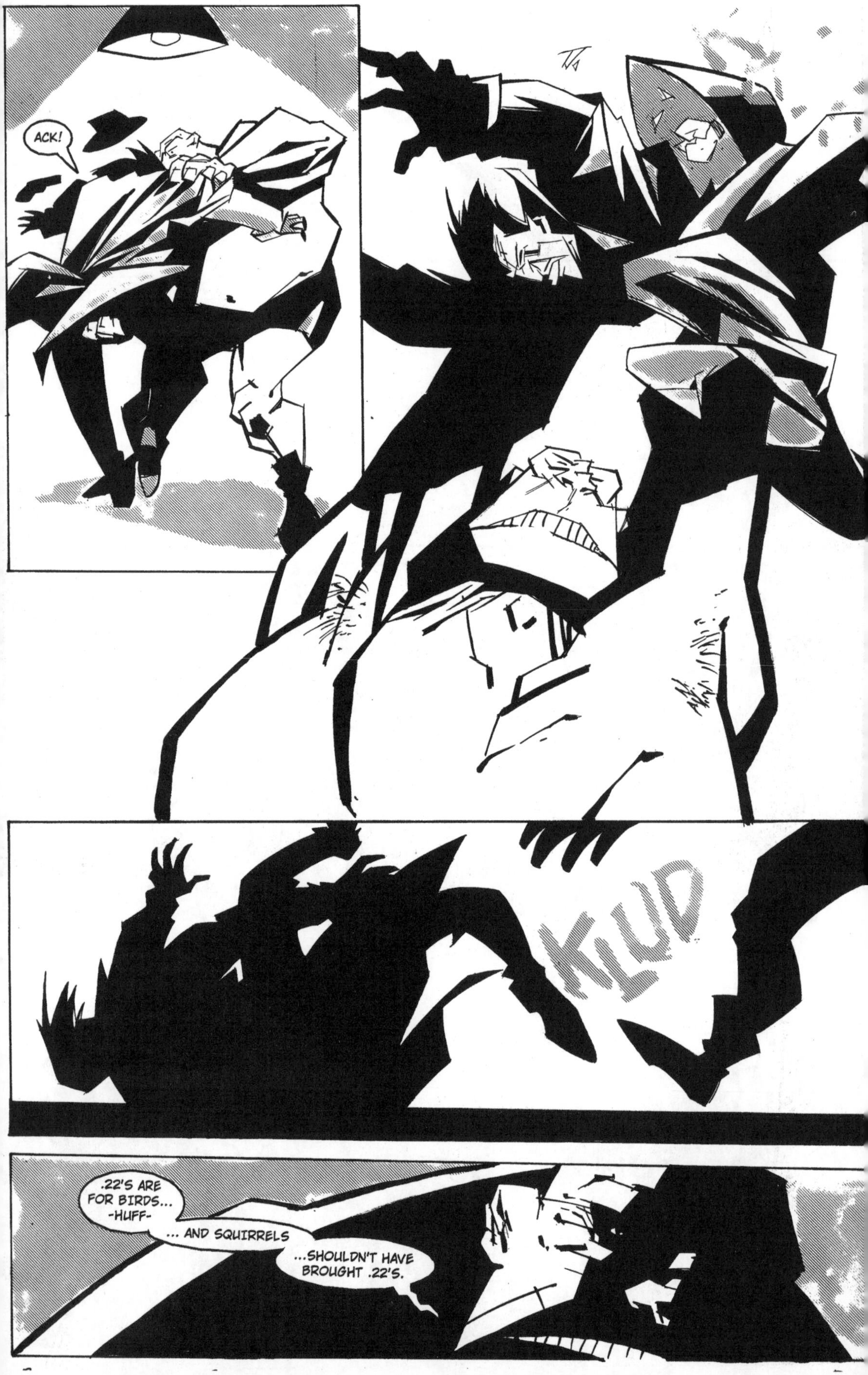
ACK!
KLUD
.22'S ARE FOR BIRDS... -HUFF-
... AND SQUIRRELS
...SHOULDN'T HAVE BROUGHT .22'S.

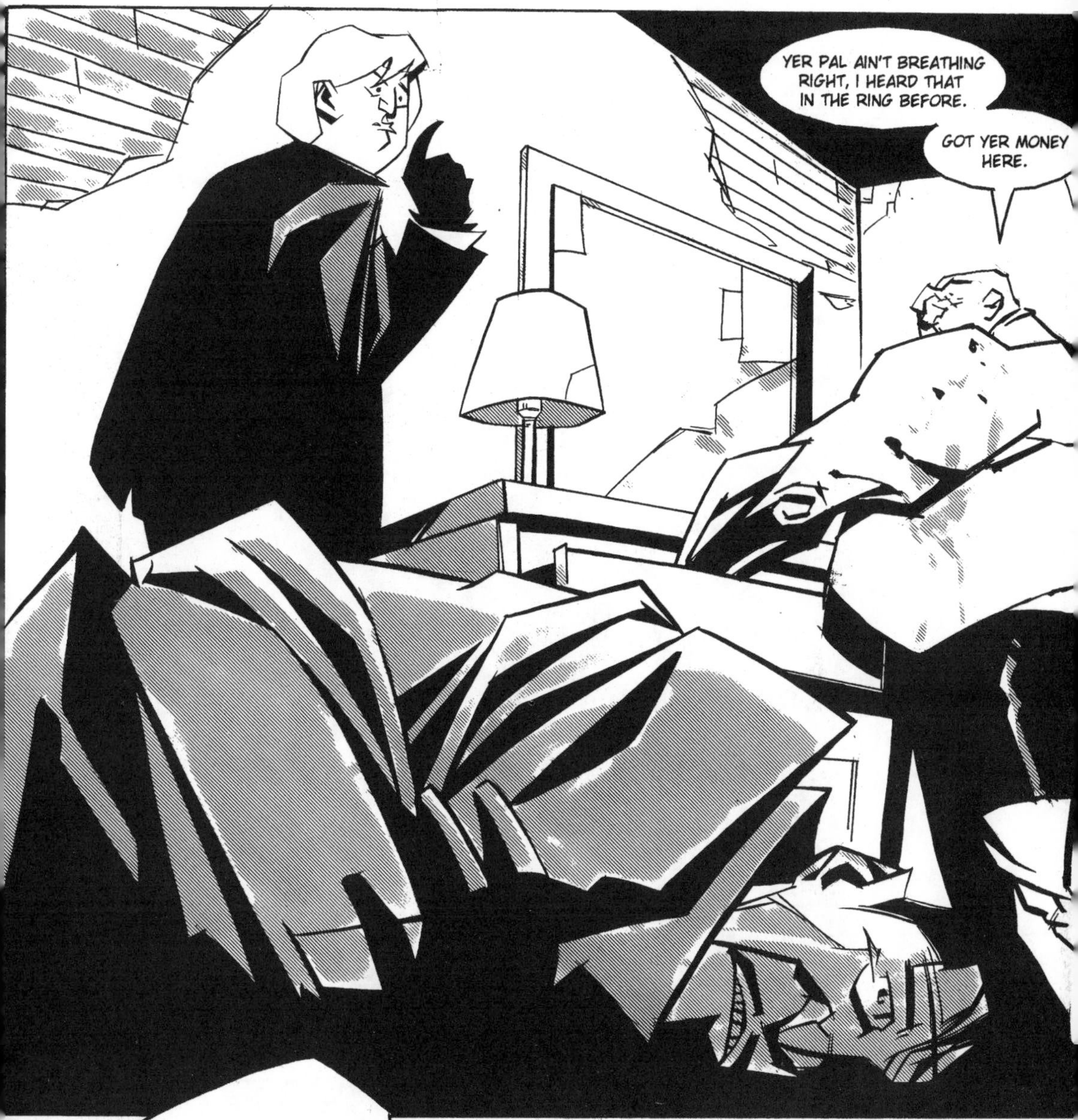
YER PAL AIN'T BREATHING RIGHT, I HEARD THAT IN THE RING BEFORE.
GOT YER MONEY HERE.

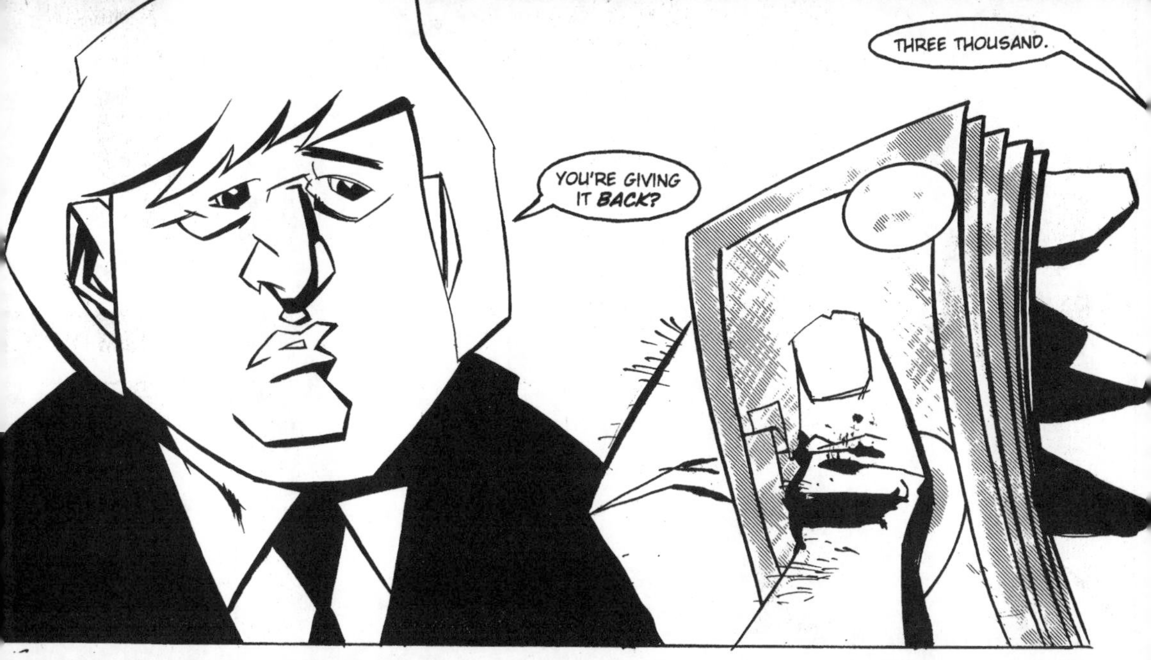
THREE THOUSAND.
YOU'RE GIVING IT *BACK?*

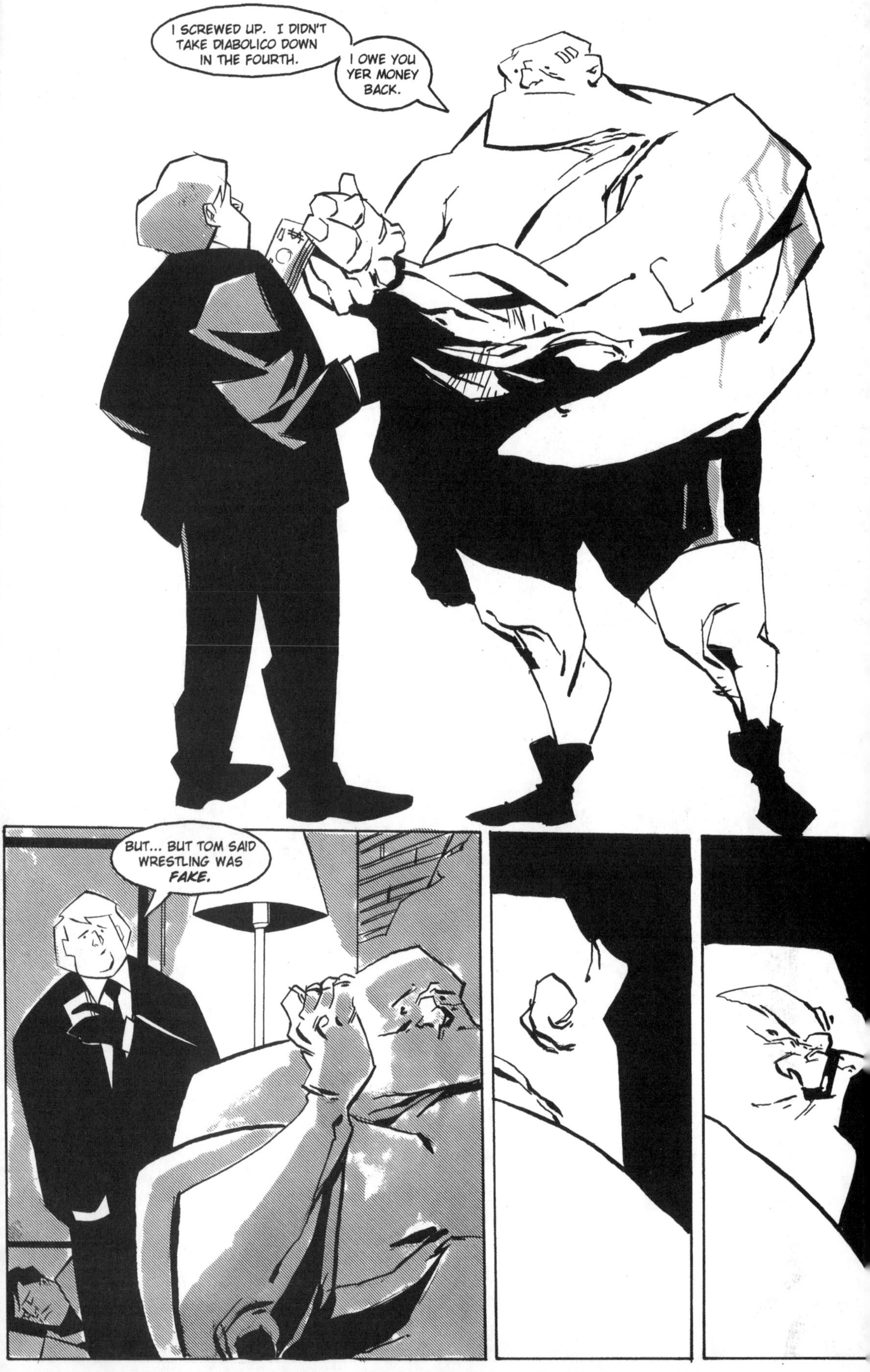
I SCREWED UP. I DIDN'T TAKE DIABOLICO DOWN IN THE FOURTH.
I OWE YOU YER MONEY BACK.
BUT... BUT TOM SAID WRESTLING WAS FAKE.

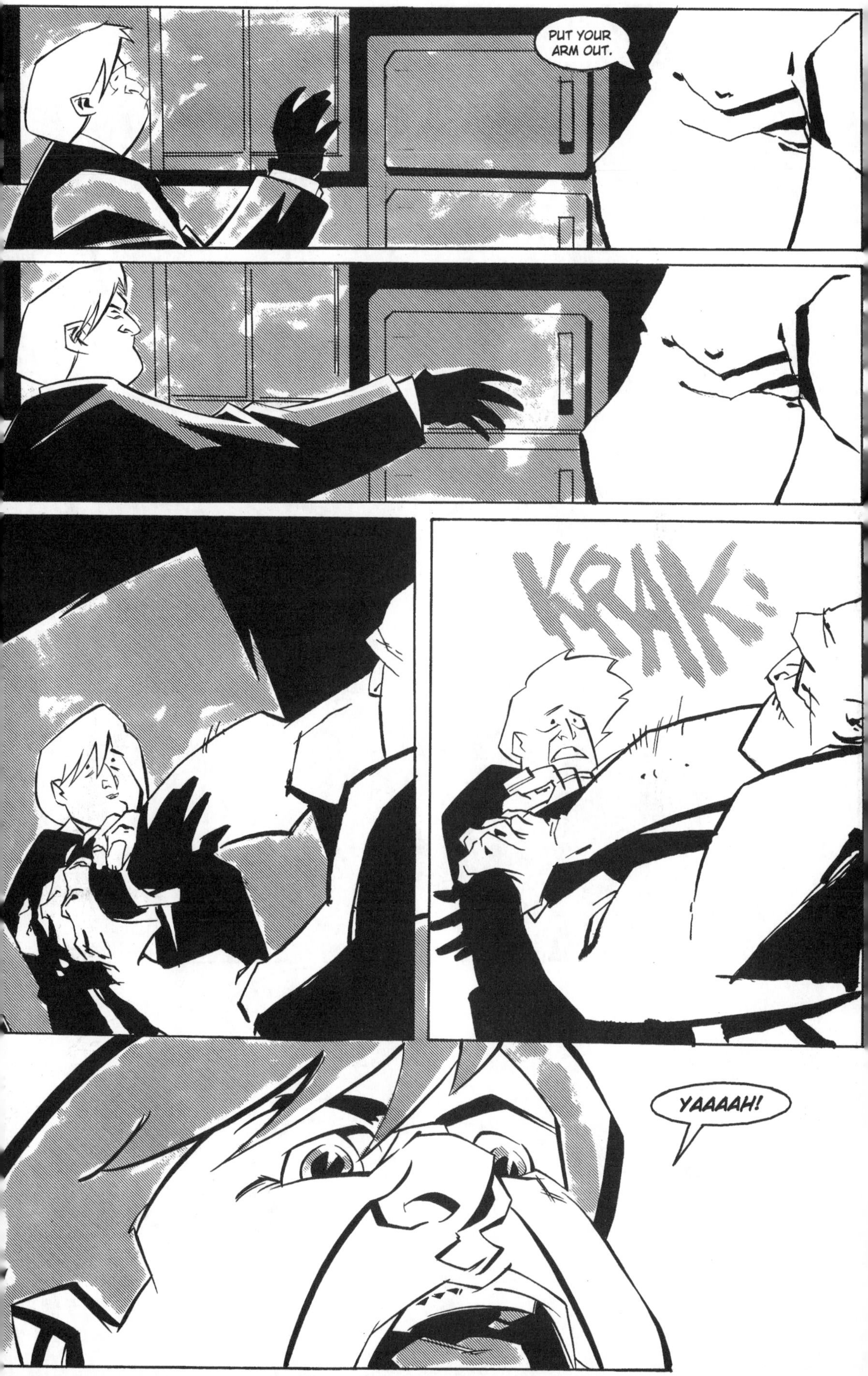
PUT YOUR ARM OUT.
KRAK!
YAAAAH!

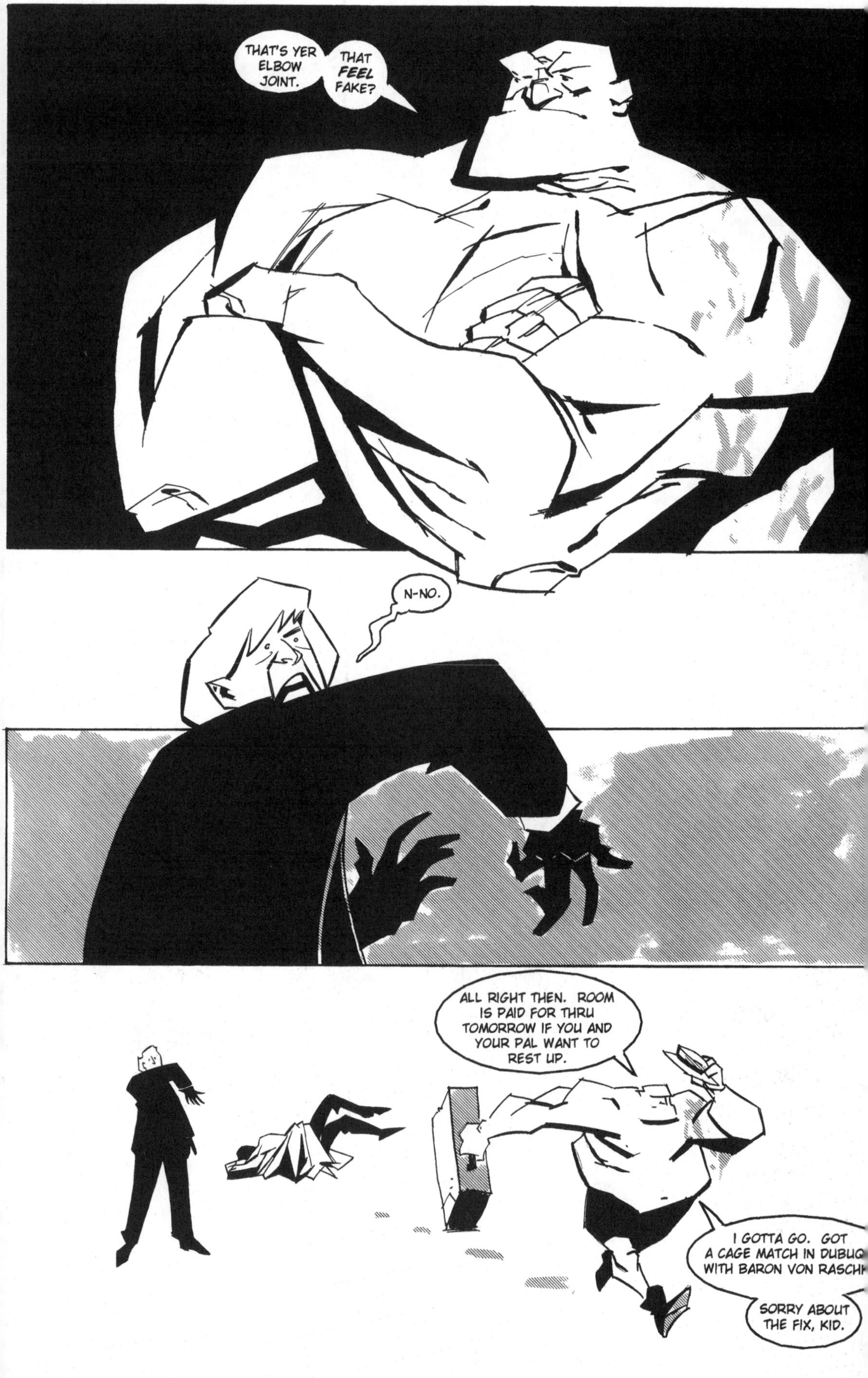
THAT'S YER ELBOW JOINT.
THAT FEEL FAKE?
N-NO.
ALL RIGHT THEN. ROOM IS PAID FOR THRU TOMORROW IF YOU AND YOUR PAL WANT TO REST UP.
I GOTTA GO. GOT A CAGE MATCH IN DUBU
WITH BARON VON RASCH
SORRY ABOUT THE FIX, KID.

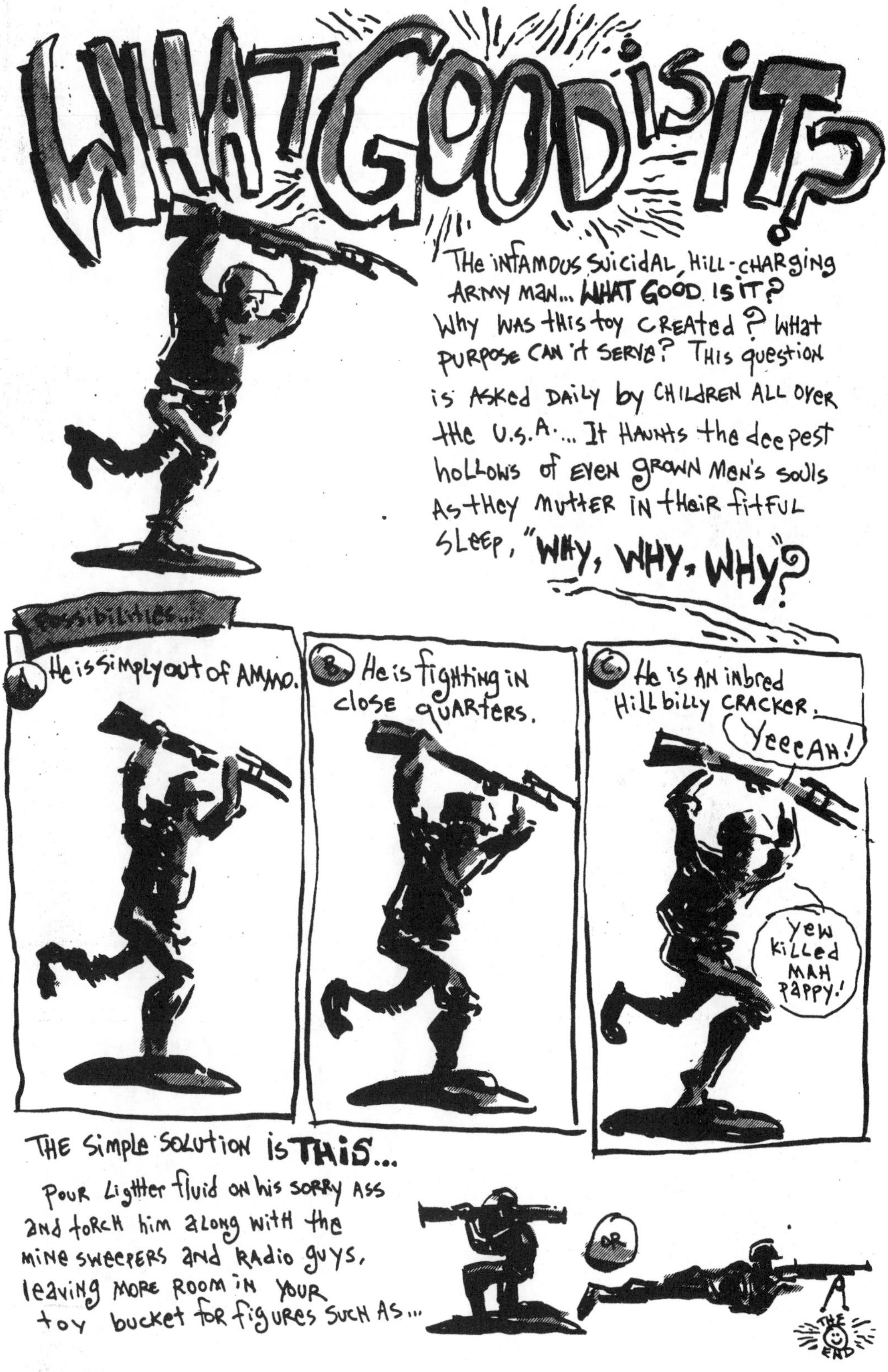
WHAT GOOD IS IT?
The infamous suicidal, hill-charging Army man... WHAT GOOD IS IT? Why was this toy created? What purpose can it serve? This question is asked daily by children all over the U.S.A.... It haunts the deepest hollows of even grown men's souls as they mutter in their fitful sleep, "Why, WHY, WHY?"
Possibilities...
A He is simply out of AMMO.
B He is fighting in close quarters.
C He is an inbred Hillbilly CRACKER.
YeecAH!
Yew killed mah pappy!
THE simple solution is THIS...
Pour lighter fluid on his sorry ass and torch him along with the mine sweepers and radio guys, leaving more room in your toy bucket for figures such as...
OR
THE END

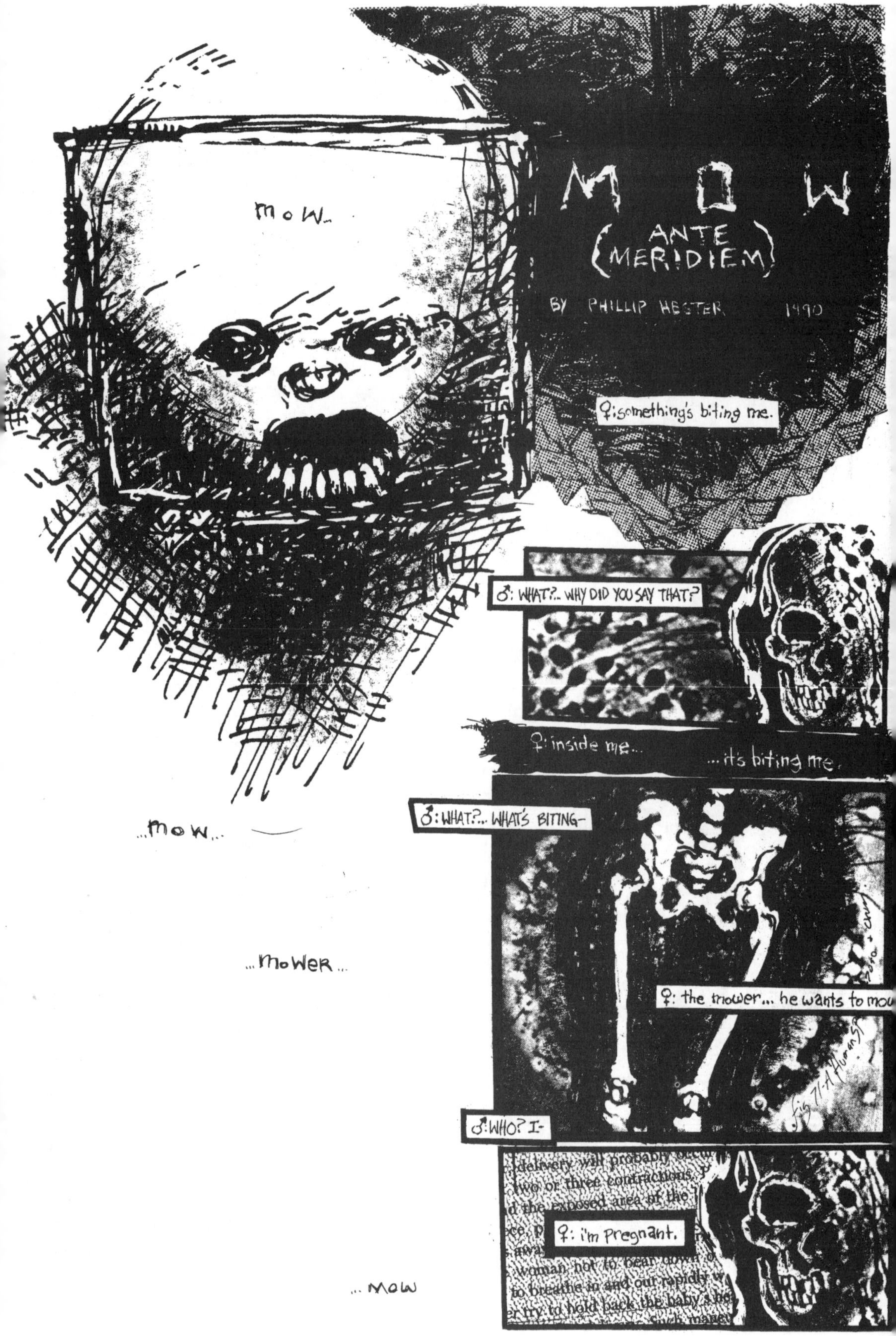
mow..
MOW
(ANTE MERIDIEM)
BY PHILLIP HESTER 1990
♀: something's biting me.
♂: WHAT?.. WHY DID YOU SAY THAT?
♀: inside me..
...it's biting me.
...mow...
♂: WHAT?... WHAT'S BITING-
...mower...
♀: the mower... he wants to mow
♂: WHO? I-
♀: i'm Pregnant.
...mow

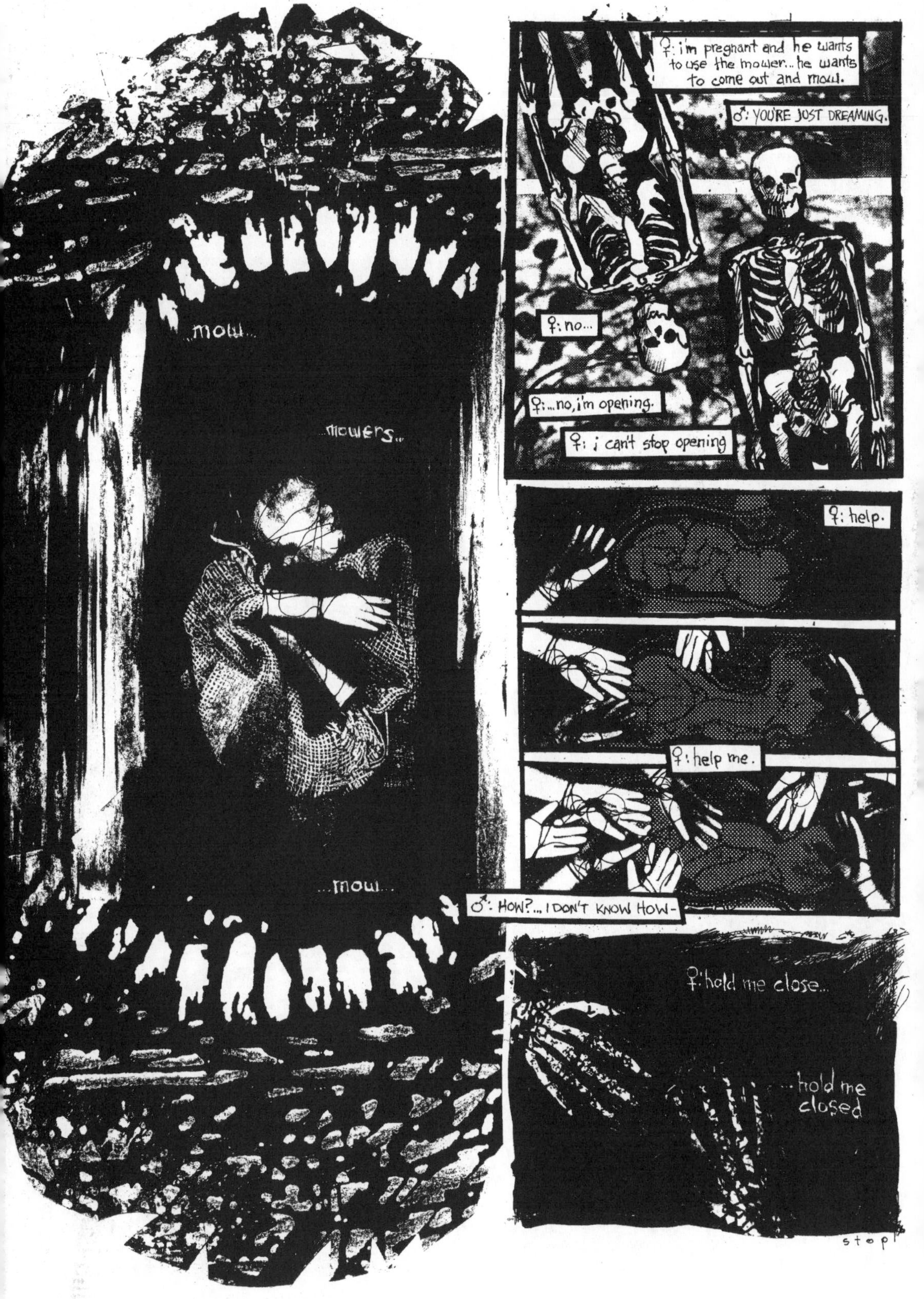

...mow...
...mowers...
...mow...
♀: i'm pregnant and he wants to use the mower... he wants to come out and mow.
♂: YOU'RE JUST DREAMING.
♀: no...
♀: ...no, i'm opening.
♀: i can't stop opening
♀: help.
♀: help me.
♂: HOW?... I DON'T KNOW HOW-
♀: hold me close...
...hold me closed
stop

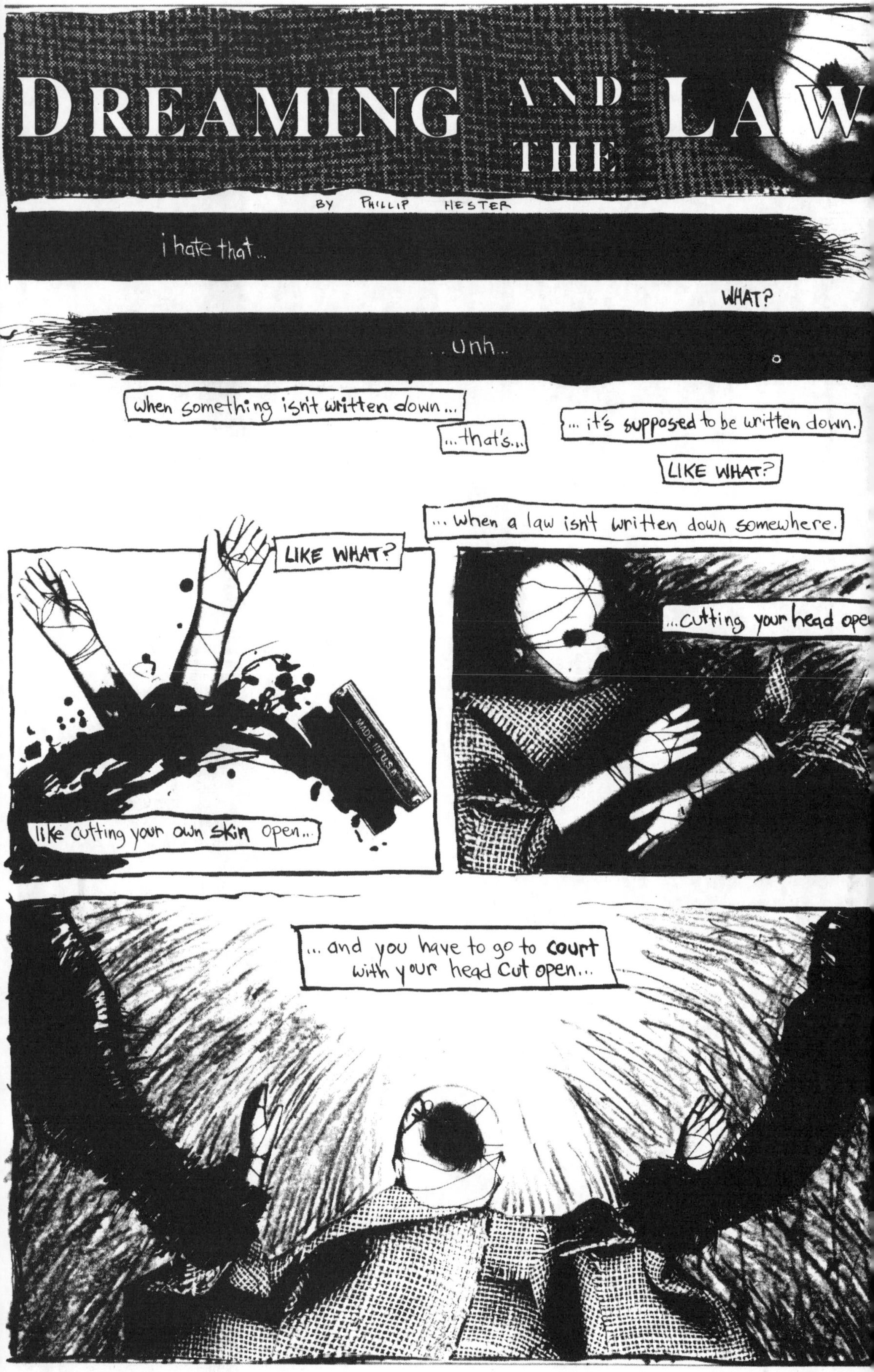

DREAMING AND THE LAW
BY PHILLIP HESTER
i hate that...
WHAT?
...unh...
when something isn't written down...
...that's...
... it's supposed to be written down.
LIKE WHAT?
... when a law isn't written down somewhere.
LIKE WHAT?
like cutting your own skin open...
MADE IN U.S.A.
...cutting your head ope
... and you have to go to court with your head cut open...

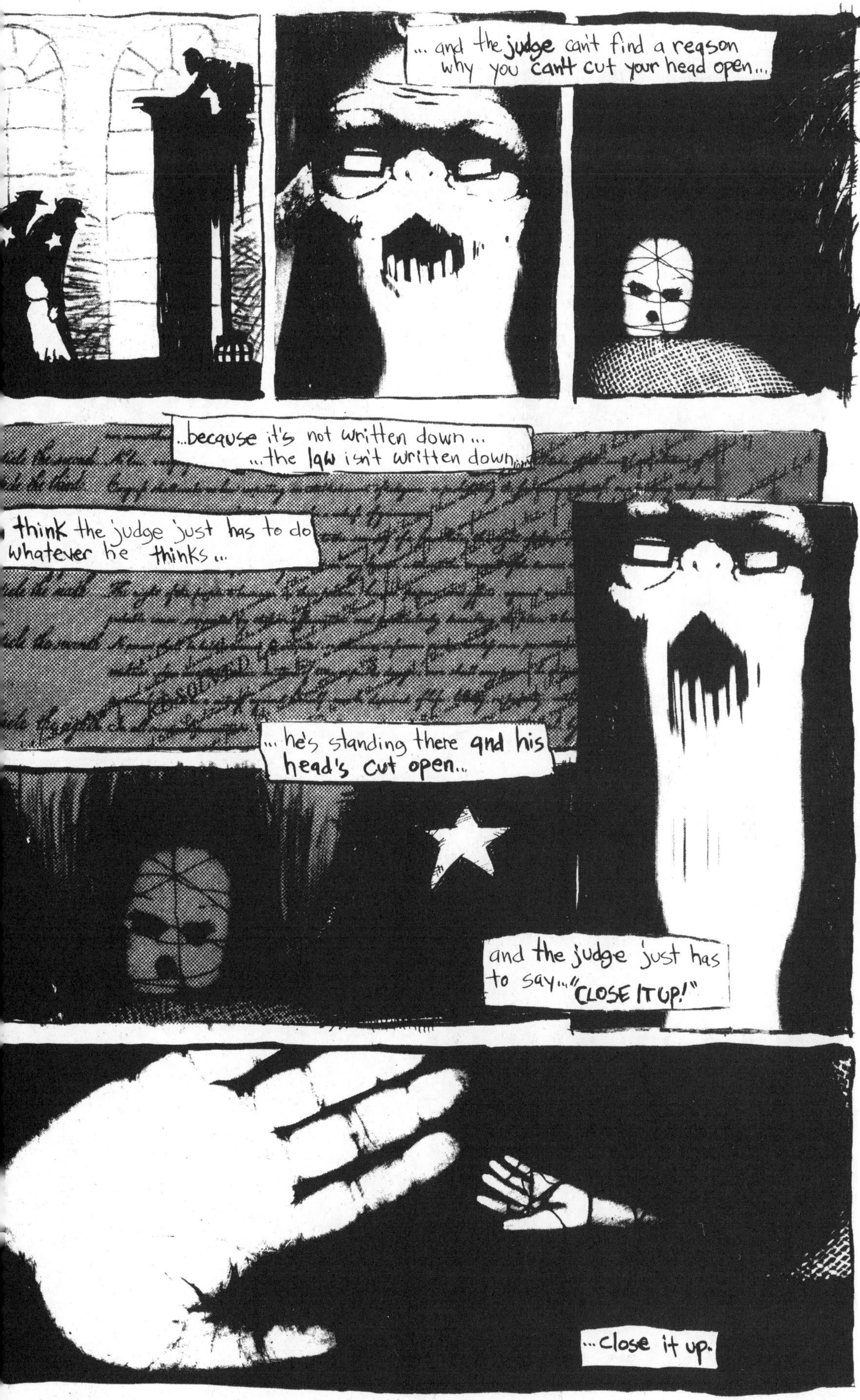
... and the judge can't find a reason why you can't cut your head open...
...because it's not written down...
...the law isn't written down...
think the judge just has to do whatever he thinks...
... he's standing there and his head's cut open...
and the judge just has to say..."CLOSE IT UP!"
...close it up.

C O N D i t i O N E D

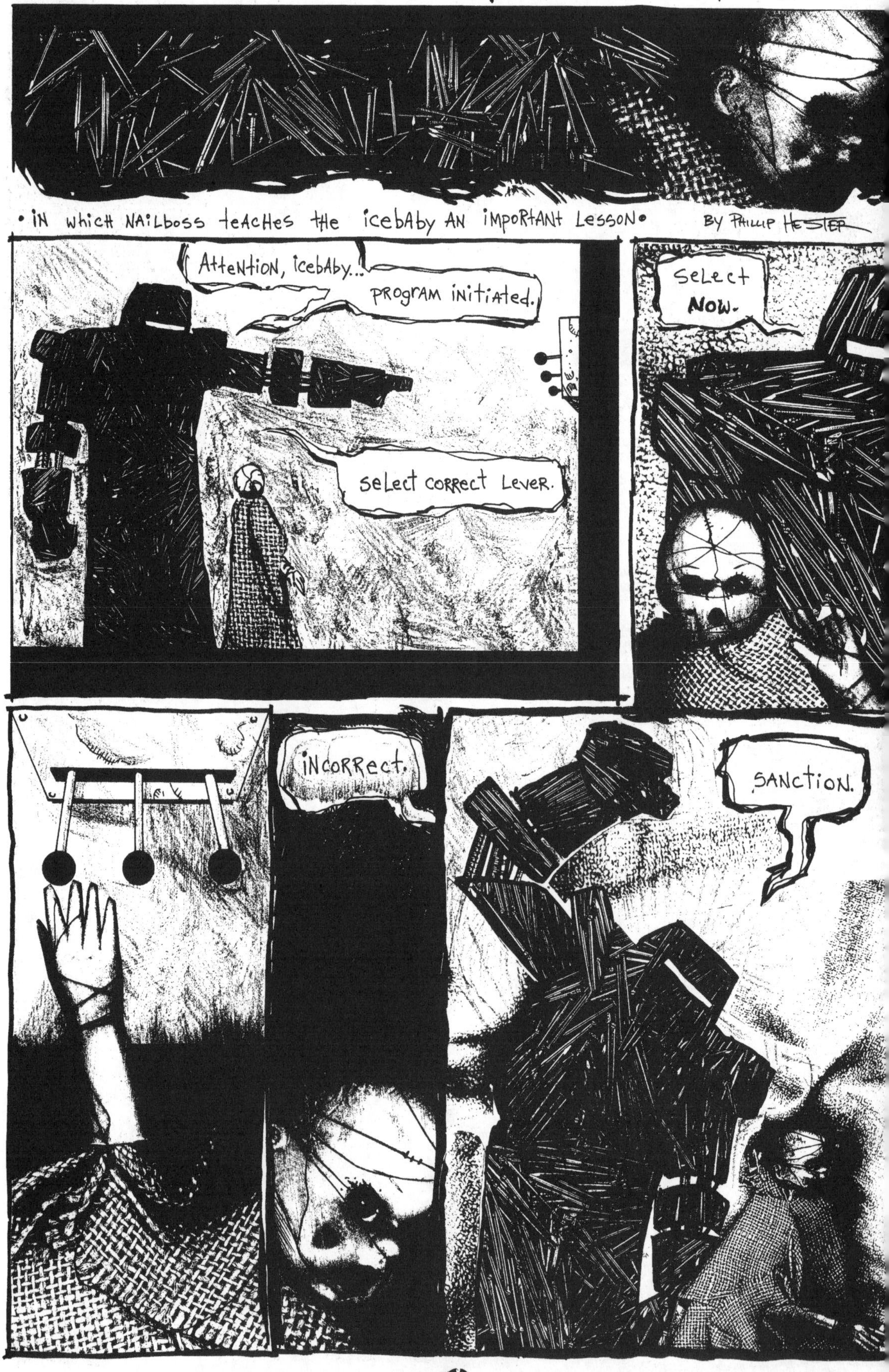

•iN which NAiLboss teAcHes the icebAby AN iMPoRtANt LessoN•
BY PHiLLiP HESTER
AttENtiON, icebAby...
pRogRAM iNitiAted.
seLect correct Lever.
SeLect NOW.
iNcoRRect.
SANction.

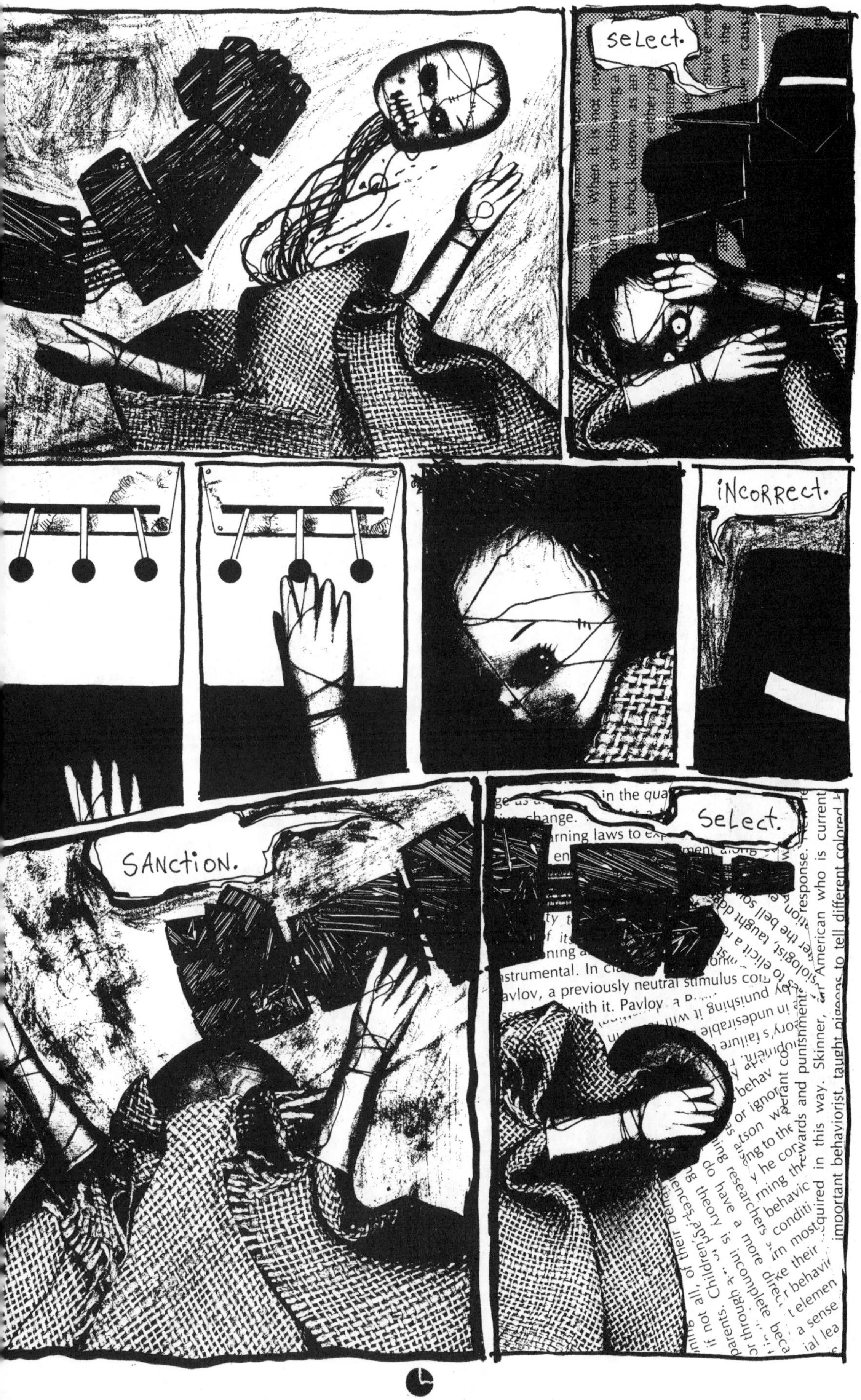
select.
incorrect.
SANCTION.
Select.

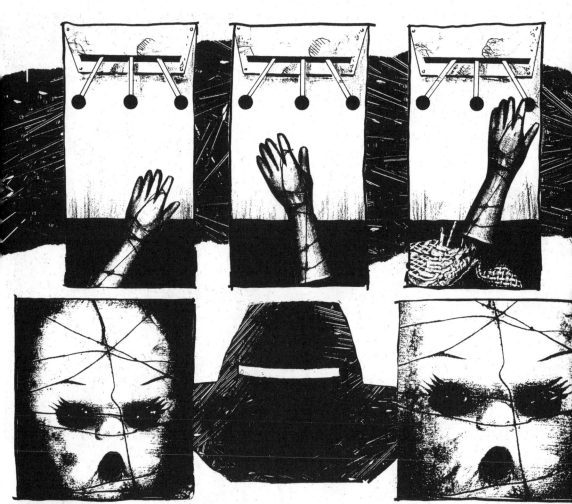

CORRECT.

ReWArD.

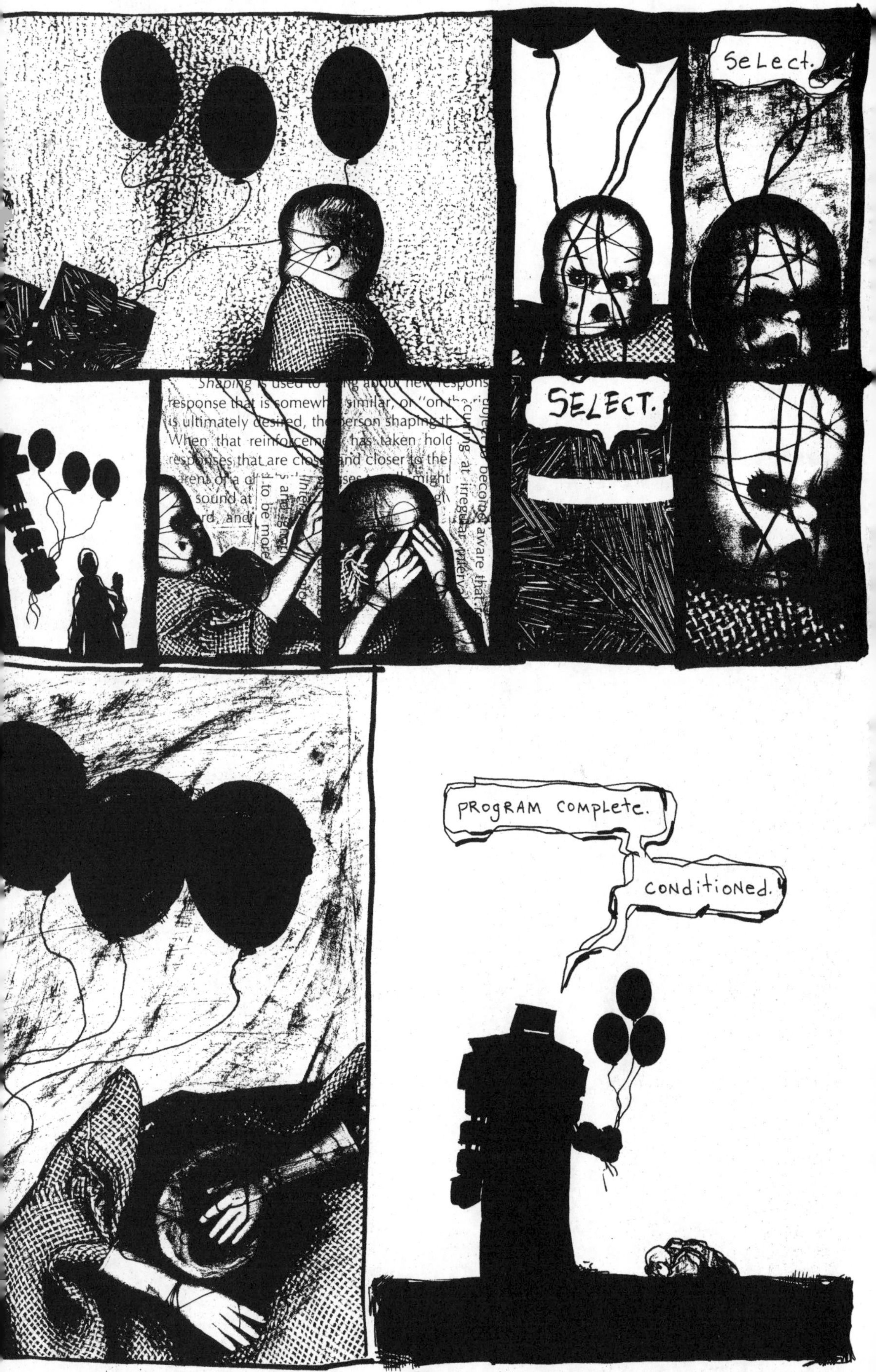
Select.
SELECT.
PROGRAM COMPLETE.
CONDITIONED.

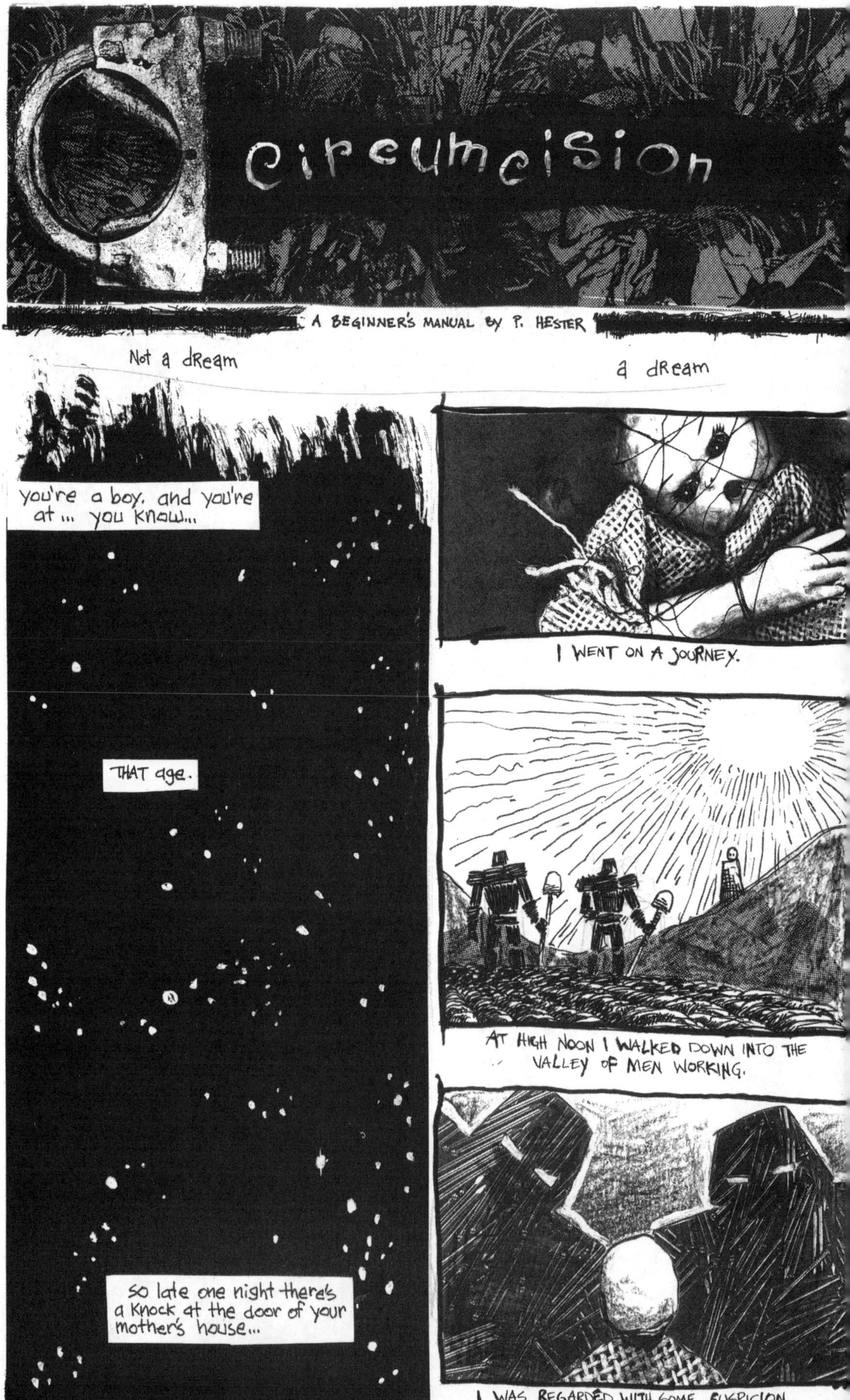
circumcision
A BEGINNER'S MANUAL BY P. HESTER
Not a dream
you're a boy, and you're at... you know...
THAT age.
so late one night there's a knock at the door of your mother's house...
a dream
I WENT ON A JOURNEY.
AT HIGH NOON I WALKED DOWN INTO THE VALLEY OF MEN WORKING.
I WAS REGARDED WITH SOME SUSPICION.

and all the men from the town come in... and they're all painted with their own caked blood.

WE DISCUSSED THE QUALITY OF THE SOIL.

THEY JUDGED MY ASSESSMENT OF THE RICH EARTH WITH MARKED INTENSITY.

feathers stick out from the wounds they've just made all over their naked skin...

...they have no front teeth.

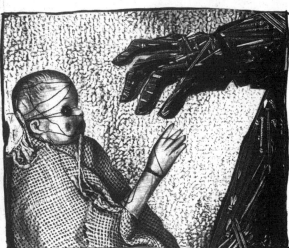

THEY ACCEPTED MY OPINION WHOLEHEARTEDLY.

THEY GAVE ME A COAT.

your mother tries to protect you, but the men push her away.

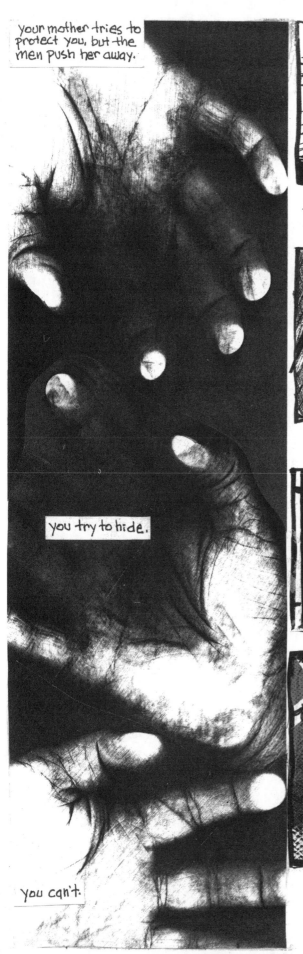

you try to hide.

you can't.

AFTER AN AFTERNOON OF FARMING WE DECIDED TO LEAVE THE VALLEY IN ORDER TO EXAMINE THE SOIL BEYOND.

NEAR SUNDOWN WE CAME UPON AN ABANDONED BARN.

THERE WAS NO HAY IN THE LOFT...

ONLY NOOSES...
BARBED WIRE NOOSES...

... RUSTED WITH BLOOD.

they take you to the woods and stand around you in a circle...

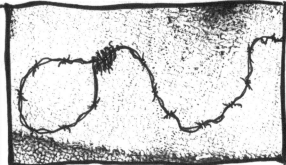

THE OLDER MAN MENTIONED HOW HE HAD SEEN PHOTOGRAPHS OF MEN HANGED BY THE BARBED WIRE NOOSE AS FAR BACK AS THE COWBOY DAYS.

...one at a time they punch you in the face until your front teeth just fly out.

BUT THERE WERE MANY ROLLS OF NEW WIRE, NOT YET TIED INTO NOOSES. UPON CLOSE EXAMINATION WE FOUND THAT EACH NOOSE HAD A CORRESPONDING PLANK OF LUMBER IN THE WALL OF THE BARN. EACH PLANK HAD CARVED IN IT A LIMERICK DESCRIBING THE NATURE OF THE CRIME AND THE DATE OF THE EXECUTION...

...AND EACH POEM WAS SIGNED:

The Daycare Center

they pin you down on the ground. all of them...

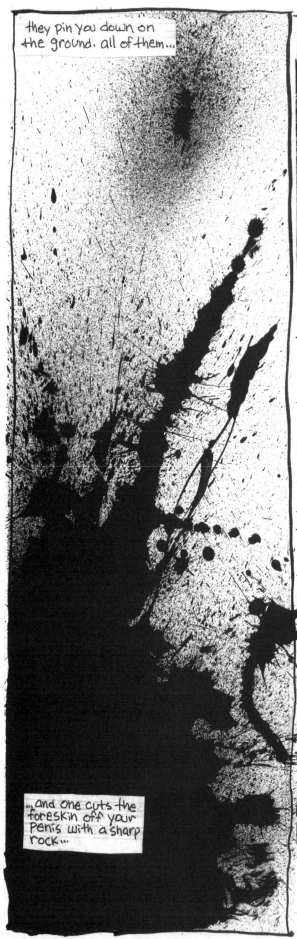

...and one cuts the foreskin off your penis with a sharp rock...

WE STOOD BLIND IN THE GRIP OF OUR OWN FEAR AND IGNORANCE...

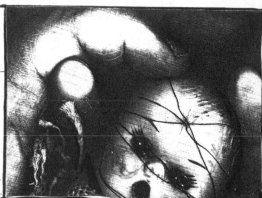

WAS THIS AGAIN THE WORK OF WOMEN?

WE WERE STARTLED BY A NOISE AT THE BARN DOOR. IT WAS THREE BOYS WHO HAD JUST COME FROM WORK AT THE NEARBY McDONALD'S.

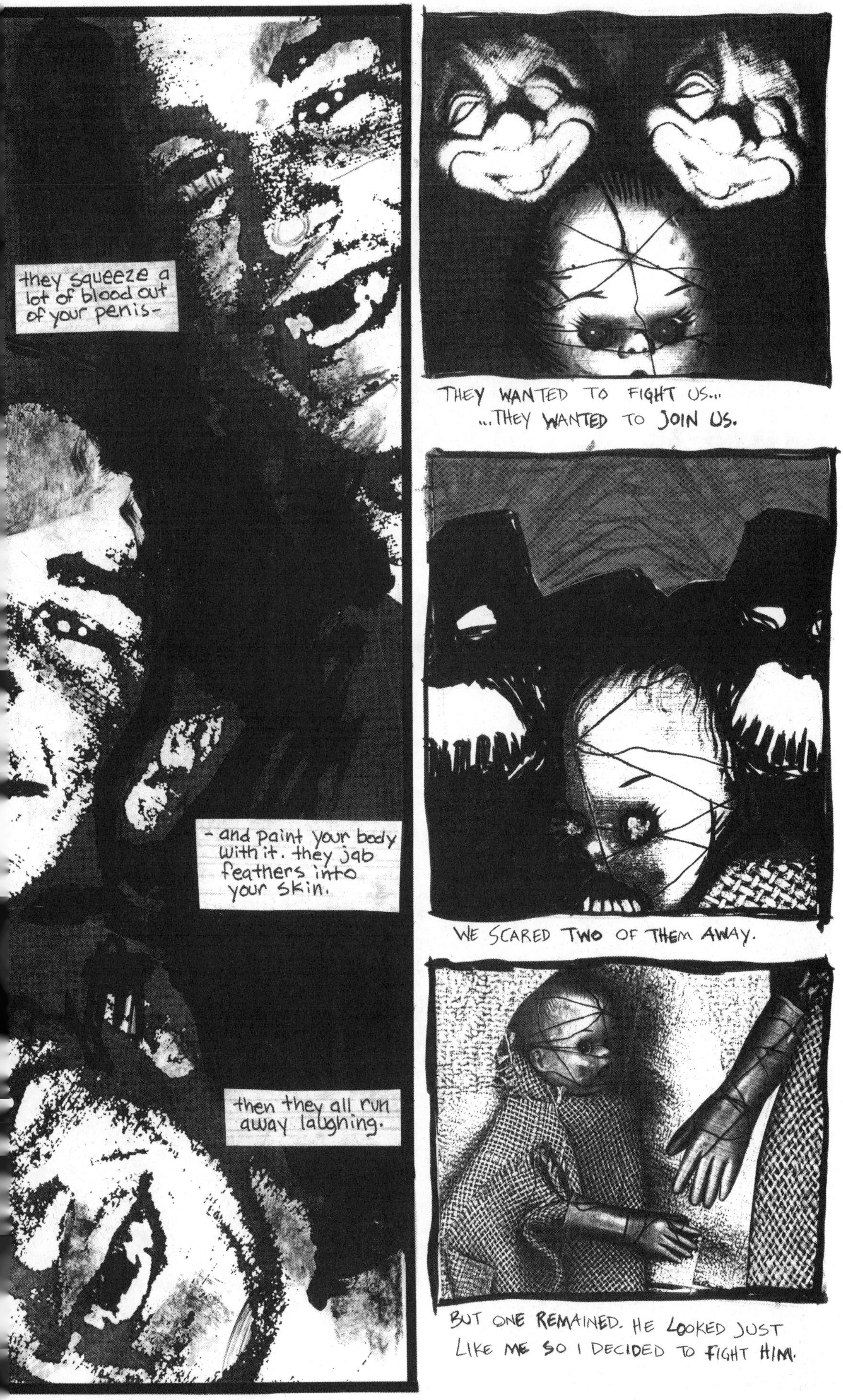
they squeeze a lot of blood out of your penis-
- and paint your body with it. they jab feathers into your skin.
then they all run away laughing.
THEY WANTED TO FIGHT US...
...THEY WANTED TO JOIN US.
WE SCARED TWO OF THEM AWAY.
BUT ONE REMAINED. HE LOOKED JUST LIKE ME SO I DECIDED TO FIGHT HIM.

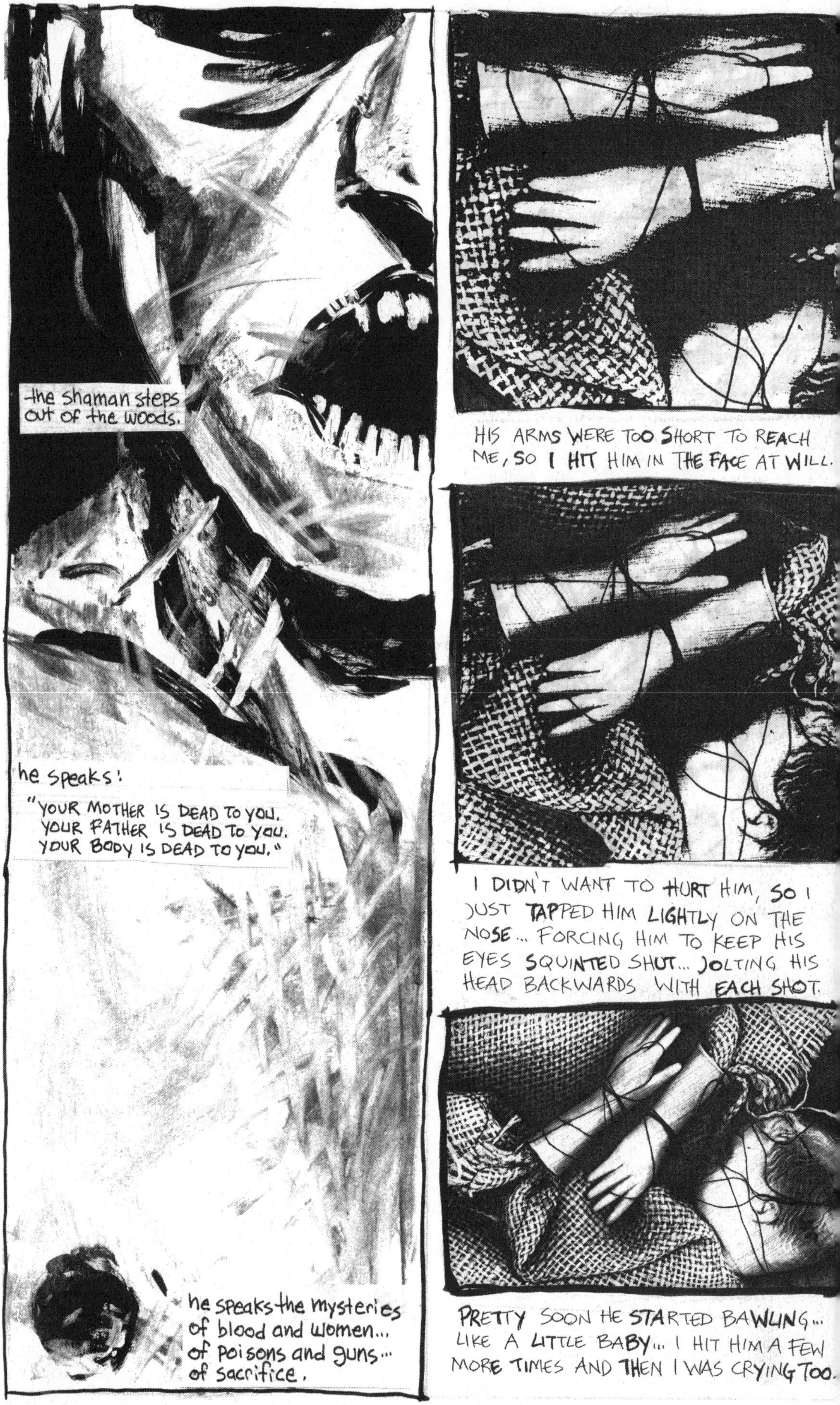
the shaman steps out of the woods.
he speaks:
"YOUR MOTHER IS DEAD TO YOU. YOUR FATHER IS DEAD TO YOU. YOUR BODY IS DEAD TO YOU."
he speaks the mysteries of blood and women... of poisons and guns... of sacrifice.
HIS ARMS WERE TOO SHORT TO REACH ME, SO I HIT HIM IN THE FACE AT WILL.
I DIDN'T WANT TO HURT HIM, SO I JUST TAPPED HIM LIGHTLY ON THE NOSE... FORCING HIM TO KEEP HIS EYES SQUINTED SHUT... JOLTING HIS HEAD BACKWARDS WITH EACH SHOT.
PRETTY SOON HE STARTED BAWLING... LIKE A LITTLE BABY... I HIT HIM A FEW MORE TIMES AND THEN I WAS CRYING TOO.

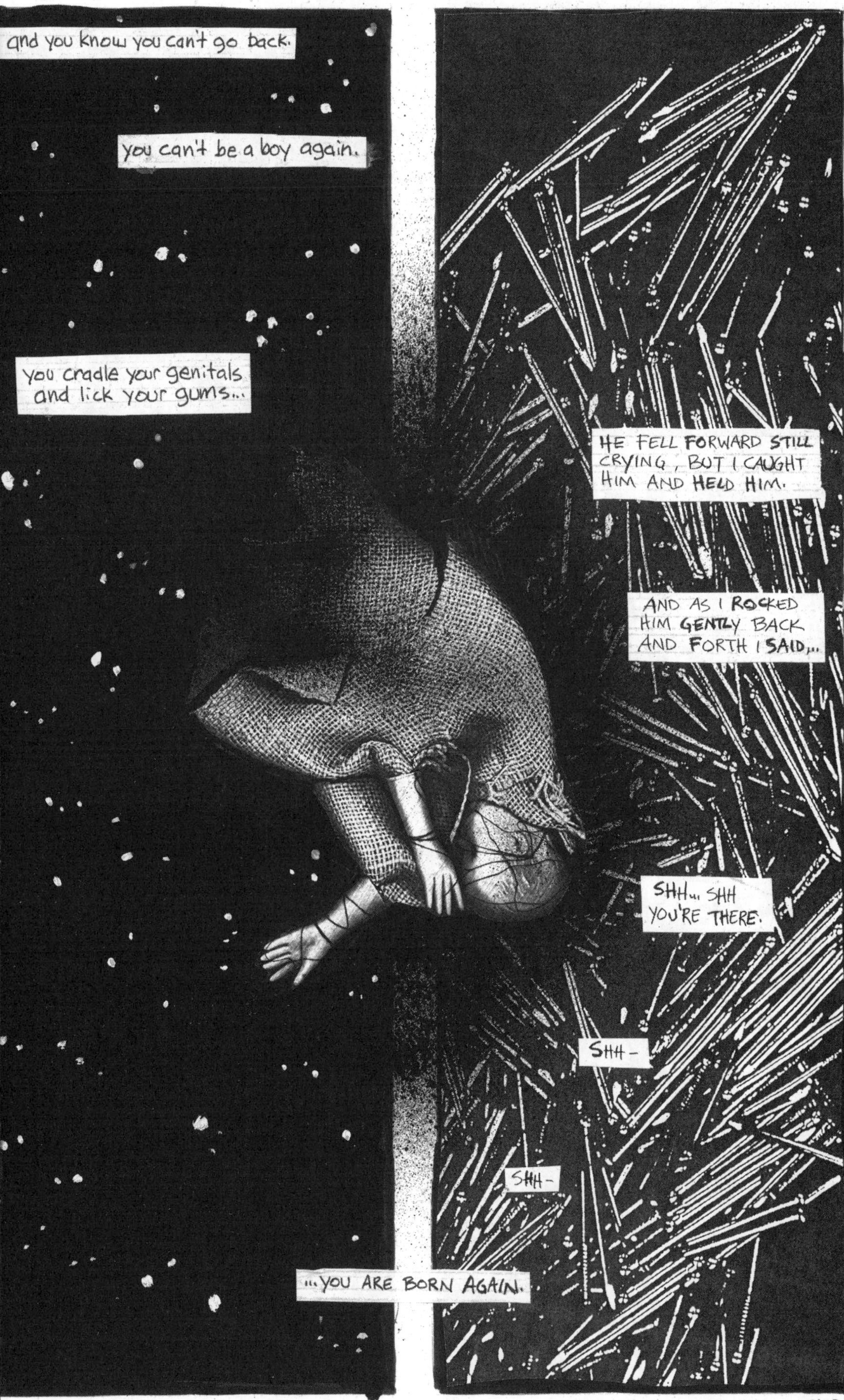
and you know you can't go back.
you can't be a boy again.
you cradle your genitals and lick your gums...
HE FELL FORWARD STILL CRYING, BUT I CAUGHT HIM AND HELD HIM.
AND AS I ROCKED HIM GENTLY BACK AND FORTH I SAID...
SHH... SHH YOU'RE THERE.
SHH-
SHH-
...YOU ARE BORN AGAIN.

stop.

HUNTING AND GATHERING

PHILLIP HESTER

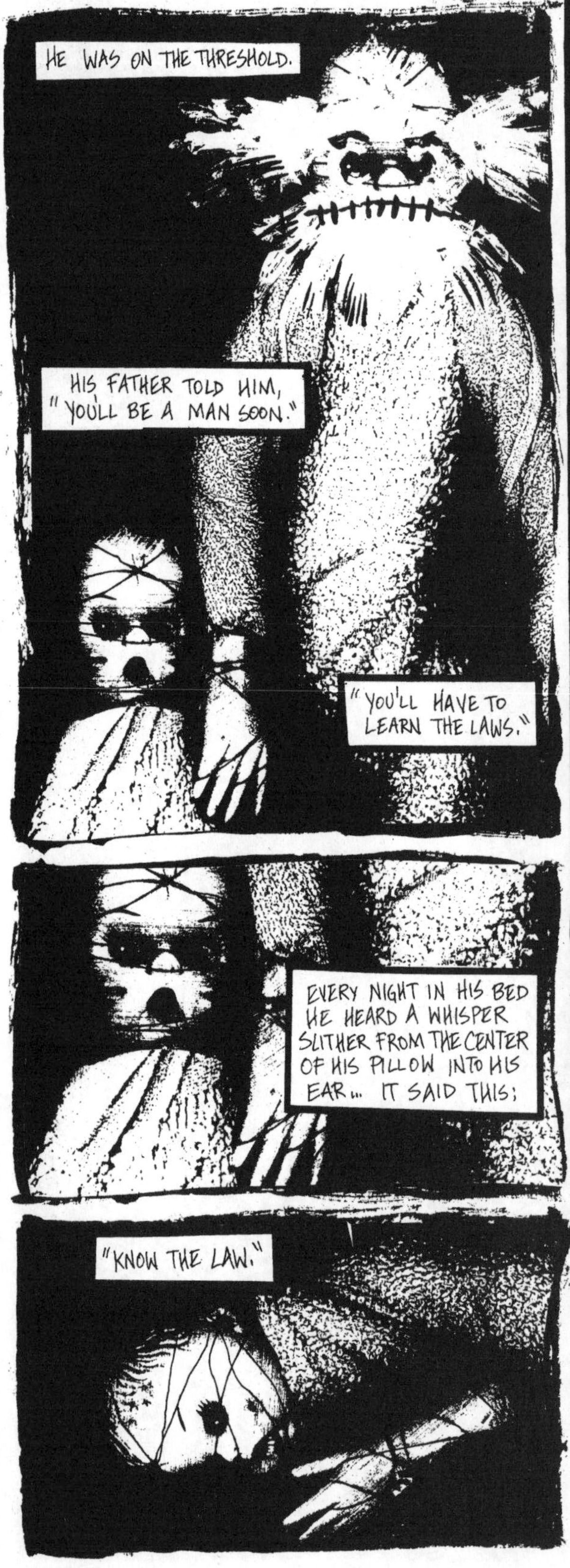
HE WAS ON THE THRESHOLD.
HIS FATHER TOLD HIM, "YOU'LL BE A MAN SOON."
"YOU'LL HAVE TO LEARN THE LAWS."
EVERY NIGHT IN HIS BED HE HEARD A WHISPER SLITHER FROM THE CENTER OF HIS PILLOW INTO HIS EAR... IT SAID THIS;
"KNOW THE LAW."

i'm maybe nine or ten, so my dad is something like twenty-six or twenty-seven years old.

very young.

it's fall, that means it's time for all the men to go shooting at animals.

fig. A (a son)

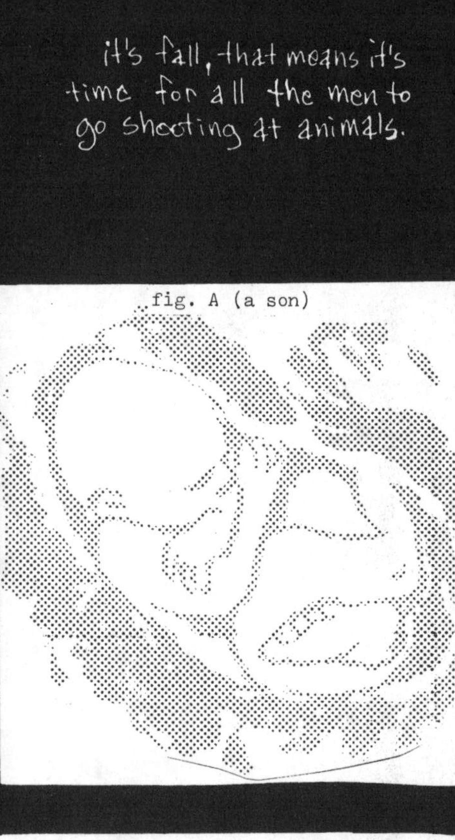

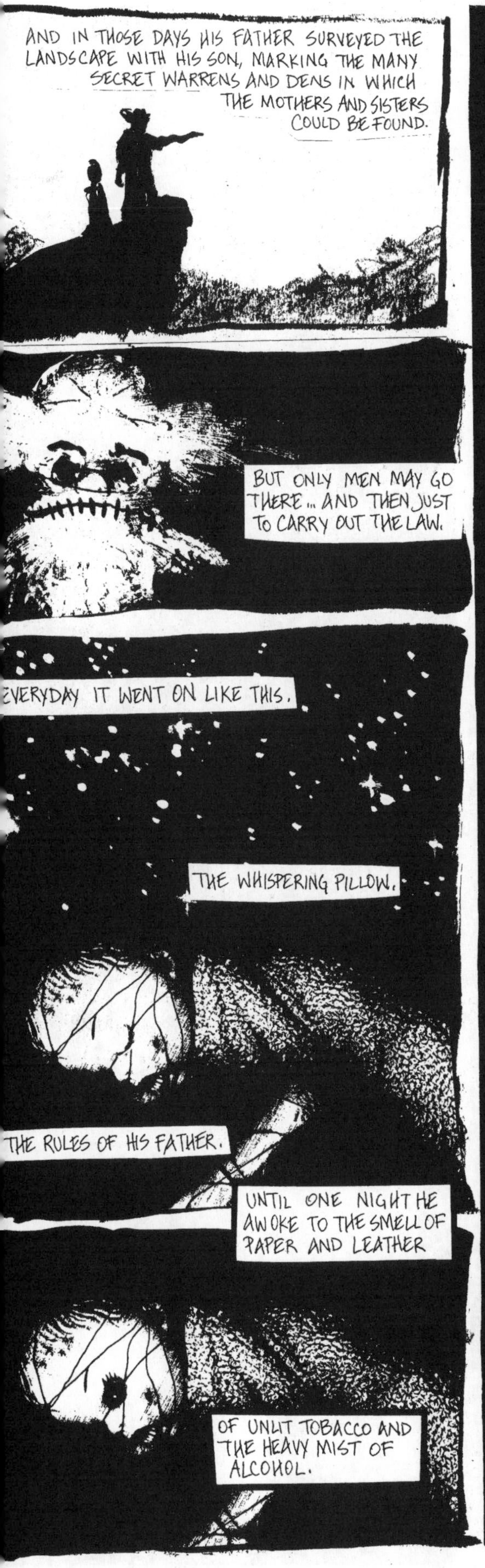
AND IN THOSE DAYS HIS FATHER SURVEYED THE LANDSCAPE WITH HIS SON, MARKING THE MANY SECRET WARRENS AND DENS IN WHICH THE MOTHERS AND SISTERS COULD BE FOUND.
BUT ONLY MEN MAY GO THERE... AND THEN JUST TO CARRY OUT THE LAW.
EVERYDAY IT WENT ON LIKE THIS.
THE WHISPERING PILLOW.
THE RULES OF HIS FATHER.
UNTIL ONE NIGHT HE AWOKE TO THE SMELL OF PAPER AND LEATHER
OF UNLIT TOBACCO AND THE HEAVY MIST OF ALCOHOL.

so all the men at my grandpa's farm say, "let's all go shooting at animals."

it's what men do.

at our respective ages i'm just starting to think about becoming a man and my dad's pretty new to it himself.

so we divvy up firearms.

my dad picks a .22 caliber rifle. you can't kill much with that. you could shoot a president with it three or four times and he'd just get better.

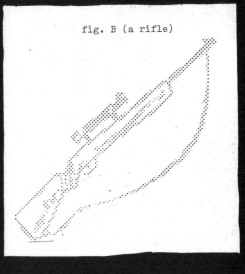

fig. B (a rifle)

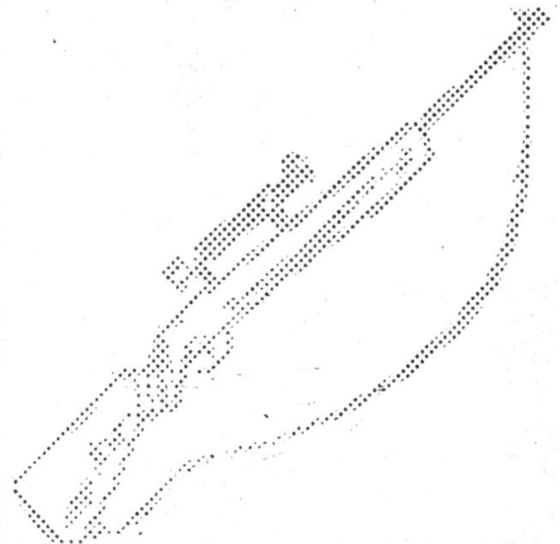

THE MEN HAD COME.

LAWMEN.

we head out and split up all over the farm. my dad and i patrol a cold, grey creek bed.

after a while my dad stops and sits down on the gritty sand.
i don't ask why.

i don't talk a lot at this age.

he confesses, "im not going to kill anything."
"i guess i'm just a pussy."

i'm not quite sure what he means, but i sit down and say, "me too."

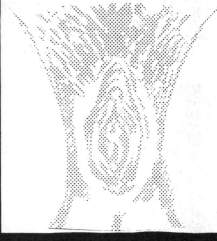

fig. C (a pussy)

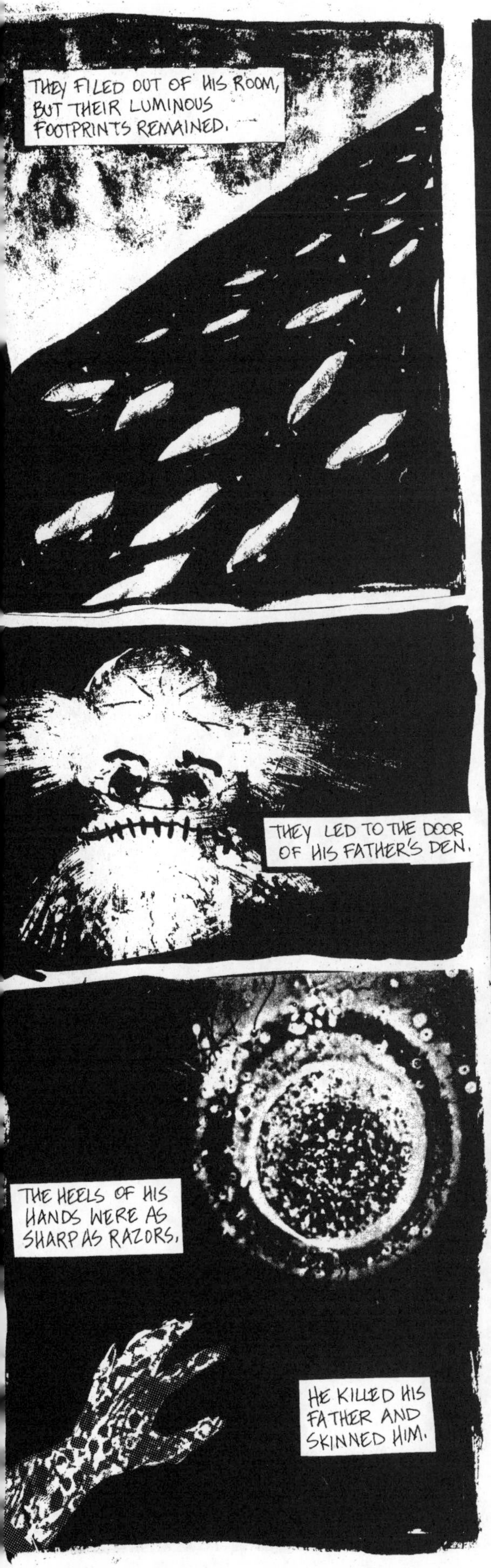
THEY FILED OUT OF HIS ROOM, BUT THEIR LUMINOUS FOOTPRINTS REMAINED.
THEY LED TO THE DOOR OF HIS FATHER'S DEN.
THE HEELS OF HIS HANDS WERE AS SHARP AS RAZORS.
HE KILLED HIS FATHER AND SKINNED HIM.

my dad gets up and pulls a rubber ball and a playing card with a rabbit printed on the back from his pocket.

he's prepared.

as he's wedging the card in the bark of a nearby tree he tells me about how he threw up the time he saw a skinned squirrel.

we pace off about 50 feet and take turns blowing the hell out of that picture rabbit.

fig. D (a rabbit)

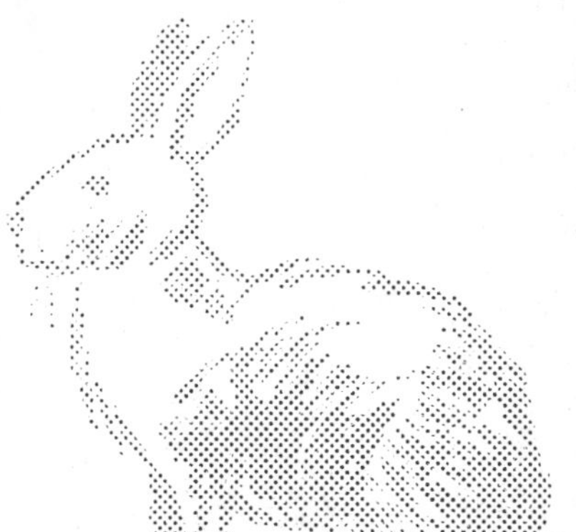

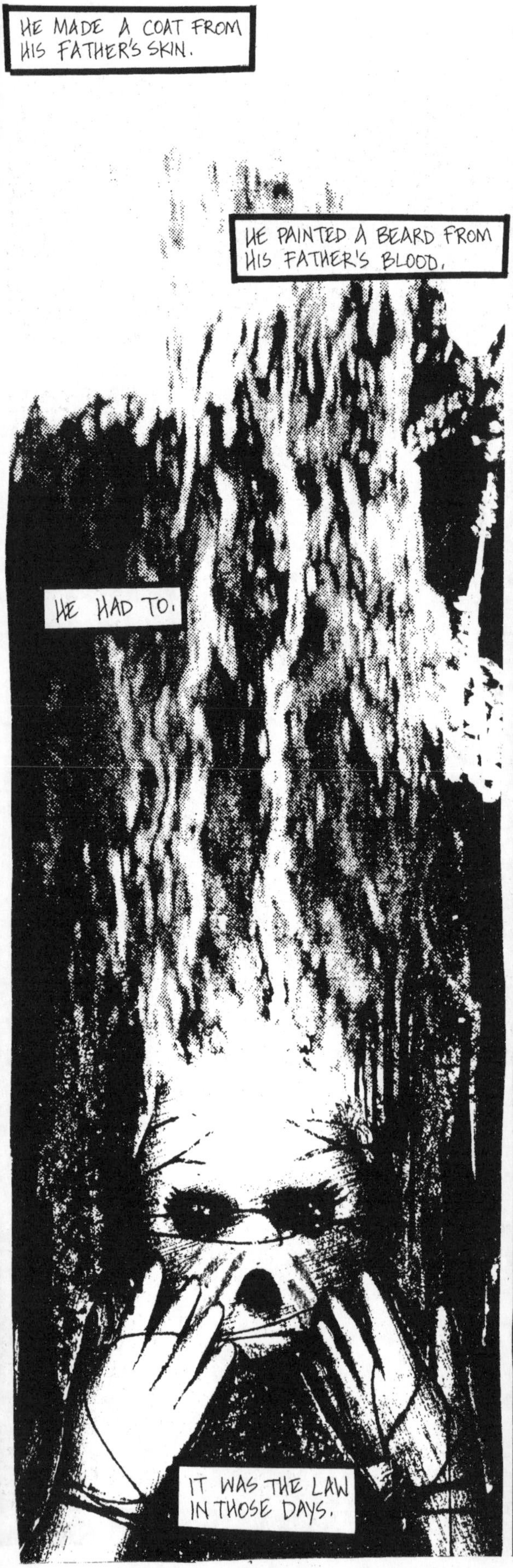
HE MADE A COAT FROM HIS FATHER'S SKIN.
HE PAINTED A BEARD FROM HIS FATHER'S BLOOD.
HE HAD TO.
IT WAS THE LAW IN THOSE DAYS.

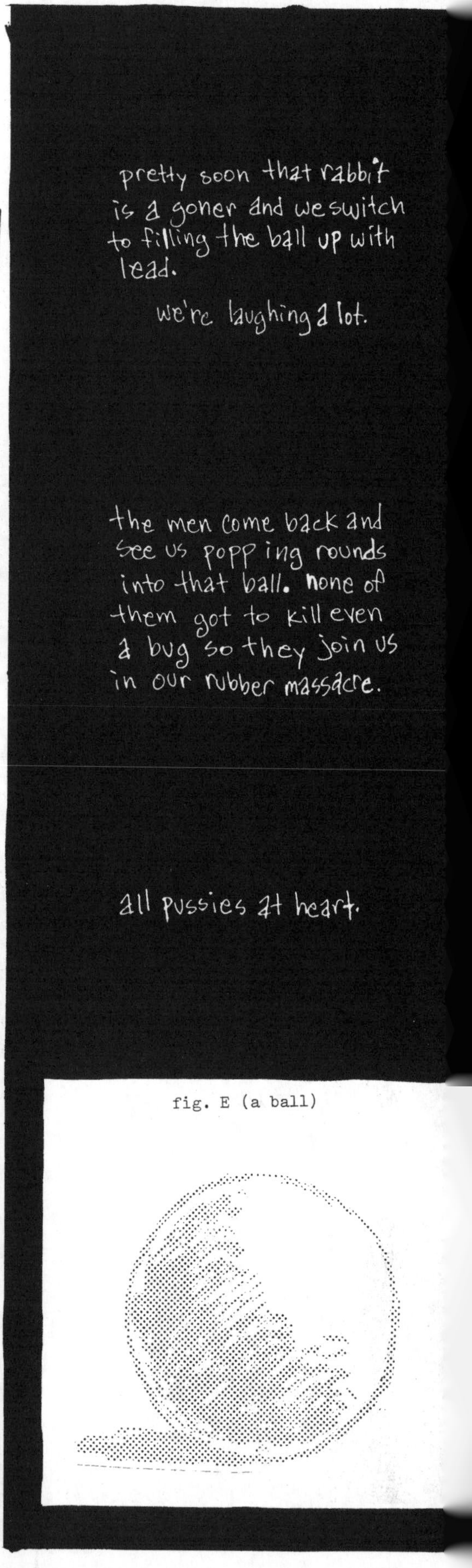
pretty soon that rabbit is a goner and we switch to filling the ball up with lead.
we're laughing a lot.
the men come back and see us popping rounds into that ball. none of them got to kill even a bug so they join us in our rubber massacre.
all pussies at heart.
fig. E (a ball)

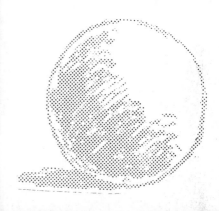

MR. MANDELBROT SAYS WE CANNOT TOUCH,

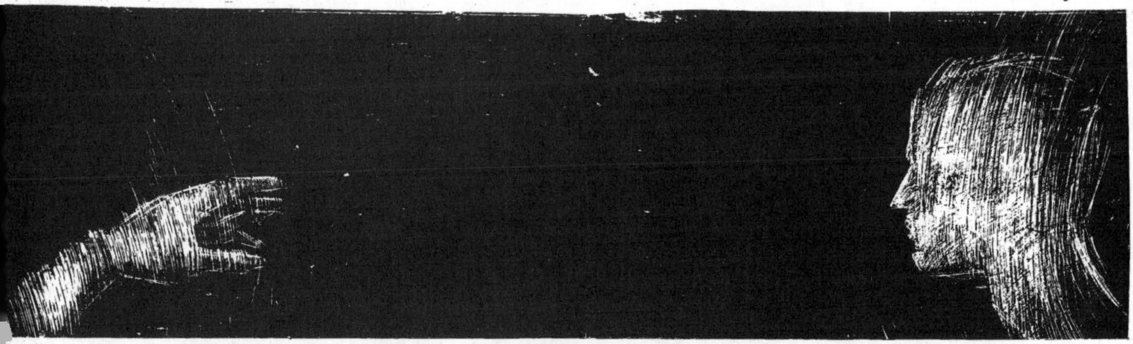

AS THE DISTANCE BETWEEN US CAN BE HALVED

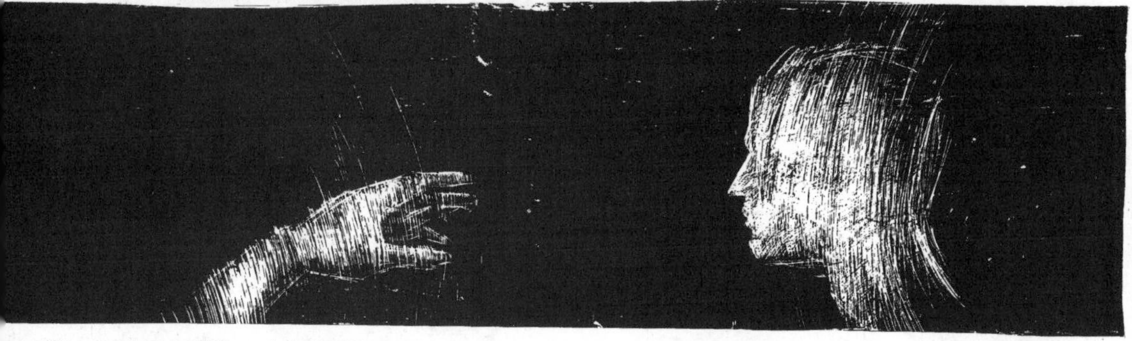

AND HALVED AGAIN. HALFWAY TO HALFWAY.

INFINITELY PARCELED.

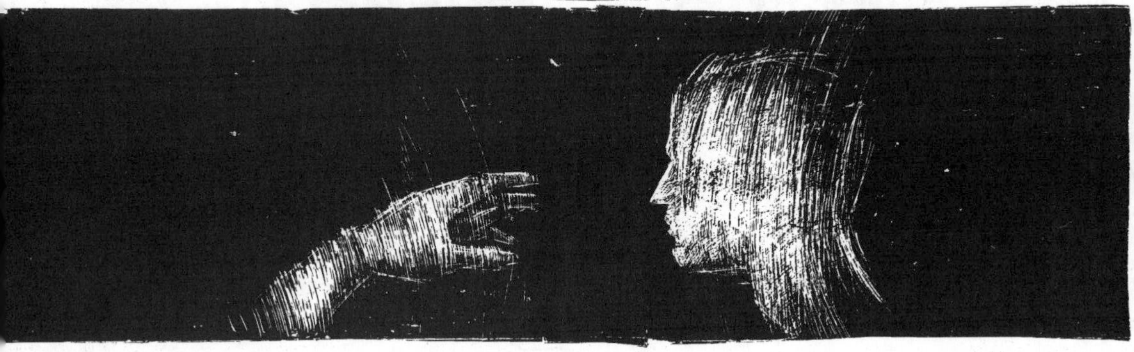

ALWAYS HALFWAY TO HALFWAY OF THE NEXT HALF.

NEVER MAKING CONTACT.

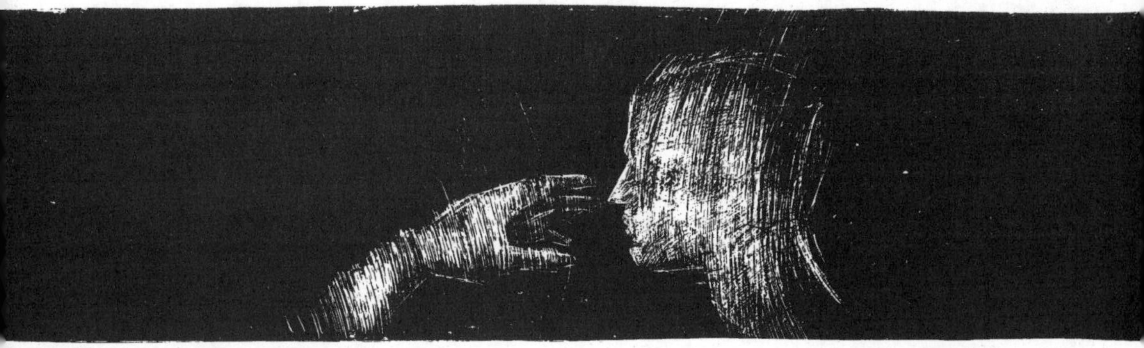

STILL, WE REACH OUT. IT'S JUST MATH.

W ETWORK

or: How Long Can You Play in the Mud
Before Your Hands Get Dirty?

A SHOCKTRAUMA STUDIOS PRODUCTION   STORY AND ART: PHILLIP HESTER   INKS: JIM WOODYARD

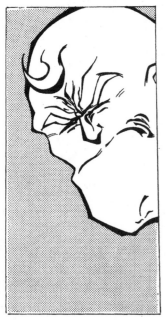

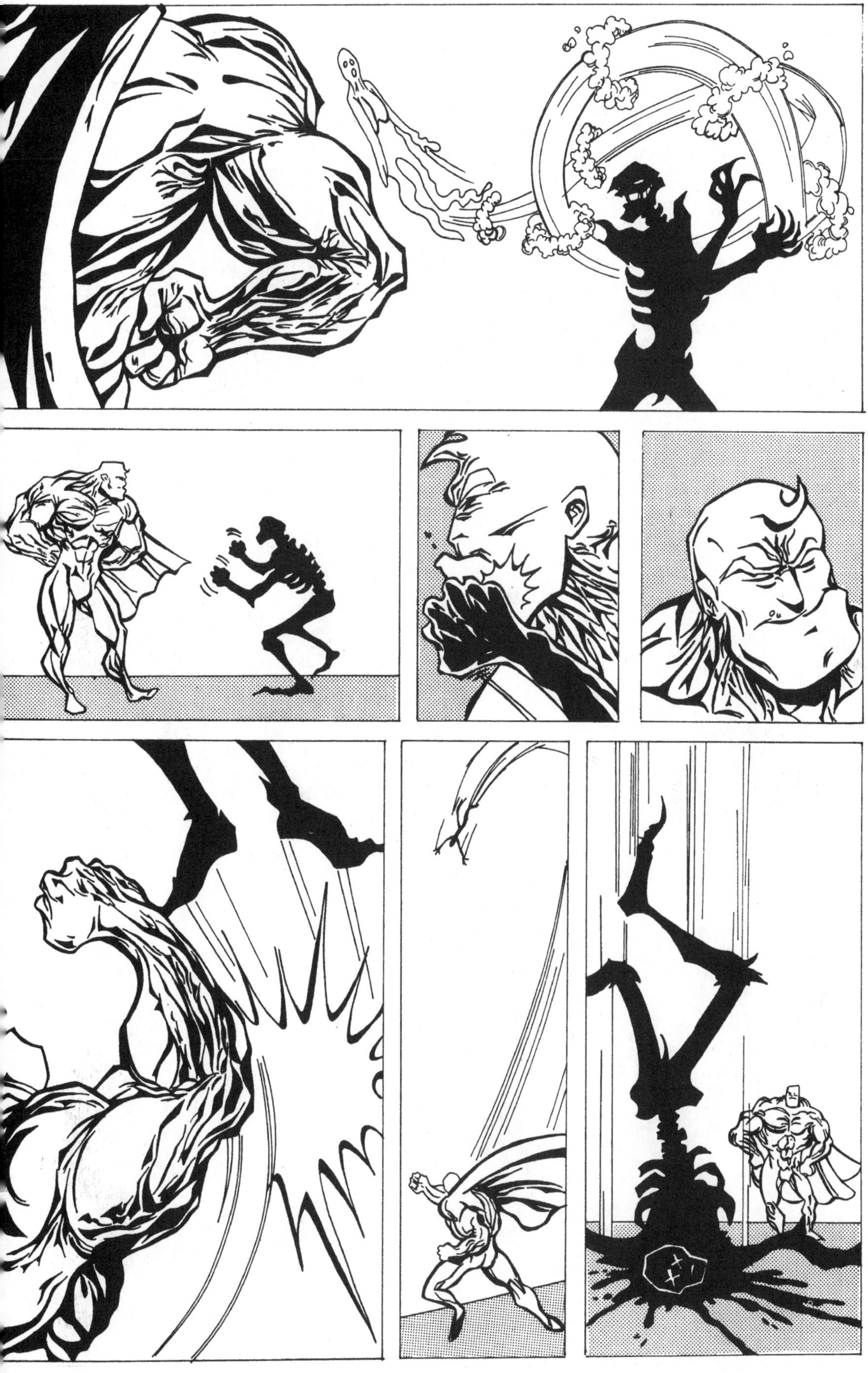

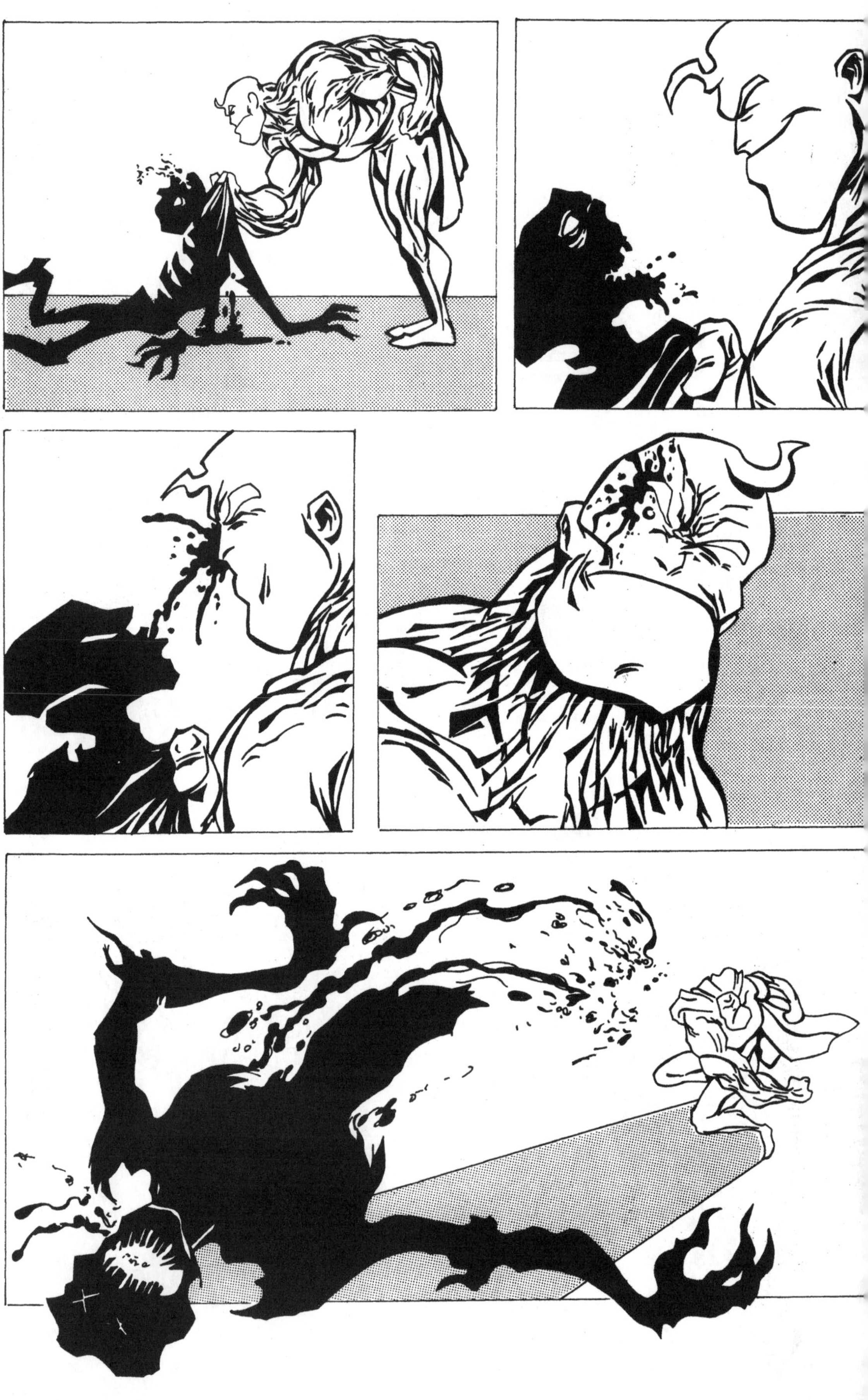

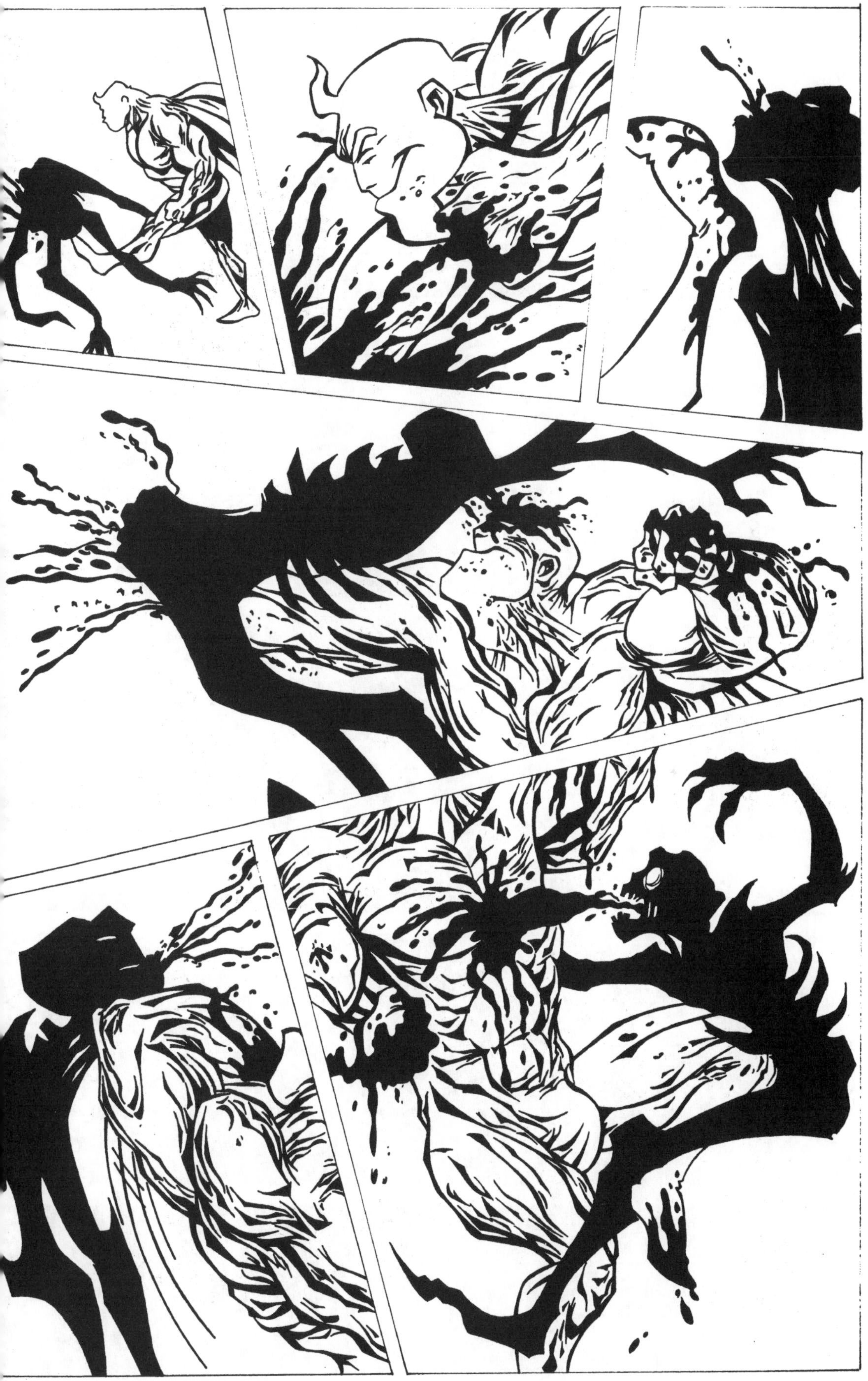

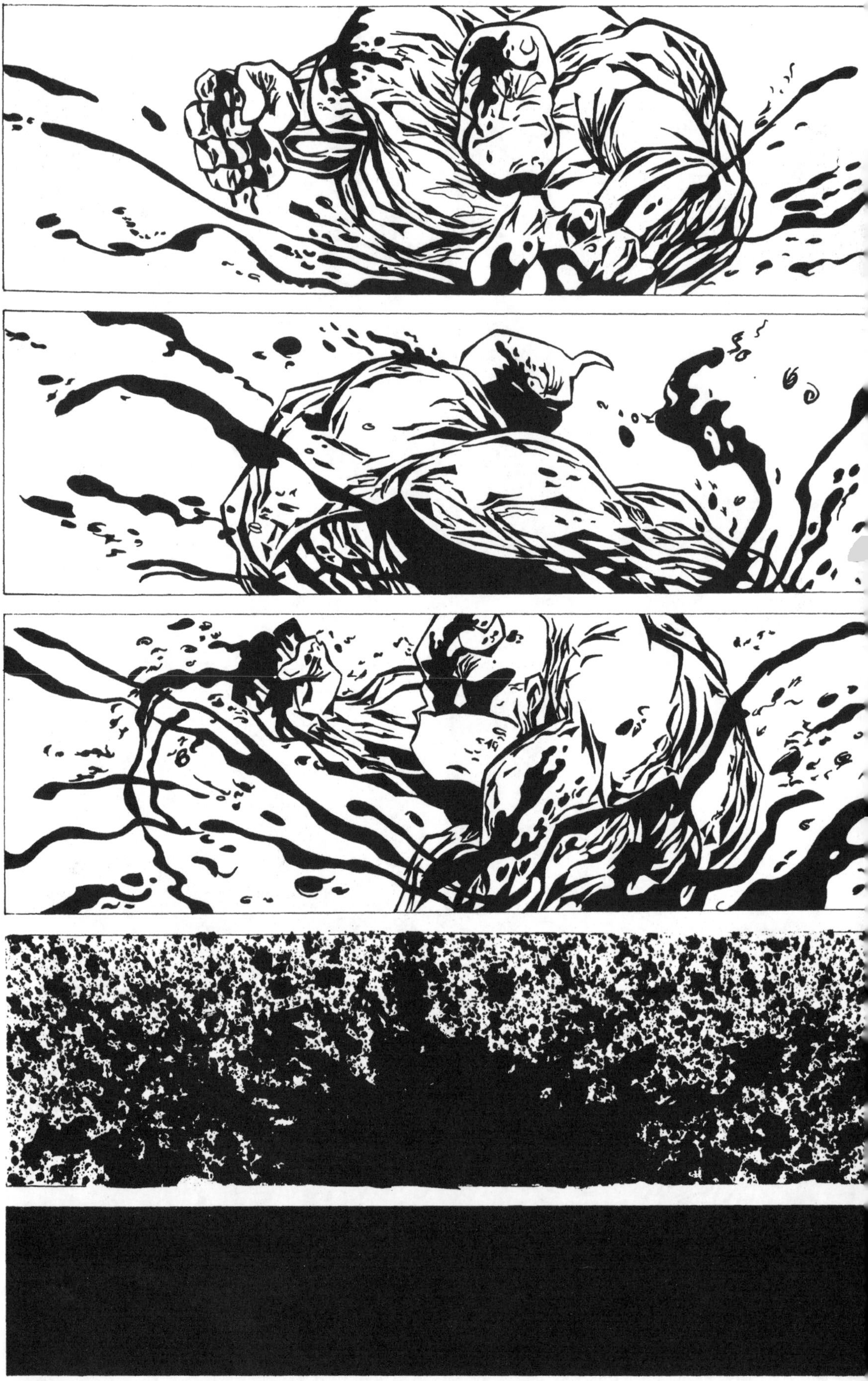

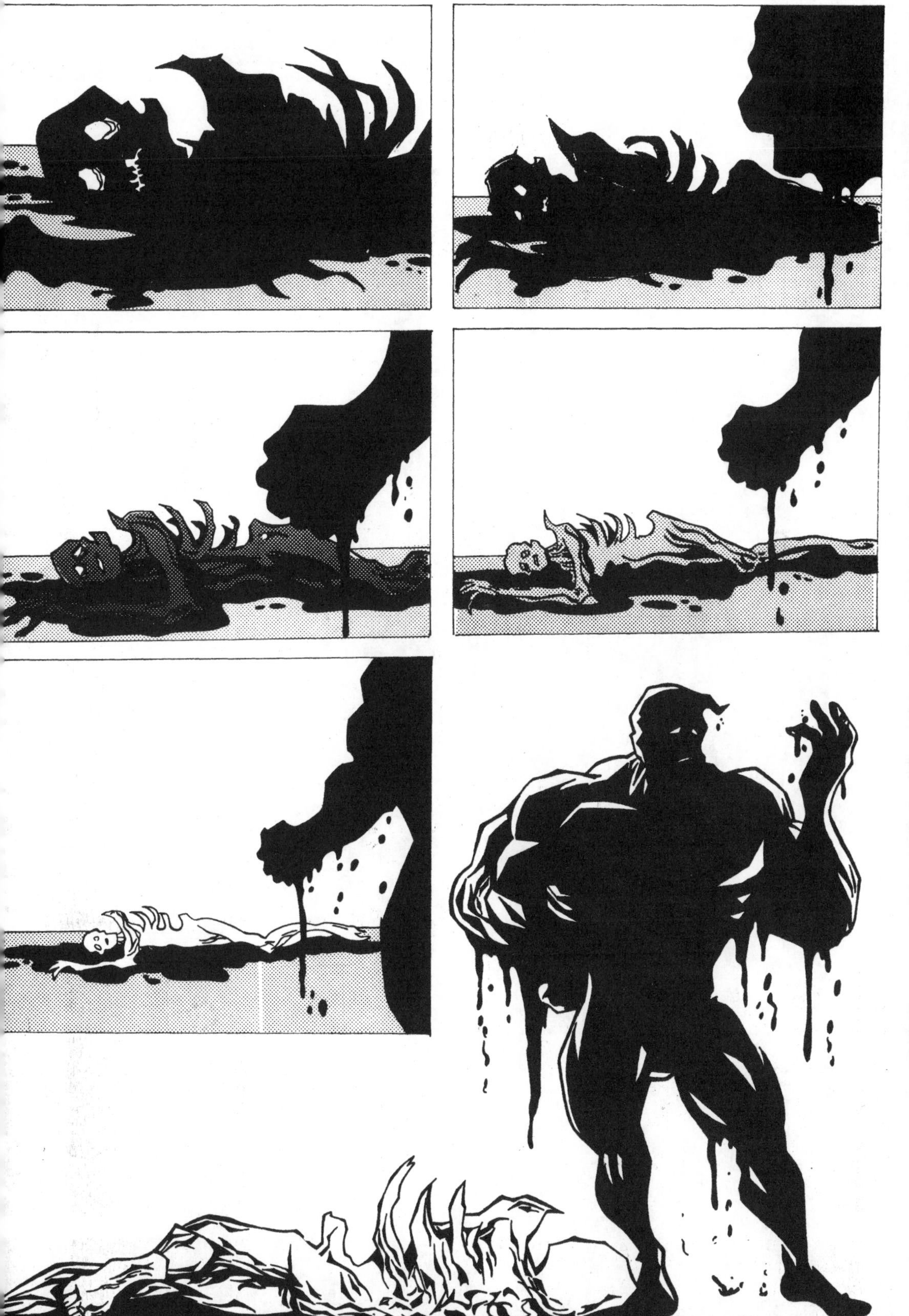
END

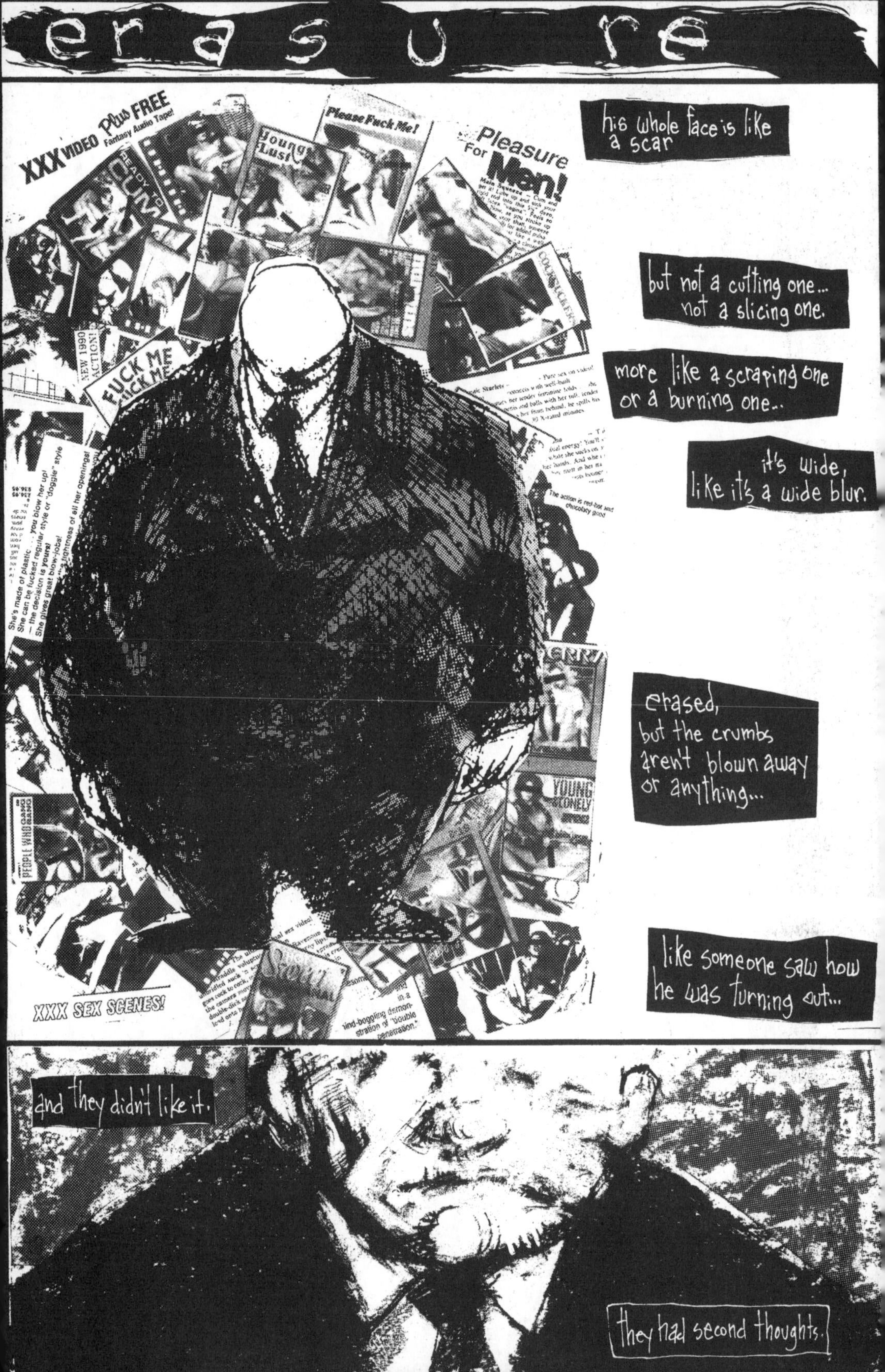
erasure
his whole face is like a scar
but not a cutting one... not a slicing one.
more like a scraping one or a burning one..
it's wide, like it's a wide blur.
erased, but the crumbs aren't blown away or anything...
like someone saw how he was turning out...
and they didn't like it.
they had second thoughts.
XXX VIDEO Plus FREE Fantasy Audio Tape!
Please Fuck Me!
Pleasure For Men!
NEW 1990 ACTION!
XXX SEX SCENES!

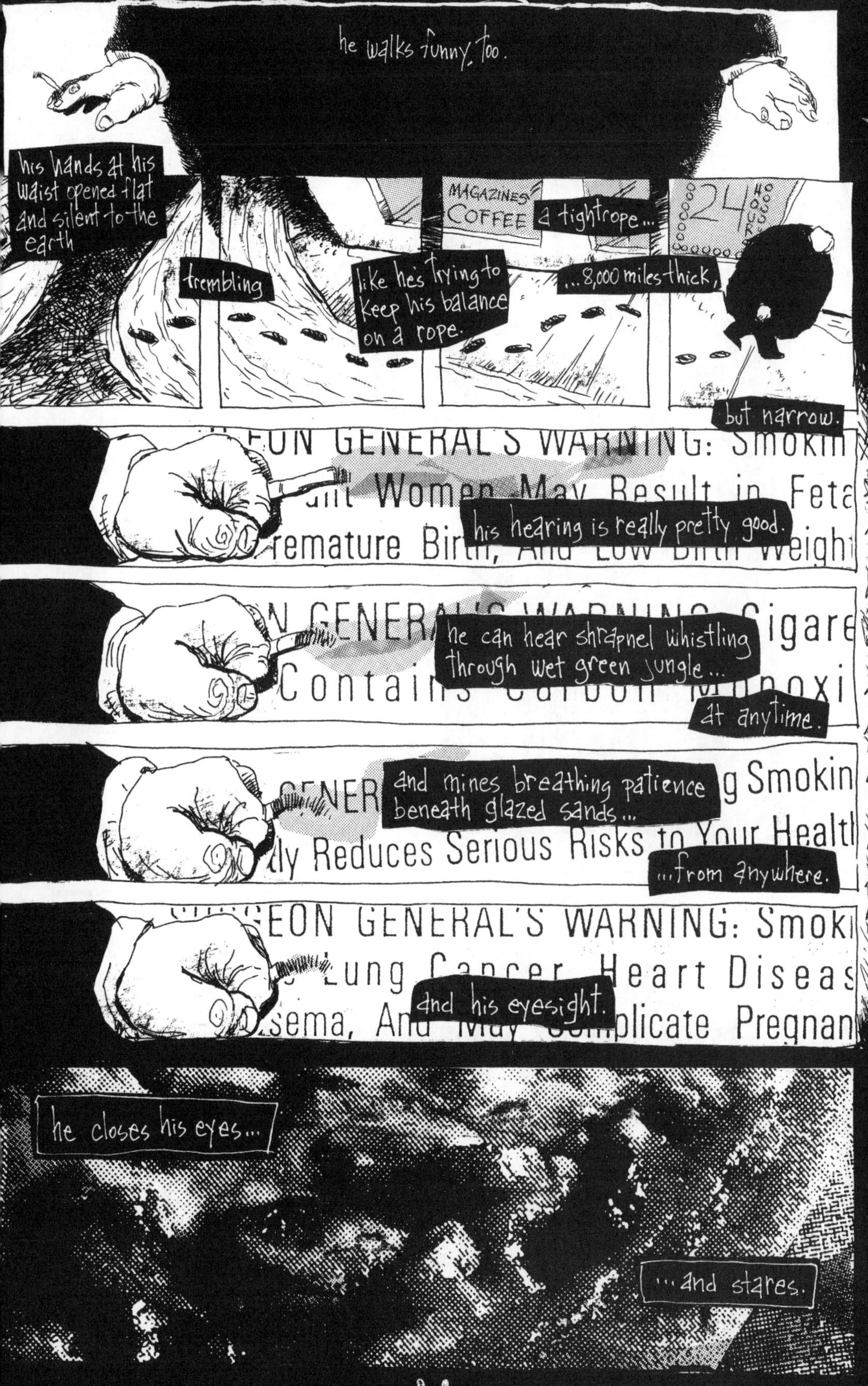
he walks funny, too.
his hands at his waist opened flat and silent to the earth
trembling
like he's trying to keep his balance on a rope.
MAGAZINES
COFFEE
a tightrope...
24
...8,000 miles thick,
but narrow.
his hearing is really pretty good.
he can hear shrapnel whistling through wet green jungle...
at anytime.
and mines breathing patience beneath glazed sands...
...from anywhere.
and his eyesight.
he closes his eyes...
...and stares.

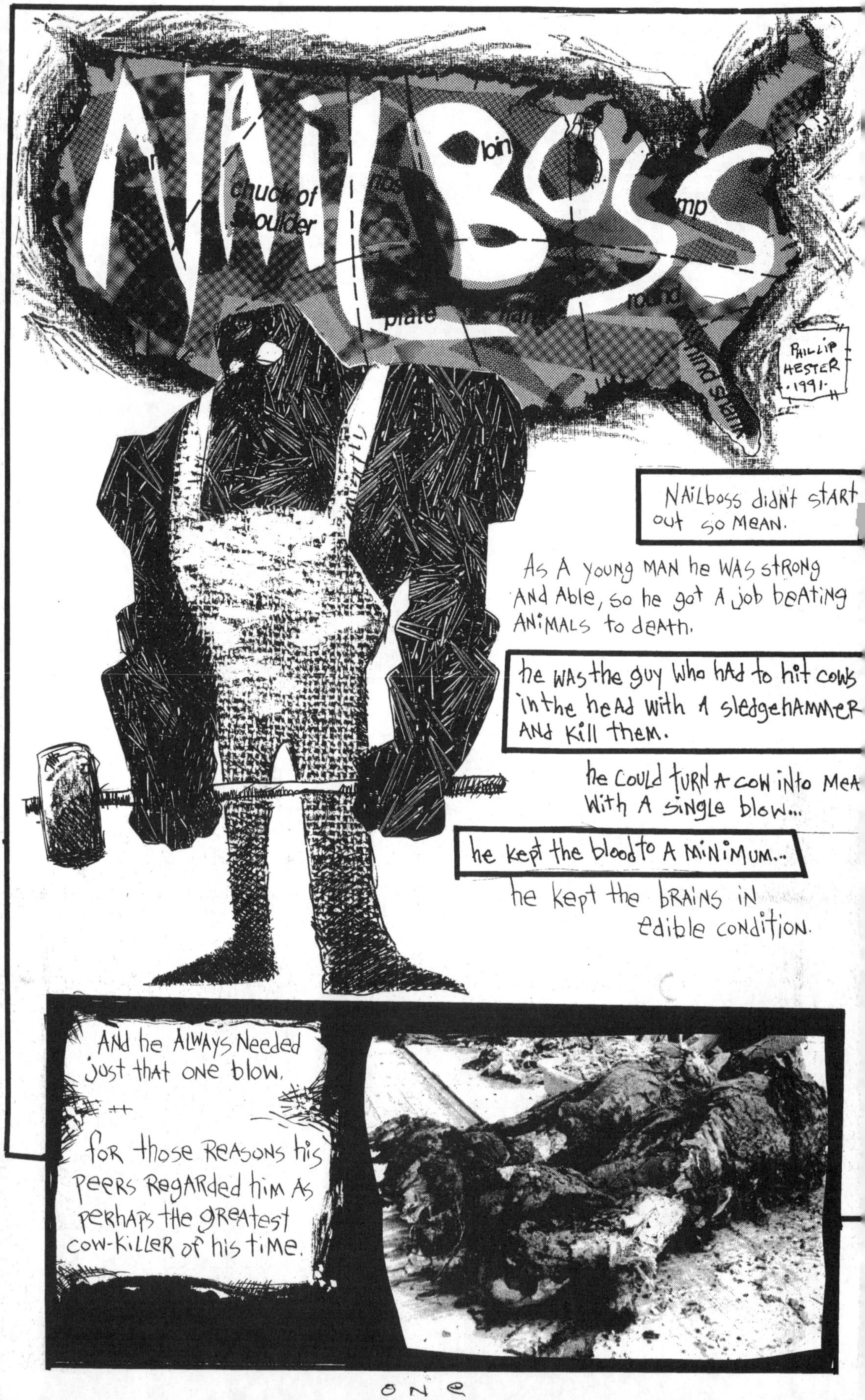
NAILBOSS
chuck of shoulder
plate
round
hind shank
PHILLIP HESTER ·1991·
NAILboss didn't start out so MEAN.
As A young MAN he WAS strong And Able, so he got A job beating ANIMALS to death.
he was the guy who had to hit cows in the head with A sledgehammer And kill them.
he could turn A cow into MEA With A single blow...
he kept the blood to A MiNiMUM...
he kept the brains in edible condition.
And he Always Needed just that one blow.
for those Reasons his peers Regarded him As perhaps the greatest cow-killer of his time.

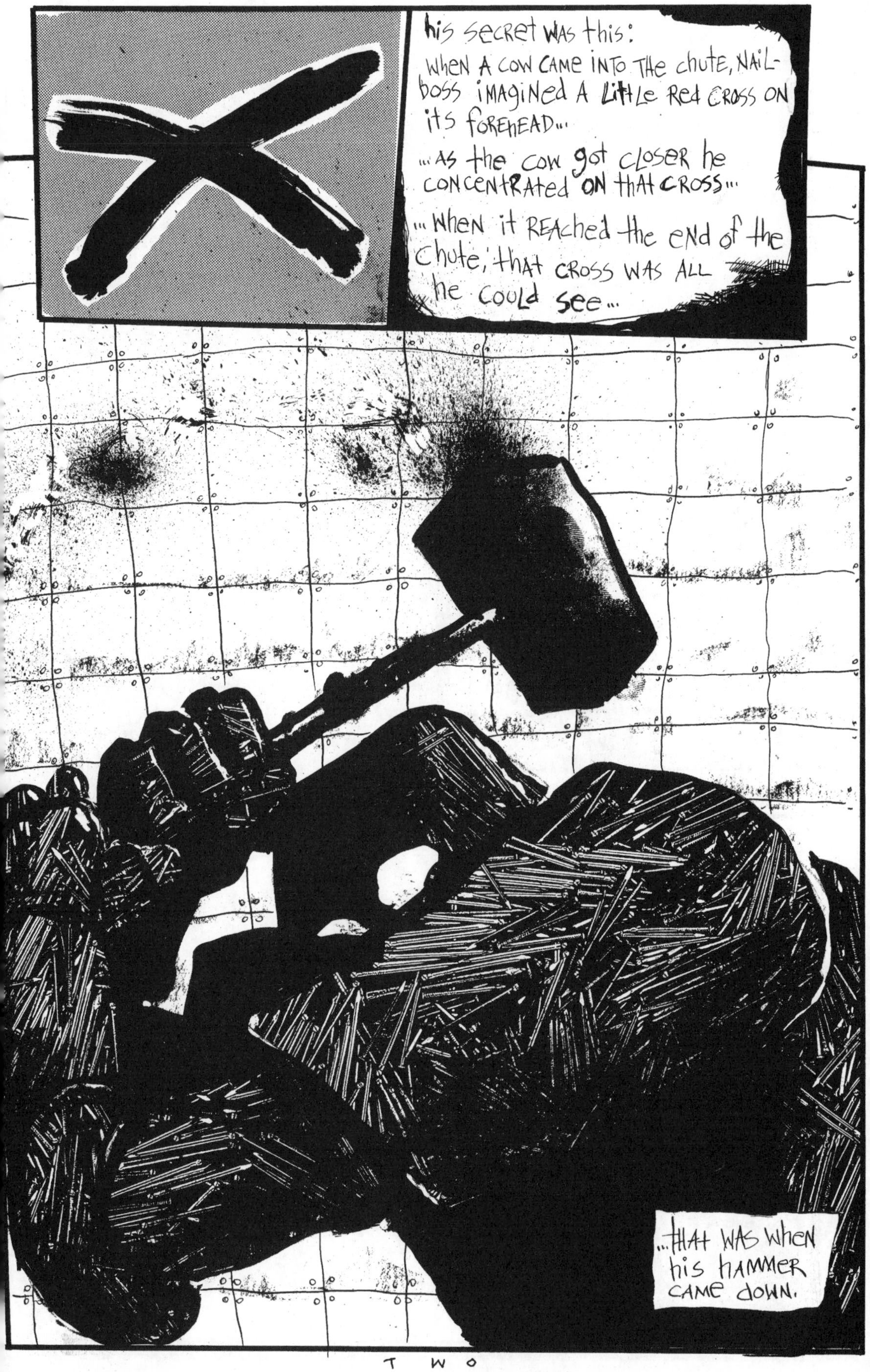
his secret was this:
when a cow came into the chute, Nail-boss imagined a little red cross on its forehead...
...as the cow got closer he concentrated on that cross...
...when it reached the end of the chute, that cross was all he could see...
...that was when his hammer came down.

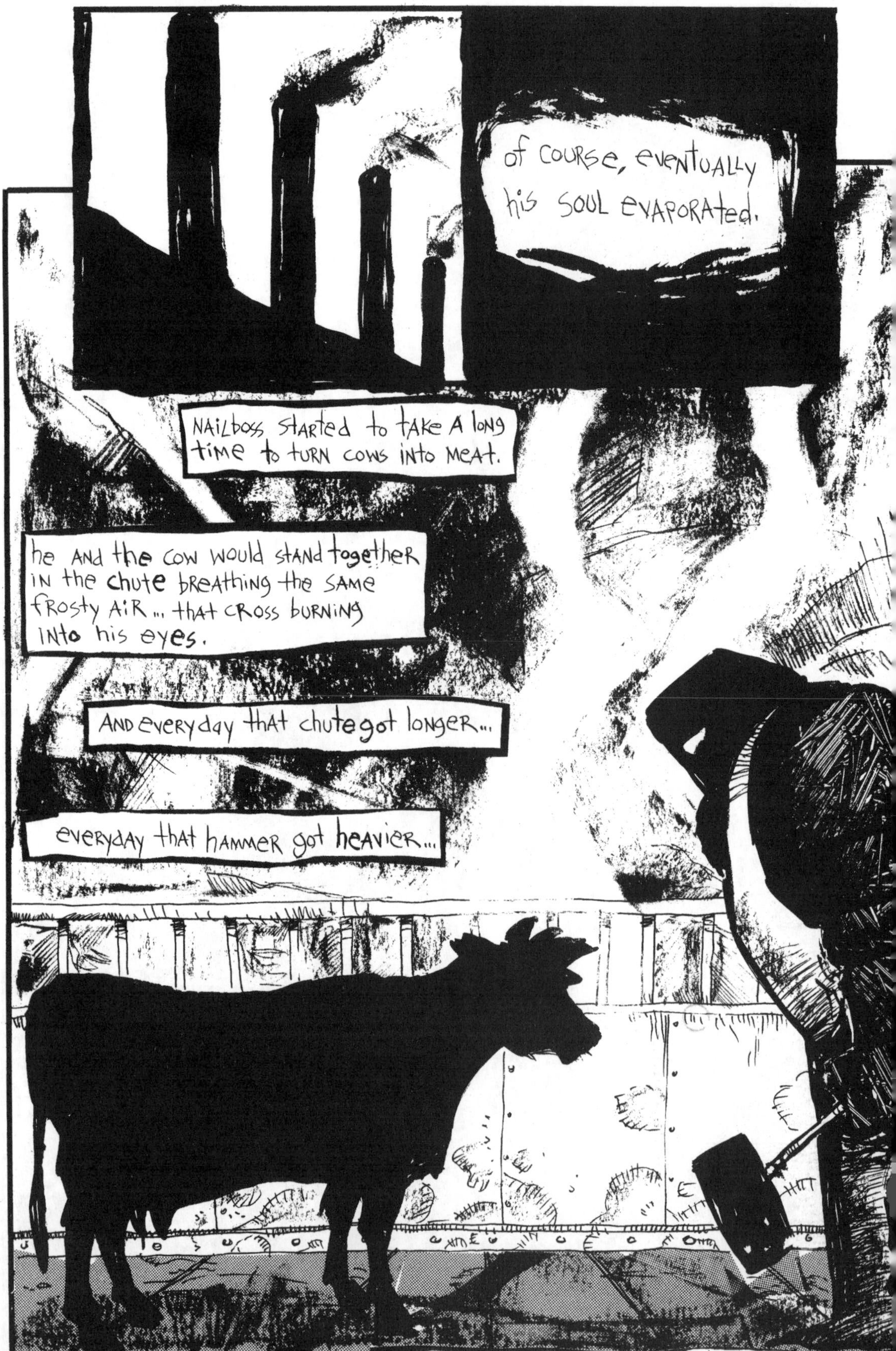
of course, eventually his soul evaporated.
NAILboss started to take a long time to turn cows into meat.
he and the cow would stand together in the chute breathing the same frosty air... that cross burning into his eyes.
And everyday that chute got longer...
everyday that hammer got heavier...
everyday that wet Noise got louder.

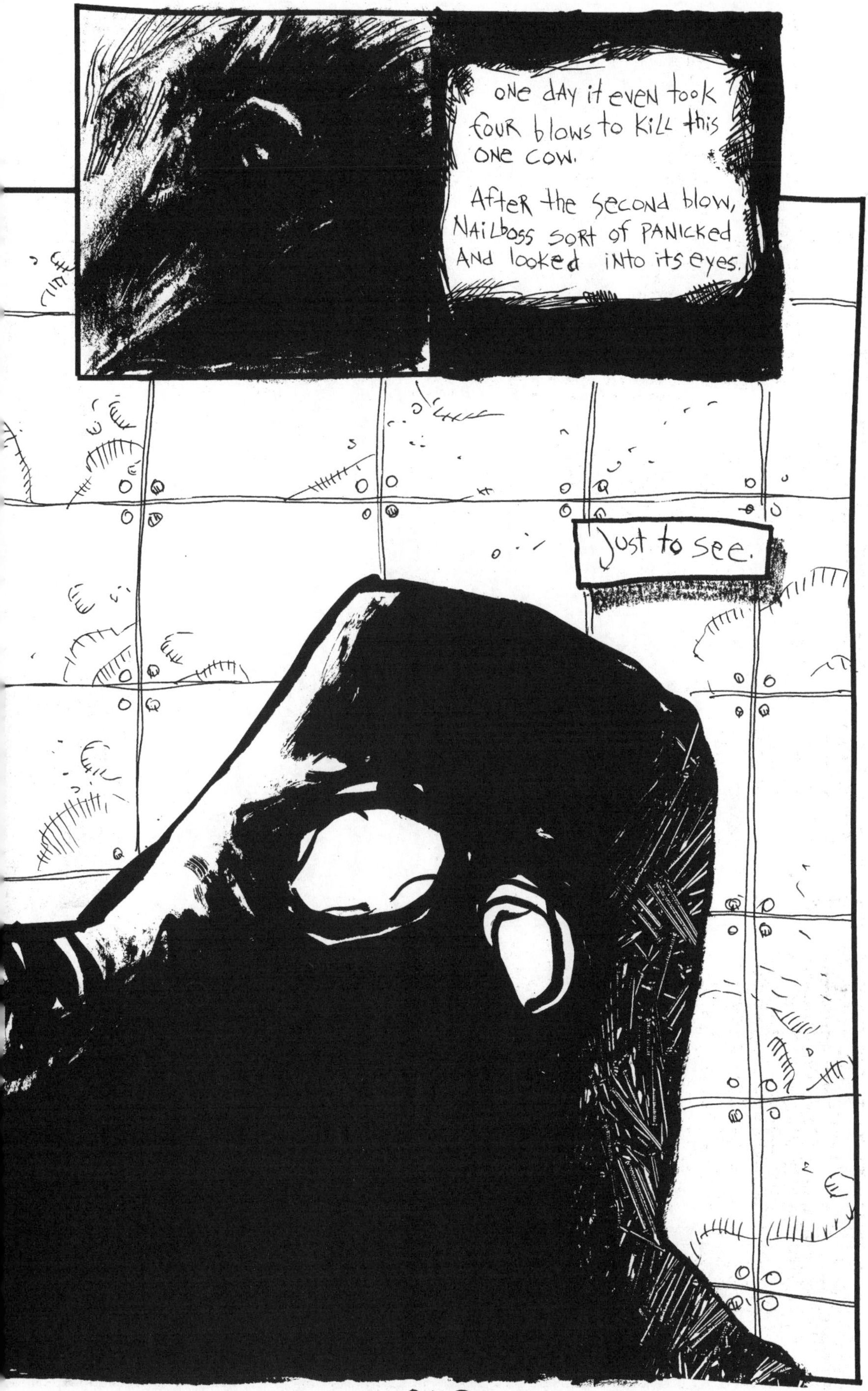
one day it even took four blows to kill this one cow.
After the second blow, Nailboss sort of panicked and looked into its eyes.
Just to see.

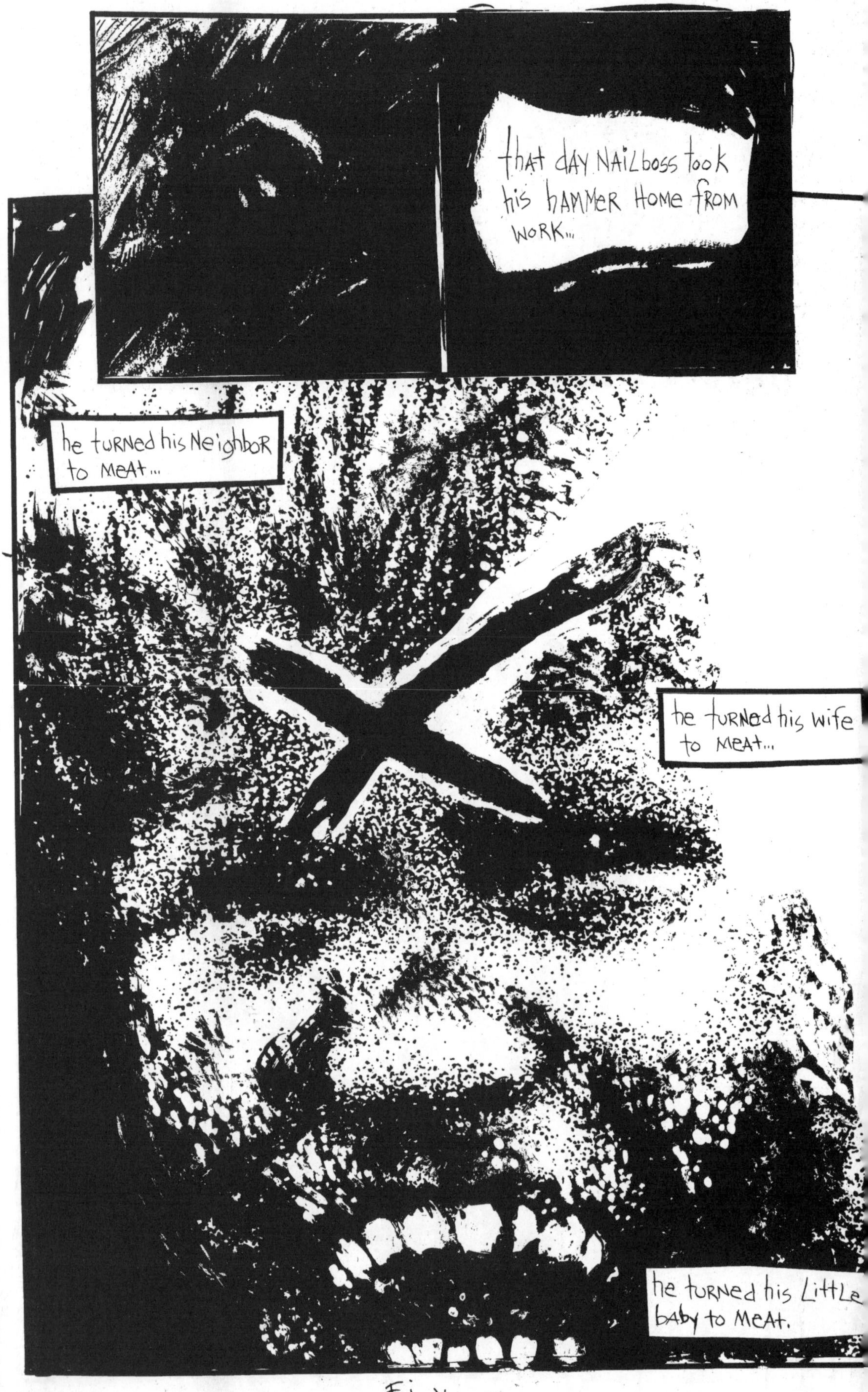
that day NAILboss took his hammer Home from work...
he turned his Neighbor to meat...
he turned his wife to meat...
he turned his little baby to meat.

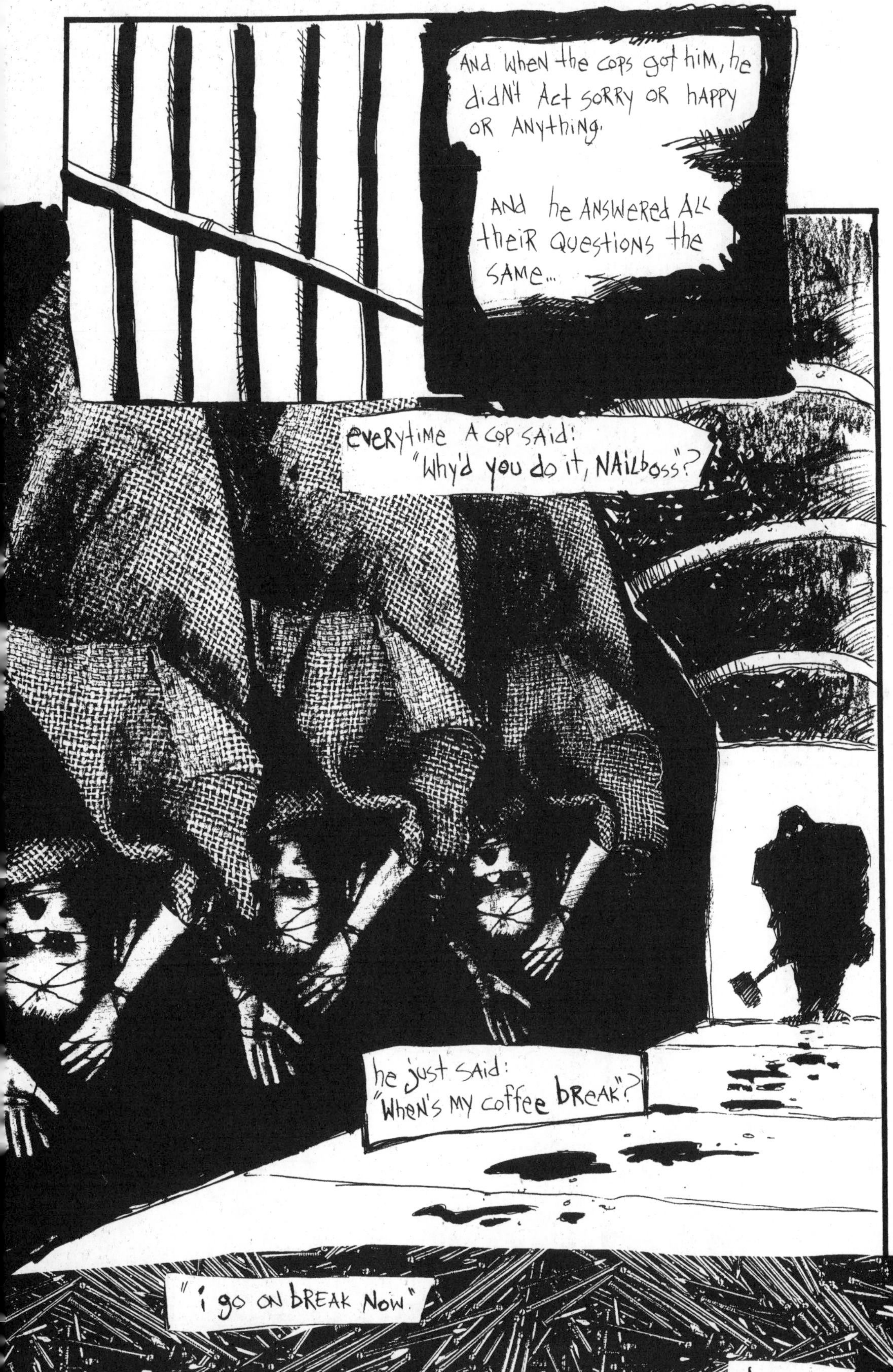
And when the cops got him, he didN't Act sorry or happy or Anything.
And he Answered All their questions the same...
everytime A cop said: "Why'd you do it, NAILboss"?
he just said: "When's my coffee break"?
"i go on break Now"
he said.

stop

How Jenny Left Earth

WHAT CROP GREW IN THAT FIELD?

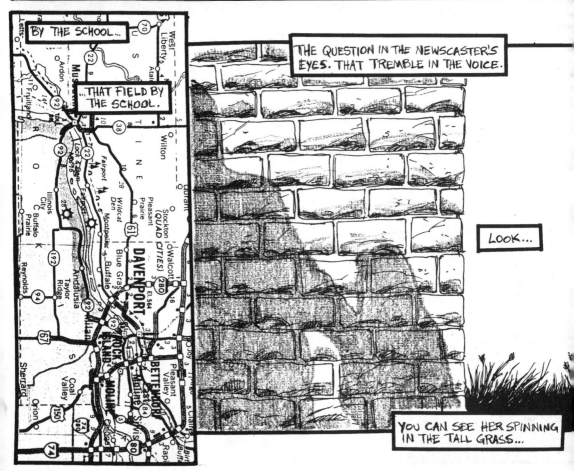

BY THE SCHOOL...

...THAT FIELD BY THE SCHOOL.

THE QUESTION IN THE NEWSCASTER'S EYES. THAT TREMBLE IN THE VOICE.

LOOK...

YOU CAN SEE HER SPINNING IN THE TALL GRASS...

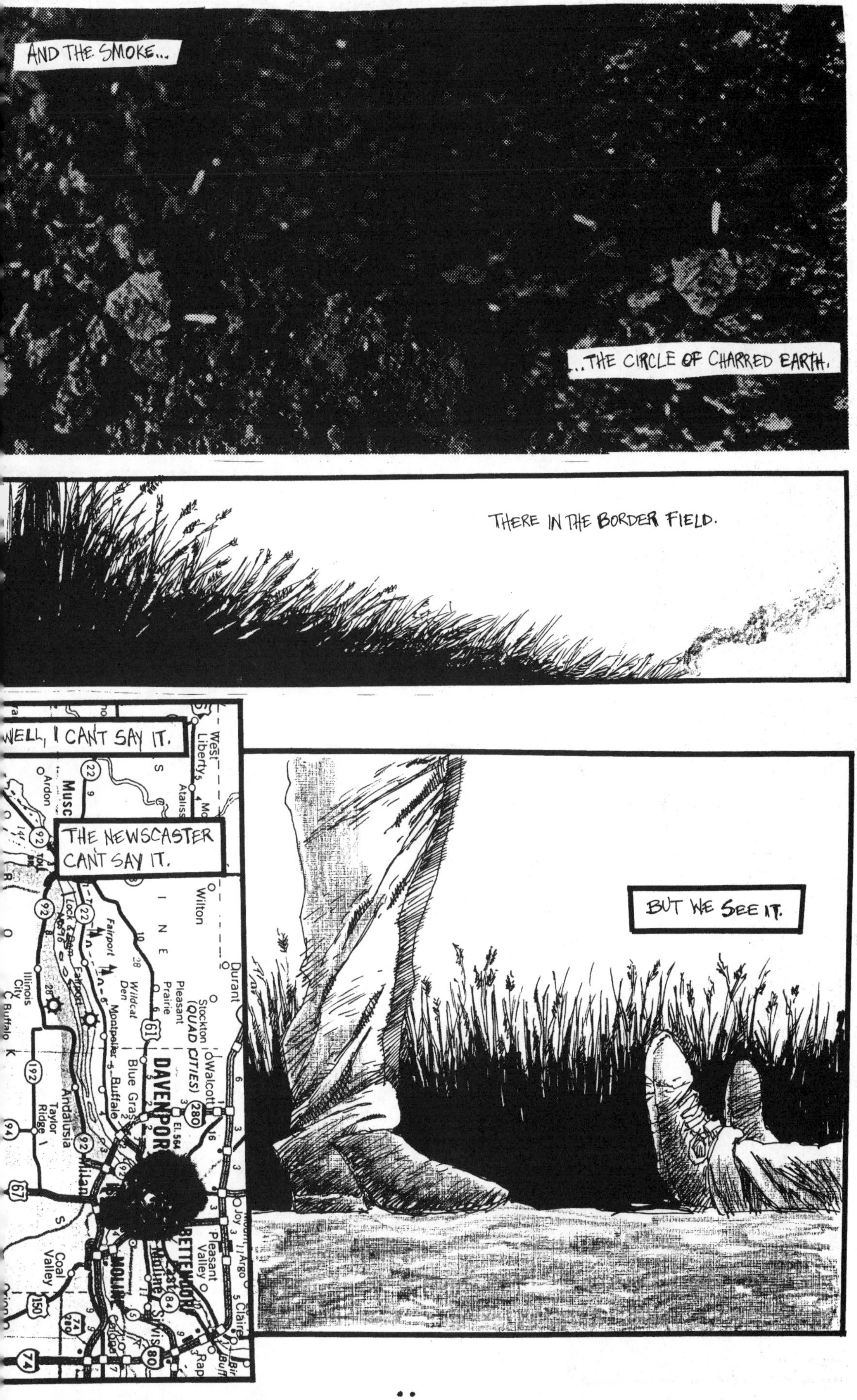
AND THE SMOKE...
...THE CIRCLE OF CHARRED EARTH.
THERE IN THE BORDER FIELD.
WELL, I CAN'T SAY IT.
THE NEWSCASTER CAN'T SAY IT.
BUT WE SEE IT.

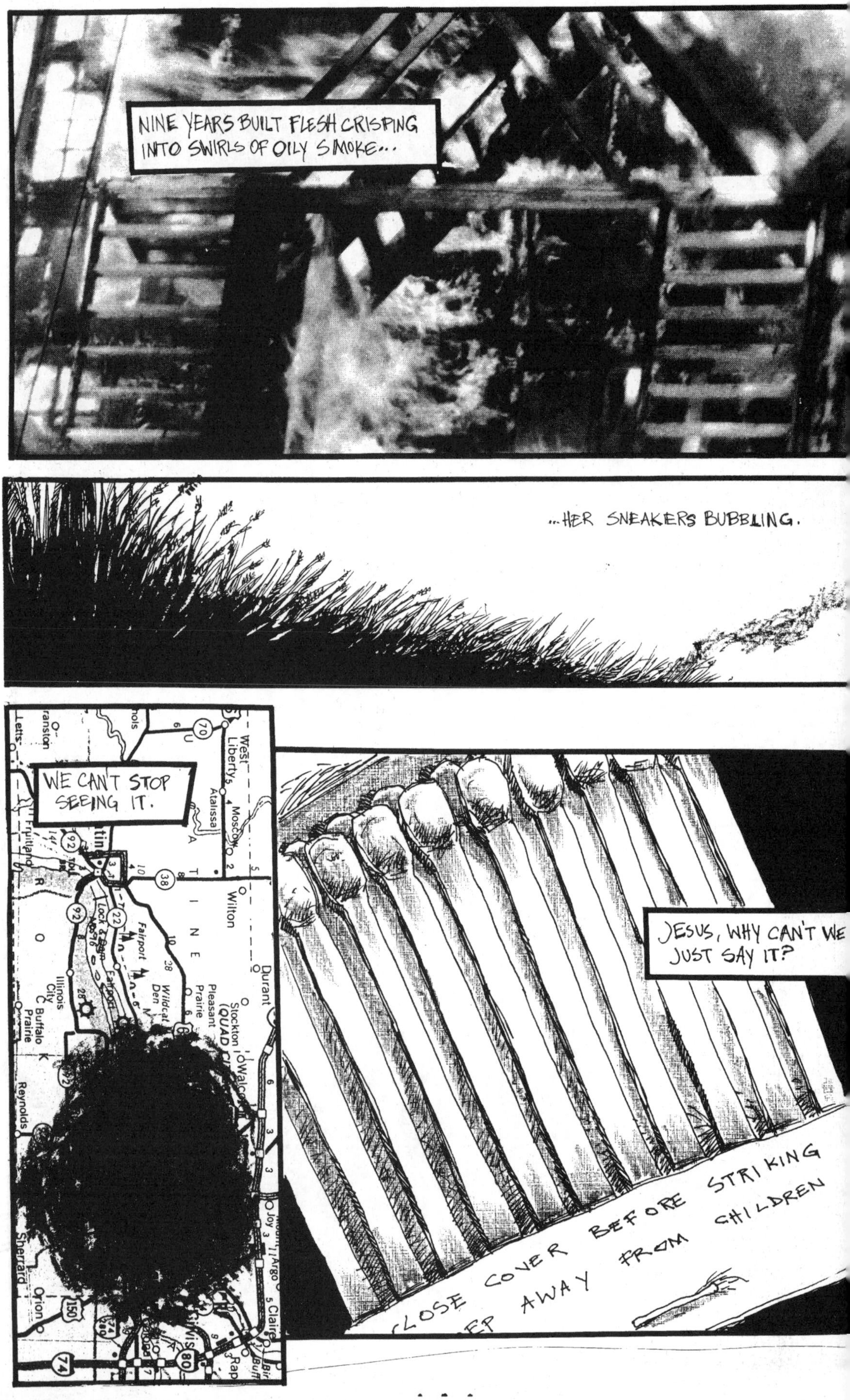
NINE YEARS BUILT FLESH CRISPING INTO SWIRLS OF OILY SMOKE...
...HER SNEAKERS BUBBLING.
WE CAN'T STOP SEEING IT.
West Liberty
Atalissa
Moscow
Wilton
Fairport
Durant
Illinois City
Buffalo Prairie
Wildcat Den
Pleasant Prairie
Stockton
Reynolds
Sherrard
Orion
Walcott
Argo
Joy
JESUS, WHY CAN'T WE JUST SAY IT?
CLOSE COVER BEFORE STRIKING
EP AWAY FROM CHILDREN

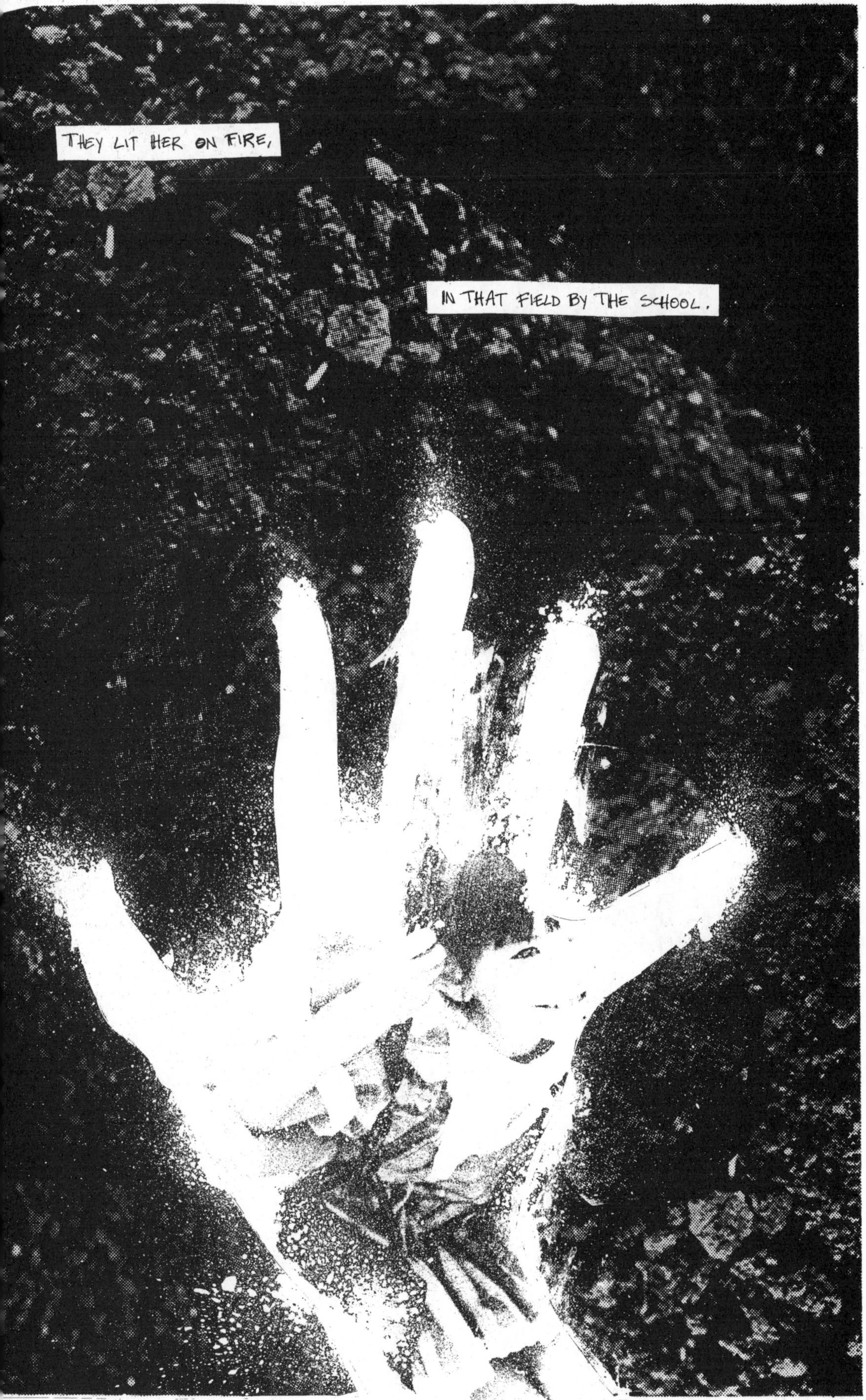
THEY LIT HER ON FIRE,
IN THAT FIELD BY THE SCHOOL.

DONE

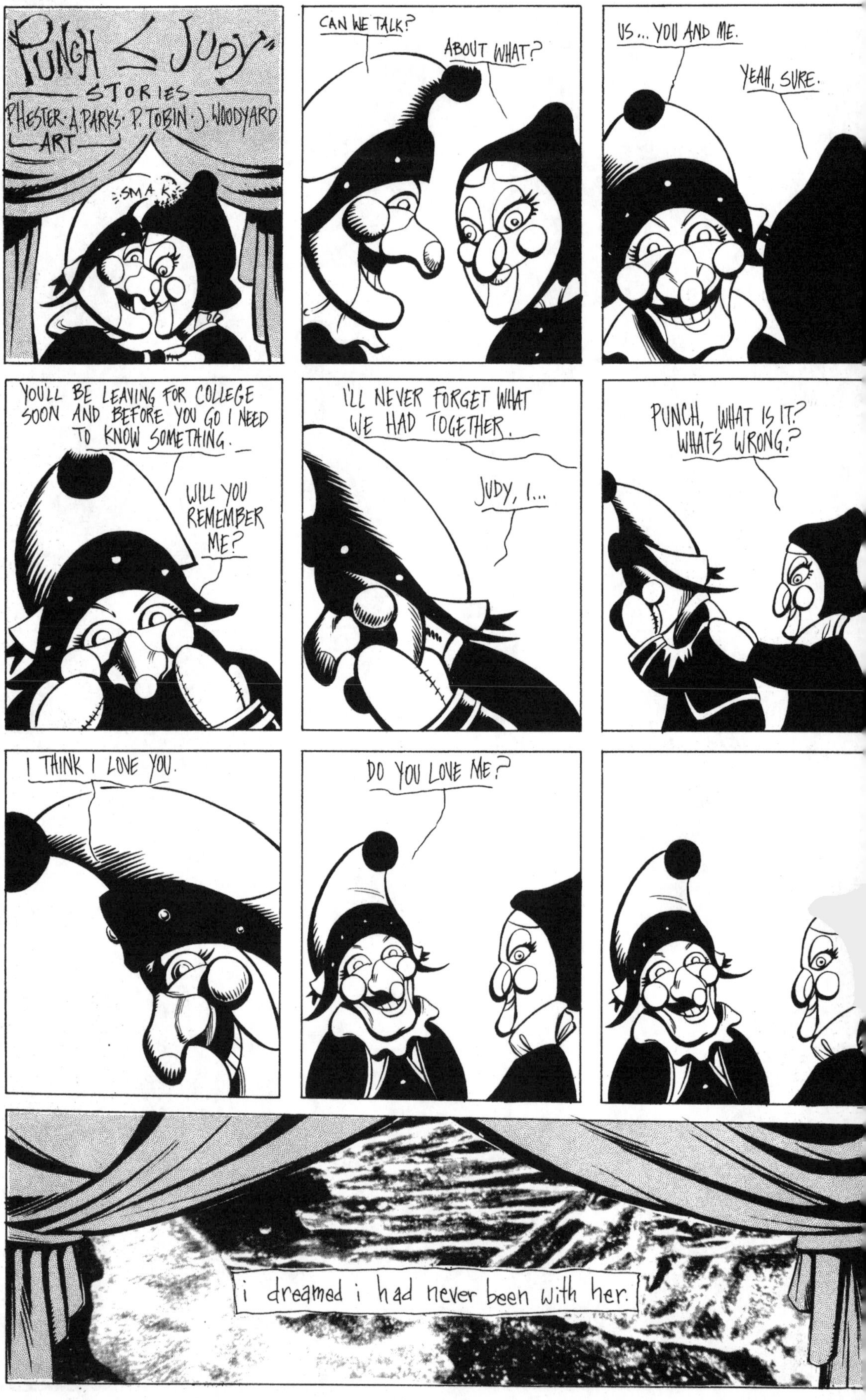
PUNCH & JUDY
STORIES
P. HESTER · A. PARKS · P. TOBIN · J. WOODYARD
ART
SMAK
CAN WE TALK?
ABOUT WHAT?
US... YOU AND ME.
YEAH, SURE.
YOU'LL BE LEAVING FOR COLLEGE SOON AND BEFORE YOU GO I NEED TO KNOW SOMETHING.
WILL YOU REMEMBER ME?
I'LL NEVER FORGET WHAT WE HAD TOGETHER.
JUDY, I...
PUNCH, WHAT IS IT? WHAT'S WRONG?
I THINK I LOVE YOU.
DO YOU LOVE ME?
i dreamed i had never been with her.

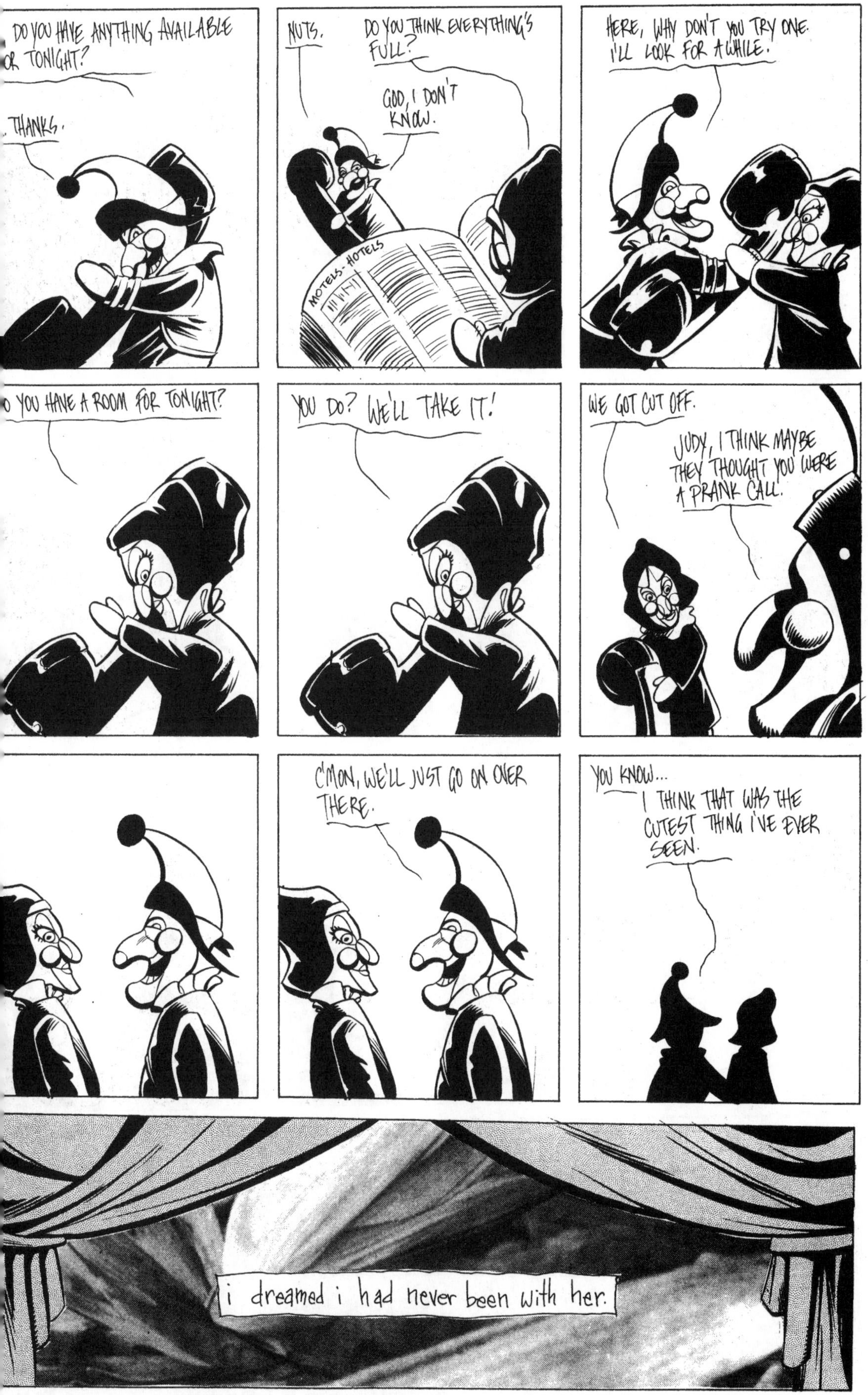
DO YOU HAVE ANYTHING AVAILABLE OR TONIGHT?
THANKS.
NUTS.
DO YOU THINK EVERYTHING'S FULL?
GOD, I DON'T KNOW.
MOTELS · HOTELS
HERE, WHY DON'T YOU TRY ONE. I'LL LOOK FOR AWHILE.
O YOU HAVE A ROOM FOR TONIGHT?
YOU DO? WE'LL TAKE IT!
WE GOT CUT OFF.
JUDY, I THINK MAYBE THEY THOUGHT YOU WERE A PRANK CALL.
C'MON, WE'LL JUST GO ON OVER THERE.
YOU KNOW...
I THINK THAT WAS THE CUTEST THING I'VE EVER SEEN.
i dreamed i had never been with her.

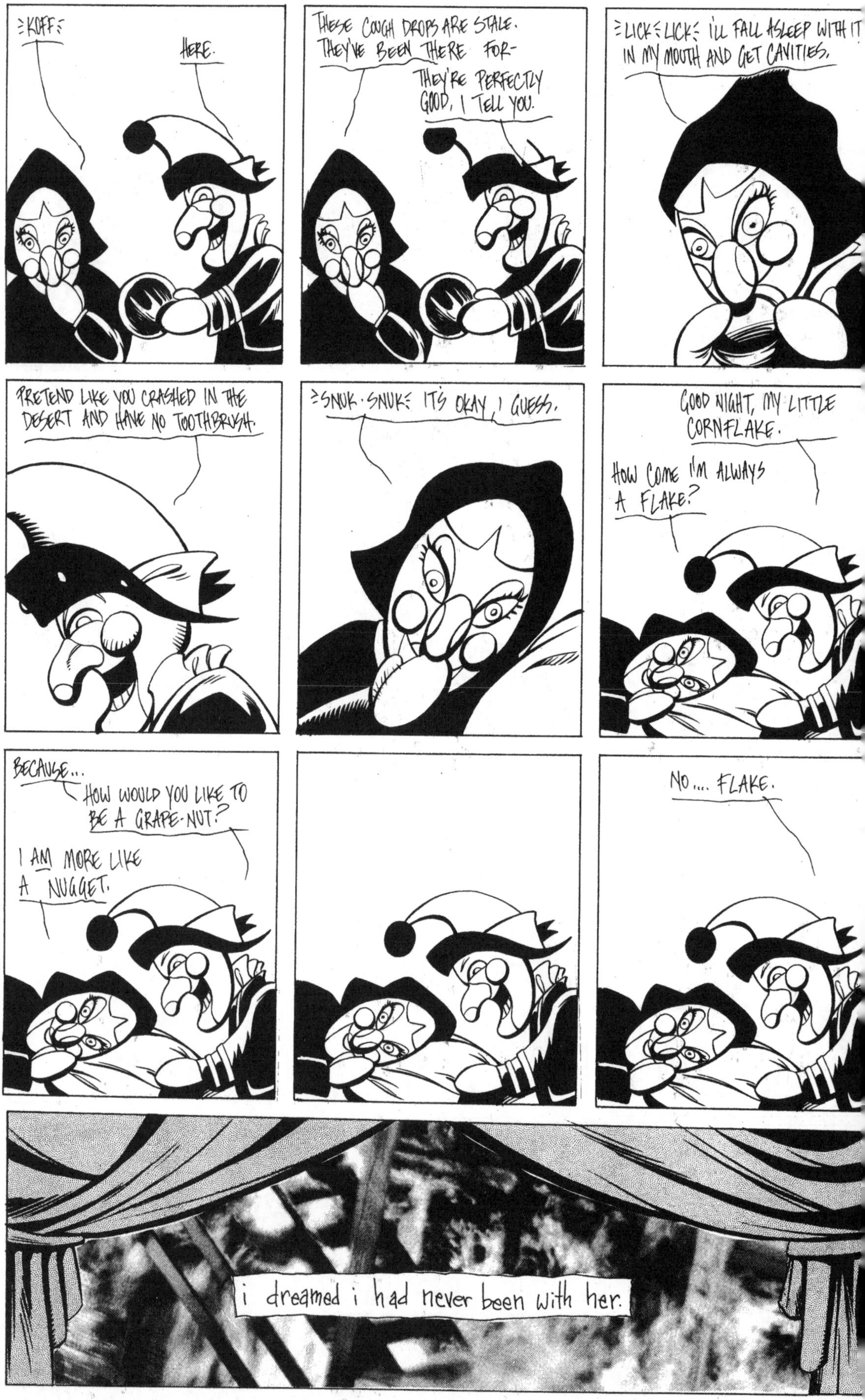

≡KOFF≡
HERE.
THESE COUGH DROPS ARE STALE. THEY'VE BEEN THERE FOR-
THEY'RE PERFECTLY GOOD, I TELL YOU.
≡LICK≡LICK≡ I'LL FALL ASLEEP WITH IT IN MY MOUTH AND GET CAVITIES.
PRETEND LIKE YOU CRASHED IN THE DESERT AND HAVE NO TOOTHBRUSH.
≡SNUK·SNUK≡ IT'S OKAY, I GUESS.
GOOD NIGHT, MY LITTLE CORNFLAKE.
HOW COME I'M ALWAYS A FLAKE?
BECAUSE...
HOW WOULD YOU LIKE TO BE A GRAPE-NUT?
I AM MORE LIKE A NUGGET.
NO.... FLAKE.
i dreamed i had never been with her.

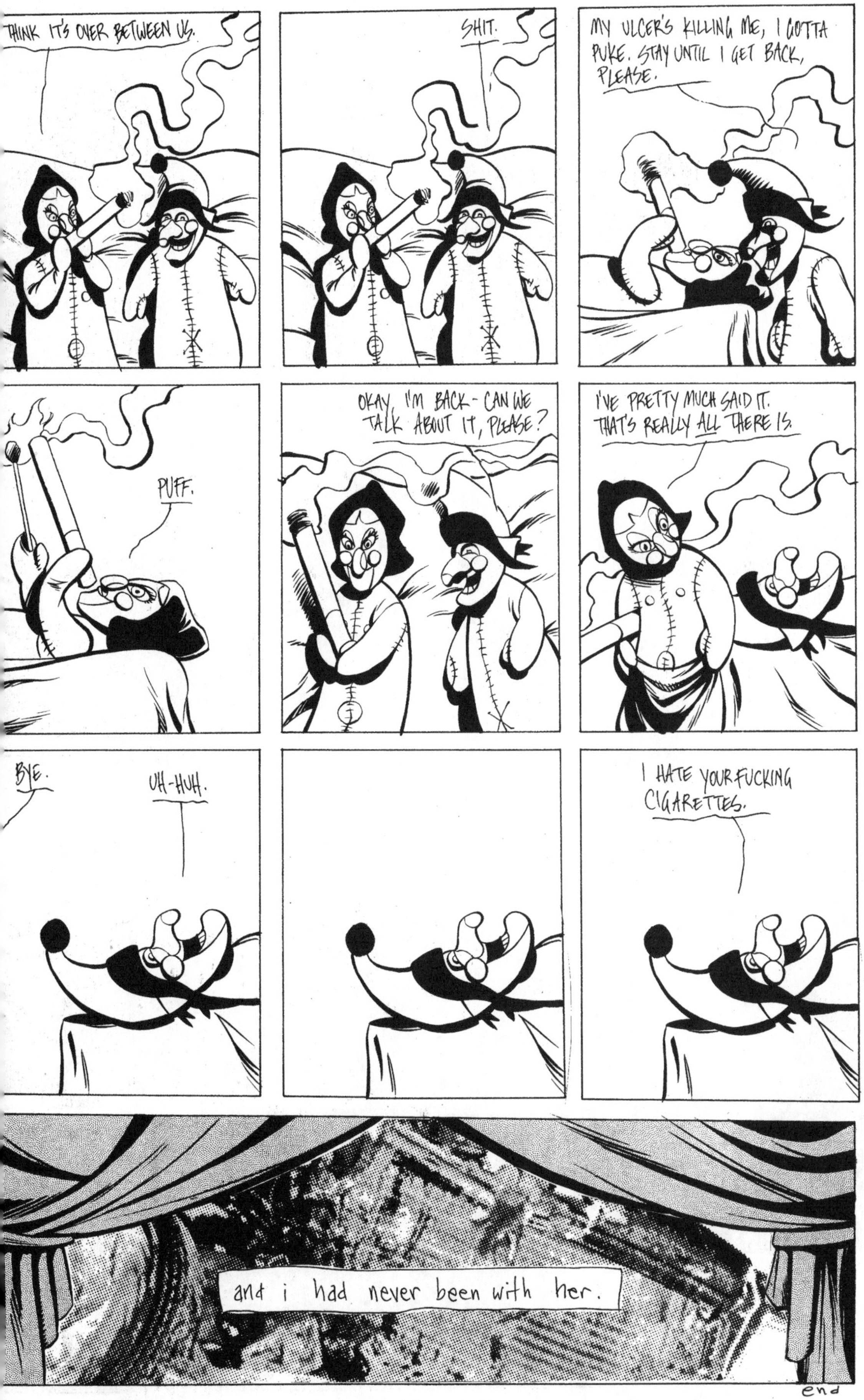
THINK IT'S OVER BETWEEN US.
SHIT.
MY ULCER'S KILLING ME, I GOTTA PUKE. STAY UNTIL I GET BACK, PLEASE.
PUFF.
OKAY, I'M BACK - CAN WE TALK ABOUT IT, PLEASE?
I'VE PRETTY MUCH SAID IT. THAT'S REALLY ALL THERE IS.
BYE.
UH-HUH.
I HATE YOUR FUCKING CIGARETTES.
and i had never been with her.
end

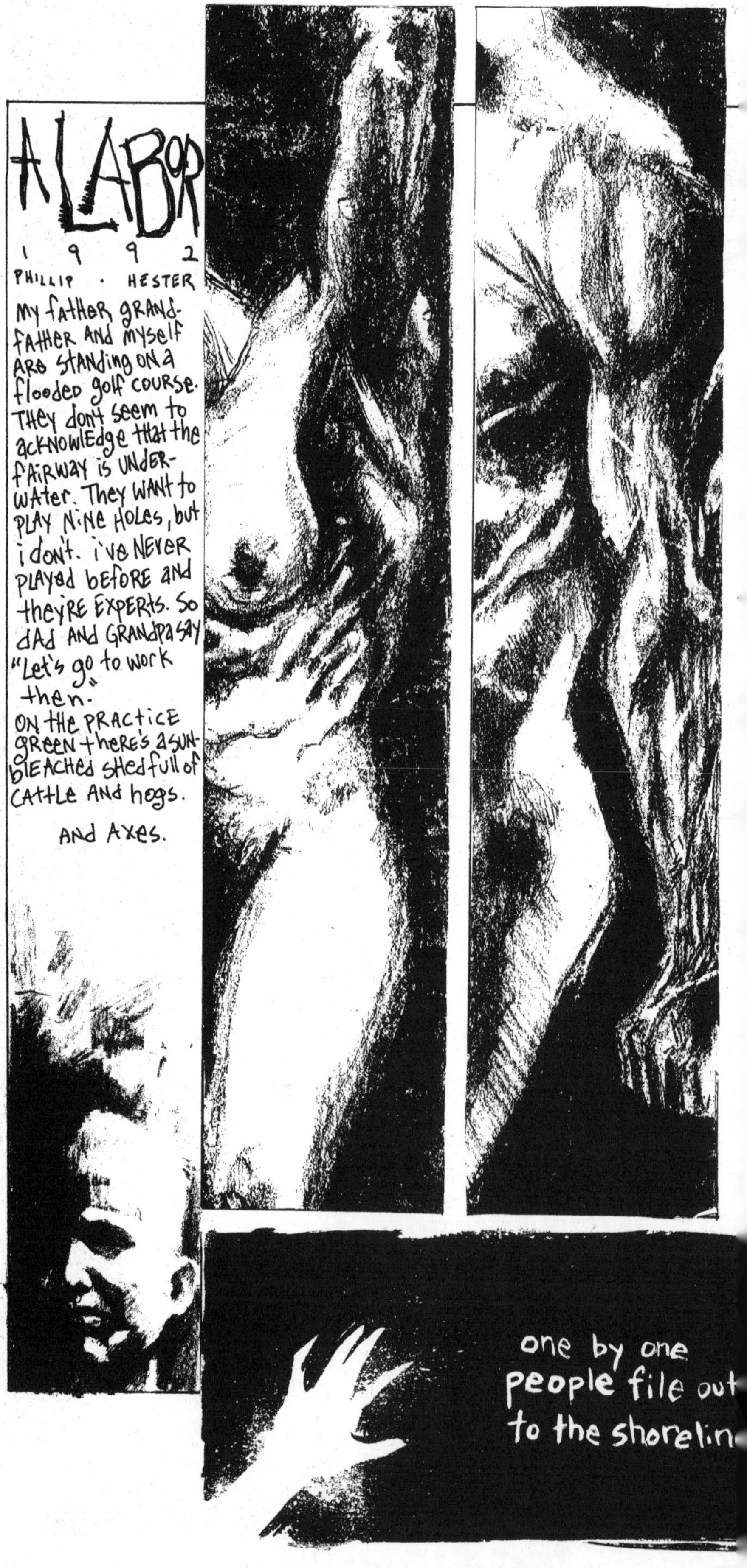

A LABOR
1 9 9 2
PHILLIP · HESTER
My father, grandfather and myself are standing on a flooded golf course. They don't seem to acknowledge that the fairway is underwater. They want to play nine holes, but i don't. i've never played before and they're experts. So dad and grandpa say "Let's go to work then."
On the practice green there's a sun-bleached shed full of cattle and hogs.
And axes.
one by one
people file out
to the shorelin

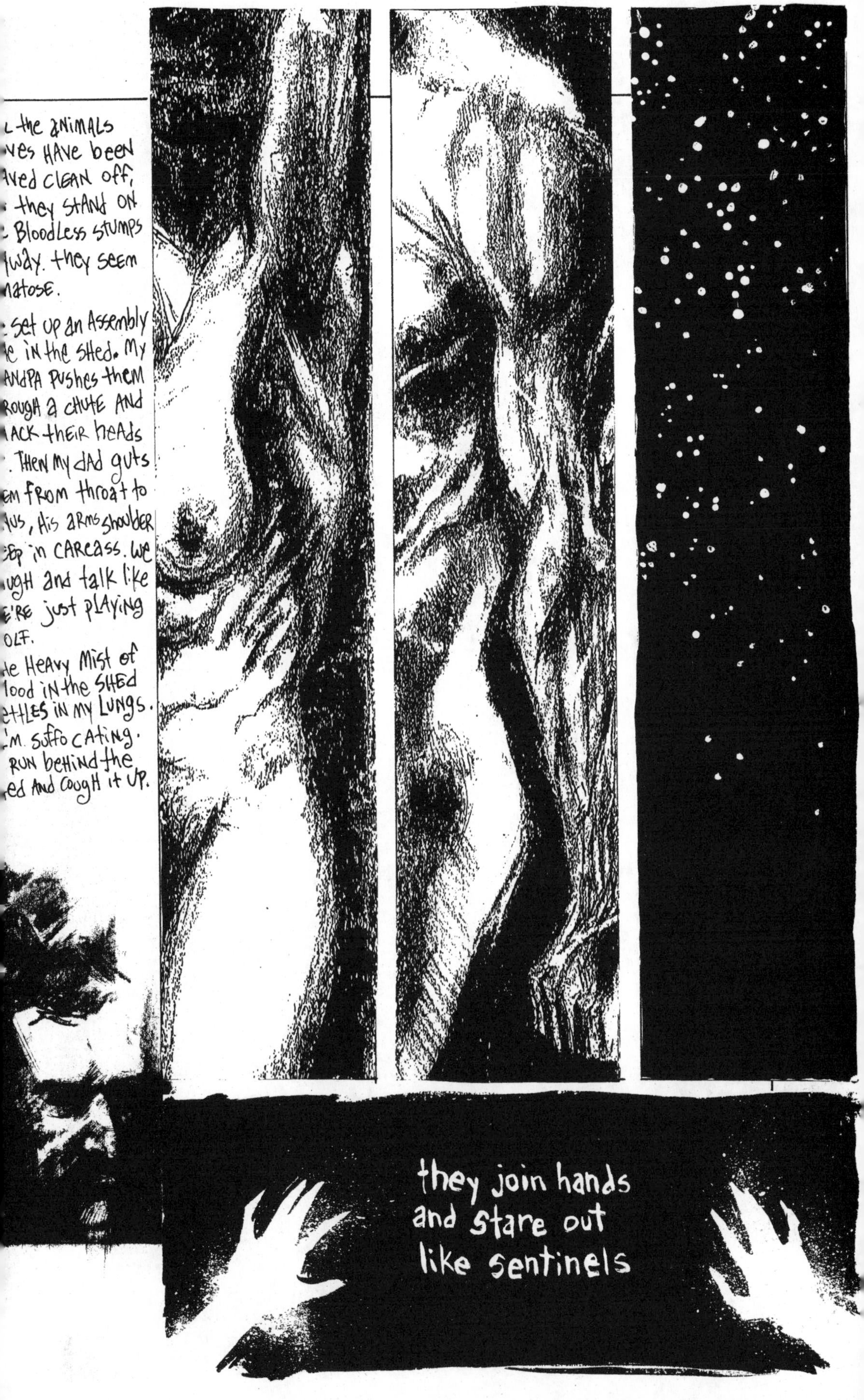

L the animals
ves have been
aved clean off,
they stand on
Bloodless stumps
lway. they seem
natose.
set up an assembly
e in the shed. my
andpa pushes them
rough a chute and
ack their heads
. then my dad guts
em from throat to
ius, his arms shoulder
ep in carcass. we
ugh and talk like
'e're just playing
olf.
e heavy mist of
lood in the shed
ettles in my lungs.
'm suffocating.
run behind the
ed and cough it up.
they join hands
and stare out
like sentinels

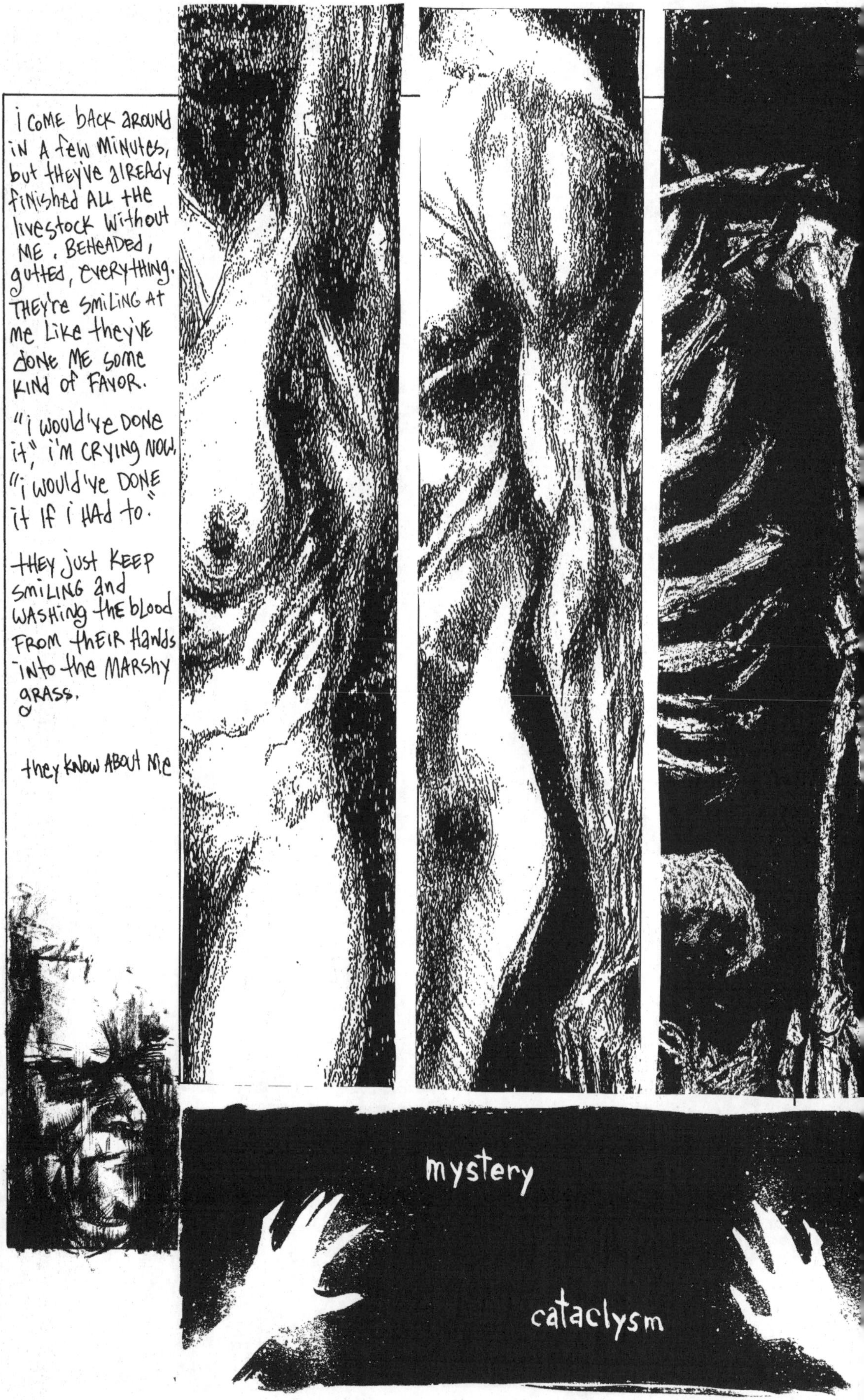
i come back around in a few minutes, but they've already finished all the livestock without me. beheaded, gutted, everything. they're smiling at me like they've done me some kind of favor.
"i would've done it," i'm crying now, "i would've done it if i had to."
they just keep smiling and washing the blood from their hands into the marshy grass.
they know about me
mystery
cataclysm

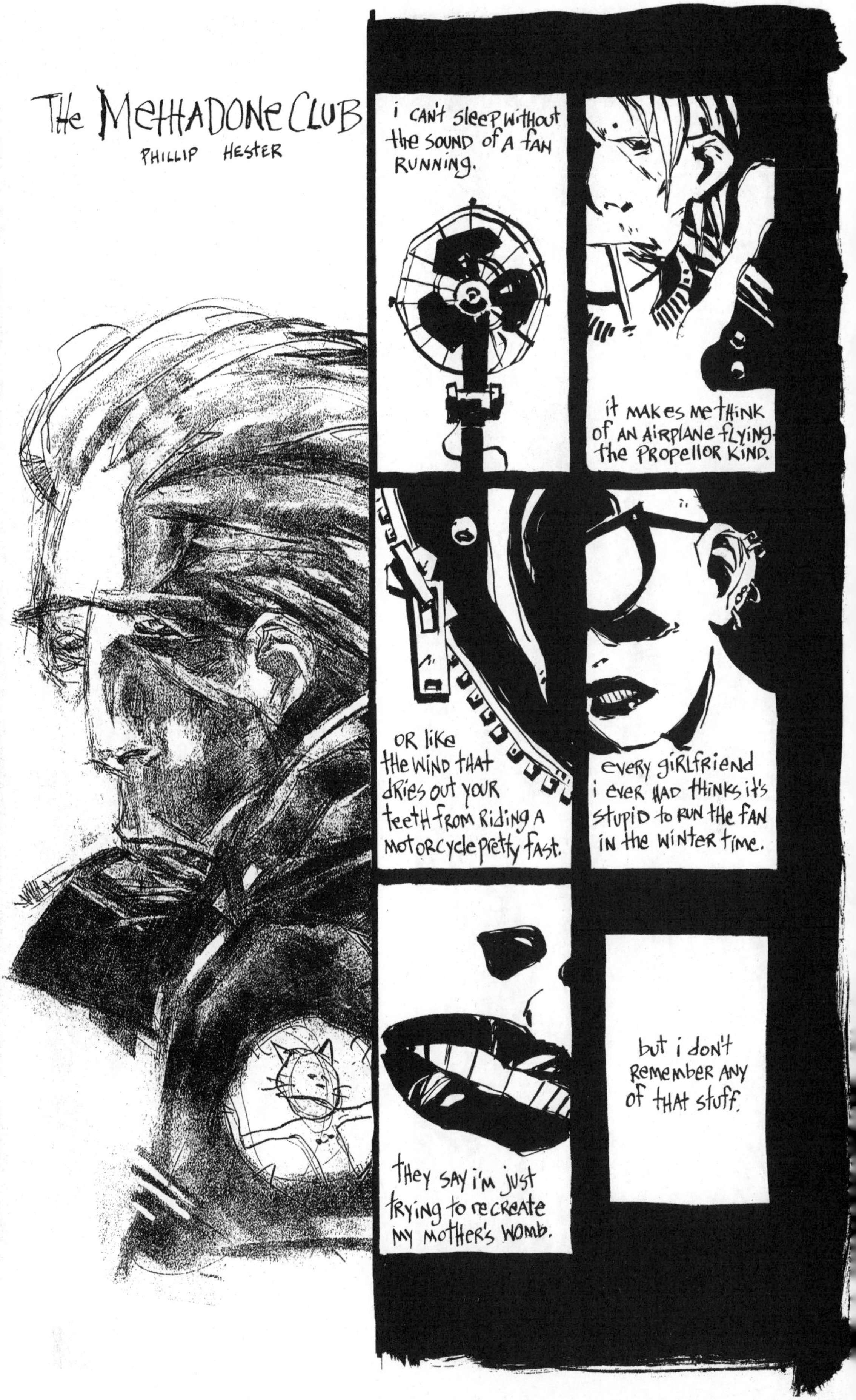
The Methadone Club
Phillip Hester
i can't sleep without the sound of a fan running.
it makes me think of an airplane flying the propellor kind.
or like the wind that dries out your teeth from riding a motorcycle pretty fast.
every girlfriend i ever had thinks it's stupid to run the fan in the winter time.
they say i'm just trying to recreate my mother's womb.
but i don't remember any of that stuff.

Witchfinger

EVEN IN THIS STATE THE MEMBRANE IS OFTEN STILL VERY TAUT.

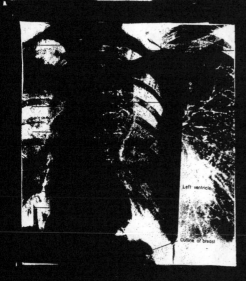

Left ventricle.

Outline of breast.

EACH INCISION MUST BE BOTH PRECISE AND ABRUPT.

AFTER COMPLETING ALL FOUR INCISIONS IN SEQUENCE, (see diagram A.)

My wife has a Witchfinger.

for most of her life it was perfectly normal.

then she sheared part of it off in a paper cutter, like paring a carrot to a point.

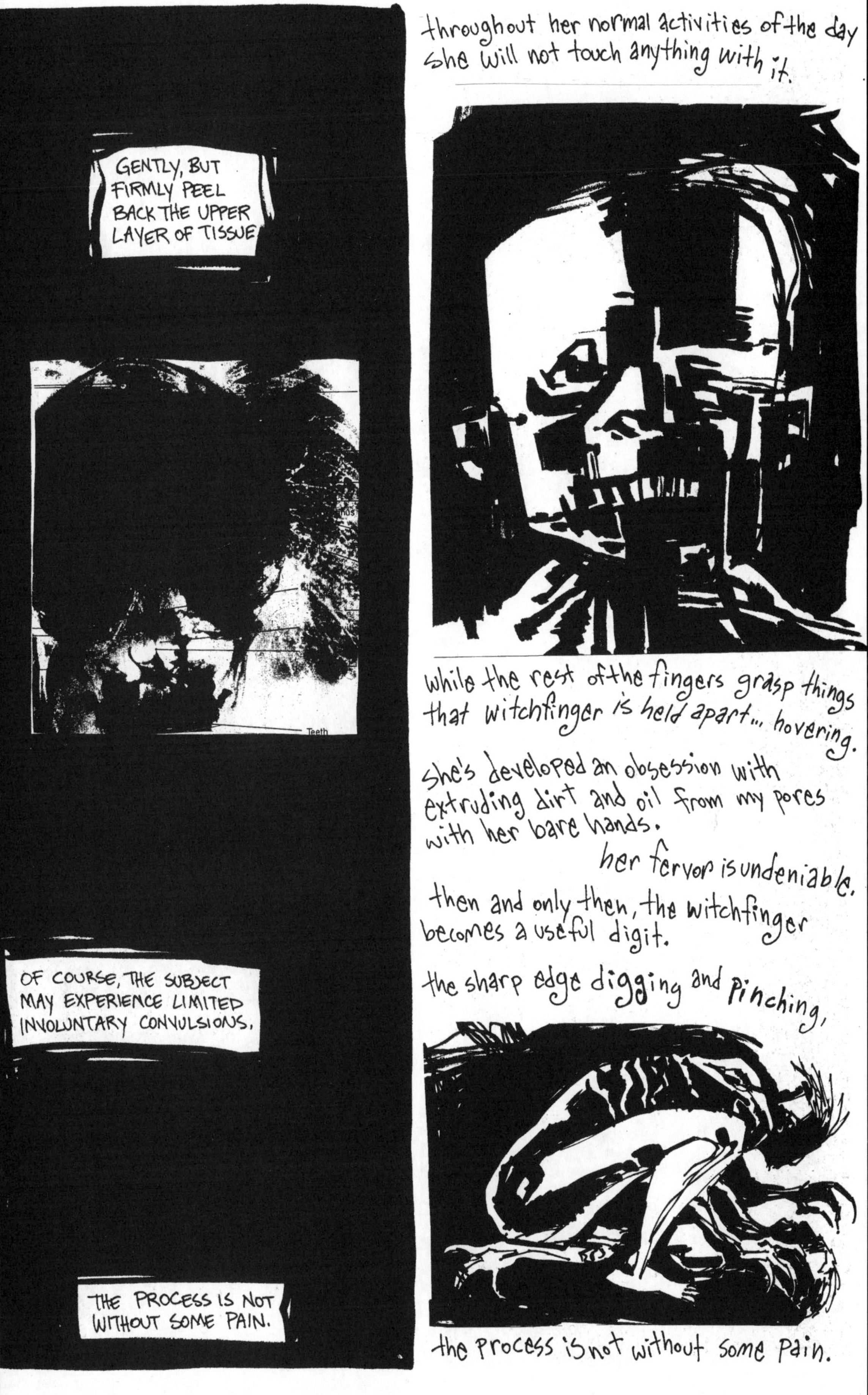
GENTLY, BUT FIRMLY PEEL BACK THE UPPER LAYER OF TISSUE
Teeth
OF COURSE, THE SUBJECT MAY EXPERIENCE LIMITED INVOLUNTARY CONVULSIONS.
THE PROCESS IS NOT WITHOUT SOME PAIN.
throughout her normal activities of the day she will not touch anything with it.
while the rest of the fingers grasp things that witchfinger is held apart... hovering.
she's developed an obsession with extruding dirt and oil from my pores with her bare hands.
her fervor is undeniable.
then and only then, the witchfinger becomes a useful digit.
the sharp edge digging and pinching,
the process is not without some pain.

YOUR INTENDED GOAL WILL BE REVEALED.
IT WILL BE AN AUTOMOBILE. A GOLF COURSE. SEVERAL KILOS OF COCAINE. A MISTRESS. IT WILL BE A WELL-APPOINTED HOME. A MARINA. LARGE DOSES OF NICOTINE AND ALCOHOL. A PUBLIC OFFICE.
IT WILL BE REVEALED. (see diagram B.)
the doctor said she should've saved the shaved off bit so he could put it back on, but it was too late.
by the time they got back to the paper cutter the morsel was a new unearthly color.
it was thrown away, just like regular garbage.
Distal transv. digital as.
Dorsal brs.
Common palmar digital a.

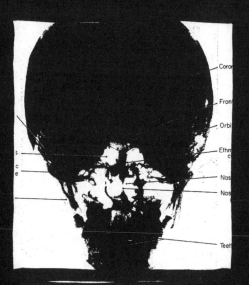

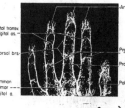

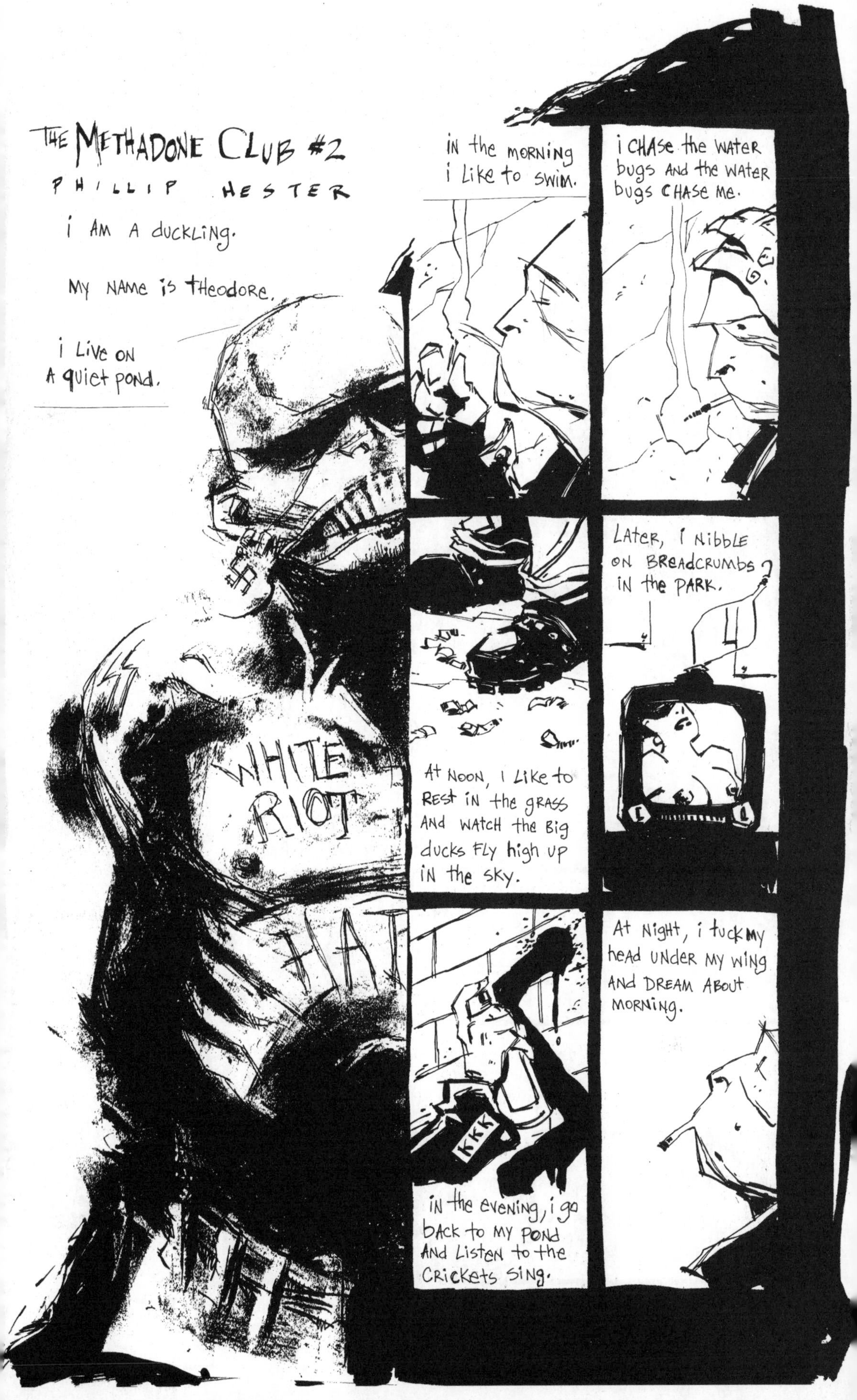
THE METHADONE CLUB #2
PHILLIP HESTER
i AM A duckling.
My NAME is theodore.
i Live ON A quiet pond.
in the morning i Like to swim.
i CHASE the water bugs And the water bugs CHASE me.
WHITE RIOT
LAter, I Nibble ON BReadcrumbs iN the PARK.
At Noon, I Like to Rest in the grass And WATCH the Big ducks FLY high up in the sky.
KKK
At Night, i tuck my head UNDER MY wing AND DREAM ABout MORNing.
in the evening, i go back to My Pond And Listen to the Crickets Sing.

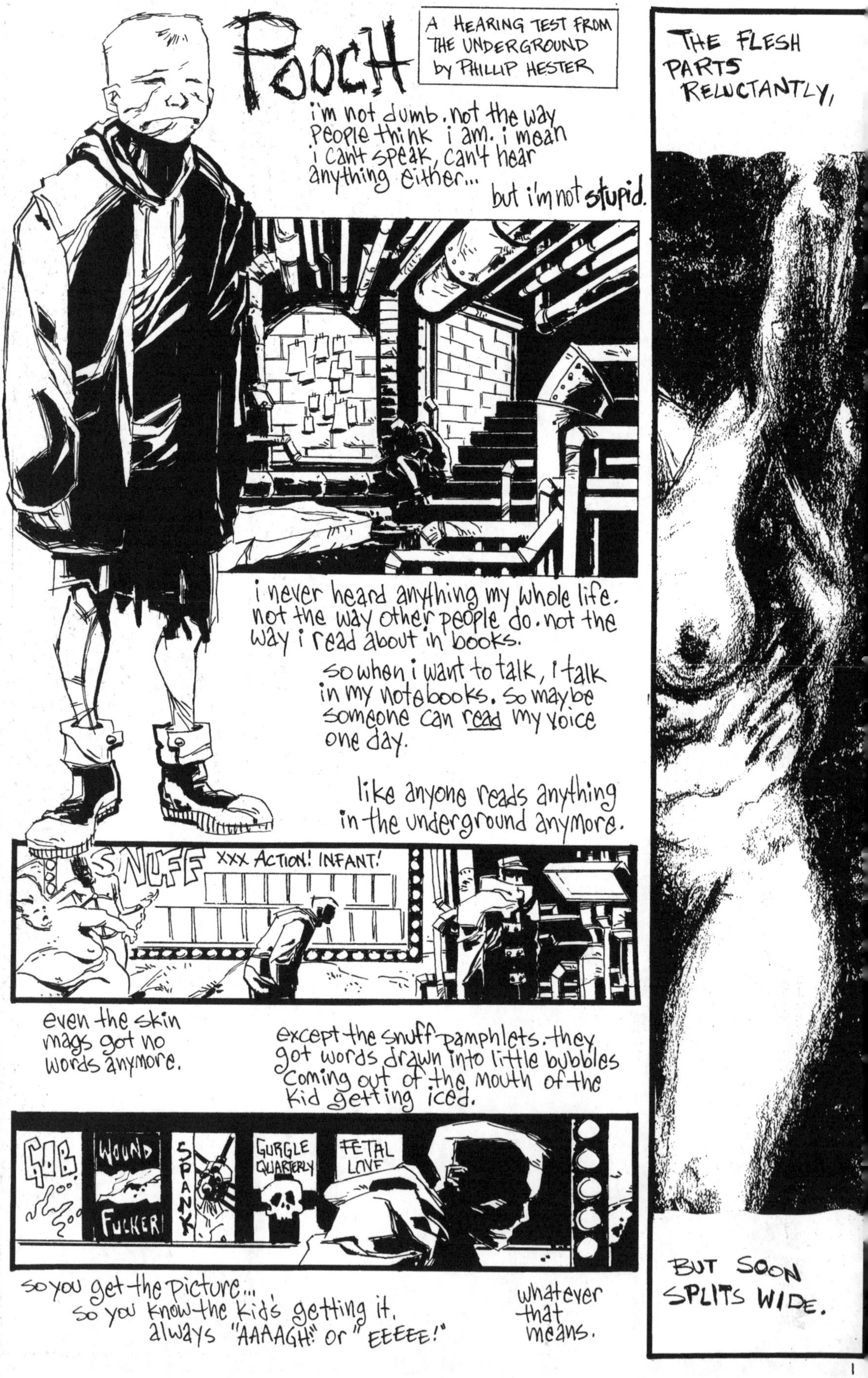
POOCH
A HEARING TEST FROM THE UNDERGROUND by PHILLIP HESTER
i'm not dumb. not the way people think i am. i mean i can't speak, can't hear anything either...
but i'm not stupid.
i never heard anything my whole life. not the way other people do. not the way i read about in books.
so when i want to talk, i talk in my notebooks. so maybe someone can read my voice one day.
like anyone reads anything in the underground anymore.
SNUFF
XXX ACTION! INFANT!
even the skin mags got no words anymore.
except the snuff pamphlets. they got words drawn into little bubbles coming out of the mouth of the kid getting iced.
GOB
WOUND FUCKER
SPANK
GURGLE QUARTERLY
FETAL LOVE
so you get the picture...
so you know the kid's getting it.
always "AAAAGH!" or "EEEEE!"
whatever that means.
THE FLESH PARTS RELUCTANTLY,
BUT SOON SPLITS WIDE.

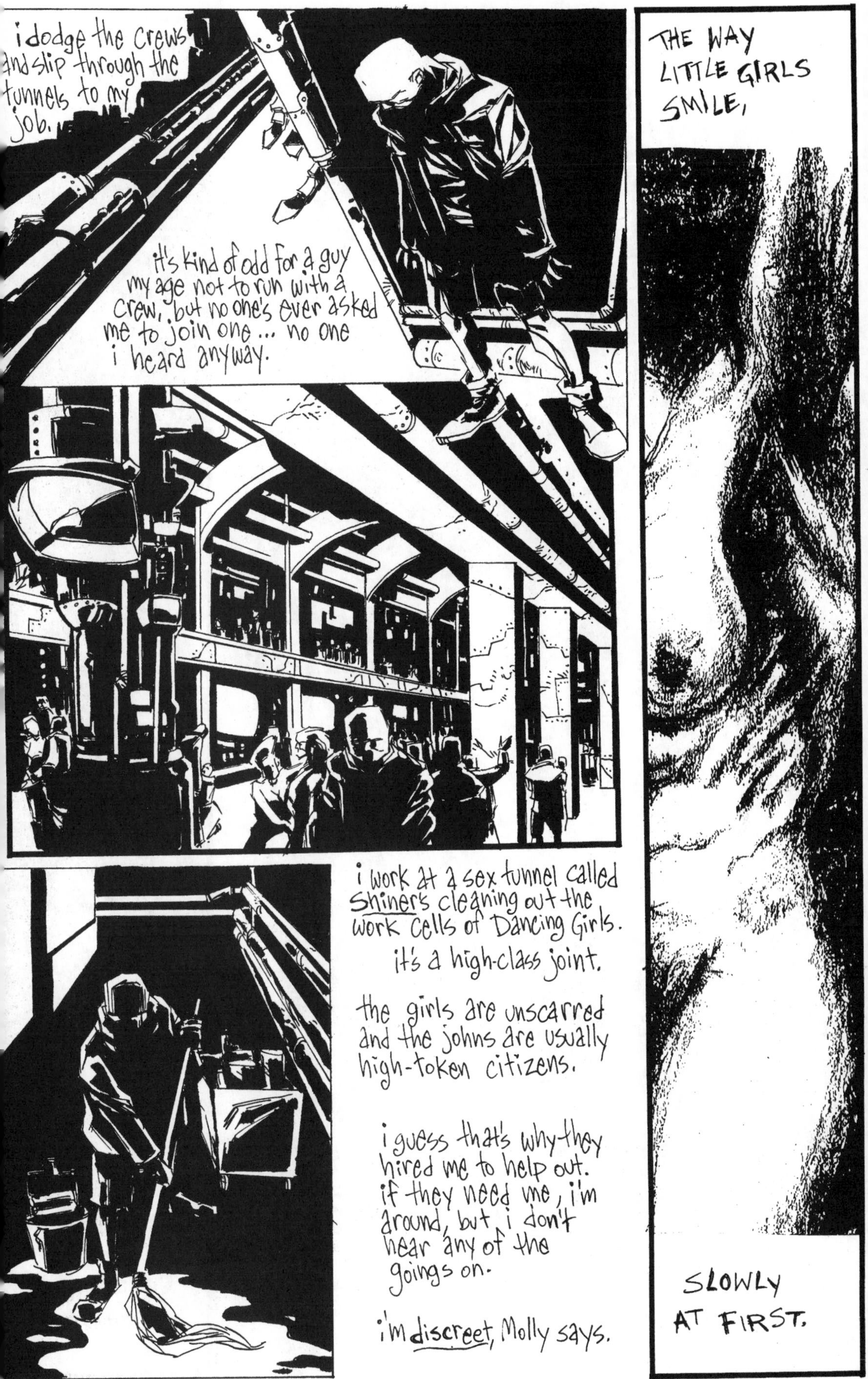

i dodge the crews and slip through the tunnels to my job.
it's kind of odd for a guy my age not to run with a crew, but no one's ever asked me to join one ... no one i heard anyway.
i work at a sex tunnel called Shiner's cleaning out the work cells of Dancing Girls.
it's a high-class joint.
the girls are unscarred and the johns are usually high-token citizens.
i guess that's why they hired me to help out. if they need me, i'm around, but i don't hear any of the goings on.
i'm discreet, Molly says.
THE WAY LITTLE GIRLS SMILE,
SLOWLY AT FIRST.

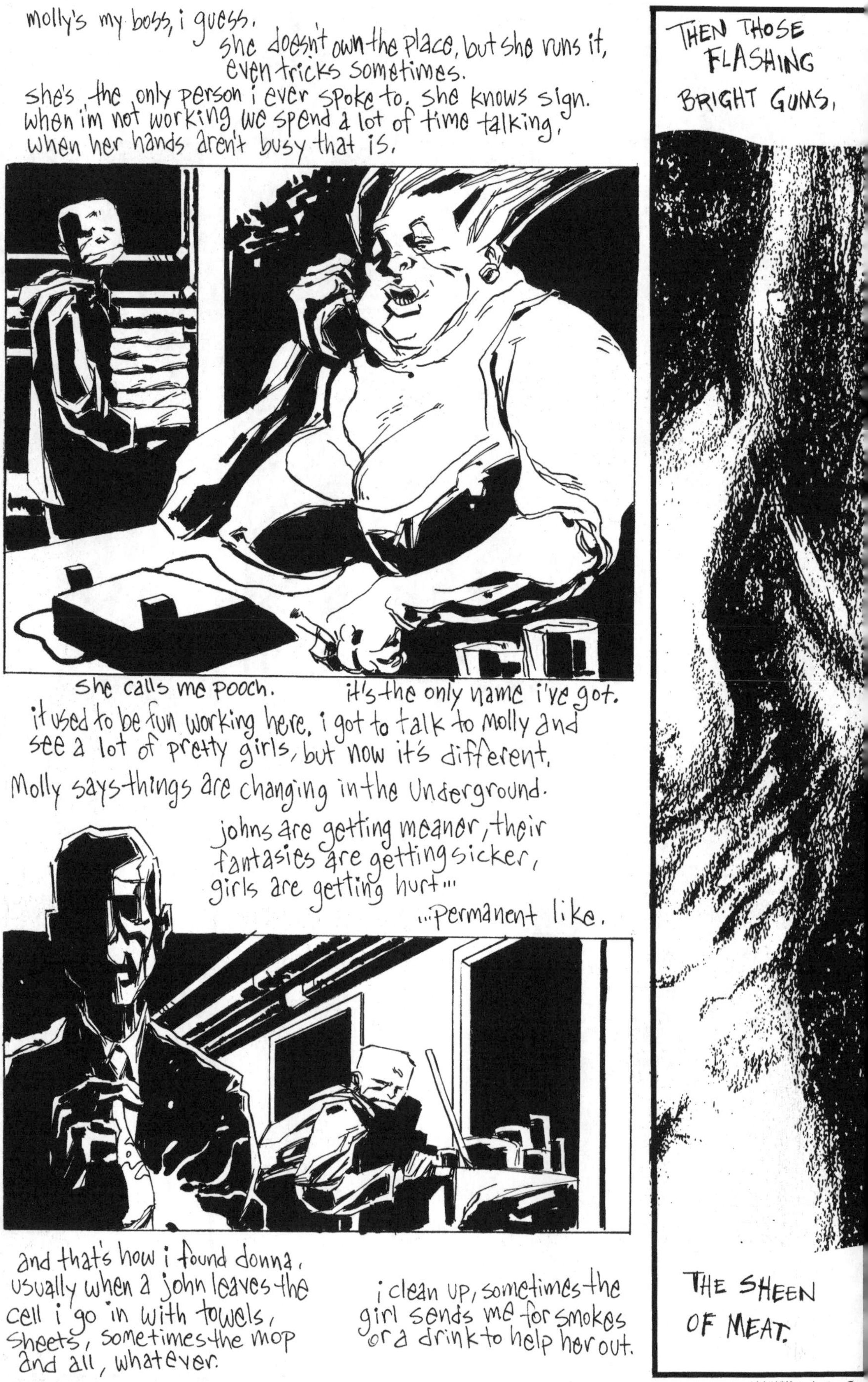
molly's my boss, i guess.
she doesn't own the place, but she runs it, even tricks sometimes.
she's the only person i ever spoke to. she knows sign. when i'm not working we spend a lot of time talking, when her hands aren't busy that is.
she calls me pooch.
it's the only name i've got.
it used to be fun working here. i got to talk to molly and see a lot of pretty girls, but now it's different.
Molly says things are changing in the Underground.
johns are getting meaner, their fantasies are getting sicker, girls are getting hurt...
...permanent like.
and that's how i found donna. usually when a john leaves the cell i go in with towels, sheets, sometimes the mop and all, whatever.
i clean up, sometimes the girl sends me for smokes or a drink to help her out.
THEN THOSE FLASHING BRIGHT GUMS,
THE SHEEN OF MEAT.

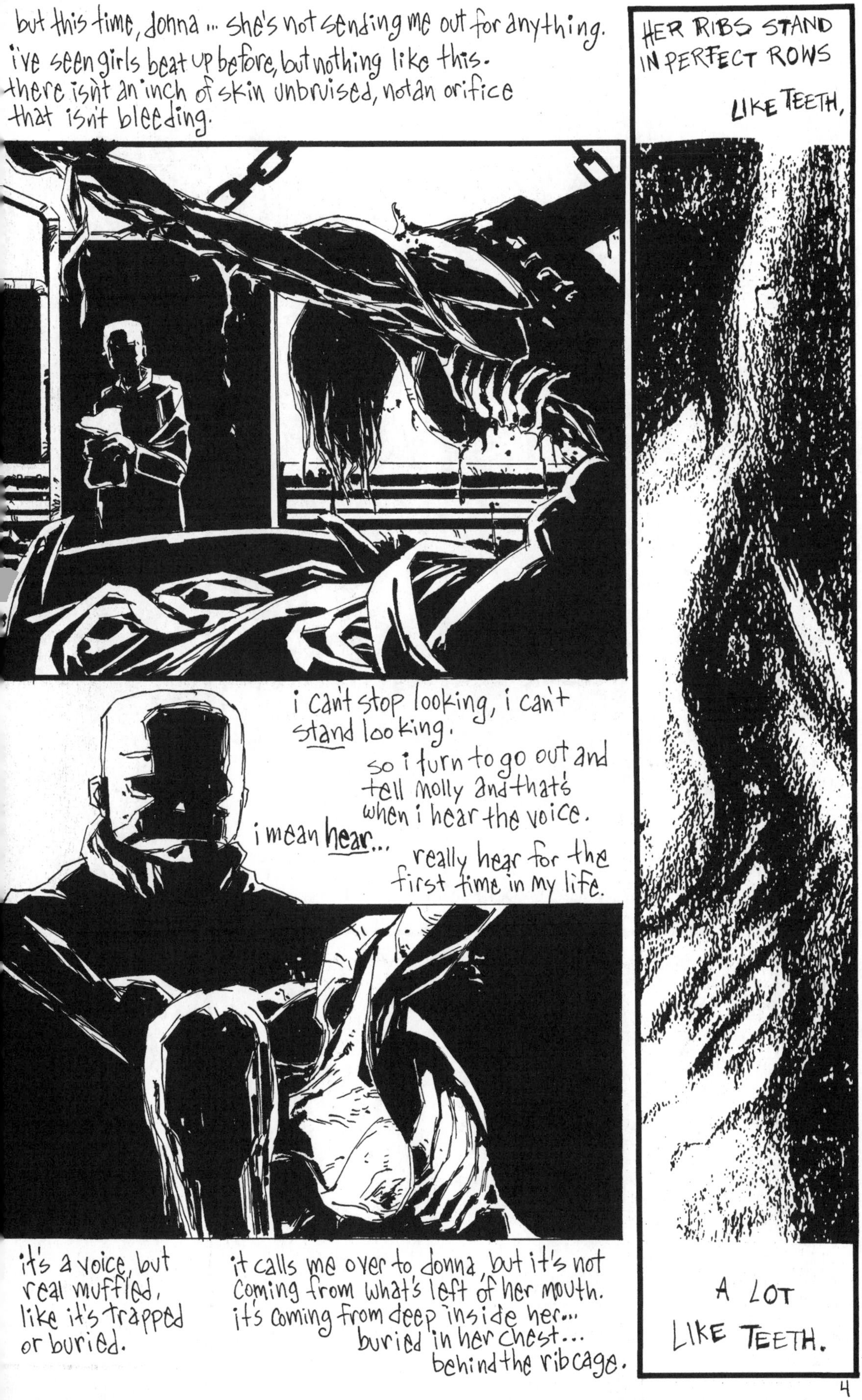

but this time, donna ... she's not sending me out for anything.
i've seen girls beat up before, but nothing like this.
there isn't an inch of skin unbruised, not an orifice that isn't bleeding.
i can't stop looking, i can't stand looking.
so i turn to go out and tell molly and that's when i hear the voice.
i mean hear...
really hear for the first time in my life.
it's a voice, but real muffled, like it's trapped or buried.
it calls me over to donna, but it's not coming from what's left of her mouth.
it's coming from deep inside her...
buried in her chest...
behind the ribcage.
HER RIBS STAND IN PERFECT ROWS
LIKE TEETH,
A LOT LIKE TEETH.

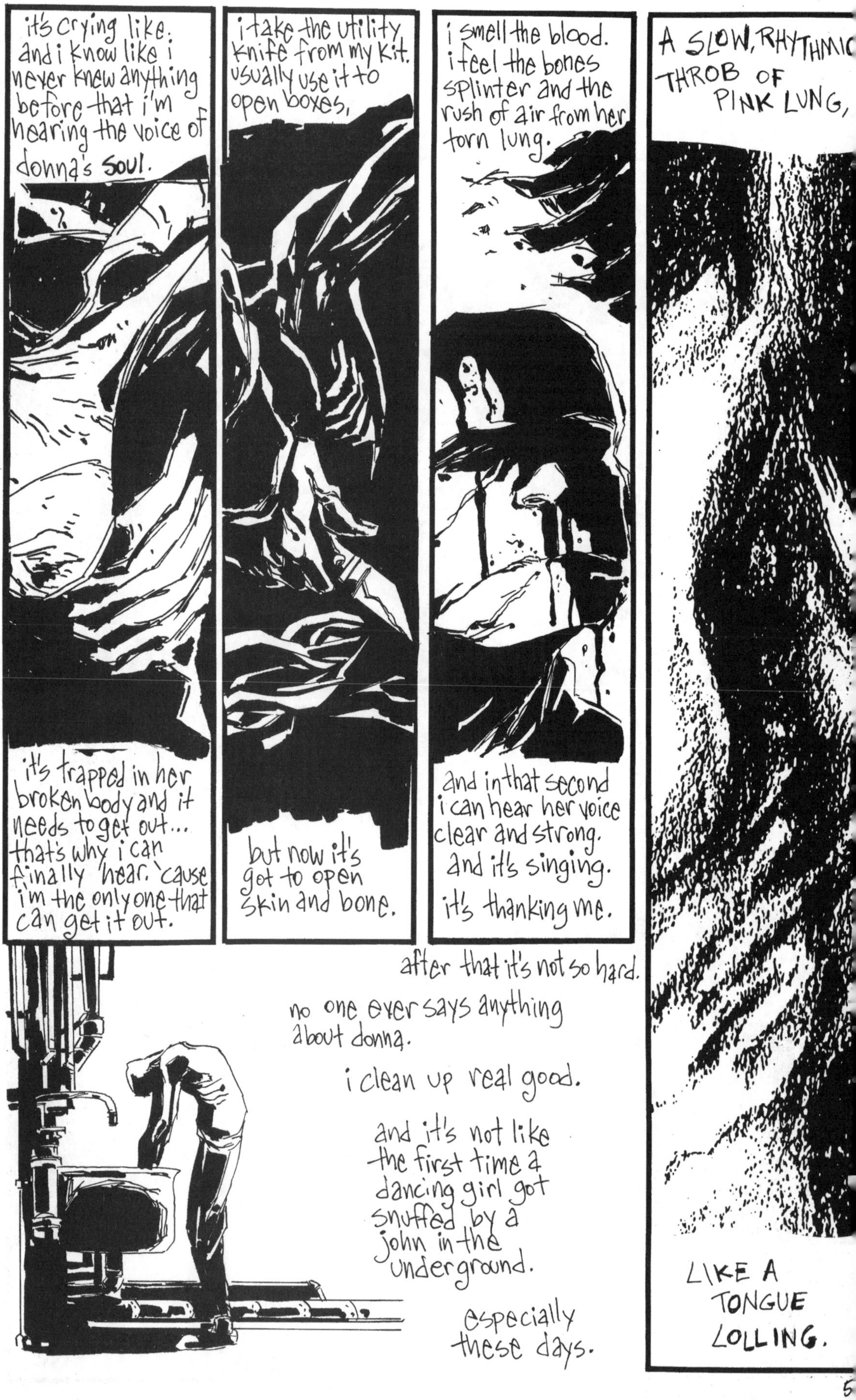
it's crying like. and i know like i never knew anything before that i'm hearing the voice of donna's soul.
it's trapped in her broken body and it needs to get out... that's why i can finally hear. 'cause i'm the only one that can get it out.
i take the utility knife from my kit. usually use it to open boxes,
but now it's got to open skin and bone.
i smell the blood. i feel the bones splinter and the rush of air from her torn lung.
and in that second i can hear her voice clear and strong.
and it's singing.
it's thanking me.
A SLOW, RHYTHMIC THROB OF PINK LUNG,
LIKE A TONGUE LOLLING.
after that it's not so hard.
no one ever says anything about donna.
i clean up real good.
and it's not like the first time a dancing girl got snuffed by a john in the underground.
especially these days.

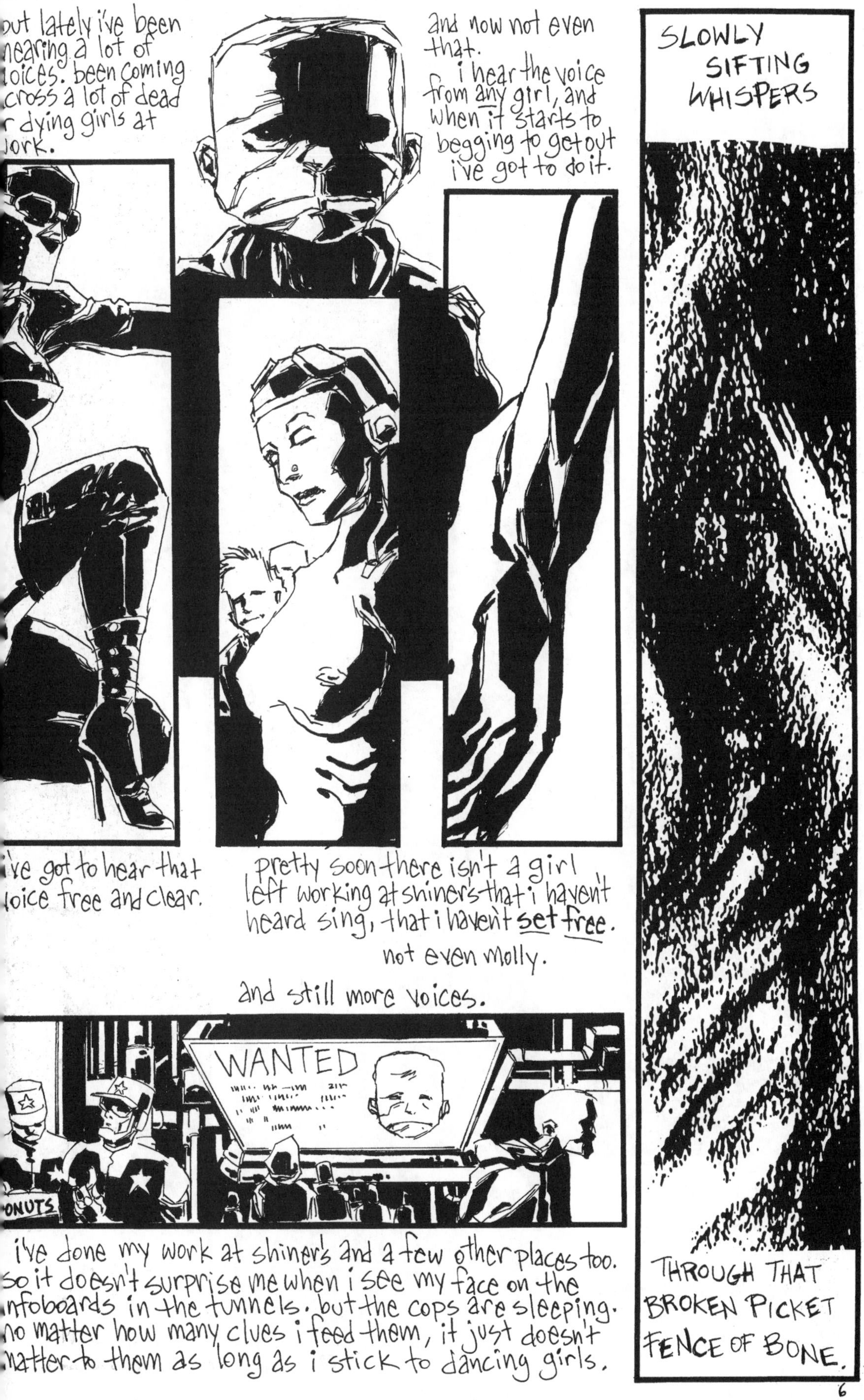
out lately i've been nearing a lot of oices. been coming cross a lot of dead r dying girls at ork.
and now not even that.
i hear the voice from any girl, and when it starts to begging to get out i've got to do it.
SLOWLY SIFTING WHISPERS
i've got to hear that oice free and clear.
pretty soon there isn't a girl left working at shiner's that i haven't heard sing, that i haven't set free.
not even molly.
and still more voices.
WANTED
ONUTS
i've done my work at shiner's and a few other places too. so it doesn't surprise me when i see my face on the nfoboards in the tunnels. but the cops are sleeping. no matter how many clues i feed them, it just doesn't matter to them as long as i stick to dancing girls.
THROUGH THAT BROKEN PICKET FENCE OF BONE.

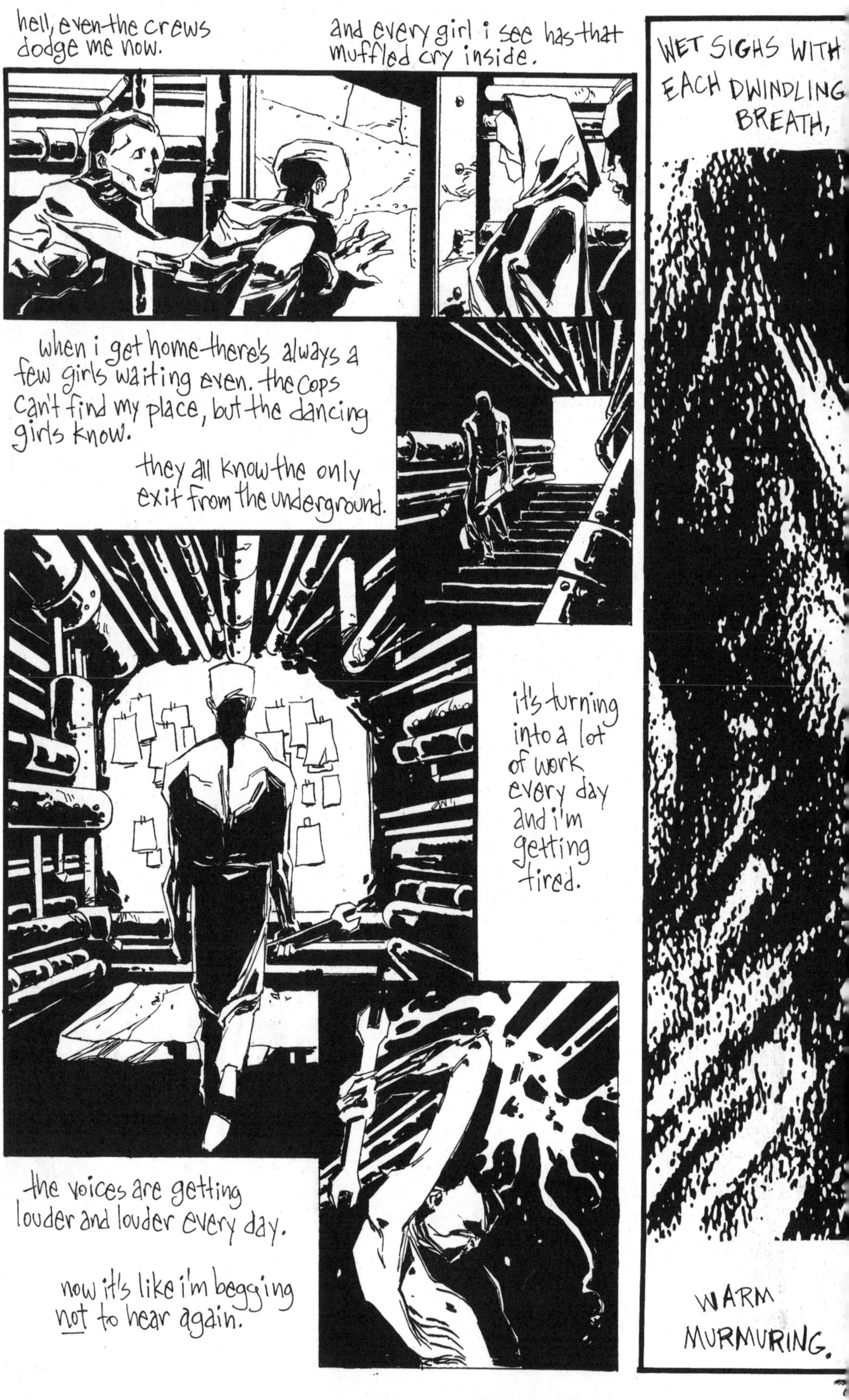
hell, even the crews dodge me now.
and every girl i see has that muffled cry inside.
when i get home there's always a few girls waiting even. the cops can't find my place, but the dancing girls know.
they all know the only exit from the underground.
it's turning into a lot of work every day and i'm getting tired.
the voices are getting louder and louder every day.
now it's like i'm begging not to hear again.
WET SIGHS WITH EACH DWINDLING BREATH,
WARM MURMURING.

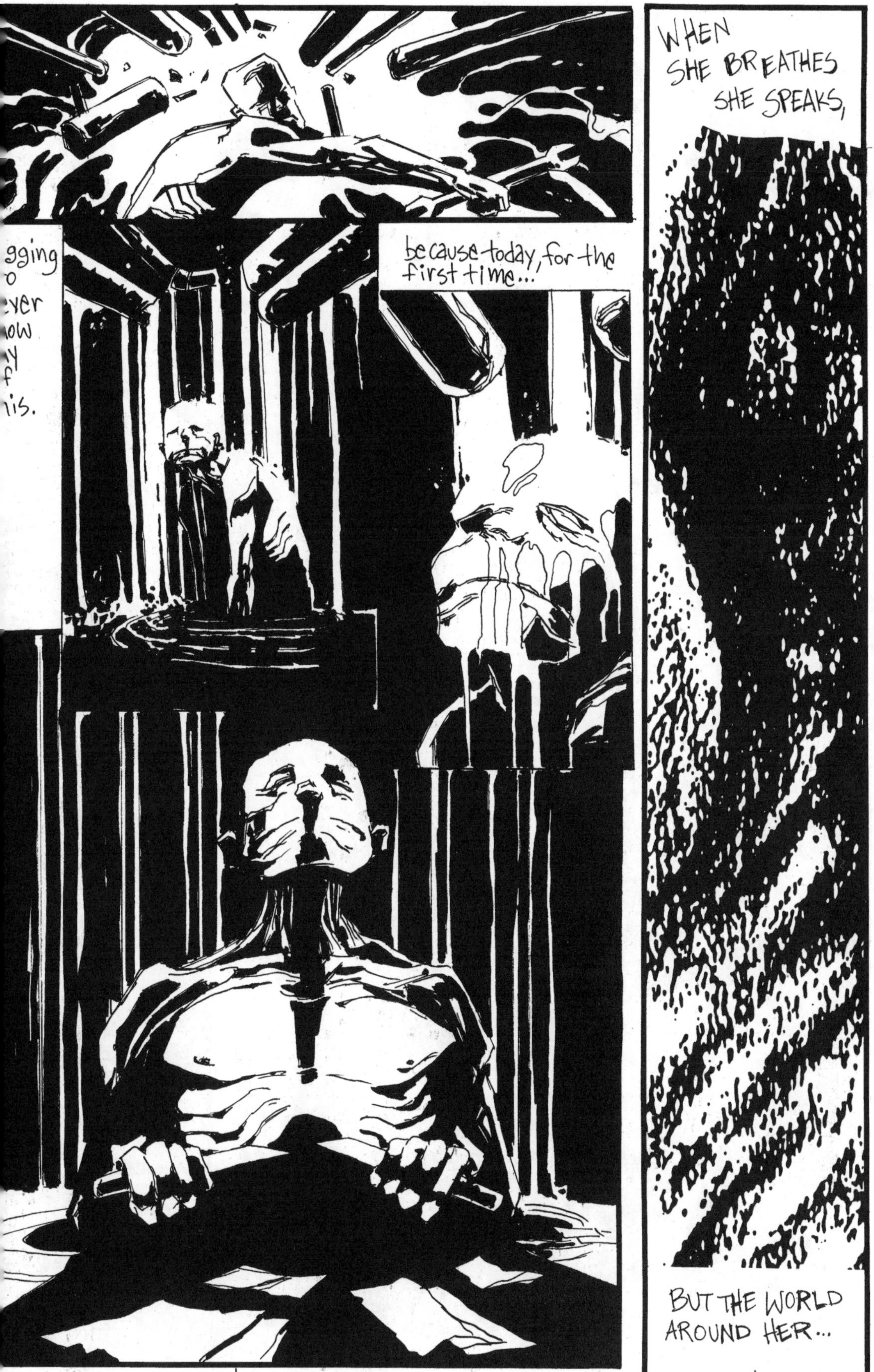

WHEN SHE BREATHES SHE SPEAKS,
BUT THE WORLD AROUND HER...
IT'S DEAF.
gging
o
ver
ow
y
f
is.
because today, for the first time...
i heard my own voice.

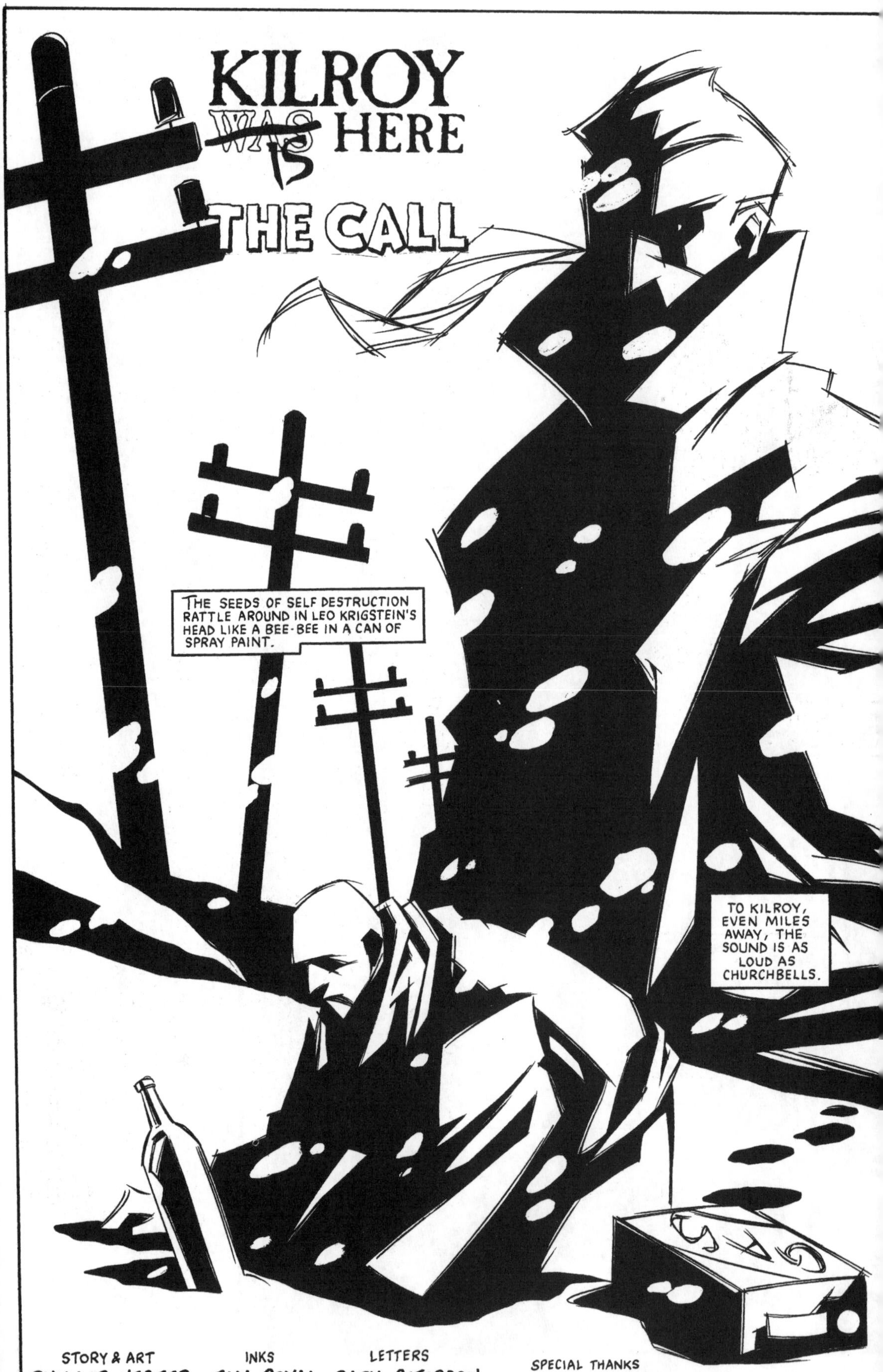

KILROY WAS IS HERE
THE CALL
THE SEEDS OF SELF DESTRUCTION RATTLE AROUND IN LEO KRIGSTEIN'S HEAD LIKE A BEE-BEE IN A CAN OF SPRAY PAINT.
TO KILROY, EVEN MILES AWAY, THE SOUND IS AS LOUD AS CHURCHBELLS.
STORY & ART PHILLIP HESTER · INKS JIM ROYAL · LETTERS GARY PETERSON
SPECIAL THANKS AARON GILLESPIE

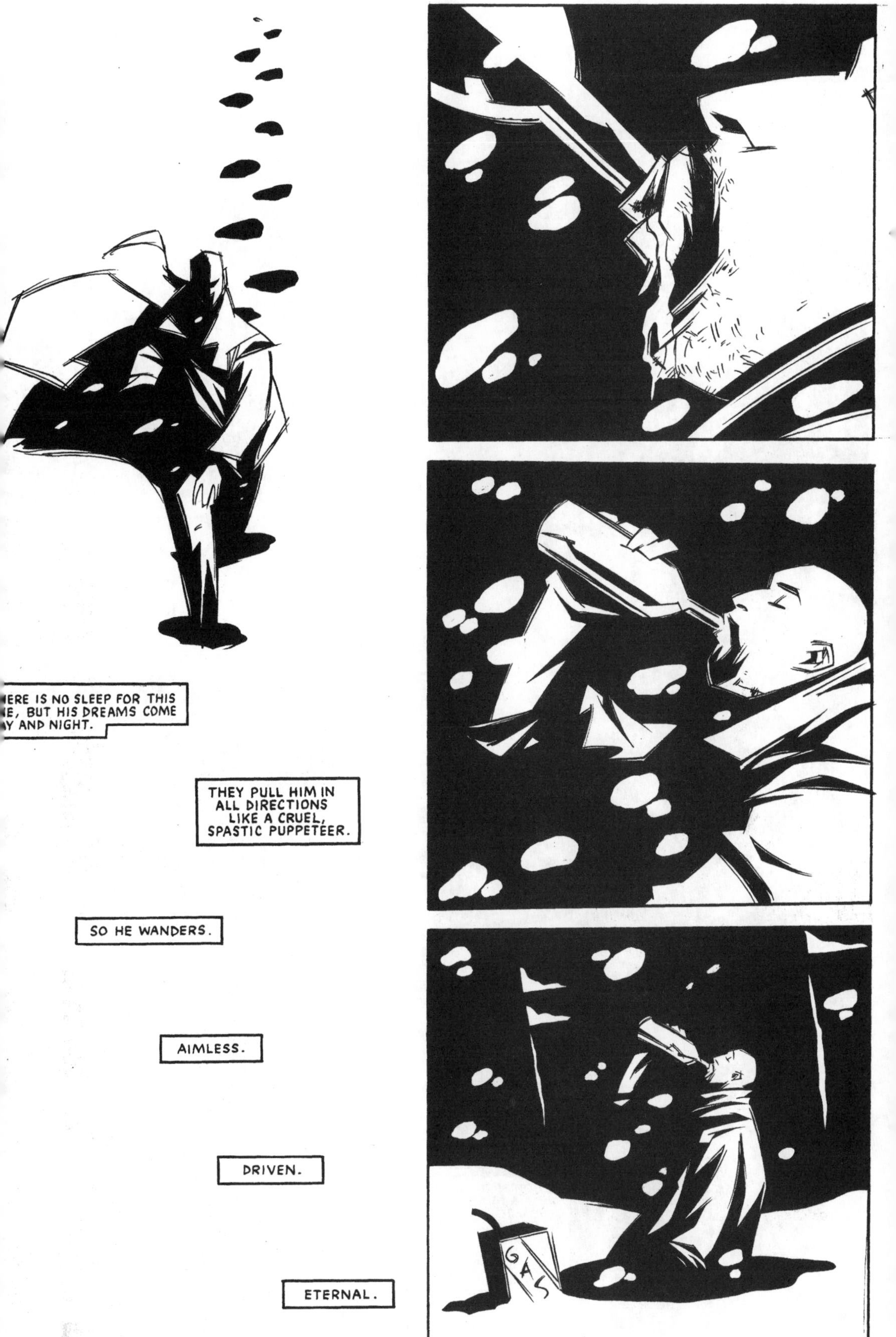

ERE IS NO SLEEP FOR THIS E, BUT HIS DREAMS COME Y AND NIGHT.
THEY PULL HIM IN ALL DIRECTIONS LIKE A CRUEL, SPASTIC PUPPETEER.
SO HE WANDERS.
AIMLESS.
DRIVEN.
ETERNAL.
GAS

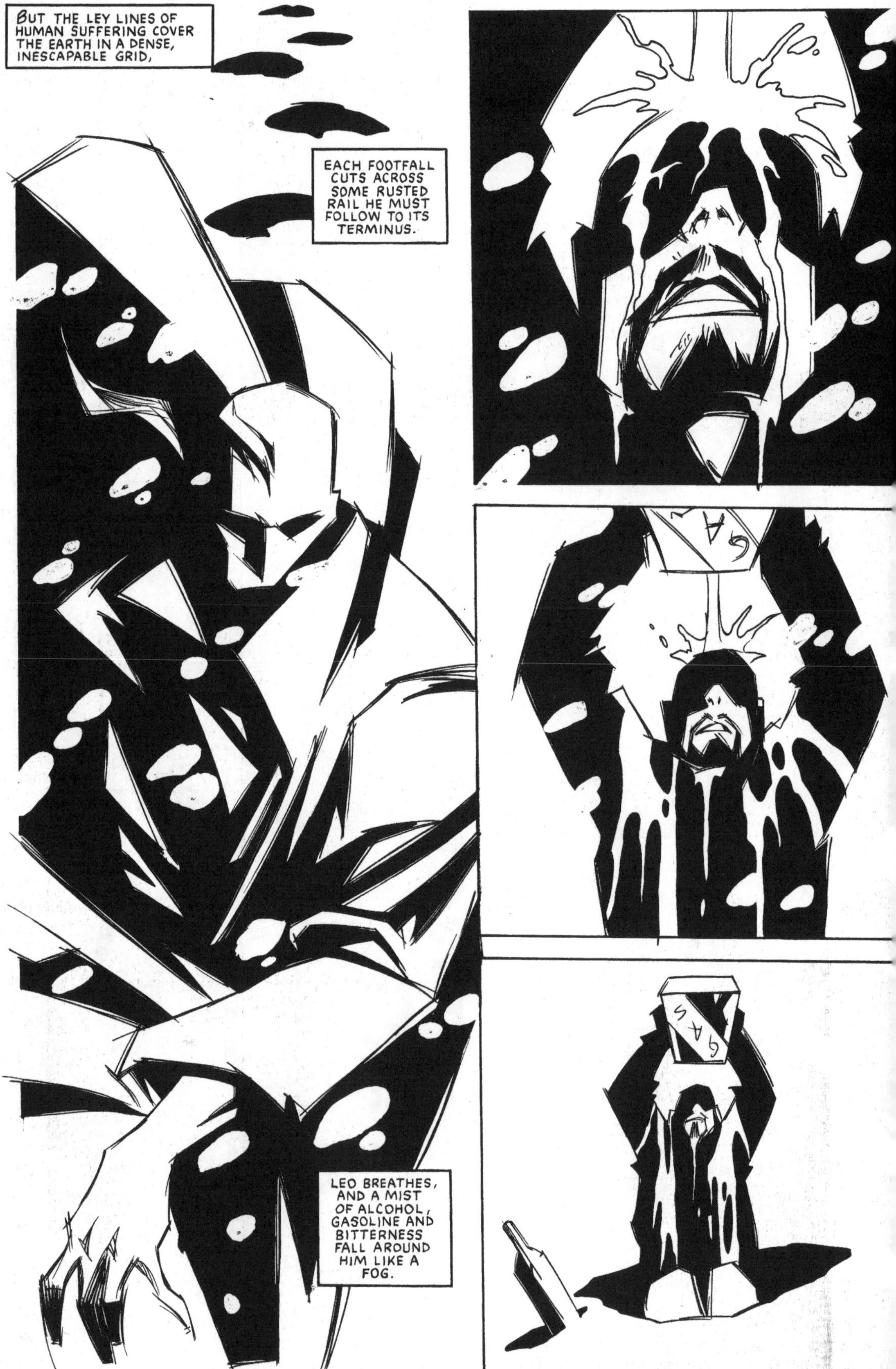
BUT THE LEY LINES OF HUMAN SUFFERING COVER THE EARTH IN A DENSE, INESCAPABLE GRID,
EACH FOOTFALL CUTS ACROSS SOME RUSTED RAIL HE MUST FOLLOW TO ITS TERMINUS.
GAS
LEO BREATHES, AND A MIST OF ALCOHOL, GASOLINE AND BITTERNESS FALL AROUND HIM LIKE A FOG.
GAS

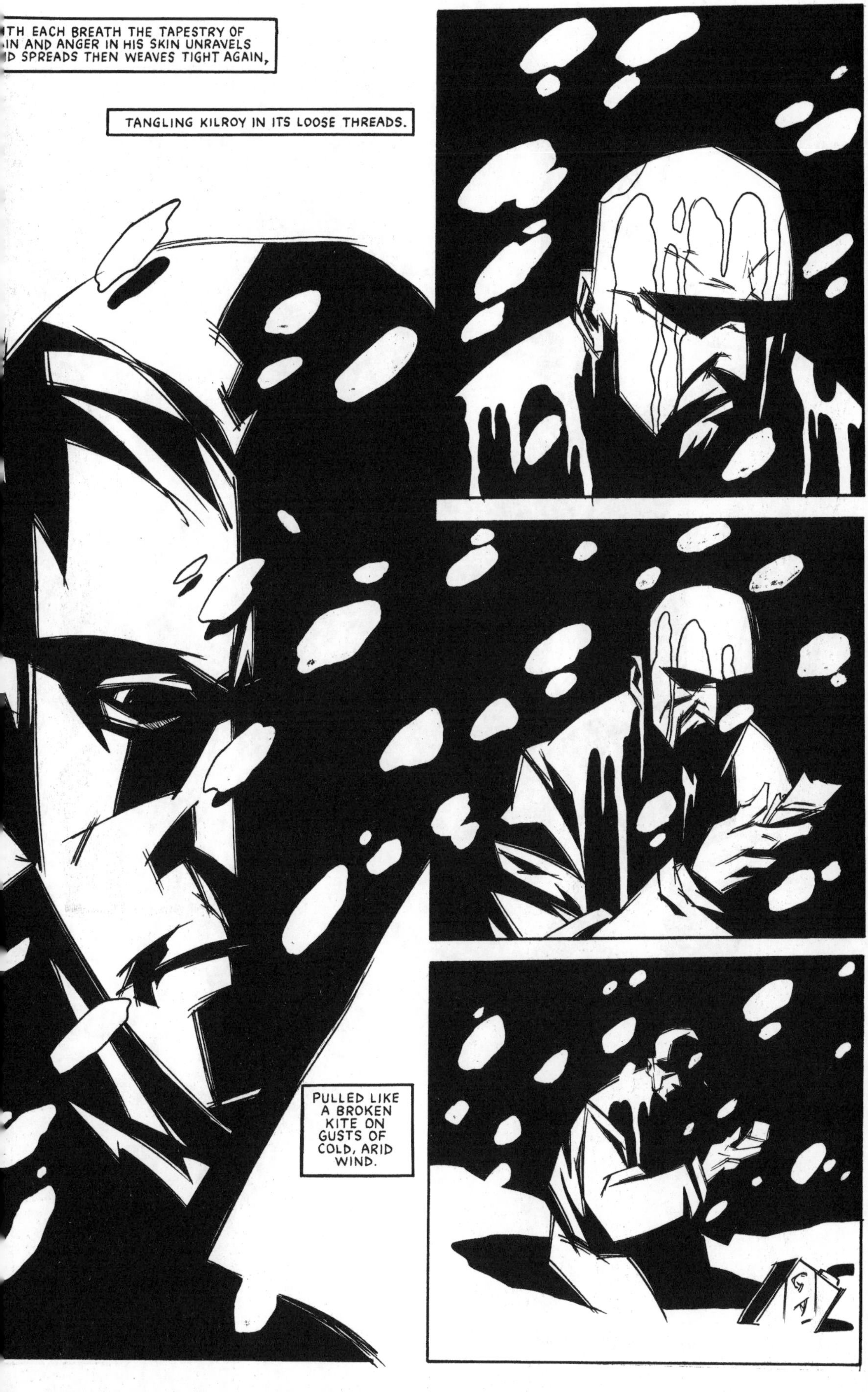
TH EACH BREATH THE TAPESTRY OF
IN AND ANGER IN HIS SKIN UNRAVELS
D SPREADS THEN WEAVES TIGHT AGAIN,
TANGLING KILROY IN ITS LOOSE THREADS.
PULLED LIKE A BROKEN KITE ON GUSTS OF COLD, ARID WIND.

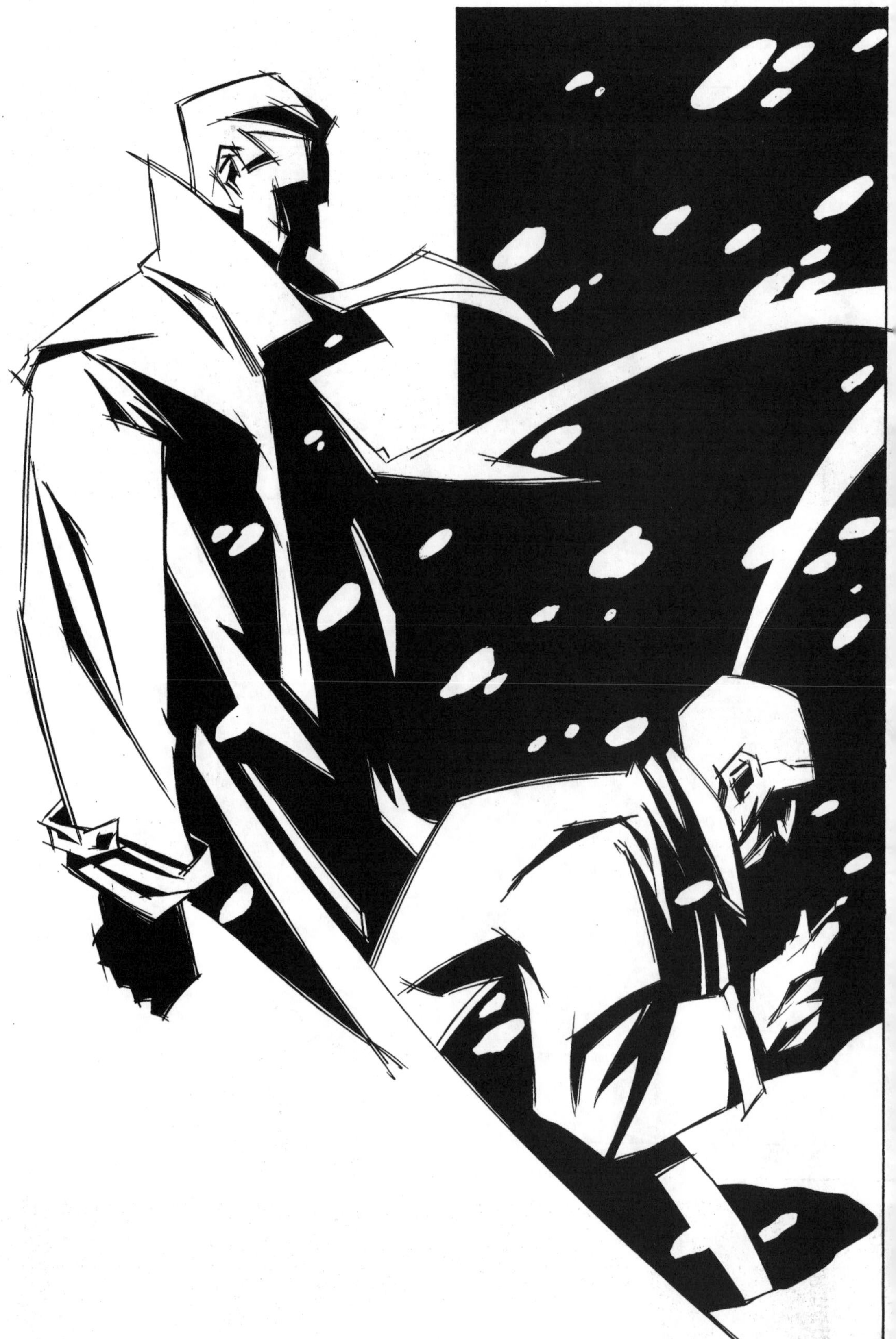

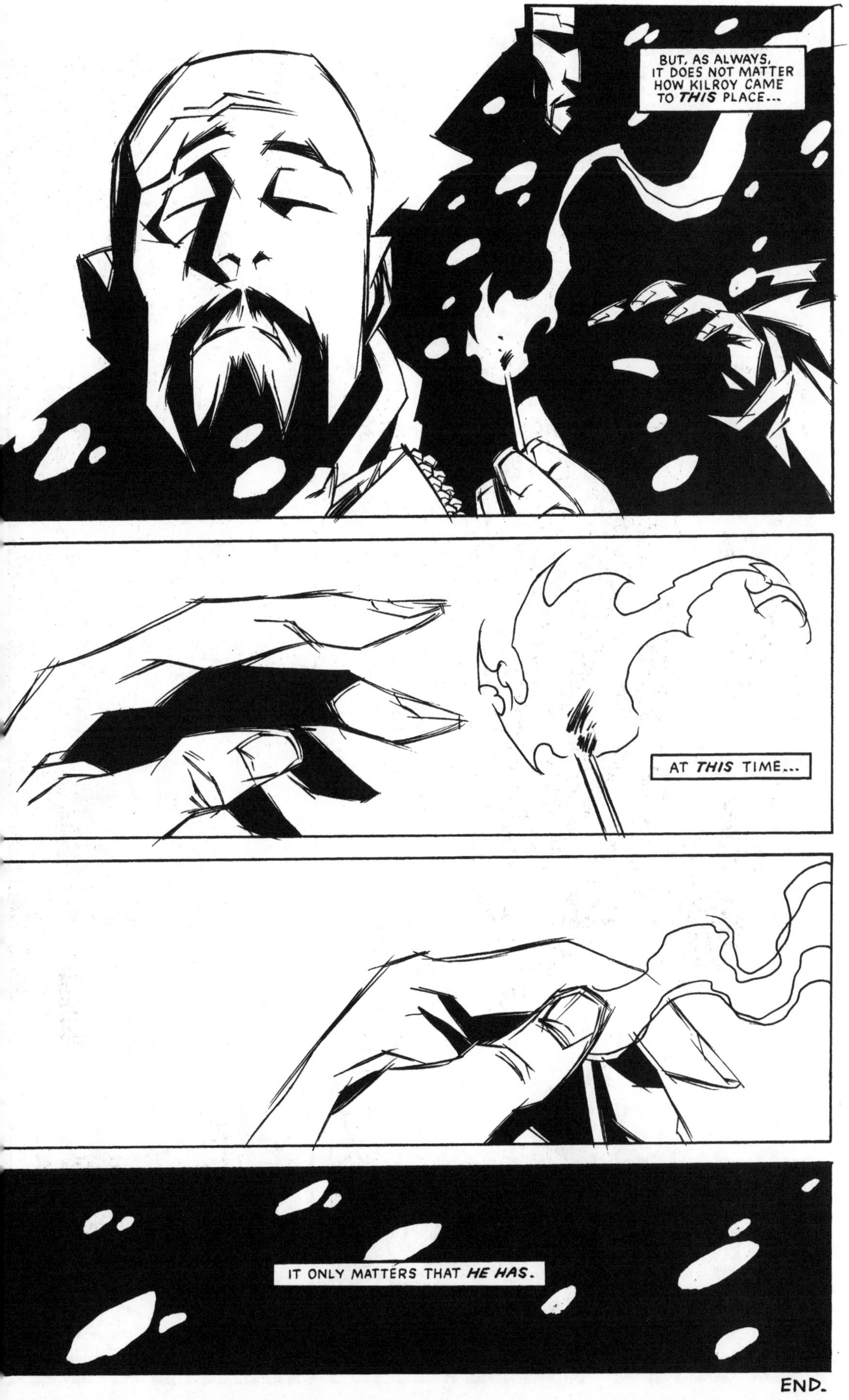

BUT, AS ALWAYS, IT DOES NOT MATTER HOW KILROY CAME TO *THIS* PLACE...
AT *THIS* TIME...
IT ONLY MATTERS THAT *HE HAS*.
END.

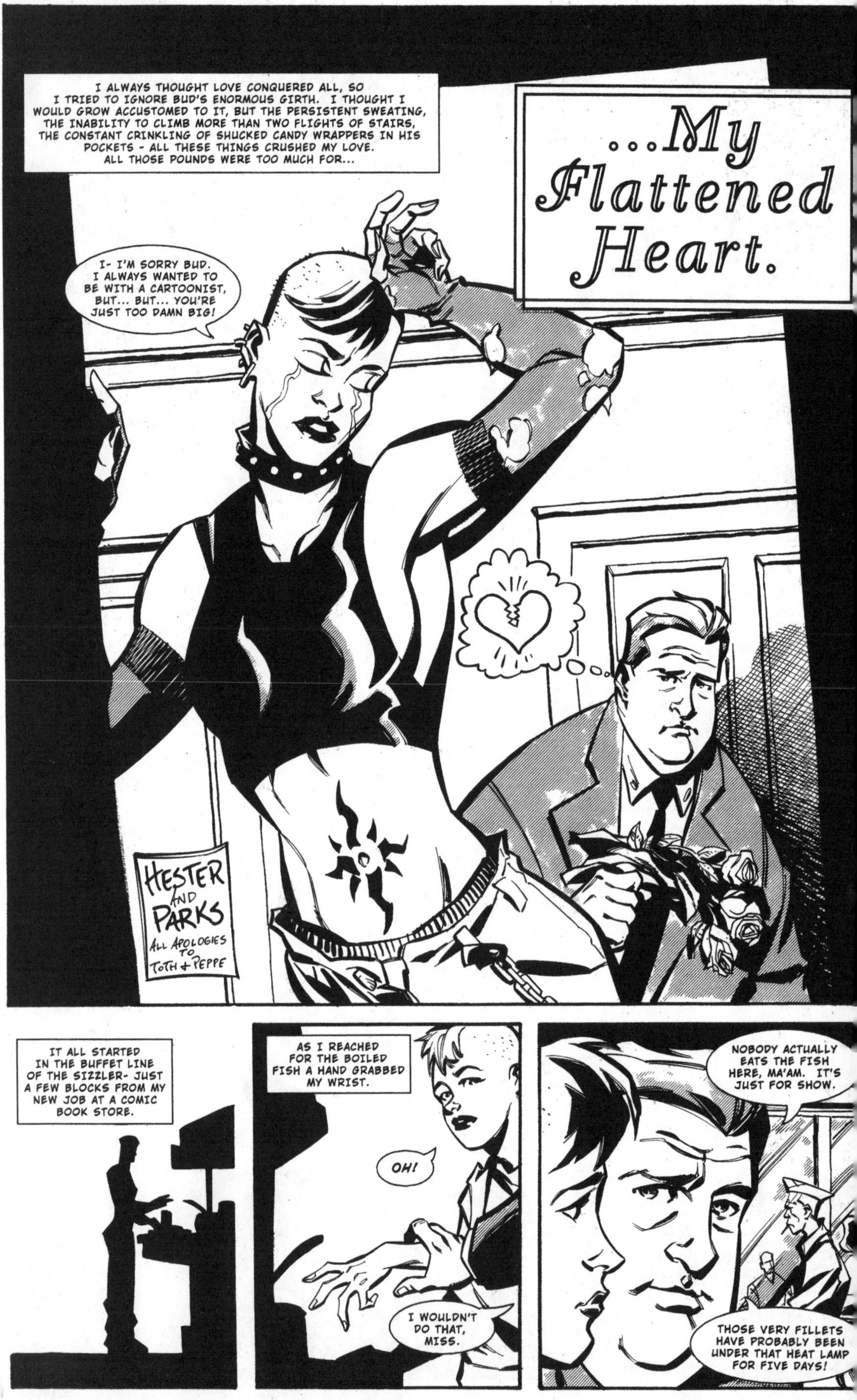
I ALWAYS THOUGHT LOVE CONQUERED ALL, SO I TRIED TO IGNORE BUD'S ENORMOUS GIRTH. I THOUGHT I WOULD GROW ACCUSTOMED TO IT, BUT THE PERSISTENT SWEATING, THE INABILITY TO CLIMB MORE THAN TWO FLIGHTS OF STAIRS, THE CONSTANT CRINKLING OF SHUCKED CANDY WRAPPERS IN HIS POCKETS - ALL THESE THINGS CRUSHED MY LOVE. ALL THOSE POUNDS WERE TOO MUCH FOR...
...My Flattened Heart.
I- I'M SORRY BUD. I ALWAYS WANTED TO BE WITH A CARTOONIST, BUT... BUT... YOU'RE JUST TOO DAMN BIG!
HESTER AND PARKS
ALL APOLOGIES TO TOTH & PEPPE
IT ALL STARTED IN THE BUFFET LINE OF THE SIZZLER- JUST A FEW BLOCKS FROM MY NEW JOB AT A COMIC BOOK STORE.
AS I REACHED FOR THE BOILED FISH A HAND GRABBED MY WRIST.
OH!
I WOULDN'T DO THAT, MISS.
NOBODY ACTUALLY EATS THE FISH HERE, MA'AM. IT'S JUST FOR SHOW.
THOSE VERY FILLETS HAVE PROBABLY BEEN UNDER THAT HEAT LAMP FOR FIVE DAYS!

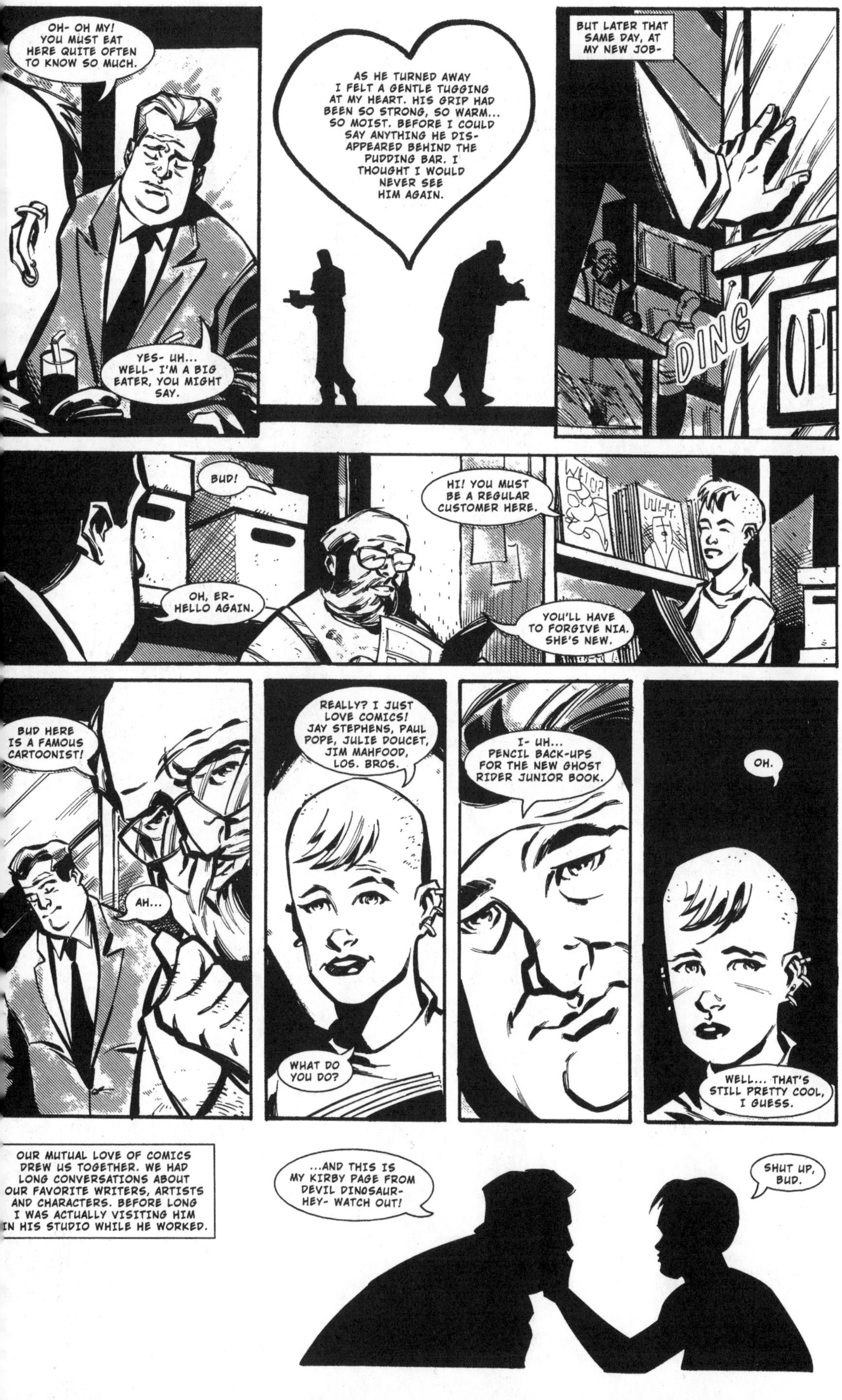
OH- OH MY! YOU MUST EAT HERE QUITE OFTEN TO KNOW SO MUCH.
YES- UH... WELL- I'M A BIG EATER, YOU MIGHT SAY.
AS HE TURNED AWAY I FELT A GENTLE TUGGING AT MY HEART. HIS GRIP HAD BEEN SO STRONG, SO WARM... SO MOIST. BEFORE I COULD SAY ANYTHING HE DIS-APPEARED BEHIND THE PUDDING BAR. I THOUGHT I WOULD NEVER SEE HIM AGAIN.
BUT LATER THAT SAME DAY, AT MY NEW JOB-
DING
BUD!
OH, ER- HELLO AGAIN.
HI! YOU MUST BE A REGULAR CUSTOMER HERE.
YOU'LL HAVE TO FORGIVE NIA. SHE'S NEW.
BUD HERE IS A FAMOUS CARTOONIST!
AH...
REALLY? I JUST LOVE COMICS! JAY STEPHENS, PAUL POPE, JULIE DOUCET, JIM MAHFOOD, LOS. BROS.
WHAT DO YOU DO?
I- UH... PENCIL BACK-UPS FOR THE NEW GHOST RIDER JUNIOR BOOK.
OH.
WELL... THAT'S STILL PRETTY COOL, I GUESS.
OUR MUTUAL LOVE OF COMICS DREW US TOGETHER. WE HAD LONG CONVERSATIONS ABOUT OUR FAVORITE WRITERS, ARTISTS AND CHARACTERS. BEFORE LONG I WAS ACTUALLY VISITING HIM IN HIS STUDIO WHILE HE WORKED.
...AND THIS IS MY KIRBY PAGE FROM DEVIL DINOSAUR- HEY- WATCH OUT!
SHUT UP, BUD.

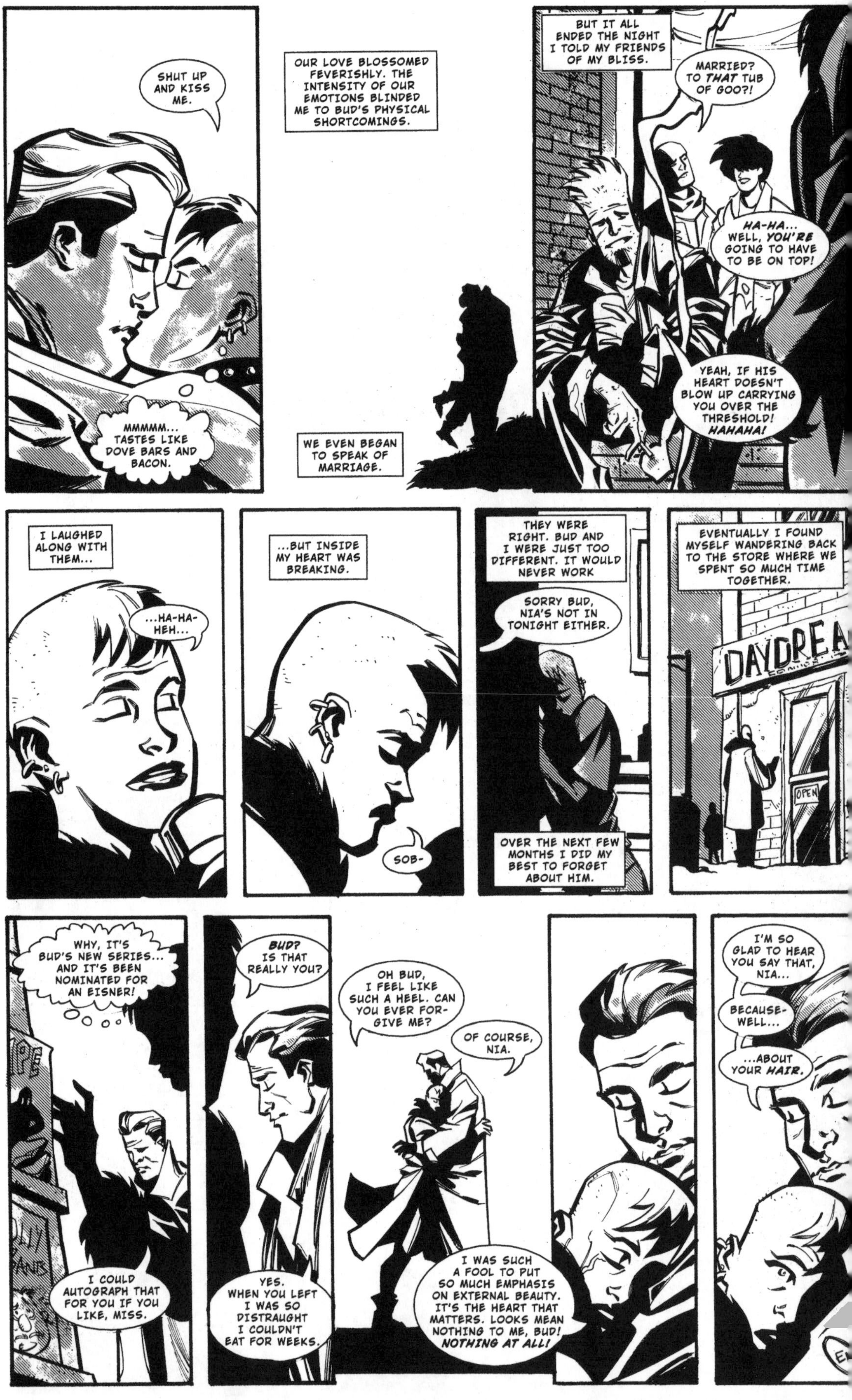
SHUT UP AND KISS ME.
MMMMM... TASTES LIKE DOVE BARS AND BACON.
OUR LOVE BLOSSOMED FEVERISHLY. THE INTENSITY OF OUR EMOTIONS BLINDED ME TO BUD'S PHYSICAL SHORTCOMINGS.
WE EVEN BEGAN TO SPEAK OF MARRIAGE.
BUT IT ALL ENDED THE NIGHT I TOLD MY FRIENDS OF MY BLISS.
MARRIED? TO *THAT* TUB OF GOO?!
HA-HA... WELL, *YOU'RE* GOING TO HAVE TO BE ON TOP!
YEAH, IF HIS HEART DOESN'T BLOW UP CARRYING YOU OVER THE THRESHOLD! *HAHAHA!*
I LAUGHED ALONG WITH THEM...
...HA-HA-HEH...
...BUT INSIDE MY HEART WAS BREAKING.
SOB-
THEY WERE RIGHT. BUD AND I WERE JUST TOO DIFFERENT. IT WOULD NEVER WORK
SORRY BUD, NIA'S NOT IN TONIGHT EITHER.
OVER THE NEXT FEW MONTHS I DID MY BEST TO FORGET ABOUT HIM.
EVENTUALLY I FOUND MYSELF WANDERING BACK TO THE STORE WHERE WE SPENT SO MUCH TIME TOGETHER.
DAYDREA
OPEN
WHY, IT'S BUD'S NEW SERIES... AND IT'S BEEN NOMINATED FOR AN EISNER!
I COULD AUTOGRAPH THAT FOR YOU IF YOU LIKE, MISS.
BUD? IS THAT REALLY YOU?
YES. WHEN YOU LEFT I WAS SO DISTRAUGHT I COULDN'T EAT FOR WEEKS.
OH BUD, I FEEL LIKE SUCH A HEEL. CAN YOU EVER FORGIVE ME?
OF COURSE, NIA.
I WAS SUCH A FOOL TO PUT SO MUCH EMPHASIS ON EXTERNAL BEAUTY. IT'S THE HEART THAT MATTERS. LOOKS MEAN NOTHING TO ME, BUD! *NOTHING AT ALL!*
I'M SO GLAD TO HEAR YOU SAY THAT, NIA...
BECAUSE-WELL...
...ABOUT YOUR *HAIR.*

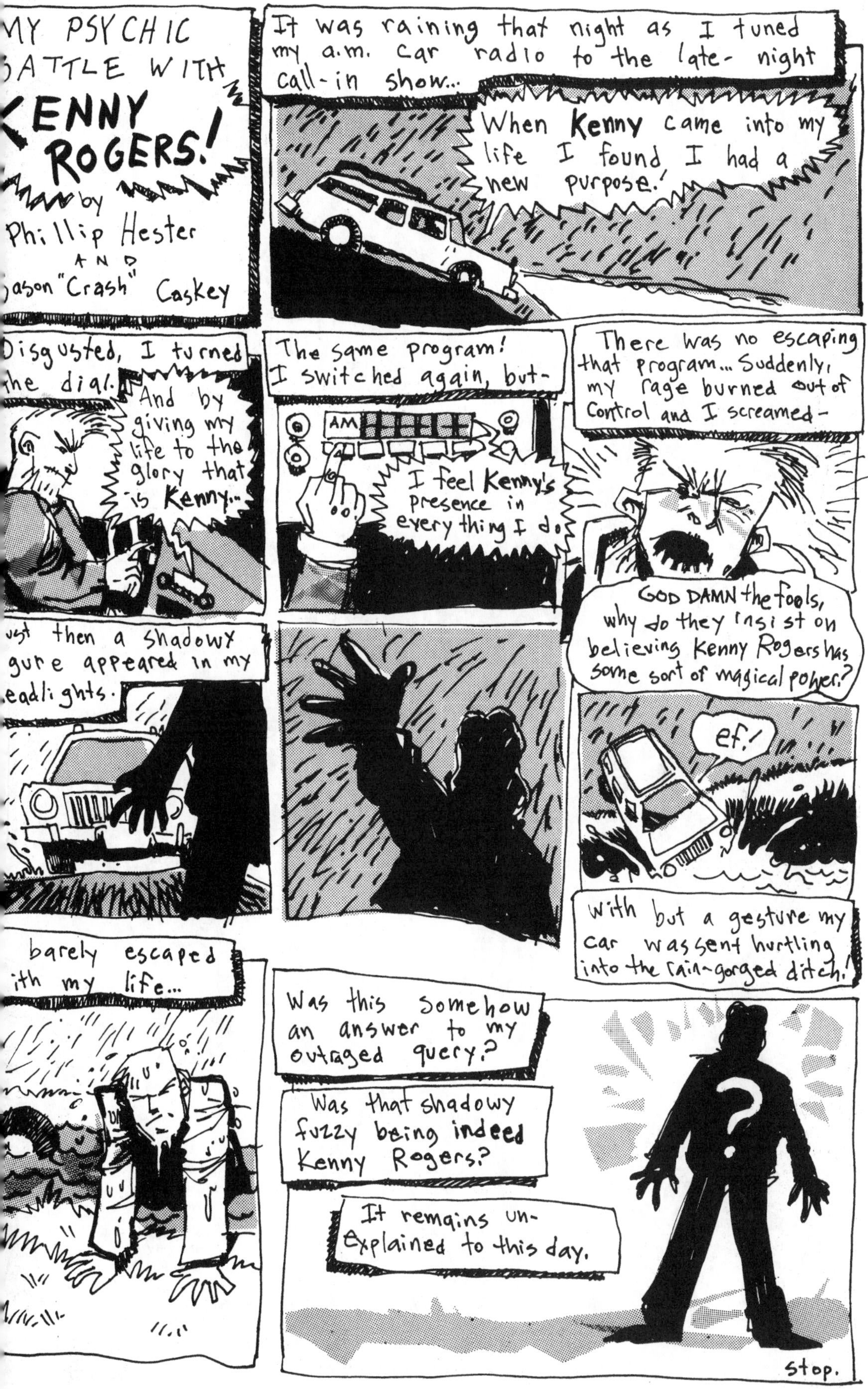

MY PSYCHIC BATTLE WITH KENNY ROGERS!
by Phillip Hester AND Jason "Crash" Caskey
It was raining that night as I tuned my a.m. car radio to the late-night call-in show...
When Kenny came into my life I found I had a new purpose.
Disgusted, I turned the dial.
And by giving my life to the glory that is Kenny...
The same program! I switched again, but-
AM
I feel Kenny's presence in every thing I do
There was no escaping that program... Suddenly, my rage burned out of control and I screamed-
GOD DAMN the fools, why do they insist on believing Kenny Rogers has some sort of magical power?
Just then a shadowy figure appeared in my headlights.
ef!
With but a gesture my car was sent hurtling into the rain-gorged ditch!
I barely escaped with my life...
Was this somehow an answer to my outraged query?
Was that shadowy fuzzy being indeed Kenny Rogers?
It remains unexplained to this day.
stop.

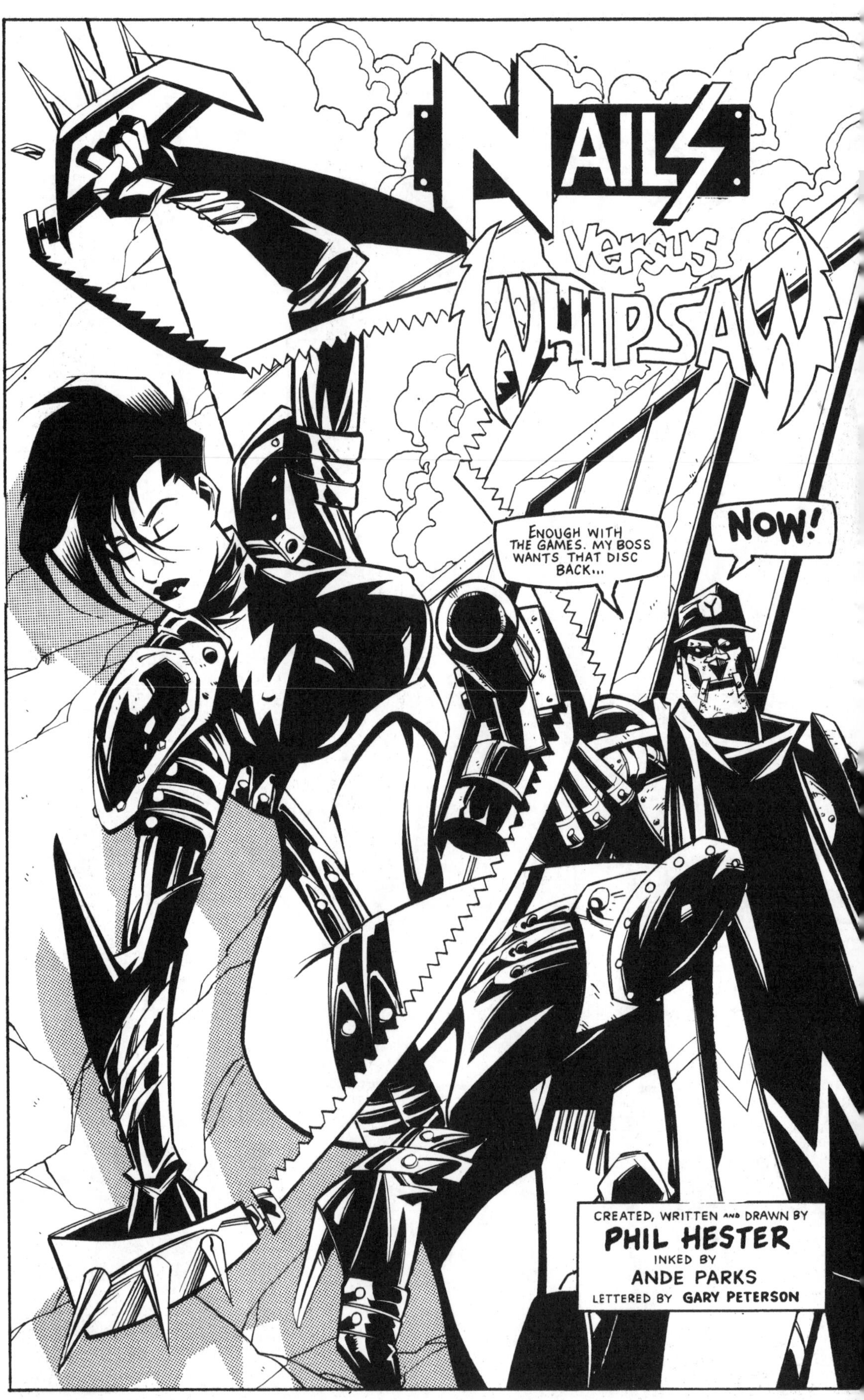
NAILS
versus
WHIPSAW
ENOUGH WITH THE GAMES. MY BOSS WANTS THAT DISC BACK...
NOW!
CREATED, WRITTEN AND DRAWN BY
PHIL HESTER
INKED BY
ANDE PARKS
LETTERED BY GARY PETERSON

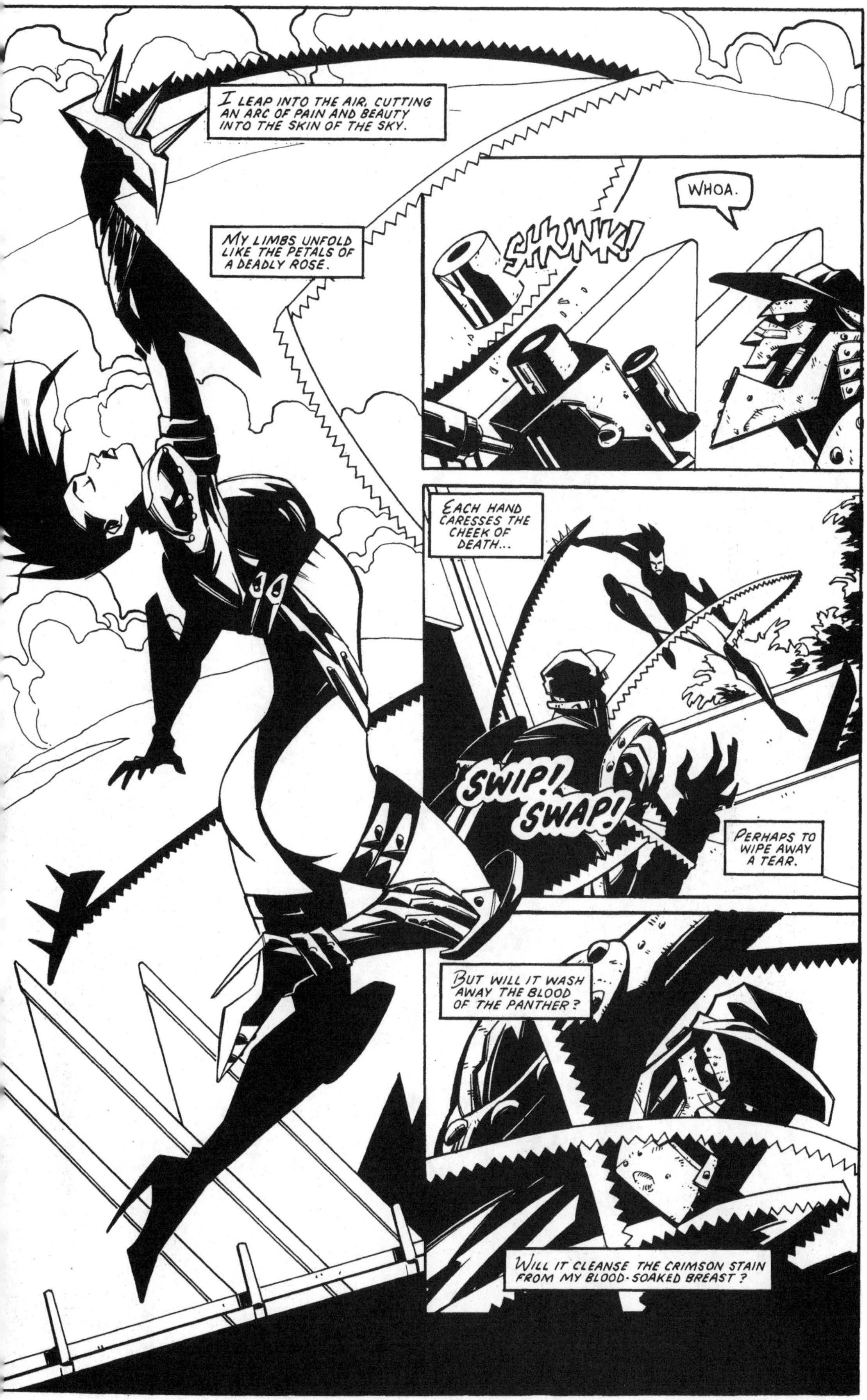
I LEAP INTO THE AIR, CUTTING AN ARC OF PAIN AND BEAUTY INTO THE SKIN OF THE SKY.
MY LIMBS UNFOLD LIKE THE PETALS OF A DEADLY ROSE.
SHUNK!
WHOA.
EACH HAND CARESSES THE CHEEK OF DEATH...
SWIP! SWAP!
PERHAPS TO WIPE AWAY A TEAR.
BUT WILL IT WASH AWAY THE BLOOD OF THE PANTHER?
WILL IT CLEANSE THE CRIMSON STAIN FROM MY BLOOD-SOAKED BREAST?

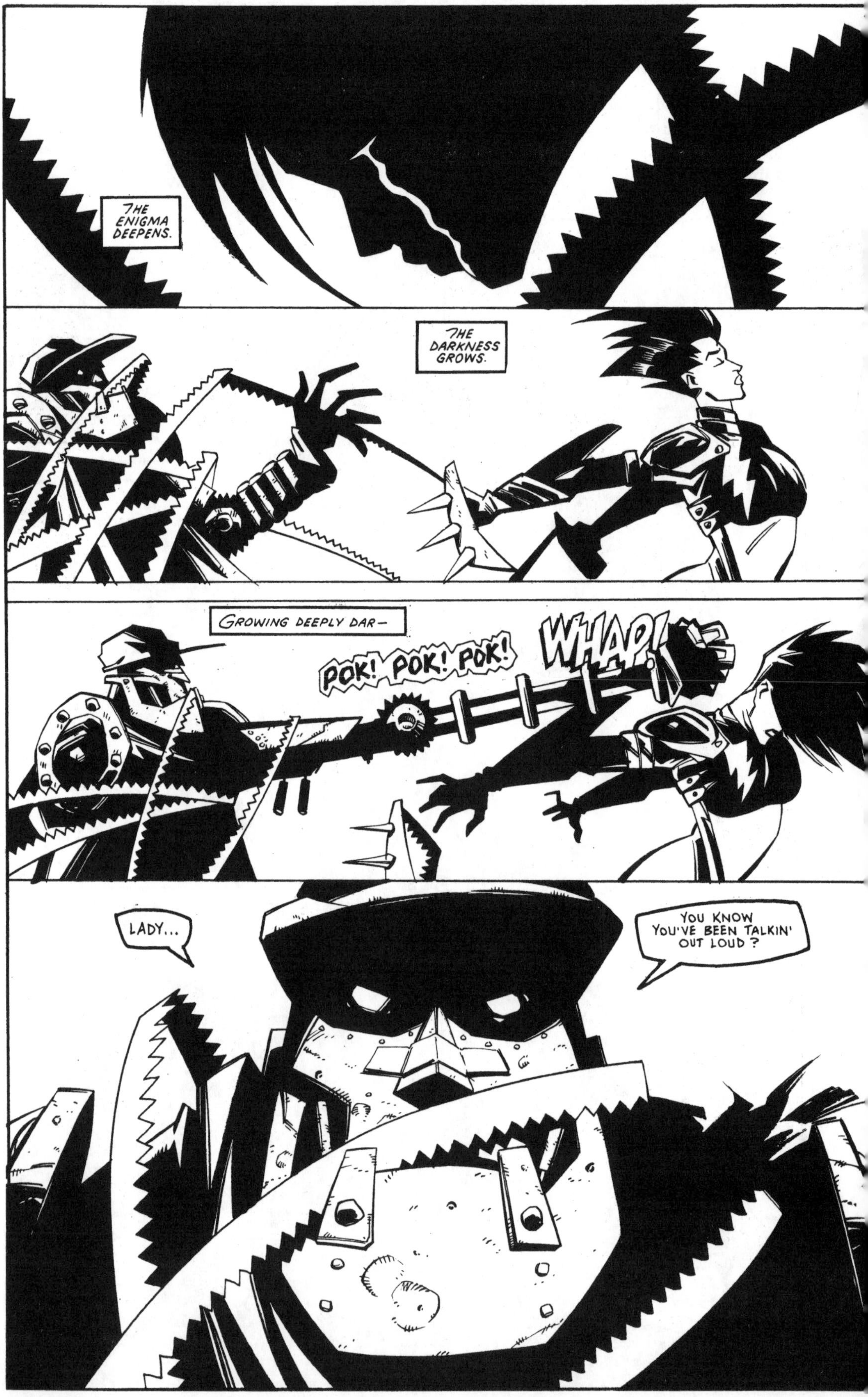

THE ENIGMA DEEPENS.
THE DARKNESS GROWS.
GROWING DEEPLY DAR—
POK! POK! POK!
WHAP!
LADY...
YOU KNOW YOU'VE BEEN TALKIN' OUT LOUD?

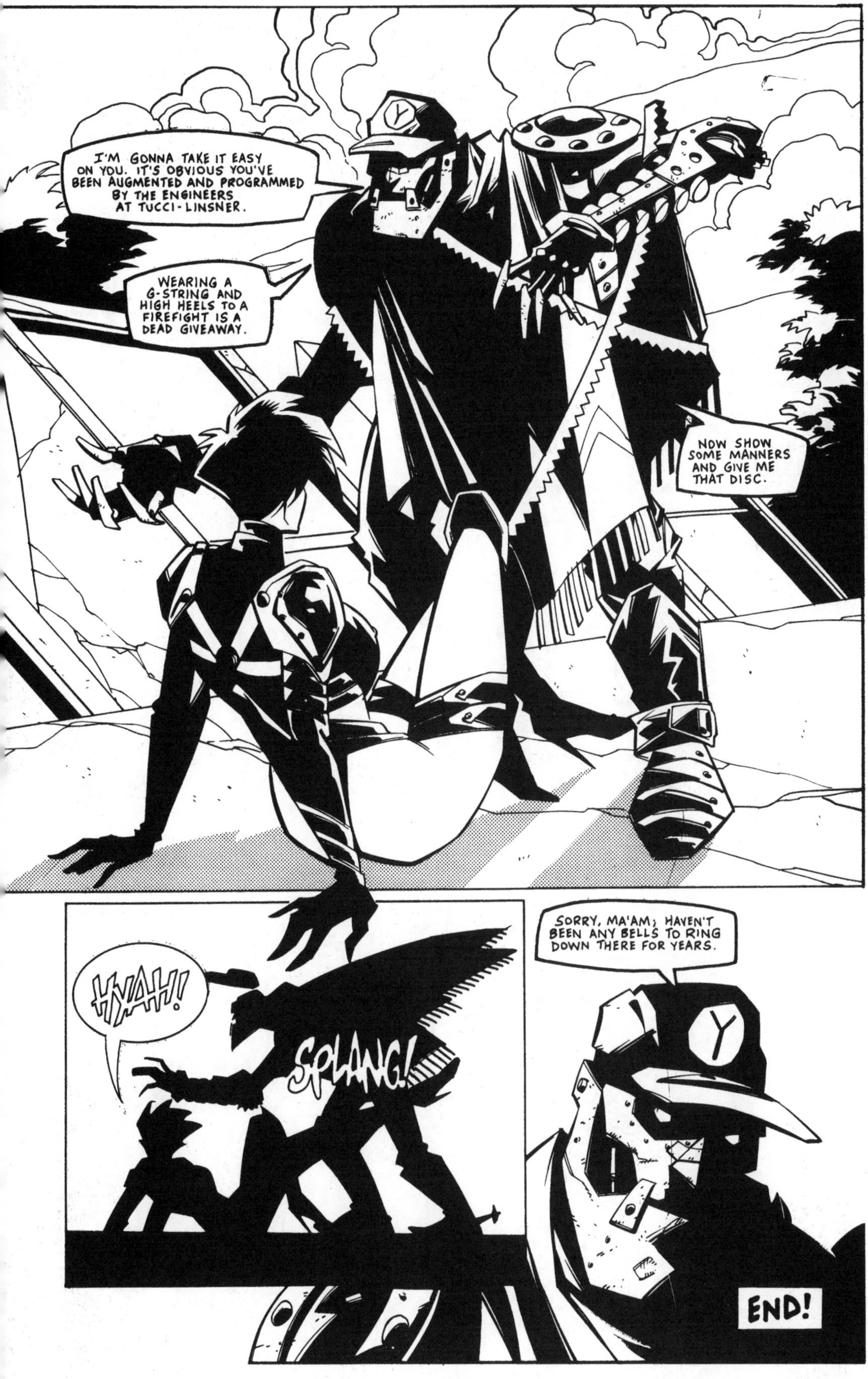
I'M GONNA TAKE IT EASY ON YOU. IT'S OBVIOUS YOU'VE BEEN AUGMENTED AND PROGRAMMED BY THE ENGINEERS AT TUCCI-LINSNER.
WEARING A G-STRING AND HIGH HEELS TO A FIREFIGHT IS A DEAD GIVEAWAY.
NOW SHOW SOME MANNERS AND GIVE ME THAT DISC.
HYAH!
SPLANG!
SORRY, MA'AM; HAVEN'T BEEN ANY BELLS TO RING DOWN THERE FOR YEARS.
END!

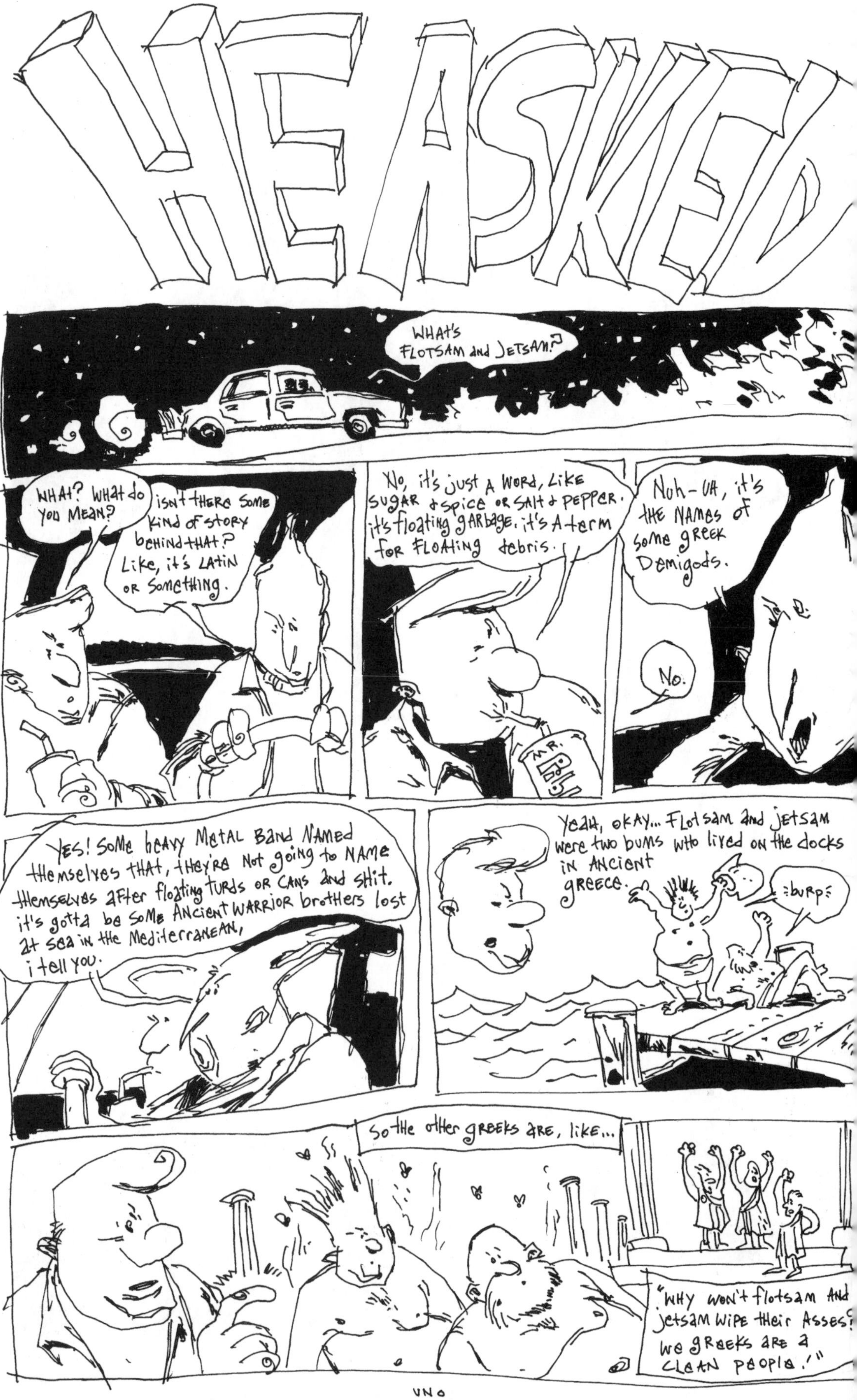
HE ASKED
WHAT'S FLOTSAM AND JETSAM?
WHAT? WHAT DO YOU MEAN?
ISN'T THERE SOME KIND OF STORY BEHIND THAT? LIKE, IT'S LATIN OR SOMETHING.
NO, IT'S JUST A WORD, LIKE SUGAR & SPICE OR SALT & PEPPER. IT'S FLOATING GARBAGE. IT'S A TERM FOR FLOATING DEBRIS.
NUH-UH, IT'S THE NAMES OF SOME GREEK DEMIGODS.
NO.
YES! SOME HEAVY METAL BAND NAMED THEMSELVES THAT, THEY'RE NOT GOING TO NAME THEMSELVES AFTER FLOATING TURDS OR CANS AND SHIT. IT'S GOTTA BE SOME ANCIENT WARRIOR BROTHERS LOST AT SEA IN THE MEDITERRANEAN, I TELL YOU.
YEAH, OKAY... FLOTSAM AND JETSAM WERE TWO BUMS WHO LIVED ON THE DOCKS IN ANCIENT GREECE.
BURP
SO THE OTHER GREEKS ARE, LIKE...
"WHY WON'T FLOTSAM AND JETSAM WIPE THEIR ASSES? WE GREEKS ARE A CLEAN PEOPLE!"

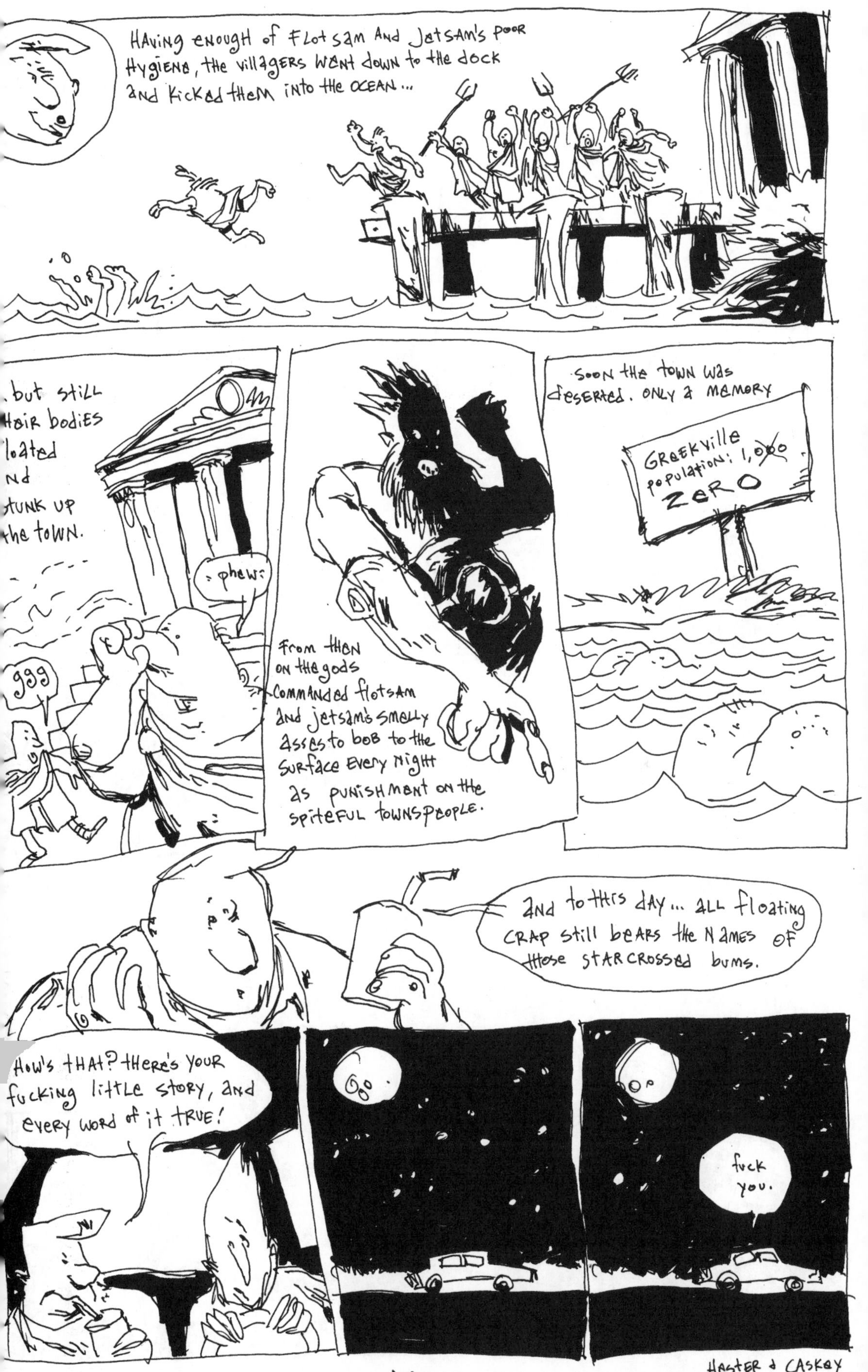
HAving enough of Flotsam And Jetsam's poor Hygiene, the villagers went down to the dock and kicked them into the ocean...
but still their bodies floated and stunk up the town.
phew:
ggg
From then on the gods commanded flotsam and jetsam's smelly asses to bob to the surface every night as punishment on the spiteful townspeople.
Soon the town was deserted. Only a memory
GREEKVILLE population: 1,000 ZERO
and to this day... all floating crap still bears the names of those starcrossed bums.
How's that? there's your fucking little story, and every word of it true!
fuck you.

Hester & Caskey

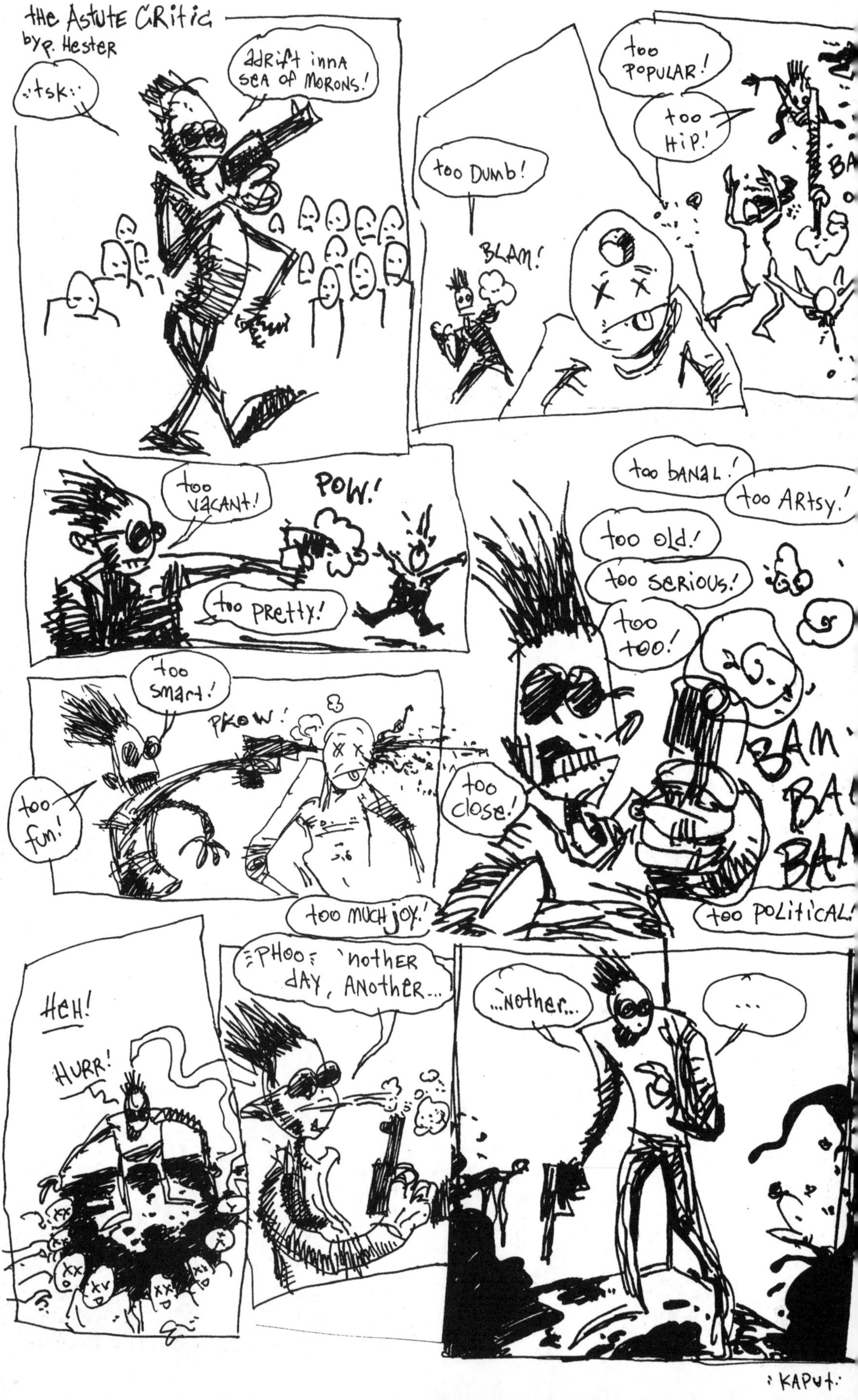
the Astute Critic
by P. Hester
..tsk..
adrift inna sea of MORONS!
too DUMB!
BLAM!
too POPULAR!
too HIP!
too VACANT!
POW!
too pretty!
too smart!
PKOW!
too fun!
too banal!
too Artsy!
too old!
too serious!
too too!
too close!
too MUCH joy!
too POLITICAL!
HEH!
HURR!
PHOO ~ 'nother day, Another...
...nother...
...
KAPUT

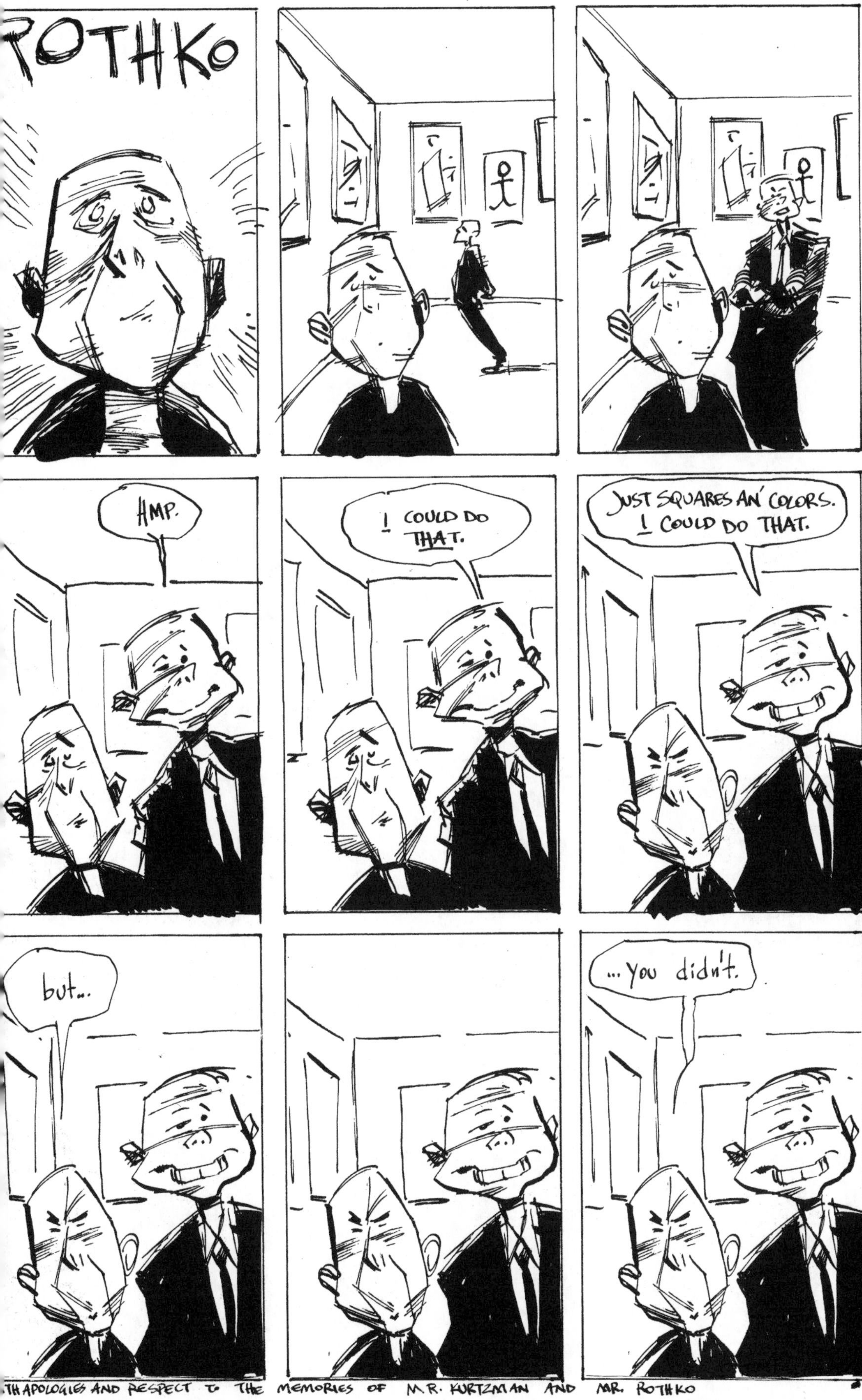
ROTHKO
HMP.
I COULD DO THAT.
JUST SQUARES AN' COLORS. I COULD DO THAT.
but...
...you didn't.

TH APOLOGIES AND RESPECT TO THE MEMORIES OF M.R. KURTZMAN AND MR. ROTHKO

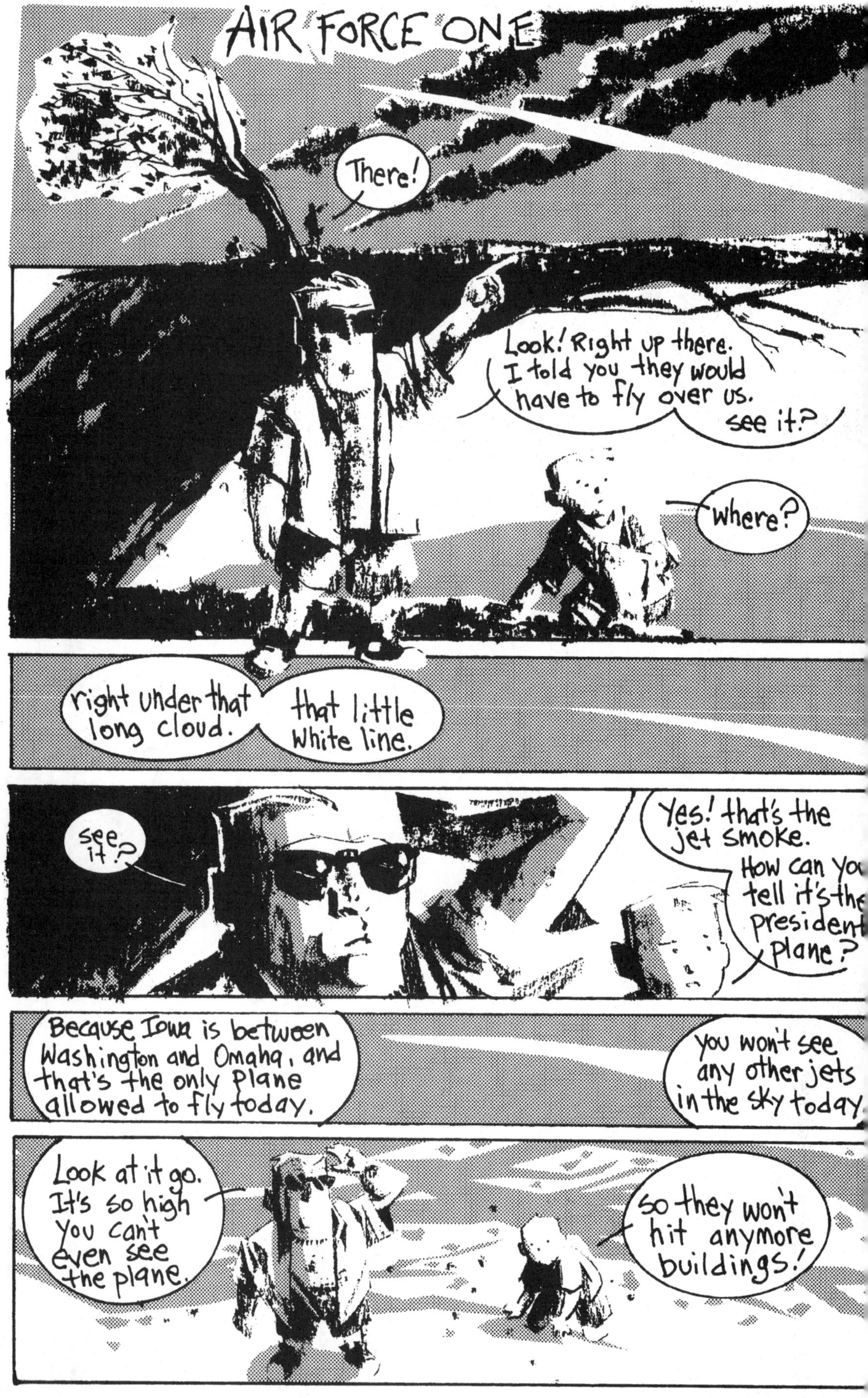
AIR FORCE ONE
There!
Look! Right up there. I told you they would have to fly over us. see it?
where?
right under that long cloud.
that little white line.
see it?
Yes! that's the jet smoke.
How can you tell it's the president's plane?
Because Iowa is between Washington and Omaha, and that's the only plane allowed to fly today.
you won't see any other jets in the sky today.
Look at it go. It's so high you can't even see the plane.
so they won't hit anymore buildings!

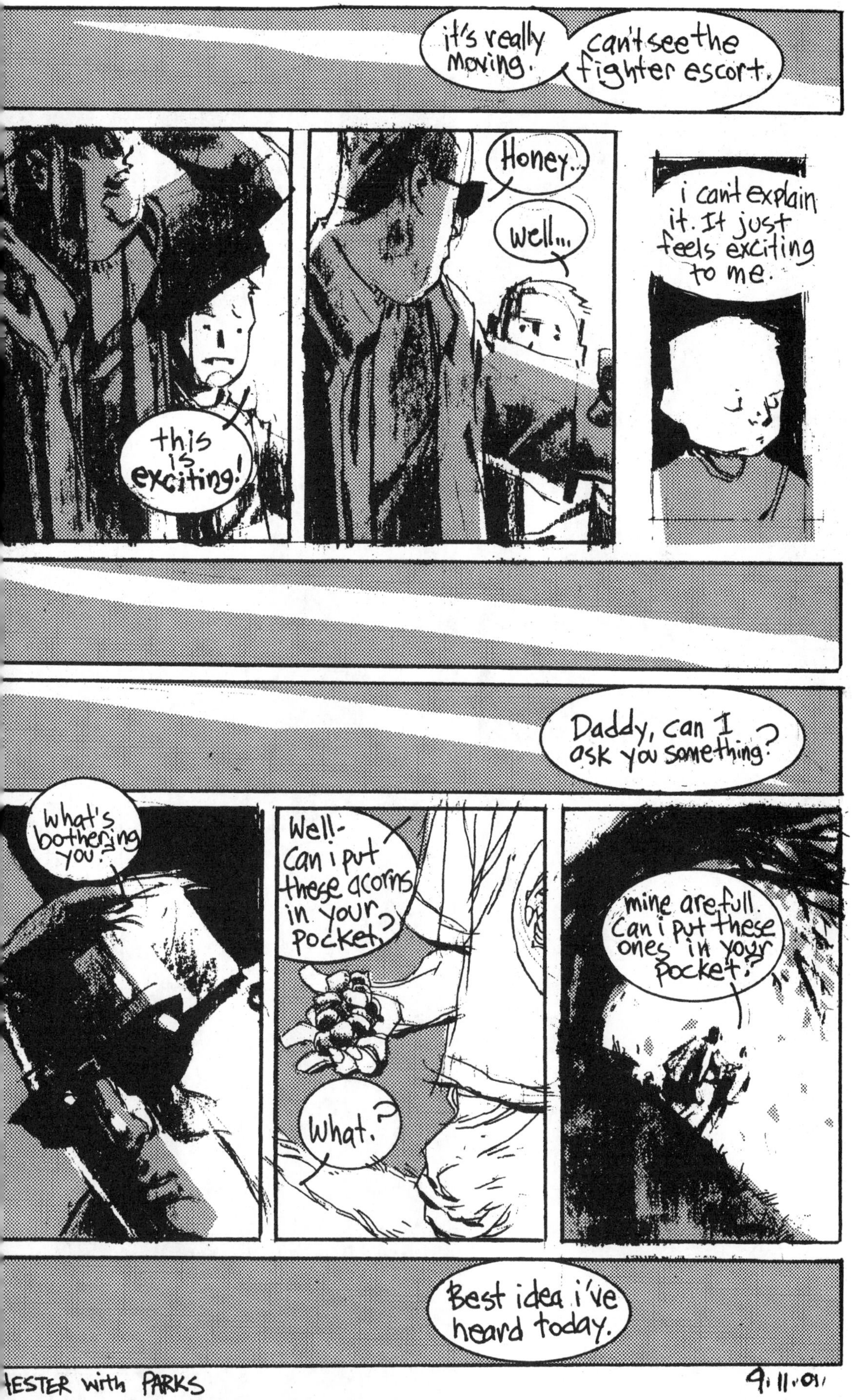
it's really moving.
can't see the fighter escort.
this is exciting!
Honey...
well...
i can't explain it. It just feels exciting to me.
Daddy, can I ask you something?
what's bothering you?
Well- can i put these acorns in your pocket?
What.?
mine are full. Can i put these ones in your pocket?
Best idea i've heard today.

HESTER with PARKS 9.11.01

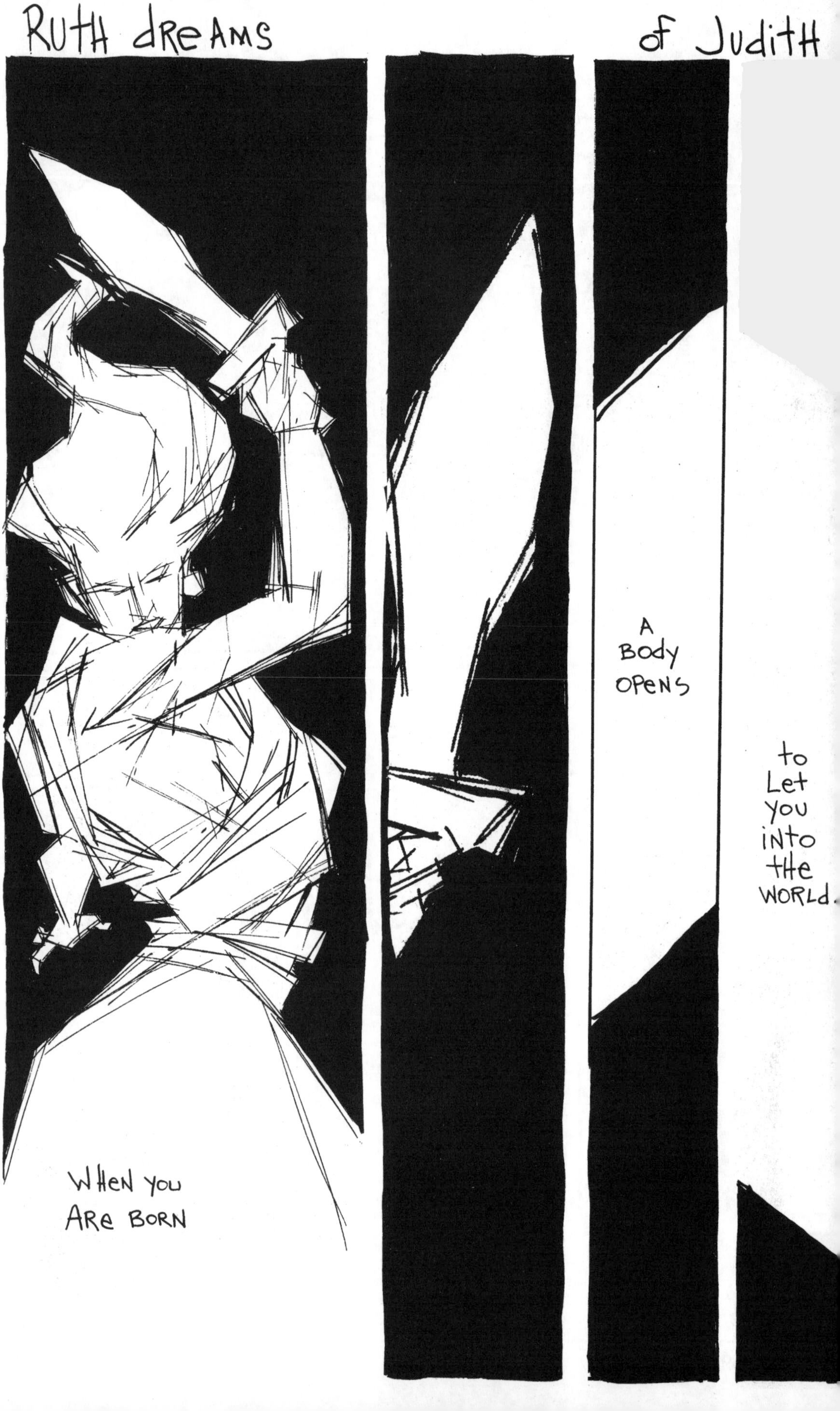
RUTH DREAMS OF JUDITH
WHEN YOU ARE BORN
A BODY OPENS
TO LET YOU INTO THE WORLD.

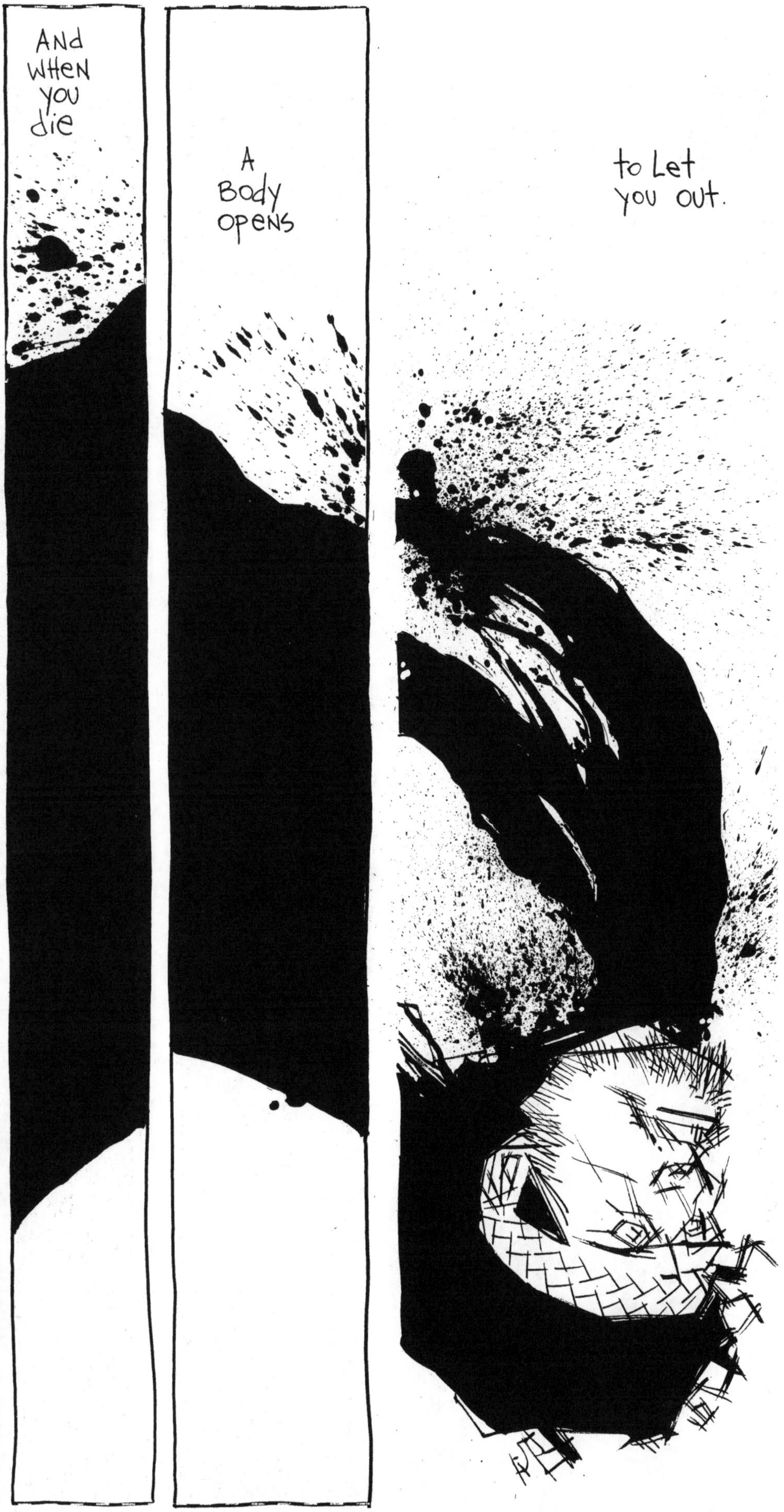
And when you die
A Body opens
to Let you out.

Ruth dreams of Naomi

I dreamed again last night, Mama.

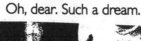

That is a good sign, I think.

I dreamed I was in the orchard, and even though the trees were bare I was holding a piece of fruit.

And even though the air was hot it was snowing. Grey snow. Oh, Mama. I was naked in the snow!

Oh, dear. Such a dream.

And when I bit the fruit the snow would fall into the opening. The snow would soak up the juice of the fruit and fill the bite mark again.

A sign. You will gain your strength back soon.

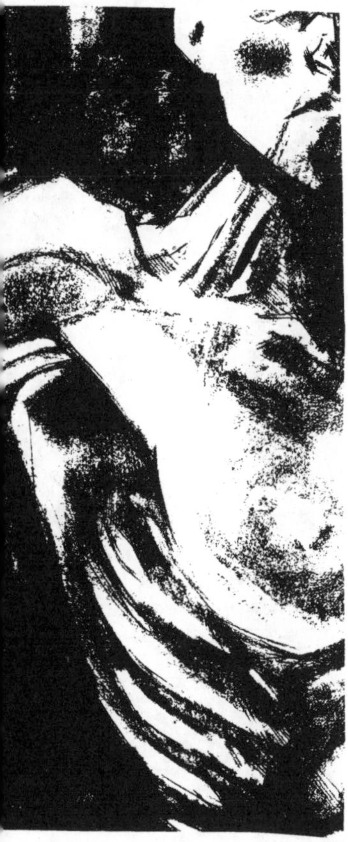

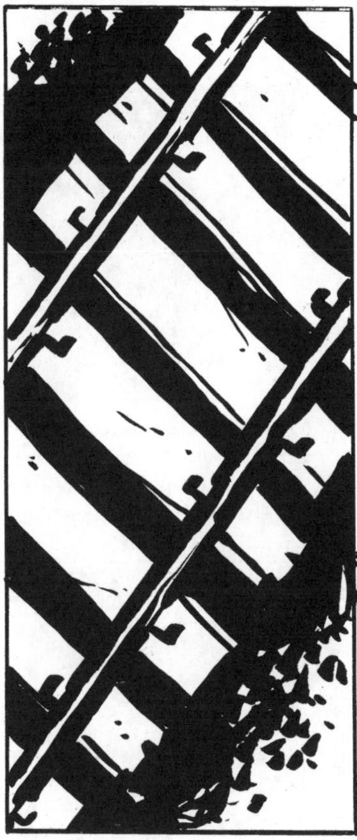

I do not think so. I hear trains when I dream.

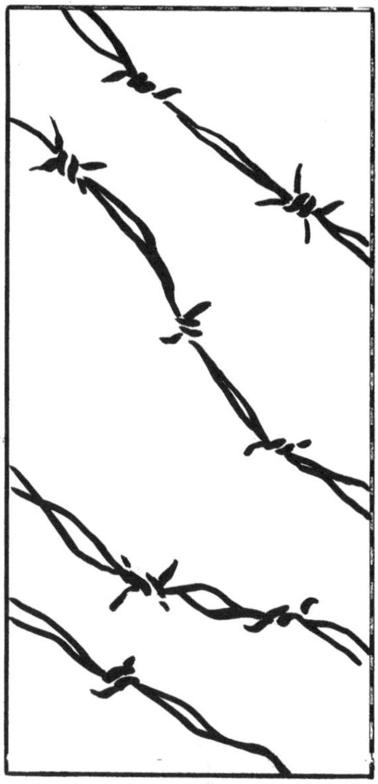

I used to sleep so well in a train- a moving train. The noise. The rocking. Like a baby riding inside you, Mama.

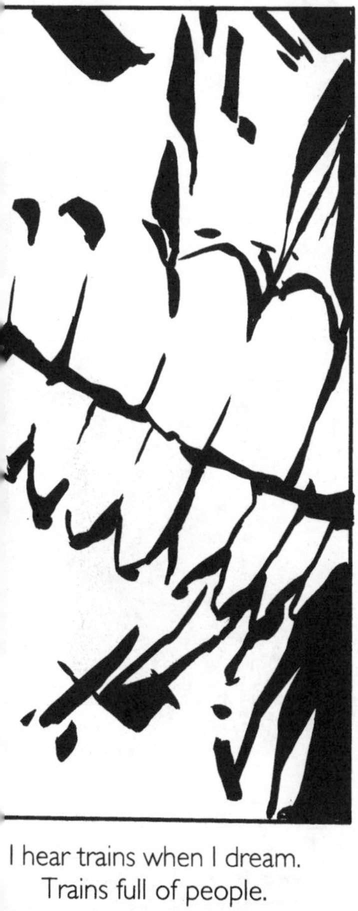

I hear trains when I dream. Trains full of people.

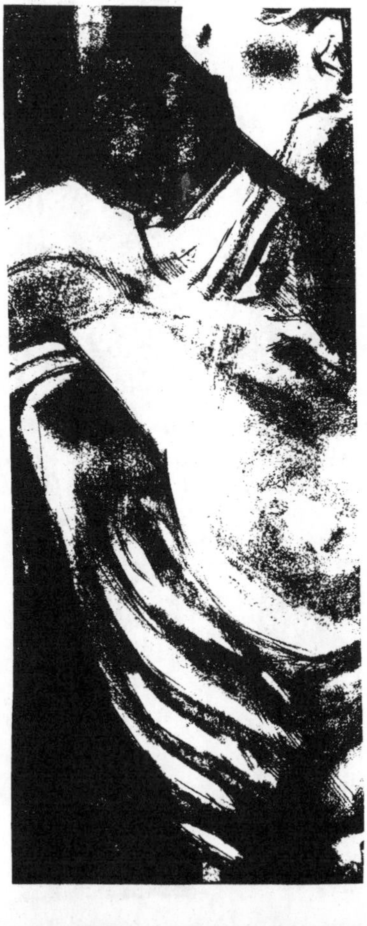

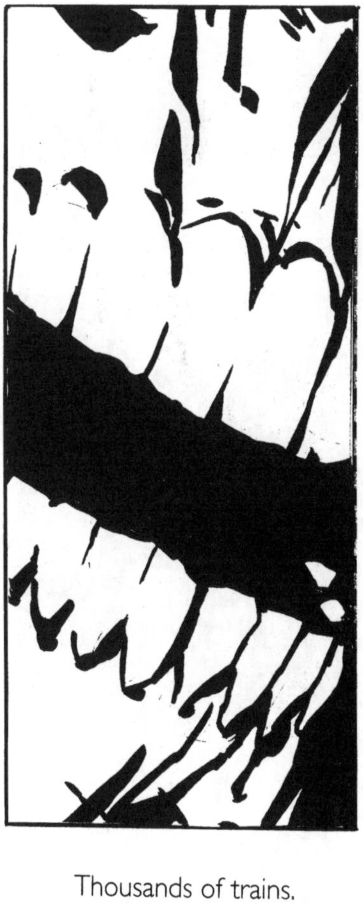

Thousands of trains.

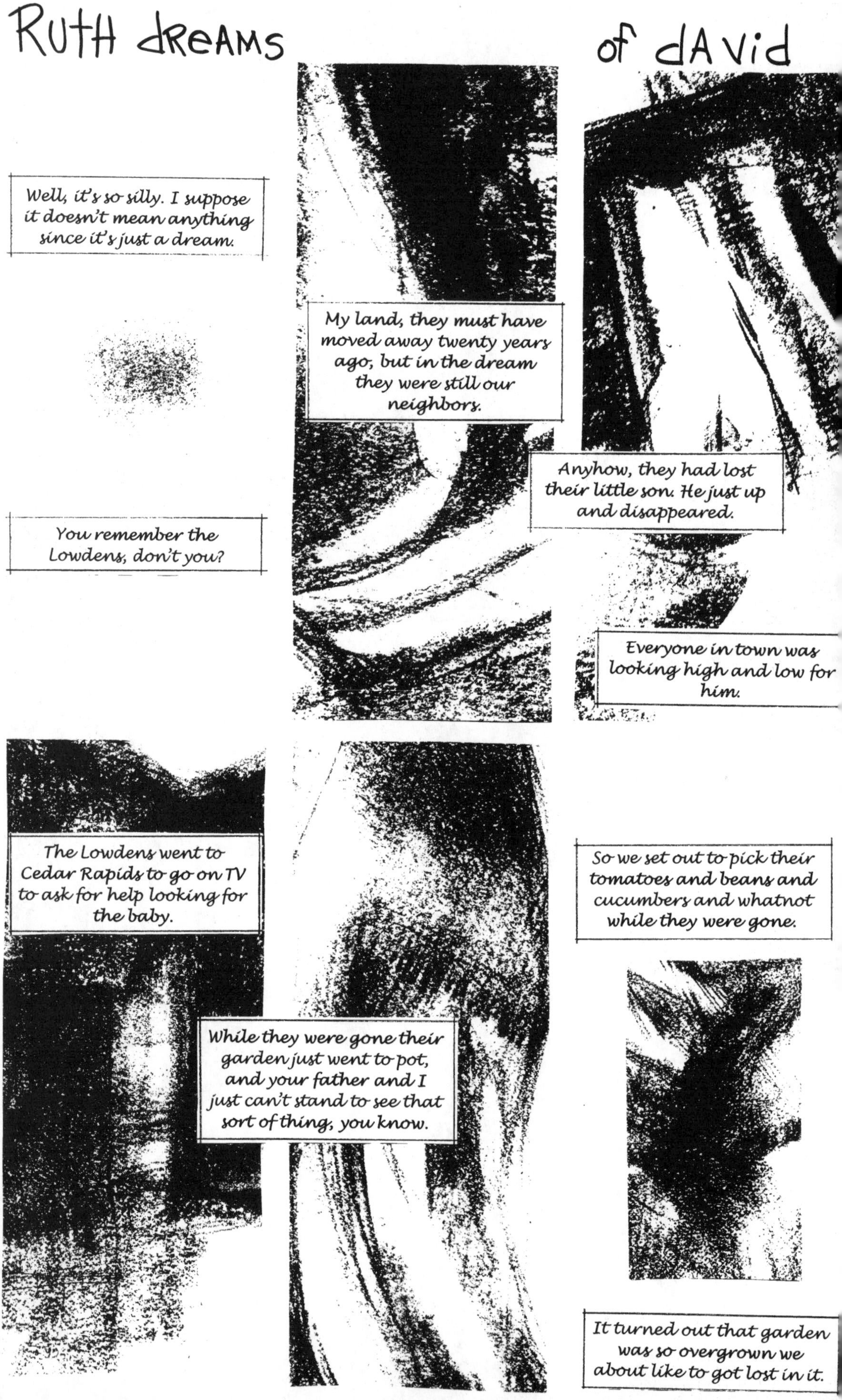
Ruth dreams of David
Well, it's so silly. I suppose it doesn't mean anything since it's just a dream.
You remember the Lowdens, don't you?
My land, they must have moved away twenty years ago, but in the dream they were still our neighbors.
Anyhow, they had lost their little son. He just up and disappeared.
Everyone in town was looking high and low for him.
The Lowdens went to Cedar Rapids to go on TV to ask for help looking for the baby.
While they were gone their garden just went to pot, and your father and I just can't stand to see that sort of thing, you know.
So we set out to pick their tomatoes and beans and cucumbers and whatnot while they were gone.
It turned out that garden was so overgrown we about like to got lost in it.

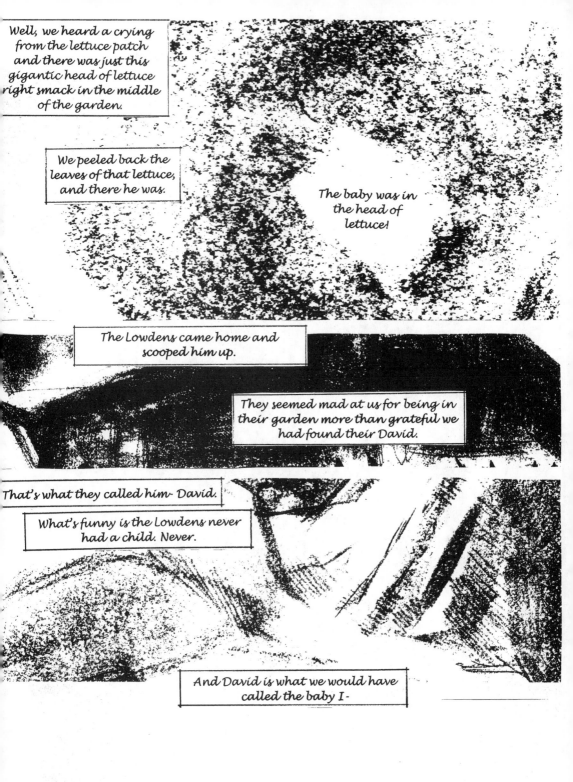

Well, we heard a crying from the lettuce patch and there was just this gigantic head of lettuce right smack in the middle of the garden.

We peeled back the leaves of that lettuce, and there he was.

The baby was in the head of lettuce!

The Lowdens came home and scooped him up.

They seemed mad at us for being in their garden more than grateful we had found their David.

That's what they called him- David.

What's funny is the Lowdens never had a child. Never.

And David is what we would have called the baby I-

Well, if you had been a boy that's what we would have named you.

David.

BONESHAKER · first part.

'92- Phillip Hester

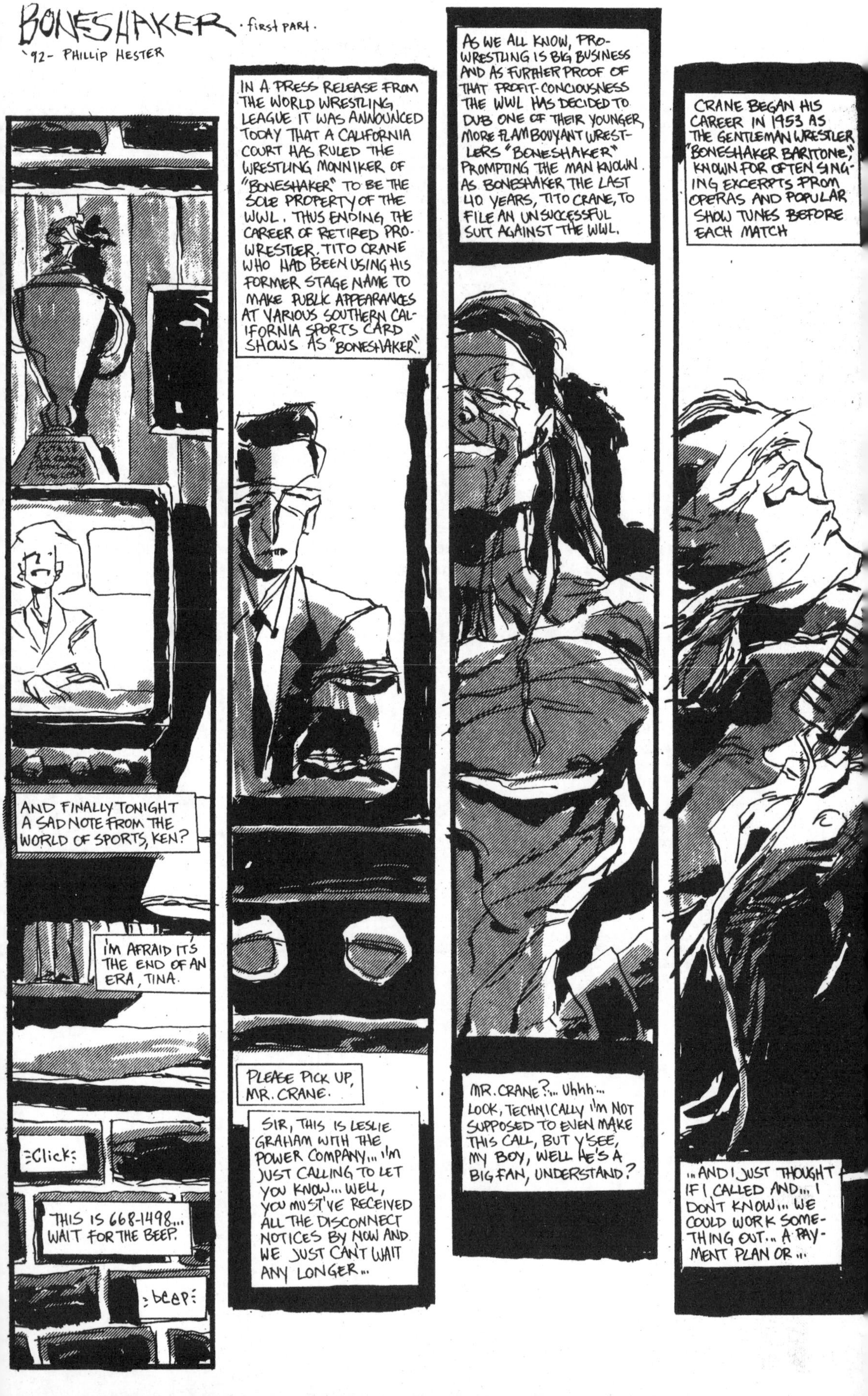
AND FINALLY TONIGHT A SAD NOTE FROM THE WORLD OF SPORTS, KEN?
I'M AFRAID IT'S THE END OF AN ERA, TINA.
:Click:
THIS IS 668-1498... WAIT FOR THE BEEP.
:beep:
IN A PRESS RELEASE FROM THE WORLD WRESTLING LEAGUE IT WAS ANNOUNCED TODAY THAT A CALIFORNIA COURT HAS RULED THE WRESTLING MONNIKER OF "BONESHAKER" TO BE THE SOLE PROPERTY OF THE WWL. THUS ENDING THE CAREER OF RETIRED PRO-WRESTLER, TITO CRANE WHO HAD BEEN USING HIS FORMER STAGE NAME TO MAKE PUBLIC APPEARANCES AT VARIOUS SOUTHERN CALIFORNIA SPORTS CARD SHOWS AS "BONESHAKER".
PLEASE PICK UP, MR. CRANE.
SIR, THIS IS LESLIE GRAHAM WITH THE POWER COMPANY... I'M JUST CALLING TO LET YOU KNOW... WELL, YOU MUST'VE RECEIVED ALL THE DISCONNECT NOTICES BY NOW AND WE JUST CAN'T WAIT ANY LONGER...
AS WE ALL KNOW, PRO-WRESTLING IS BIG BUSINESS AND AS FURTHER PROOF OF THAT PROFIT-CONCIOUSNESS THE WWL HAS DECIDED TO DUB ONE OF THEIR YOUNGER, MORE FLAMBOUYANT WRESTLERS "BONESHAKER" PROMPTING THE MAN KNOWN AS BONESHAKER THE LAST 40 YEARS, TITO CRANE, TO FILE AN UNSUCCESSFUL SUIT AGAINST THE WWL.
MR. CRANE?... Uhhh... LOOK, TECHNICALLY I'M NOT SUPPOSED TO EVEN MAKE THIS CALL, BUT Y'SEE, MY BOY, WELL HE'S A BIG FAN, UNDERSTAND?
CRANE BEGAN HIS CAREER IN 1953 AS THE GENTLEMAN WRESTLER "BONESHAKER BARITONE," KNOWN FOR OFTEN SINGING EXCERPTS FROM OPERAS AND POPULAR SHOW TUNES BEFORE EACH MATCH
...AND I JUST THOUGHT IF I CALLED AND... I DON'T KNOW... WE COULD WORK SOMETHING OUT... A PAYMENT PLAN OR...

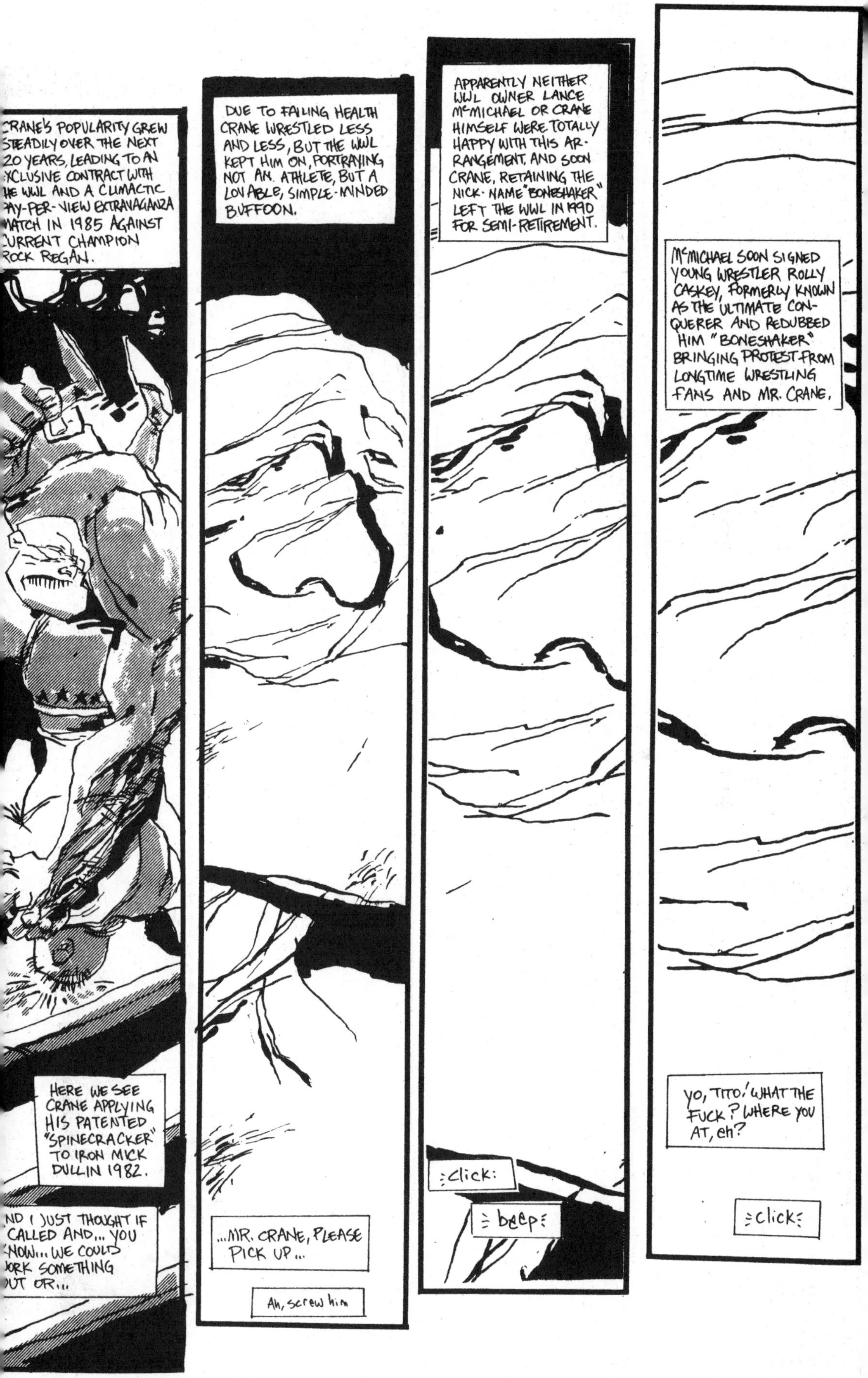
CRANE'S POPULARITY GREW STEADILY OVER THE NEXT 20 YEARS, LEADING TO AN EXCLUSIVE CONTRACT WITH THE WWL AND A CLIMACTIC PAY-PER-VIEW EXTRAVAGANZA MATCH IN 1985 AGAINST CURRENT CHAMPION ROCK REGAN.
HERE WE SEE CRANE APPLYING HIS PATENTED "SPINECRACKER" TO IRON MICK DULLIN 1982.
AND I JUST THOUGHT IF I CALLED AND... YOU KNOW... WE COULD WORK SOMETHING OUT OR...
DUE TO FAILING HEALTH CRANE WRESTLED LESS AND LESS, BUT THE WWL KEPT HIM ON, PORTRAYING NOT AN ATHLETE, BUT A LOVABLE, SIMPLE-MINDED BUFFOON.
...MR. CRANE, PLEASE PICK UP...
Ah, screw him
APPARENTLY NEITHER WWL OWNER LANCE McMICHAEL OR CRANE HIMSELF WERE TOTALLY HAPPY WITH THIS ARRANGEMENT, AND SOON CRANE, RETAINING THE NICK-NAME "BONESHAKER" LEFT THE WWL IN 1990 FOR SEMI-RETIREMENT.
click
beep
McMICHAEL SOON SIGNED YOUNG WRESTLER ROLLY CASKEY, FORMERLY KNOWN AS THE ULTIMATE CONQUERER AND REDUBBED HIM "BONESHAKER" BRINGING PROTEST FROM LONGTIME WRESTLING FANS AND MR. CRANE.
YO, TITO! WHAT THE FUCK? WHERE YOU AT, eh?
click

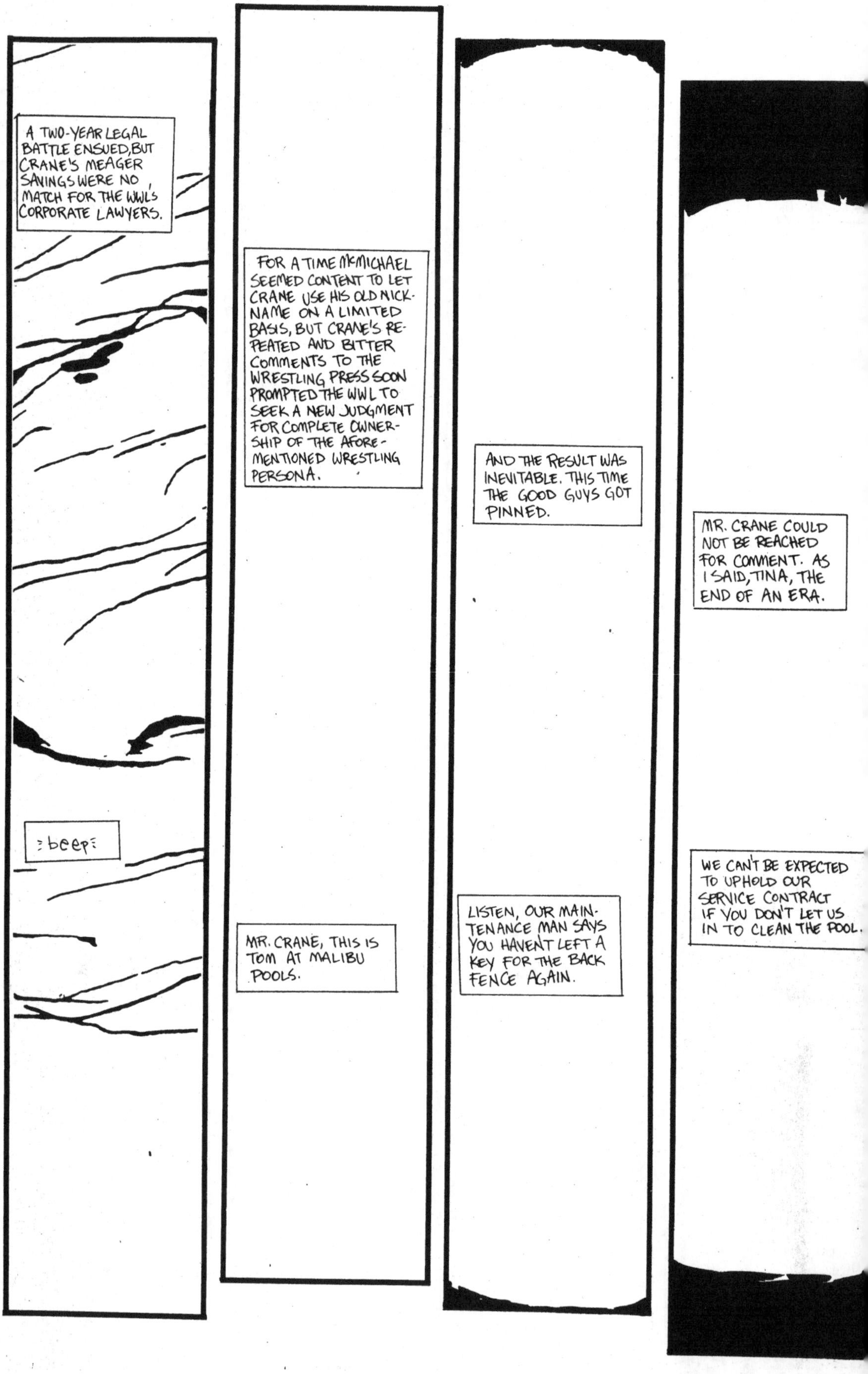

A TWO-YEAR LEGAL BATTLE ENSUED, BUT CRANE'S MEAGER SAVINGS WERE NO MATCH FOR THE WWL'S CORPORATE LAWYERS.
FOR A TIME McMICHAEL SEEMED CONTENT TO LET CRANE USE HIS OLD NICKNAME ON A LIMITED BASIS, BUT CRANE'S REPEATED AND BITTER COMMENTS TO THE WRESTLING PRESS SOON PROMPTED THE WWL TO SEEK A NEW JUDGMENT FOR COMPLETE OWNERSHIP OF THE AFOREMENTIONED WRESTLING PERSONA.
AND THE RESULT WAS INEVITABLE. THIS TIME THE GOOD GUYS GOT PINNED.
MR. CRANE COULD NOT BE REACHED FOR COMMENT. AS I SAID, TINA, THE END OF AN ERA.
:beep:
MR. CRANE, THIS IS TOM AT MALIBU POOLS.
LISTEN, OUR MAINTENANCE MAN SAYS YOU HAVEN'T LEFT A KEY FOR THE BACK FENCE AGAIN.
WE CAN'T BE EXPECTED TO UPHOLD OUR SERVICE CONTRACT IF YOU DON'T LET US IN TO CLEAN THE POOL.

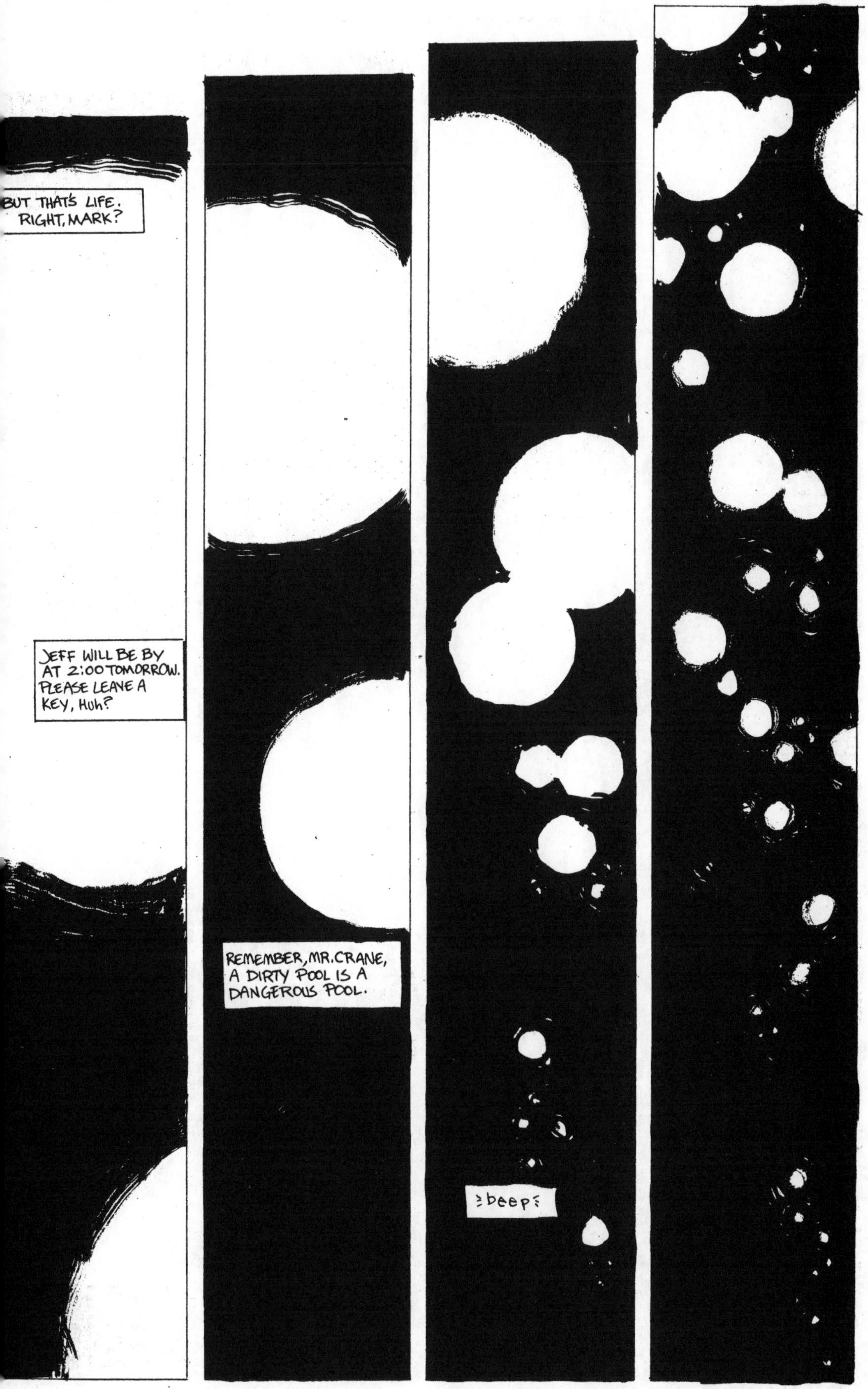
BUT THAT'S LIFE. RIGHT, MARK?
JEFF WILL BE BY AT 2:00 TOMORROW. PLEASE LEAVE A KEY, HUH?
REMEMBER, MR. CRANE, A DIRTY POOL IS A DANGEROUS POOL.
beep

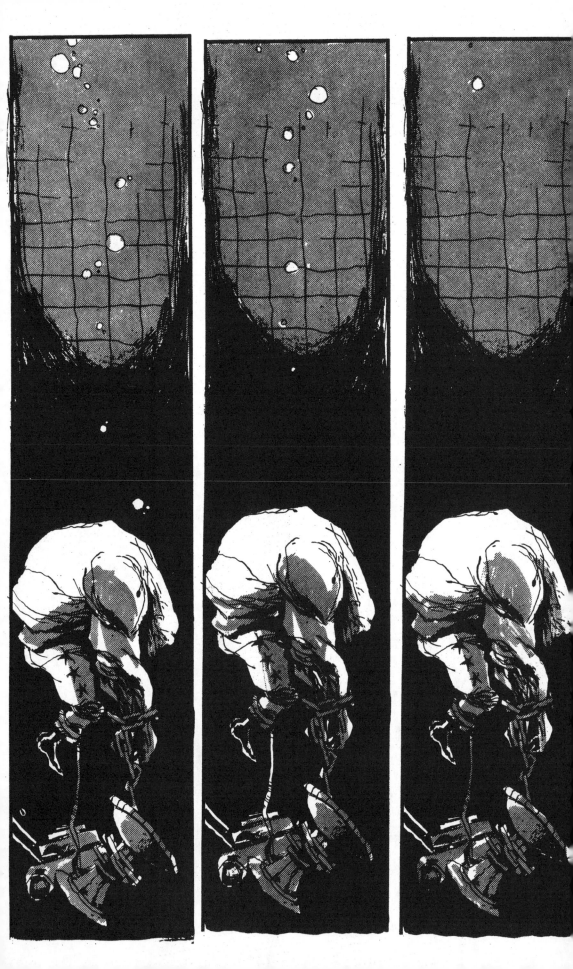

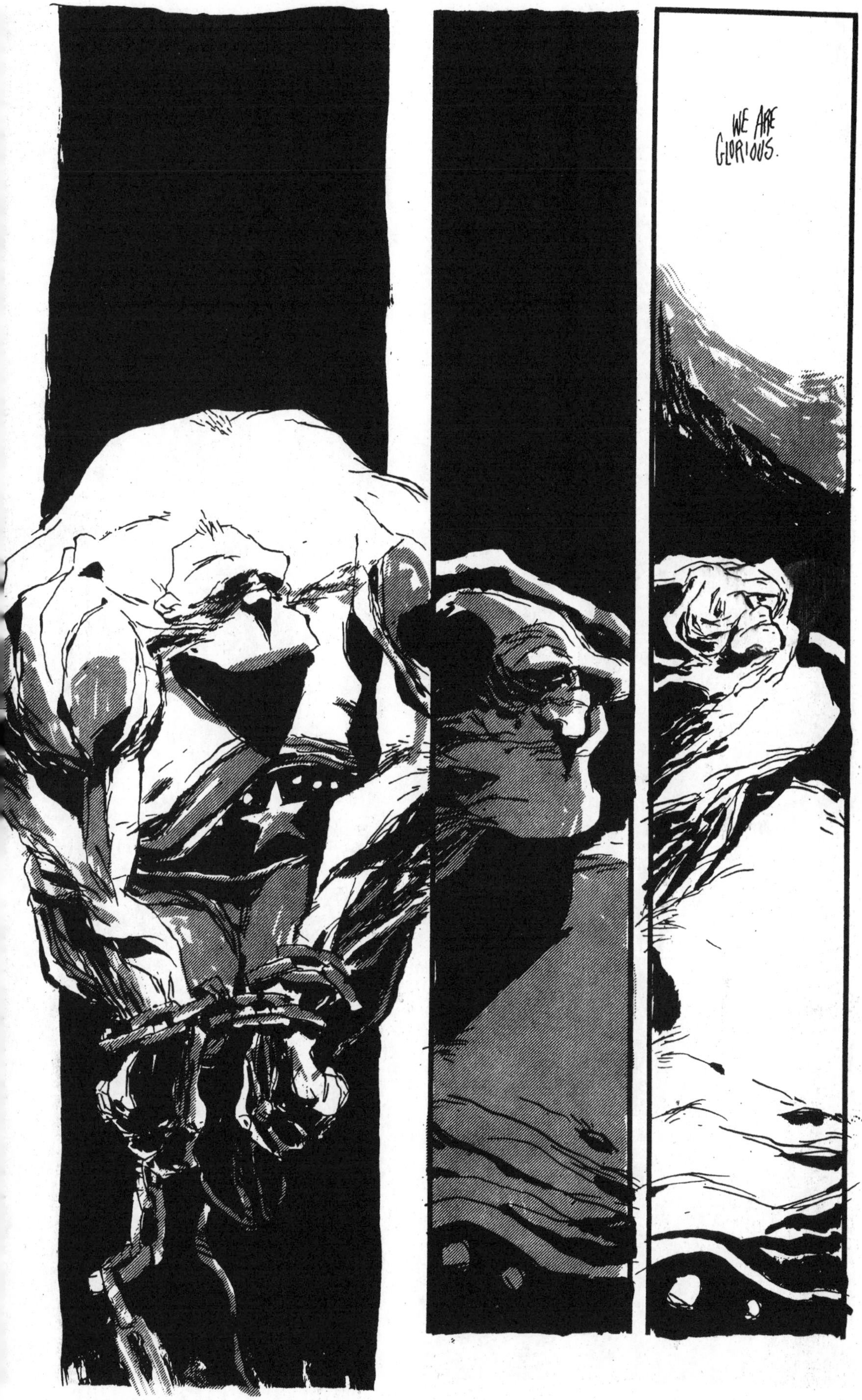
WE ARE GLORIOUS.

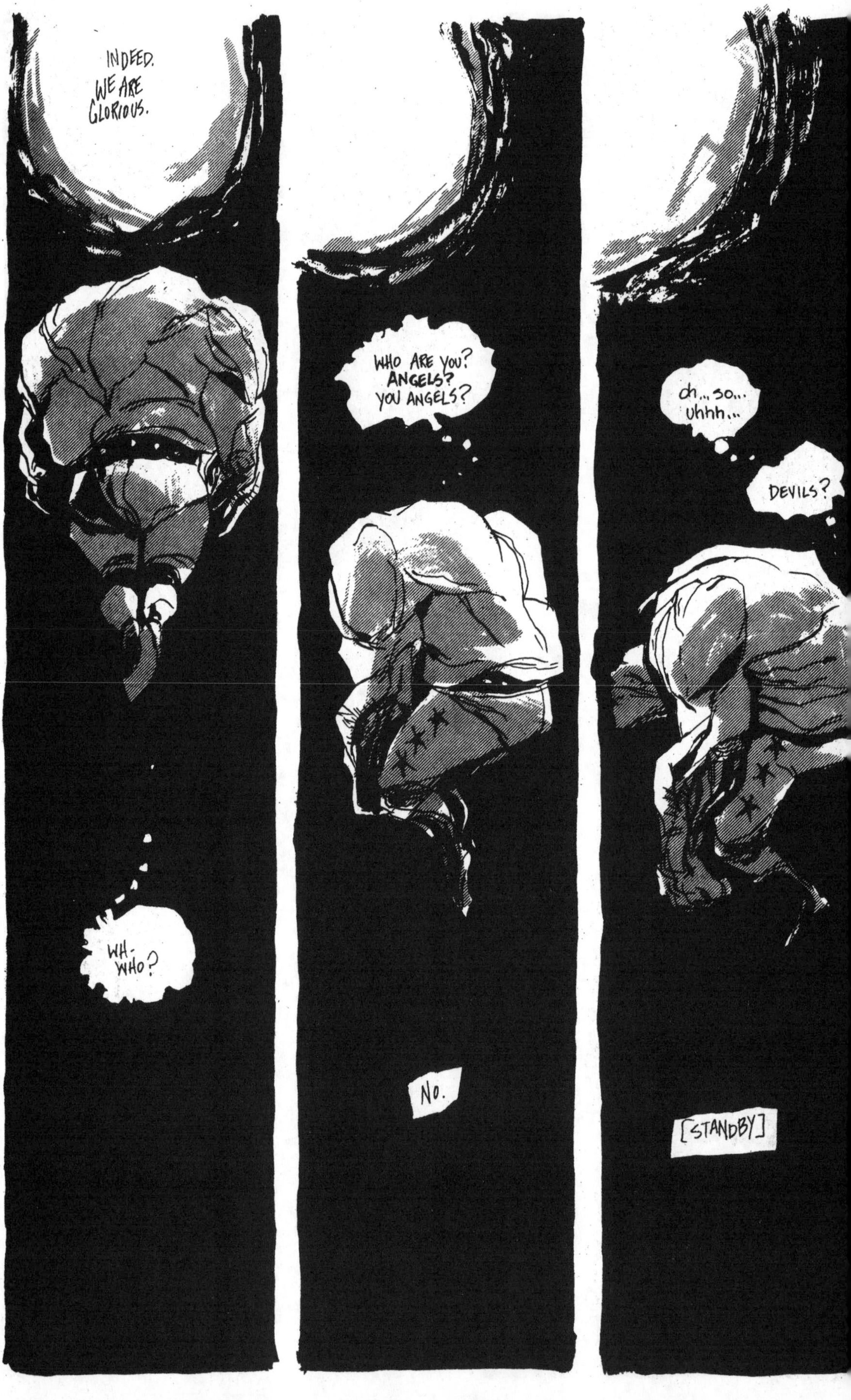
INDEED. WE ARE GLORIOUS.
WH-WHO?
WHO ARE YOU? ANGELS? YOU ANGELS?
NO.
oh... so... uhhh...
DEVILS?
[STANDBY]

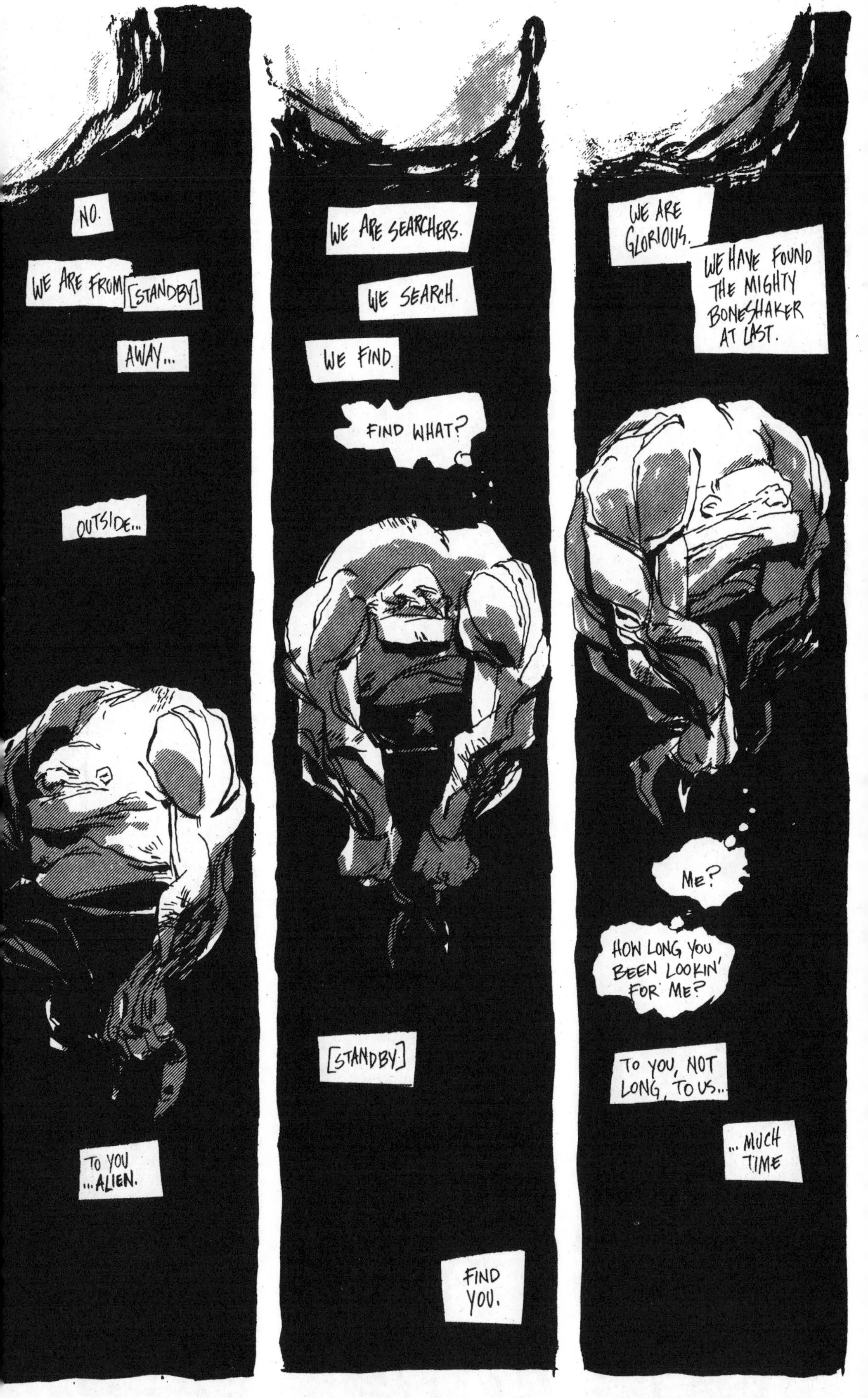
NO.
WE ARE FROM [STANDBY]
AWAY...
OUTSIDE...
TO YOU ...ALIEN.
WE ARE SEARCHERS.
WE SEARCH.
WE FIND.
FIND WHAT?
[STANDBY]
FIND YOU.
WE ARE GLORIOUS.
WE HAVE FOUND THE MIGHTY BONESHAKER AT LAST.
ME?
HOW LONG YOU BEEN LOOKIN' FOR ME?
TO YOU, NOT LONG, TO US...
...MUCH TIME

WHEN YOU SUBMERGED YOURSELF IN DENSE AIR [STANDBY]

WATER [STANDBY]

POOL...

YOU BECAME A BEACON TO US, EVEN THEN THE SEARCH WAS LONG.

HOW LONG, huh? HOW LONG I BEEN DOWN HERE?

[STANDBY]

FOURTEEN...

...DAYS

WE ARE UNCERTAIN, DO YOU CONCUR?

NO.

NO, THAT CAN'T BE RIGHT... TWO WEEKS. I CAN'T-

YOU ARE CORRECT. A TRANSLATION ERROR. IT IS DIFFICULT FOR US.

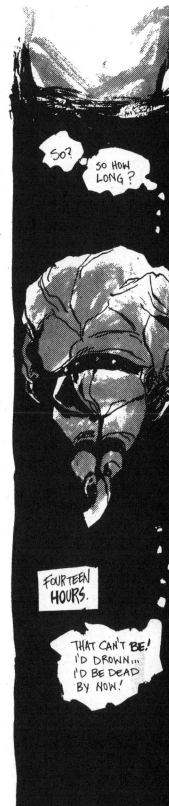

SO?

SO HOW LONG?

FOURTEEN HOURS.

THAT CAN'T BE! I'D DROWN... I'D BE DEAD BY NOW!

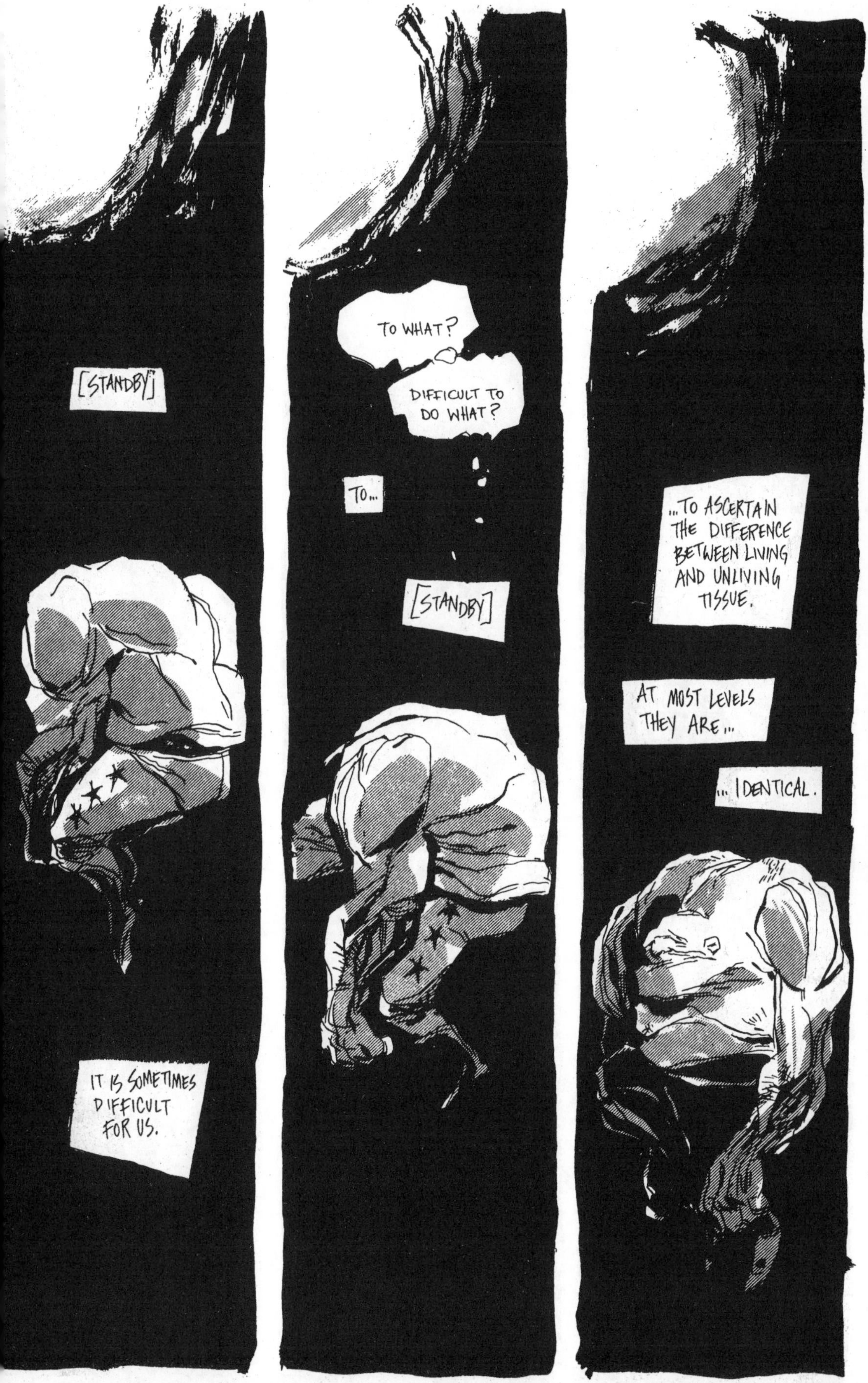
[STANDBY]
IT IS SOMETIMES DIFFICULT FOR US.
TO WHAT?
DIFFICULT TO DO WHAT?
TO...
[STANDBY]
...TO ASCERTAIN THE DIFFERENCE BETWEEN LIVING AND UNLIVING TISSUE.
AT MOST LEVELS THEY ARE...
...IDENTICAL.

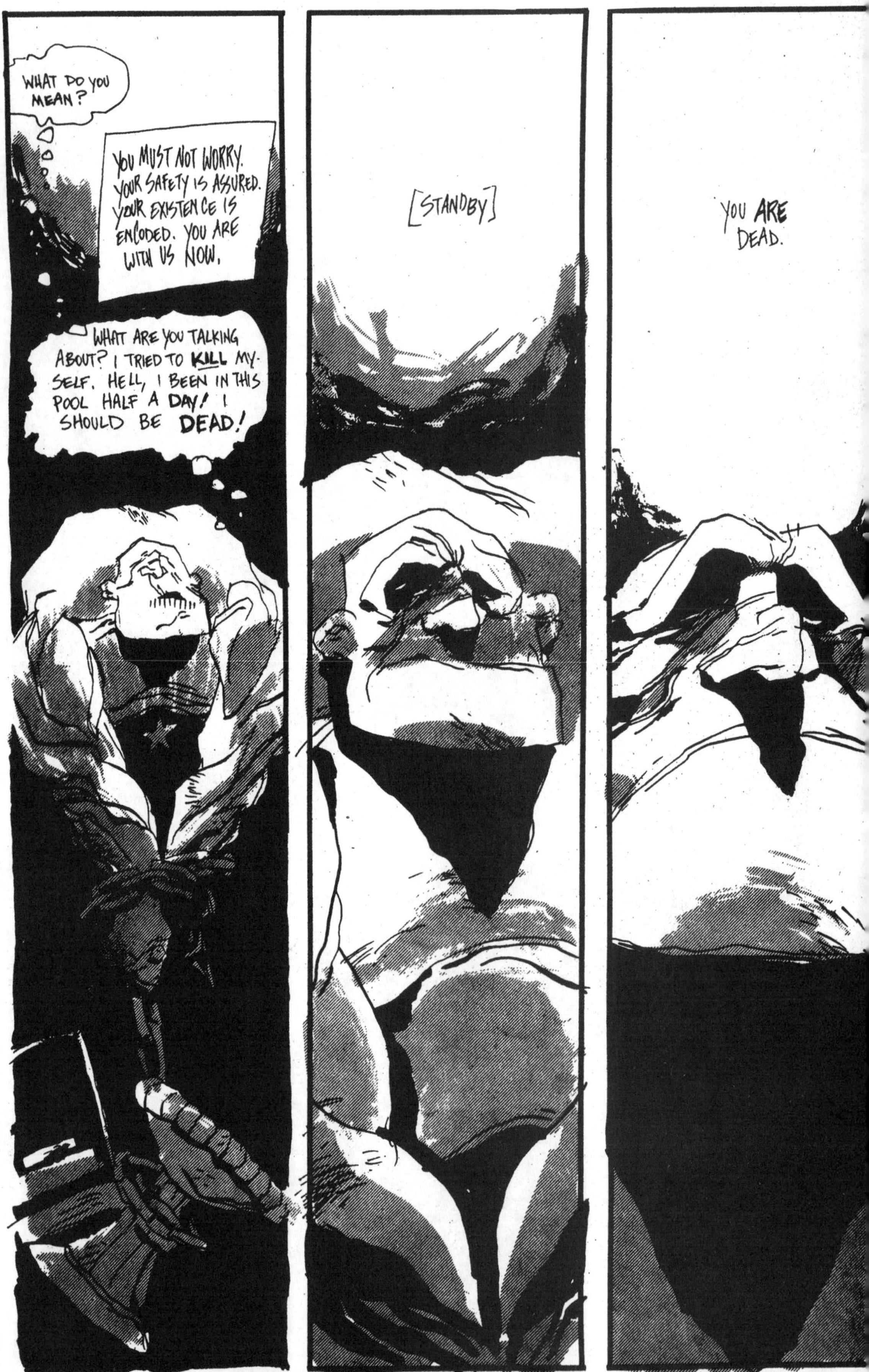
WHAT DO YOU MEAN?
YOU MUST NOT WORRY. YOUR SAFETY IS ASSURED. YOUR EXISTENCE IS ENCODED. YOU ARE WITH US NOW.
WHAT ARE YOU TALKING ABOUT? I TRIED TO KILL MYSELF. HELL, I BEEN IN THIS POOL HALF A DAY! I SHOULD BE DEAD!
[STANDBY]
YOU ARE DEAD.

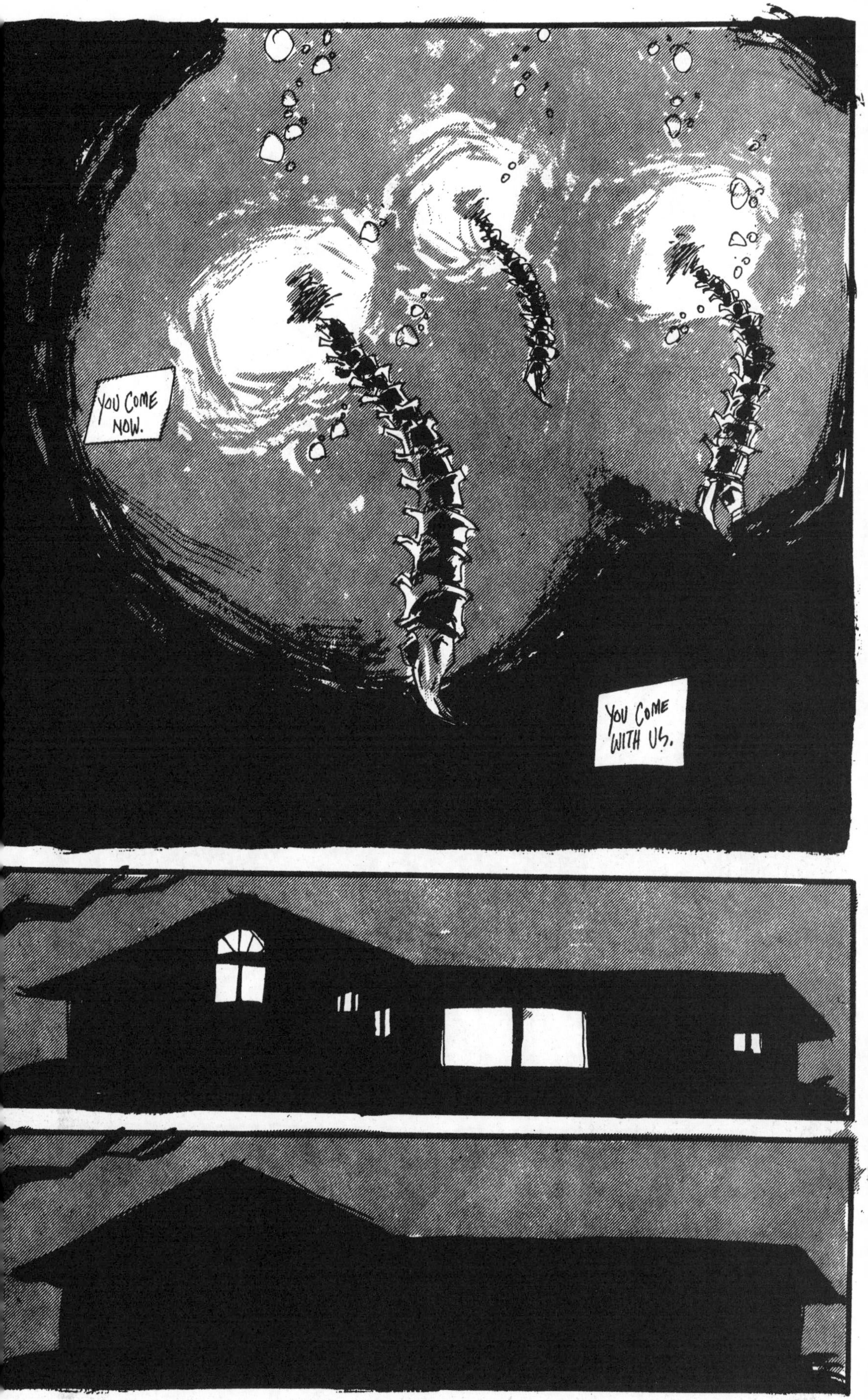
YOU COME NOW.
YOU COME WITH US.

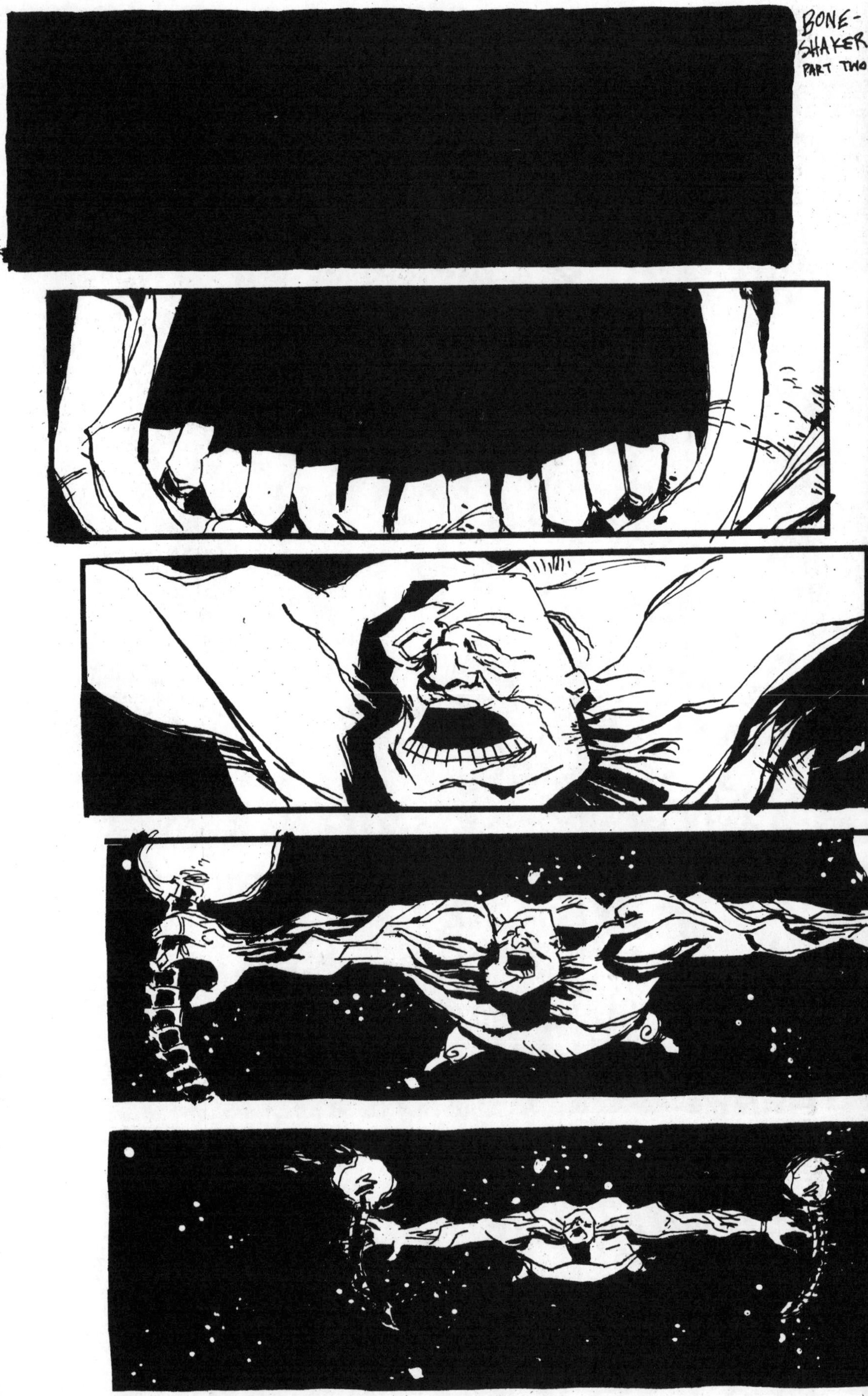
BONE-
SHAKER
PART TWO

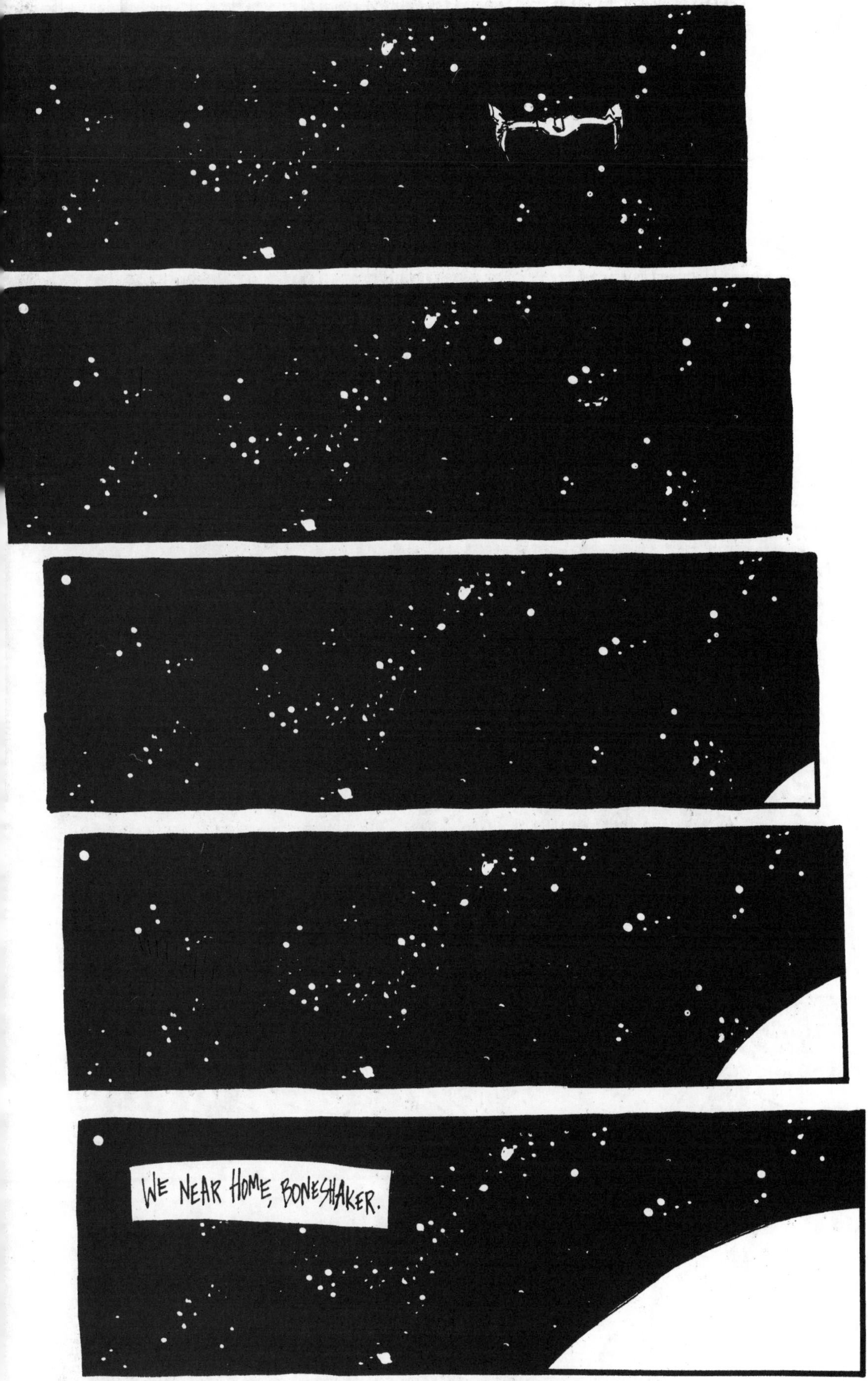
WE NEAR HOME, BONESHAKER.

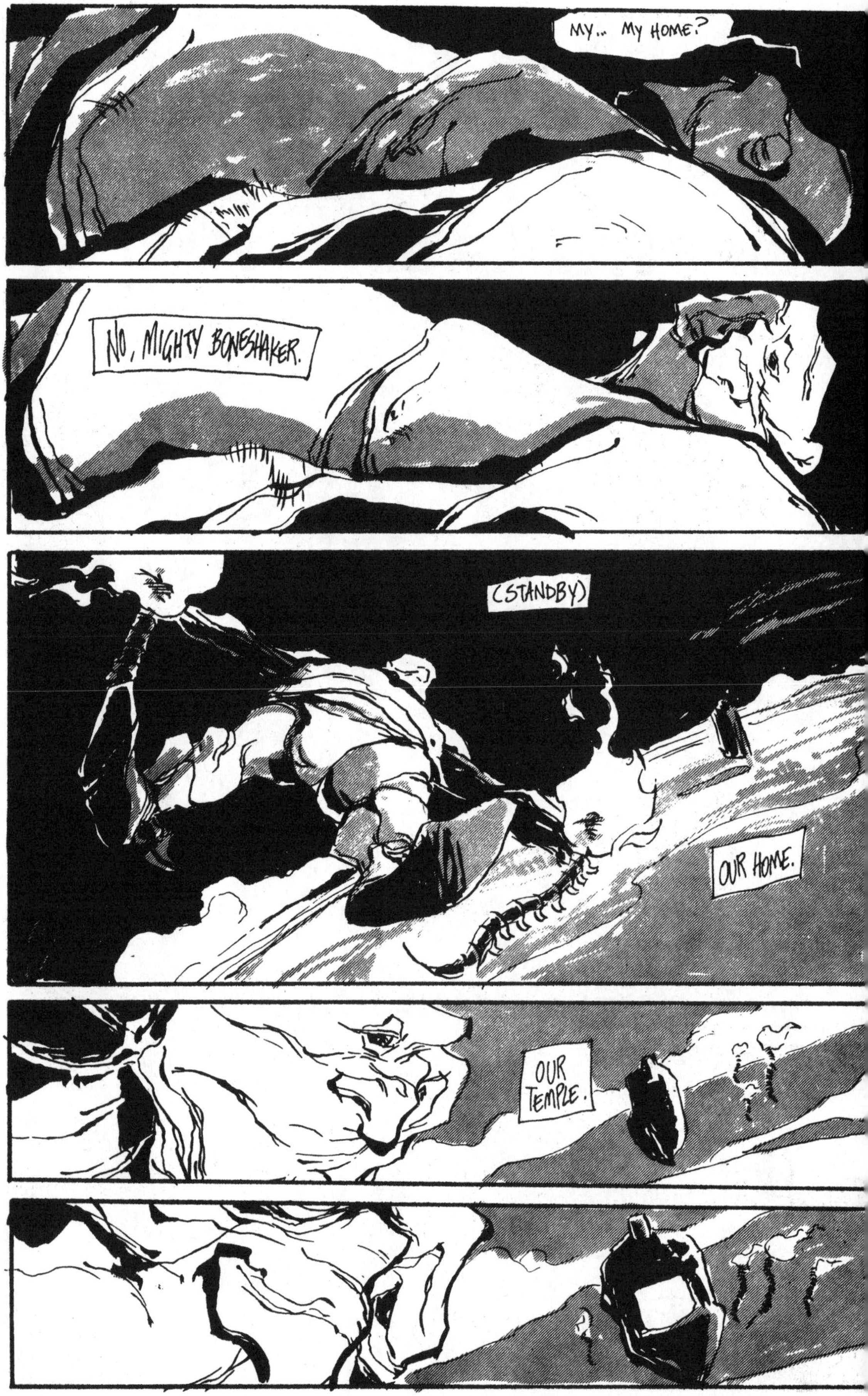
MY... MY HOME?
NO, MIGHTY BONESHAKER.
(STANDBY)
OUR HOME.
OUR TEMPLE.

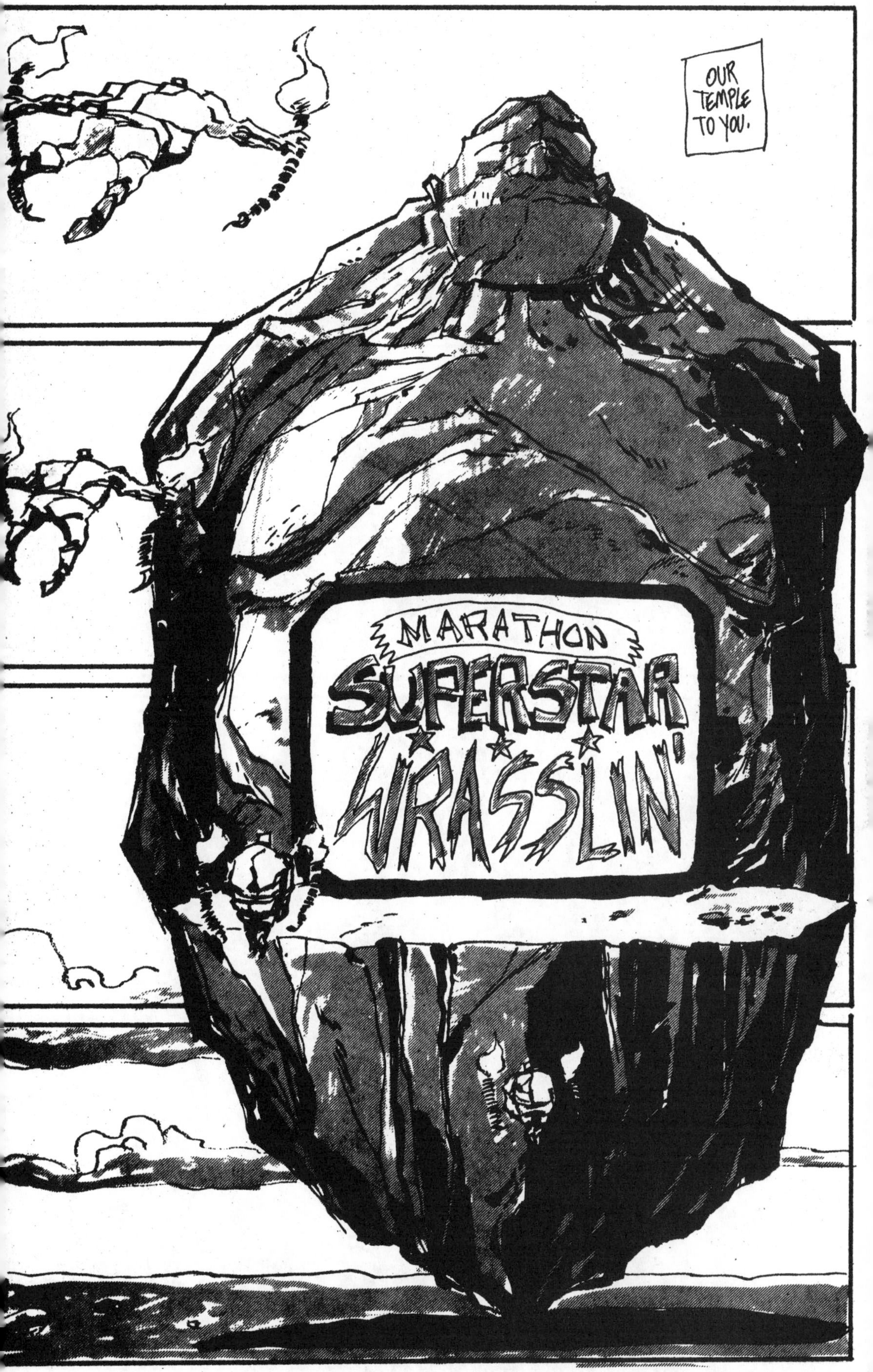
OUR TEMPLE TO YOU.
MARATHON
SUPERSTAR
WRASSLIN'

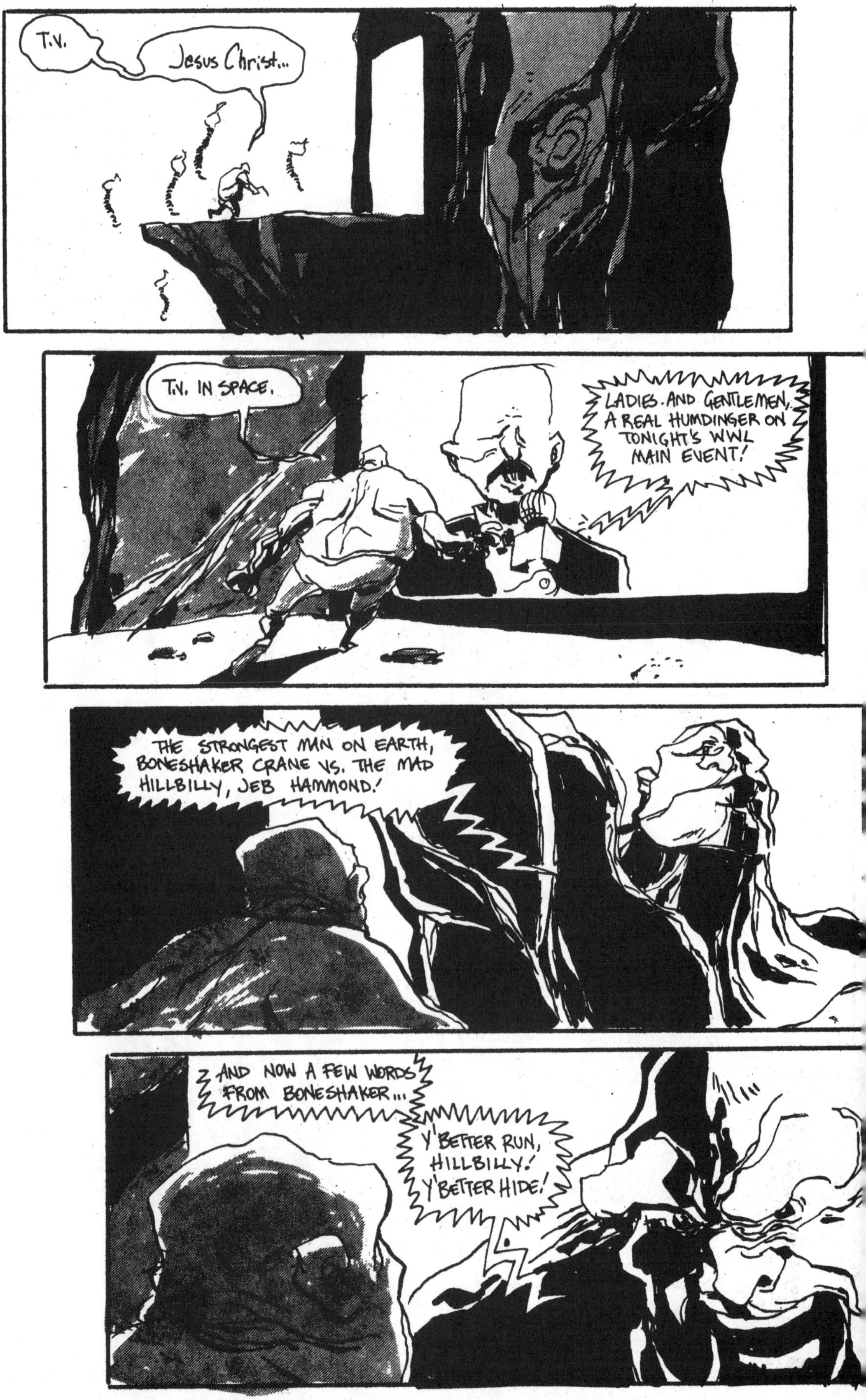
T.V.
Jesus Christ...
T.V. IN SPACE.
LADIES AND GENTLEMEN, A REAL HUMDINGER ON TONIGHT'S WWL MAIN EVENT!
THE STRONGEST MAN ON EARTH, BONESHAKER CRANE VS. THE MAD HILLBILLY, JEB HAMMOND!
AND NOW A FEW WORDS FROM BONESHAKER...
Y'BETTER RUN, HILLBILLY! Y'BETTER HIDE!

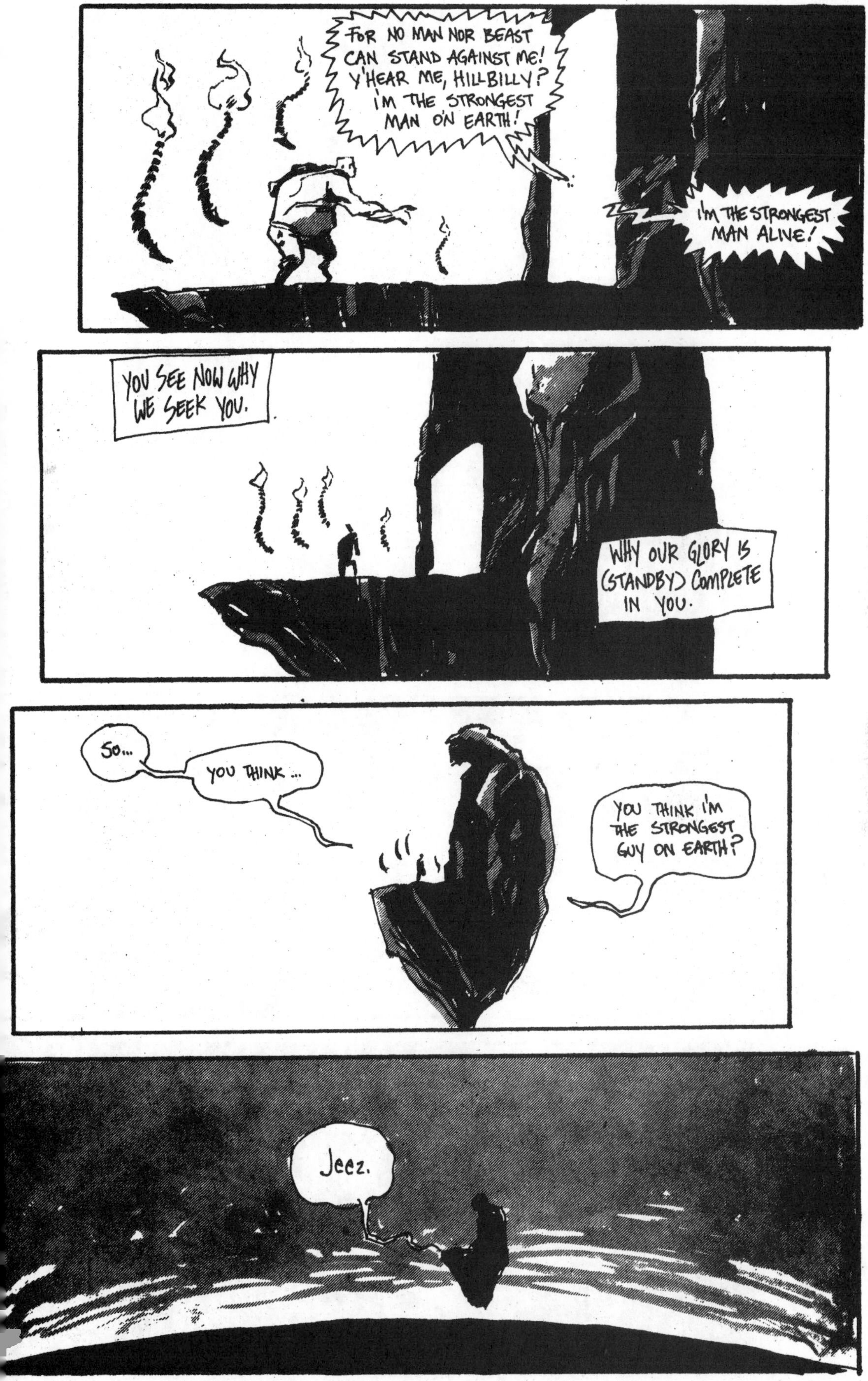
FOR NO MAN NOR BEAST CAN STAND AGAINST ME! Y'HEAR ME, HILLBILLY? I'M THE STRONGEST MAN ON EARTH!
I'M THE STRONGEST MAN ALIVE!
YOU SEE NOW WHY WE SEEK YOU.
WHY OUR GLORY IS (STANDBY) COMPLETE IN YOU.
SO...
YOU THINK...
YOU THINK I'M THE STRONGEST GUY ON EARTH?
Jeez.

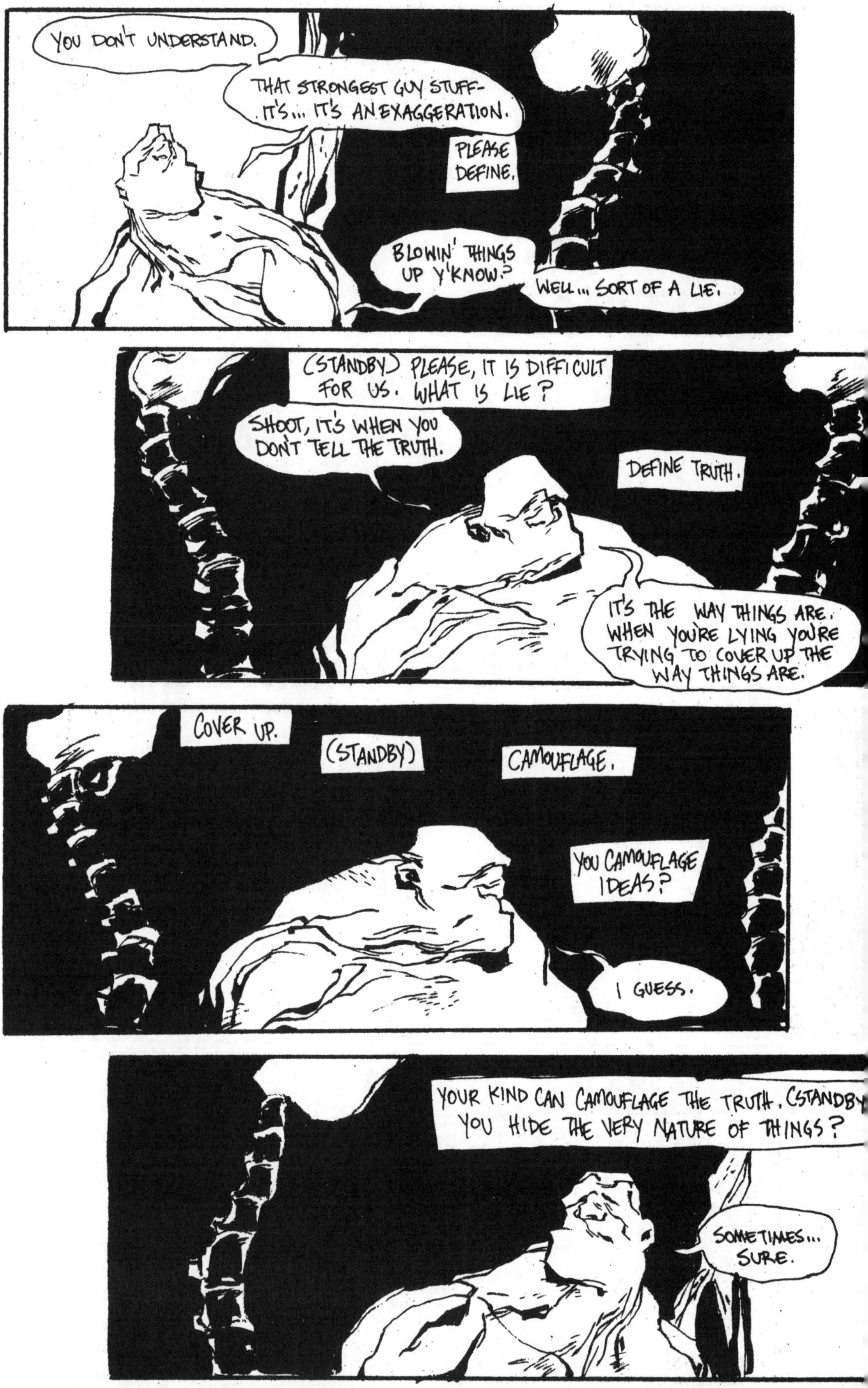
YOU DON'T UNDERSTAND.
THAT STRONGEST GUY STUFF- IT'S... IT'S AN EXAGGERATION.
PLEASE DEFINE.
BLOWIN' THINGS UP Y'KNOW?
WELL... SORT OF A LIE.
(STANDBY) PLEASE, IT IS DIFFICULT FOR US. WHAT IS LIE?
SHOOT, IT'S WHEN YOU DON'T TELL THE TRUTH.
DEFINE TRUTH.
IT'S THE WAY THINGS ARE. WHEN YOU'RE LYING YOU'RE TRYING TO COVER UP THE WAY THINGS ARE.
COVER UP.
(STANDBY)
CAMOUFLAGE.
YOU CAMOUFLAGE IDEAS?
I GUESS.
YOUR KIND CAN CAMOUFLAGE THE TRUTH. (STANDBY) YOU HIDE THE VERY NATURE OF THINGS?
SOMETIMES... SURE.

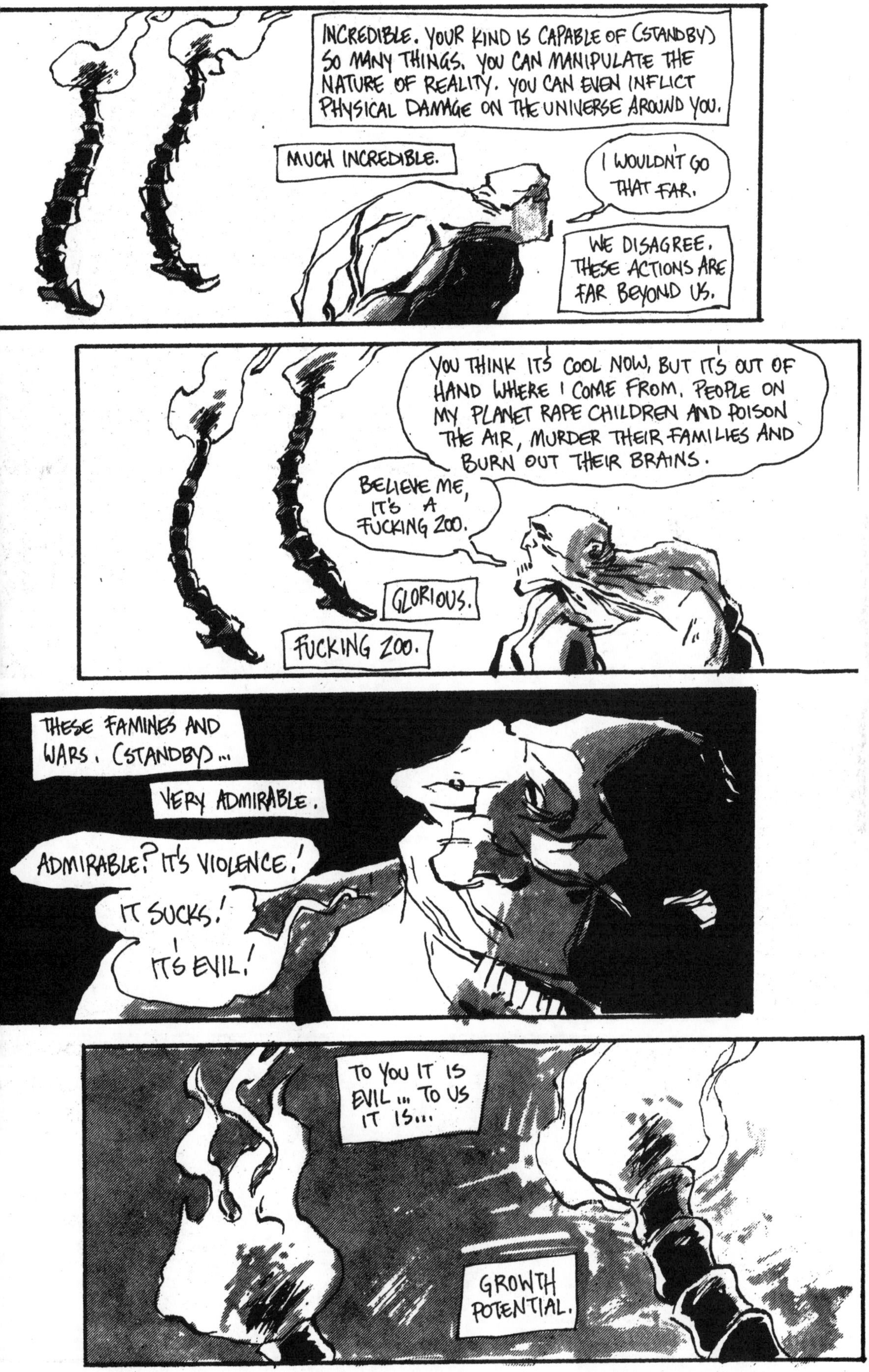
INCREDIBLE. YOUR KIND IS CAPABLE OF (STANDBY) SO MANY THINGS. YOU CAN MANIPULATE THE NATURE OF REALITY. YOU CAN EVEN INFLICT PHYSICAL DAMAGE ON THE UNIVERSE AROUND YOU.
MUCH INCREDIBLE.
I WOULDN'T GO THAT FAR.
WE DISAGREE. THESE ACTIONS ARE FAR BEYOND US.
YOU THINK IT'S COOL NOW, BUT IT'S OUT OF HAND WHERE I COME FROM. PEOPLE ON MY PLANET RAPE CHILDREN AND POISON THE AIR, MURDER THEIR FAMILIES AND BURN OUT THEIR BRAINS.
BELIEVE ME, IT'S A FUCKING ZOO.
GLORIOUS.
FUCKING ZOO.
THESE FAMINES AND WARS. (STANDBY)...
VERY ADMIRABLE.
ADMIRABLE? IT'S VIOLENCE!
IT SUCKS!
IT'S EVIL!
TO YOU IT IS EVIL... TO US IT IS...
GROWTH POTENTIAL.

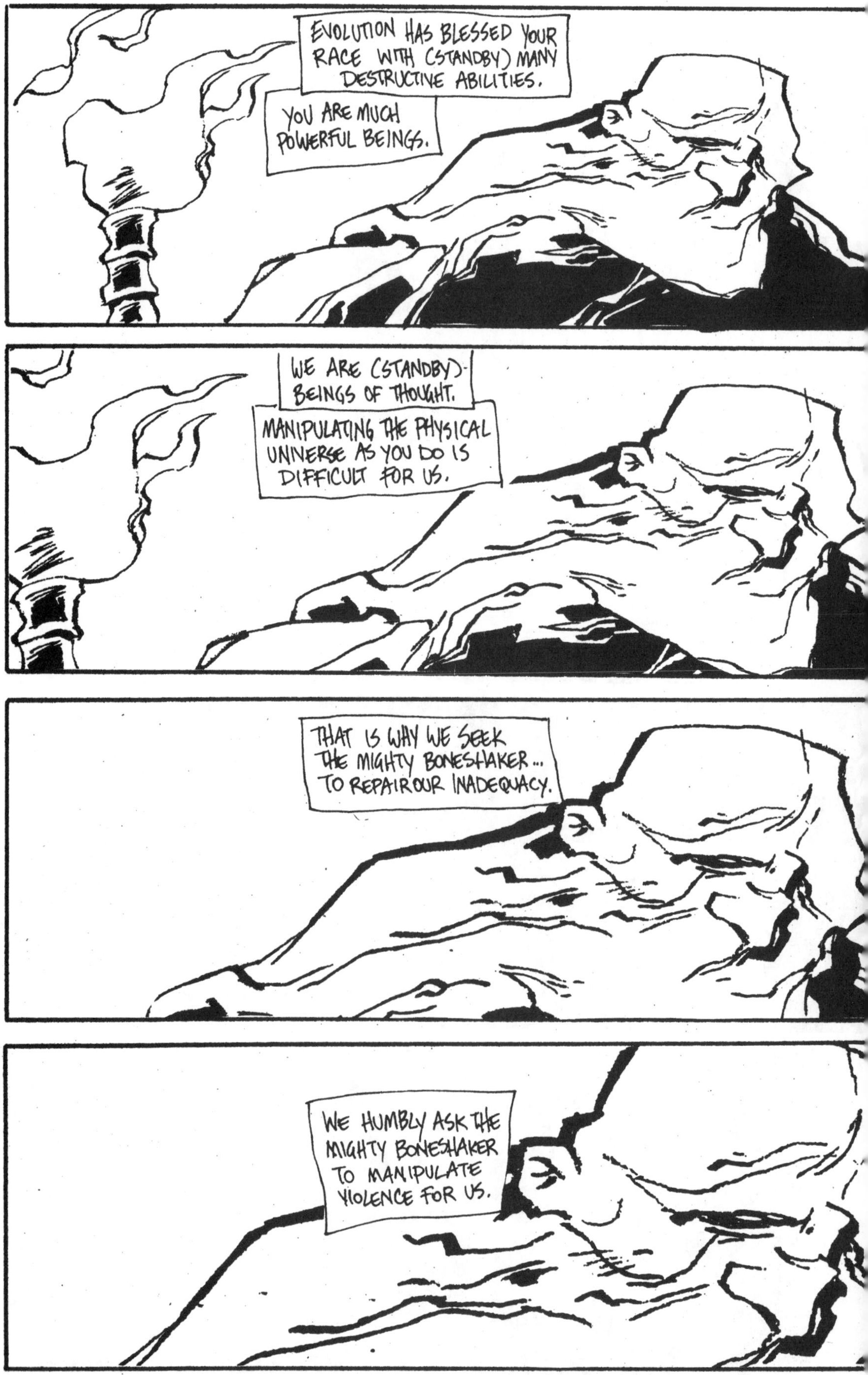
EVOLUTION HAS BLESSED YOUR RACE WITH (STANDBY) MANY DESTRUCTIVE ABILITIES.
YOU ARE MUCH POWERFUL BEINGS.
WE ARE (STANDBY) BEINGS OF THOUGHT.
MANIPULATING THE PHYSICAL UNIVERSE AS YOU DO IS DIFFICULT FOR US.
THAT IS WHY WE SEEK THE MIGHTY BONESHAKER... TO REPAIR OUR INADEQUACY.
WE HUMBLY ASK THE MIGHTY BONESHAKER TO MANIPULATE VIOLENCE FOR US.

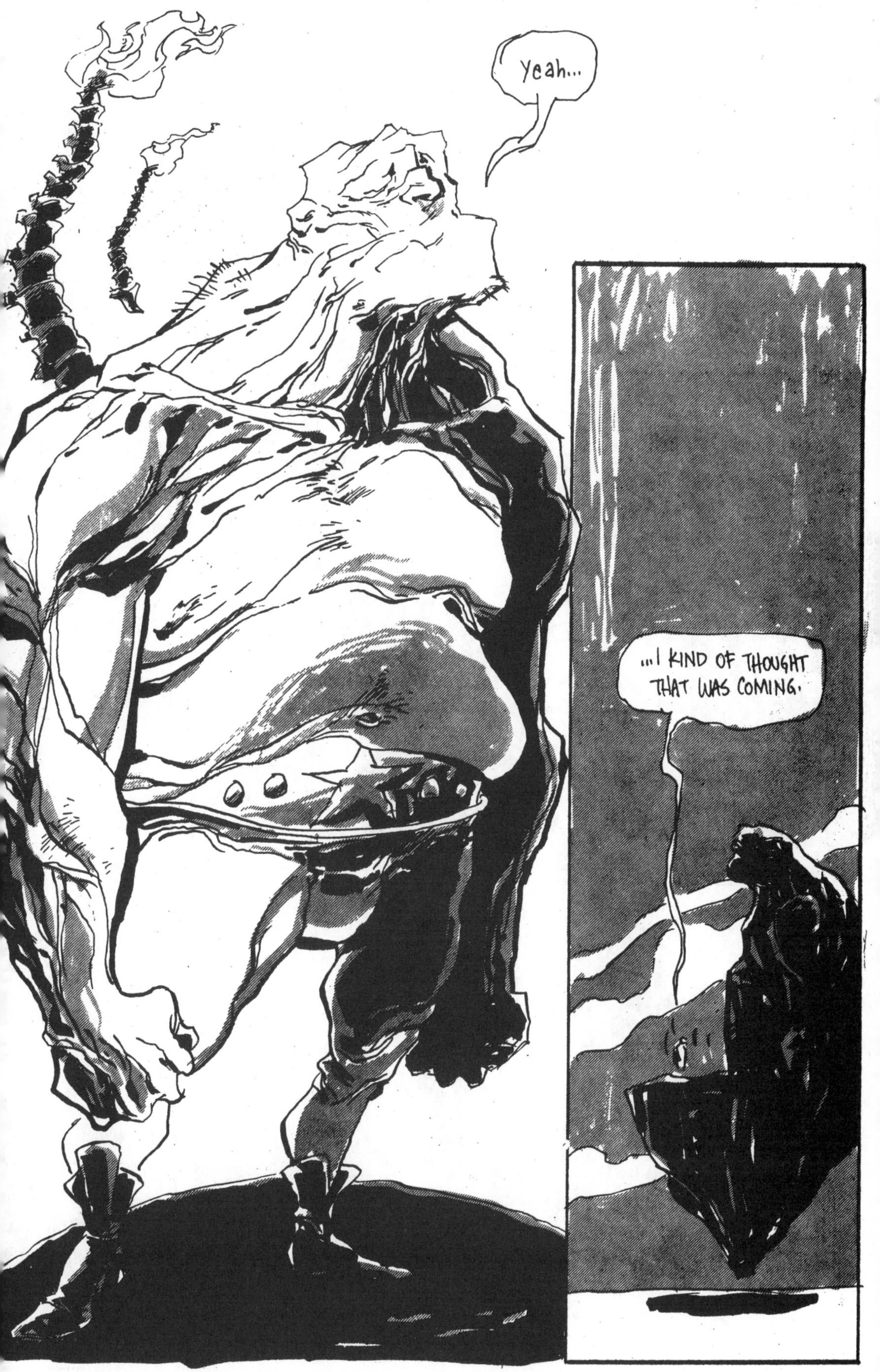
Yeah...
...I KIND OF THOUGHT THAT WAS COMING.

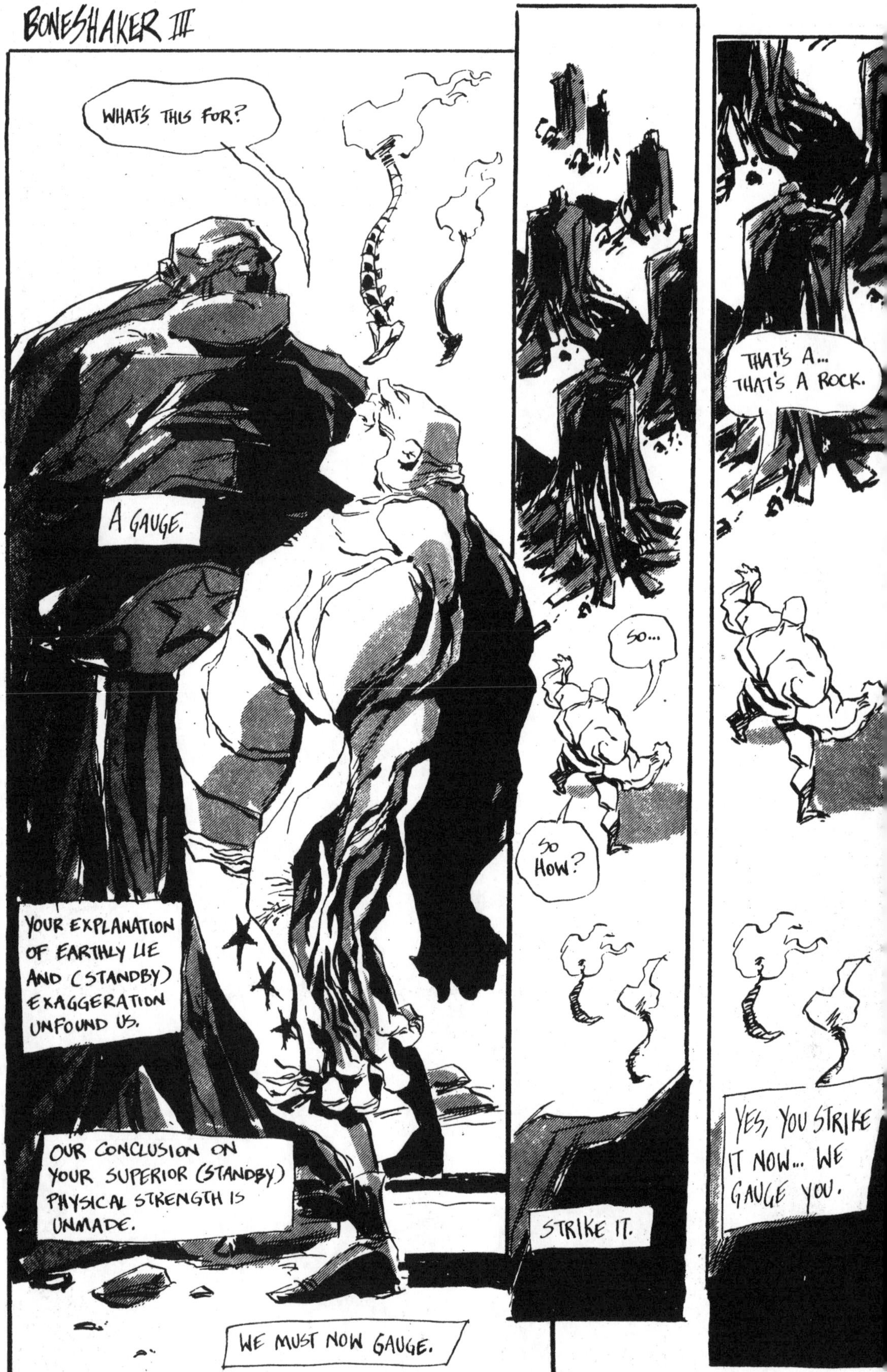
BONESHAKER III
WHAT'S THIS FOR?
A GAUGE.
YOUR EXPLANATION OF EARTHLY LIE AND (STANDBY) EXAGGERATION UNFOUND US.
OUR CONCLUSION ON YOUR SUPERIOR (STANDBY) PHYSICAL STRENGTH IS UNMADE.
WE MUST NOW GAUGE.
SO...
SO HOW?
STRIKE IT.
THAT'S A... THAT'S A ROCK.
YES, YOU STRIKE IT NOW... WE GAUGE YOU.

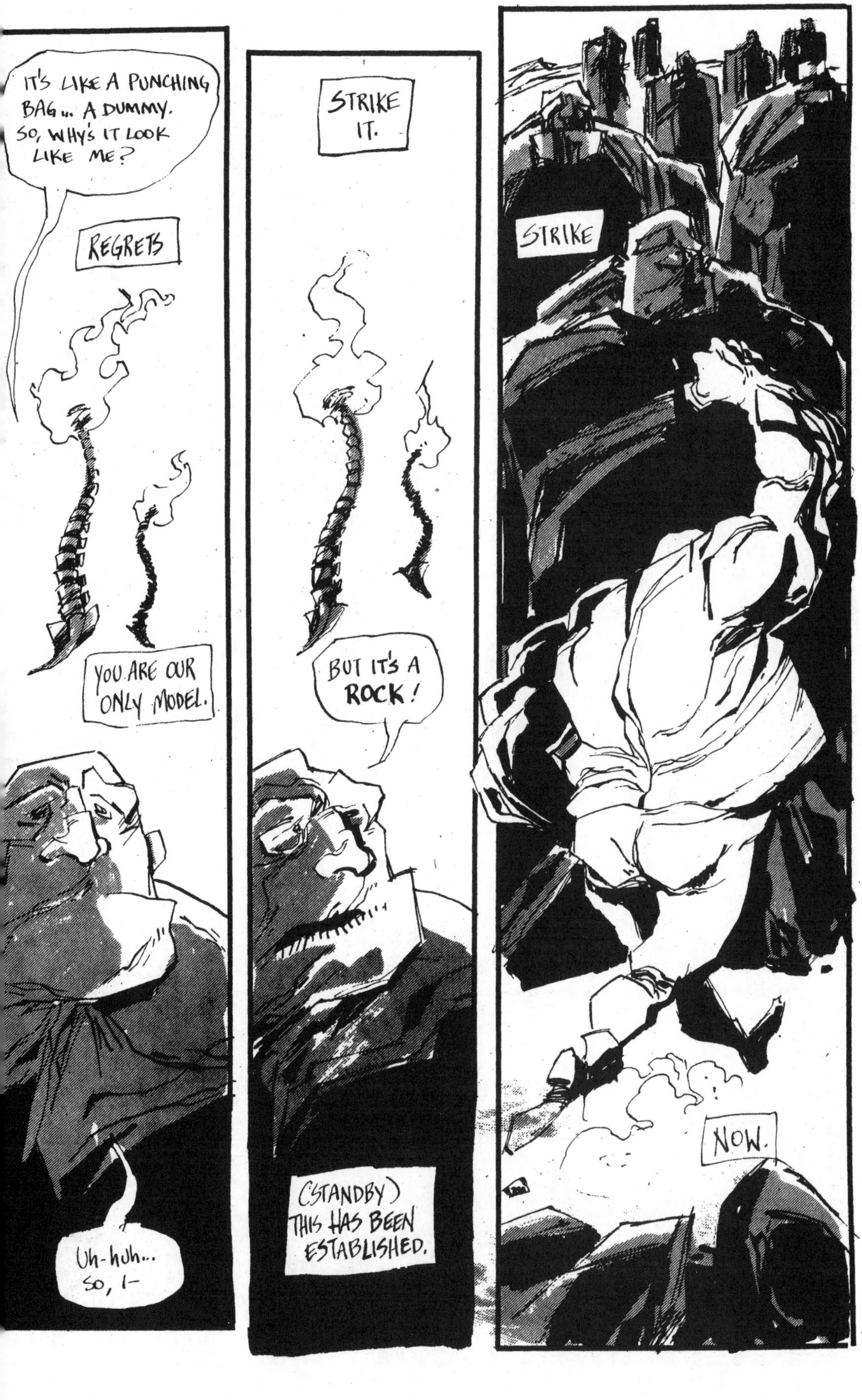
IT'S LIKE A PUNCHING BAG... A DUMMY. SO, WHY'S IT LOOK LIKE ME?
REGRETS
YOU ARE OUR ONLY MODEL.
Uh-huh... SO, I-
STRIKE IT.
BUT IT'S A ROCK!
(STANDBY) THIS HAS BEEN ESTABLISHED.
STRIKE
NOW.

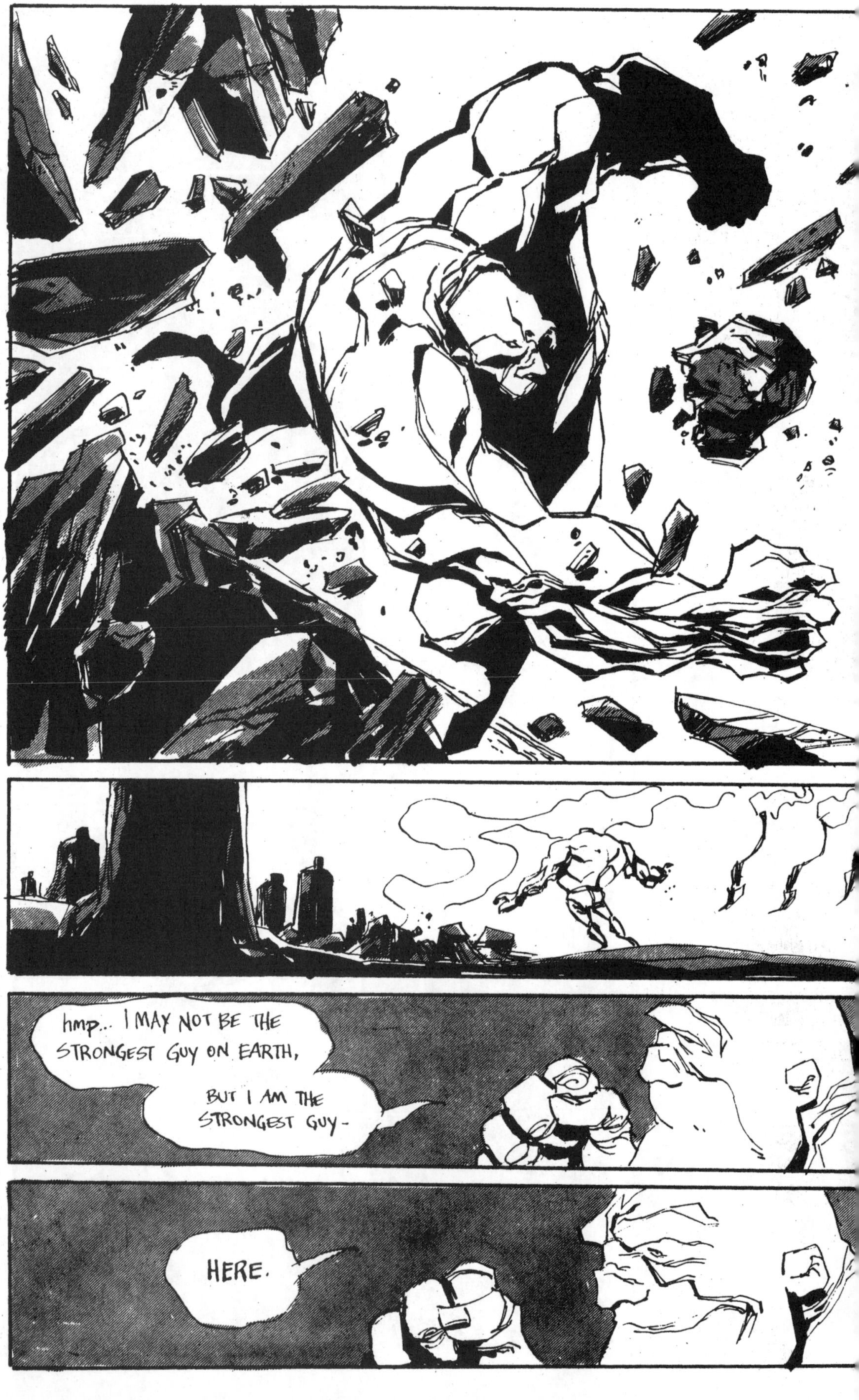
hmp... I MAY NOT BE THE STRONGEST GUY ON EARTH,
BUT I AM THE STRONGEST GUY-
HERE.

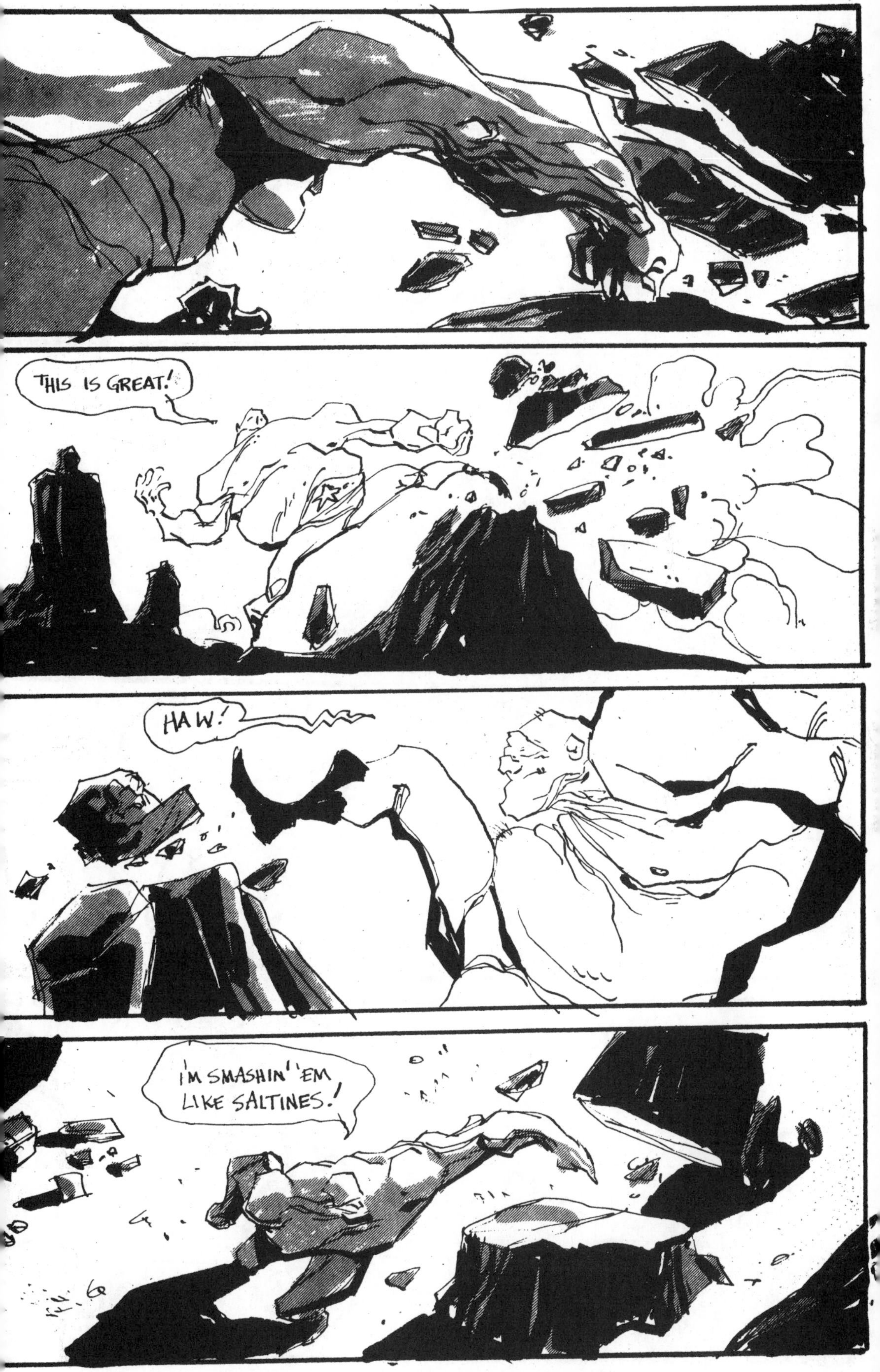

THIS IS GREAT!
HAW!
I'M SMASHIN' 'EM LIKE SALTINES!

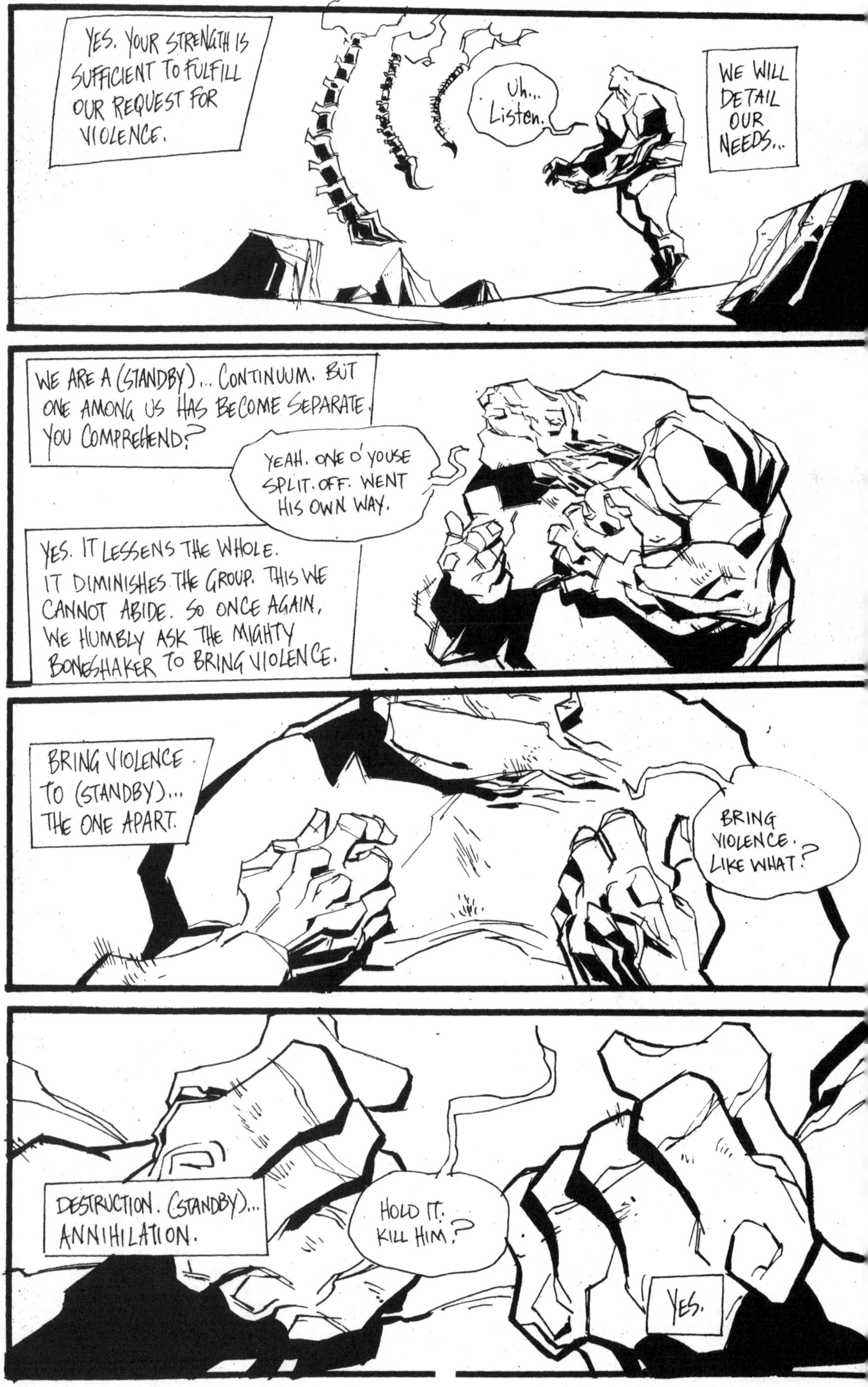
YES. YOUR STRENGTH IS SUFFICIENT TO FULFILL OUR REQUEST FOR VIOLENCE.
Uh... Listen.
WE WILL DETAIL OUR NEEDS...
WE ARE A (STANDBY)... CONTINUUM. BUT ONE AMONG US HAS BECOME SEPARATE. YOU COMPREHEND?
YEAH. ONE O' YOUSE SPLIT. OFF. WENT HIS OWN WAY.
YES. IT LESSENS THE WHOLE. IT DIMINISHES THE GROUP. THIS WE CANNOT ABIDE. SO ONCE AGAIN, WE HUMBLY ASK THE MIGHTY BONESHAKER TO BRING VIOLENCE.
BRING VIOLENCE TO (STANDBY)... THE ONE APART.
BRING VIOLENCE. LIKE WHAT?
DESTRUCTION. (STANDBY)... ANNIHILATION.
HOLD IT. KILL HIM?
YES.

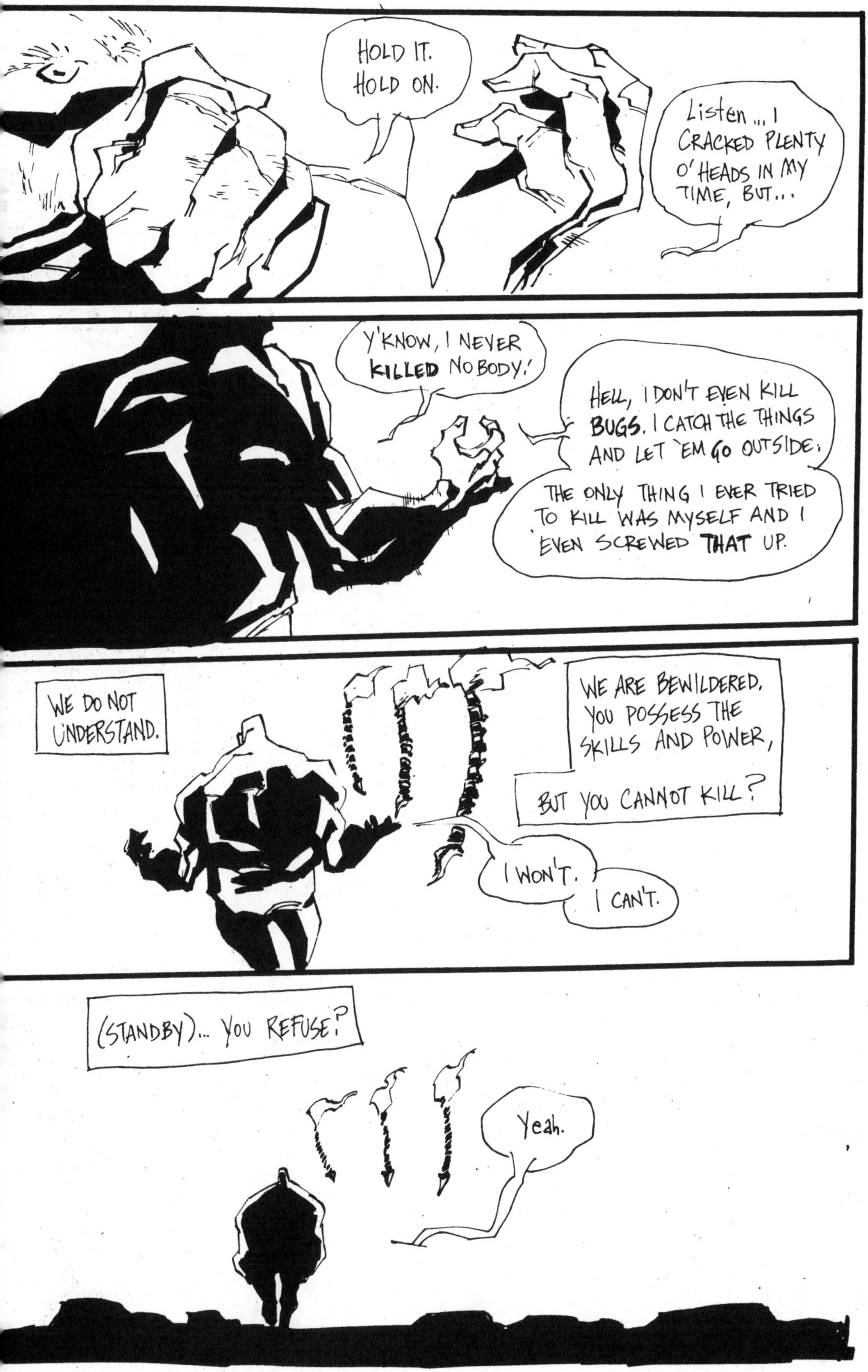
HOLD IT. HOLD ON.
Listen... I CRACKED PLENTY O' HEADS IN MY TIME, BUT...
Y'KNOW, I NEVER KILLED NOBODY.
HELL, I DON'T EVEN KILL BUGS. I CATCH THE THINGS AND LET 'EM GO OUTSIDE.
THE ONLY THING I EVER TRIED TO KILL WAS MYSELF AND I EVEN SCREWED THAT UP.
WE DO NOT UNDERSTAND.
WE ARE BEWILDERED. YOU POSSESS THE SKILLS AND POWER,
BUT YOU CANNOT KILL?
I WON'T.
I CAN'T.
(STANDBY)... YOU REFUSE?
Yeah.

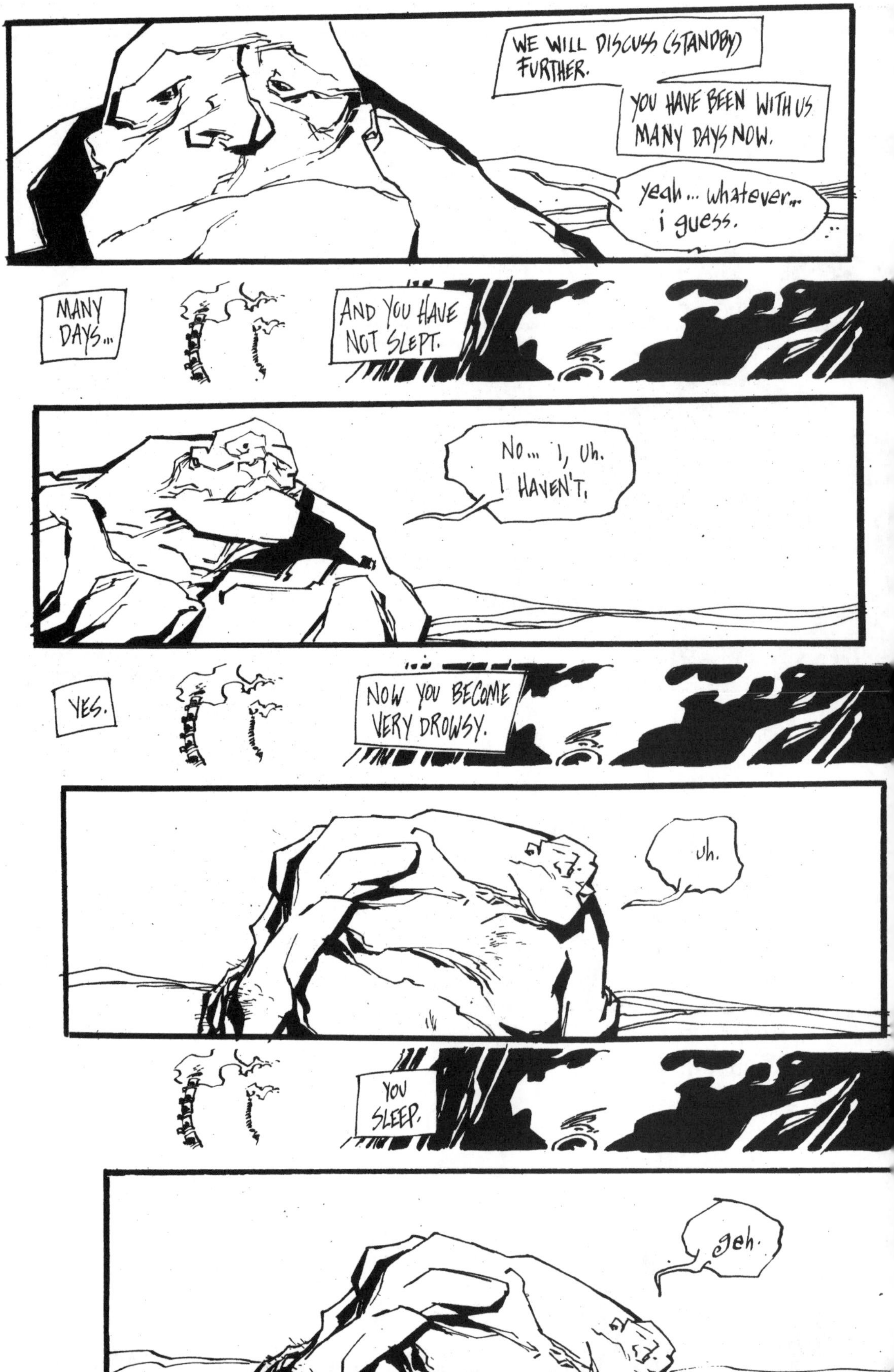
WE WILL DISCUSS (STANDBY) FURTHER.
YOU HAVE BEEN WITH US MANY DAYS NOW.
yeah... whatever... i guess.
MANY DAYS...
AND YOU HAVE NOT SLEPT.
No... I, Uh. I HAVEN'T.
YES.
NOW YOU BECOME VERY DROWSY.
uh.
YOU SLEEP.
geh.

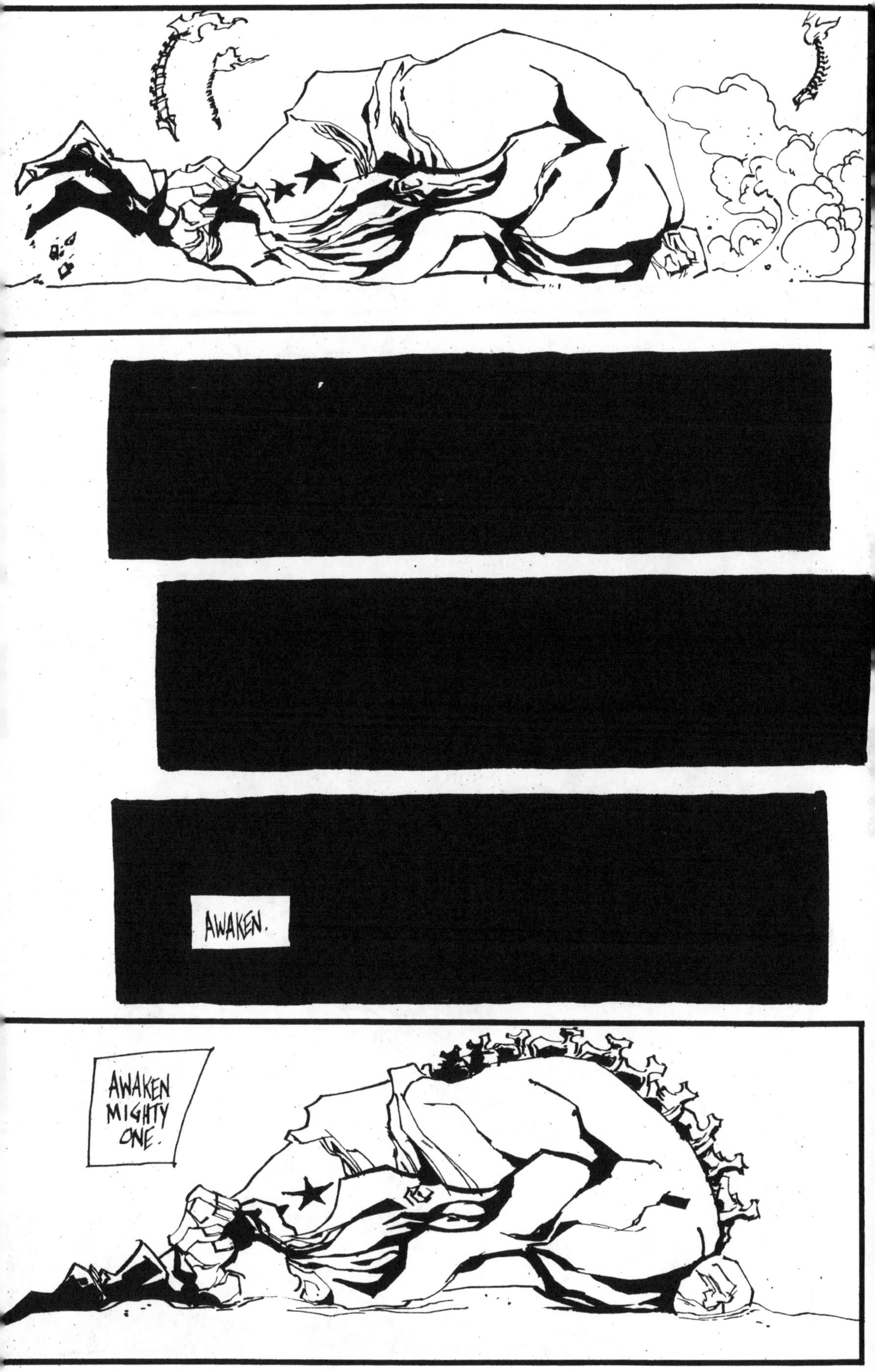
AWAKEN.
AWAKEN MIGHTY ONE.

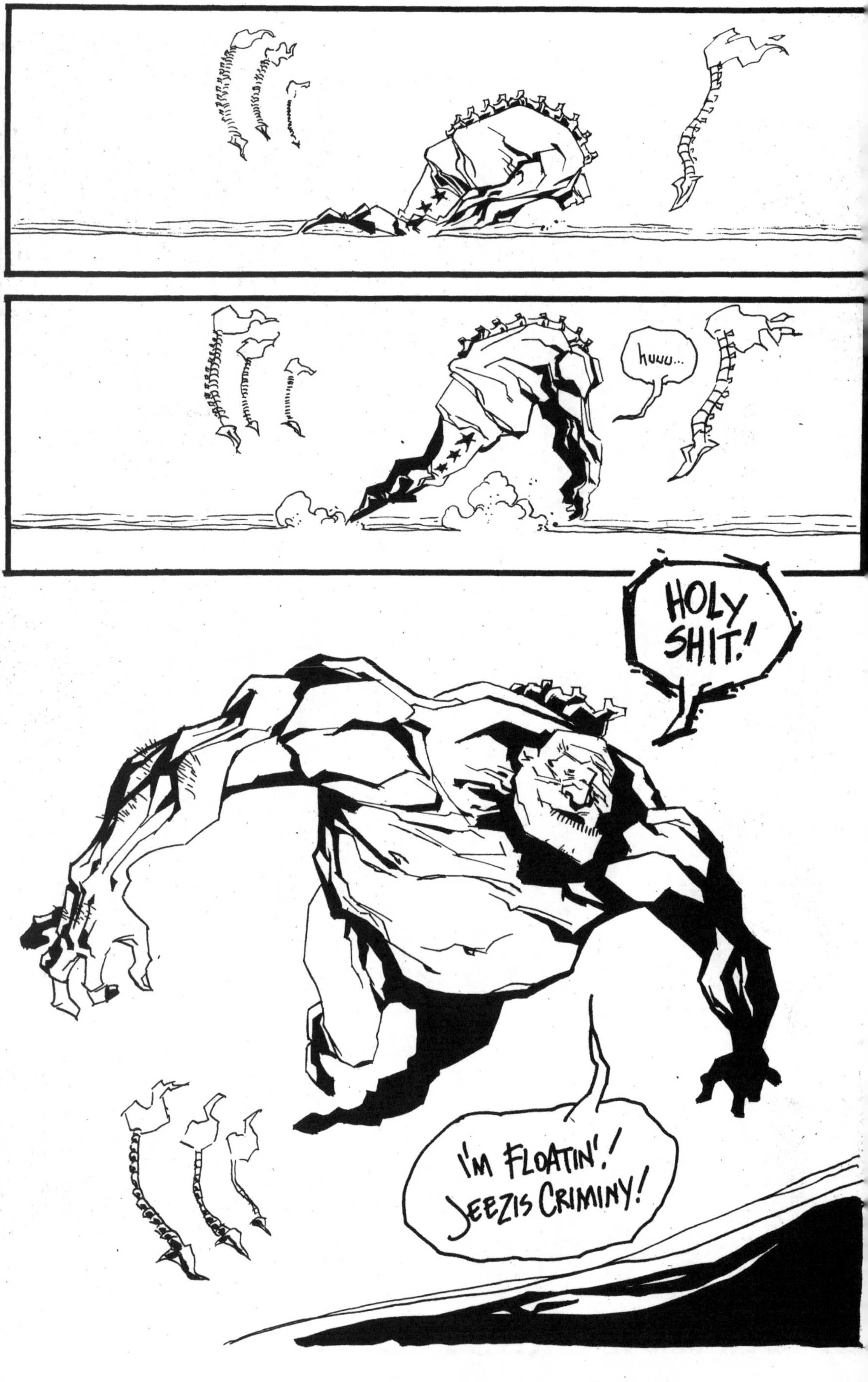
huuu...
HOLY SHIT!
I'M FLOATIN'! JEEZIS CRIMINY!

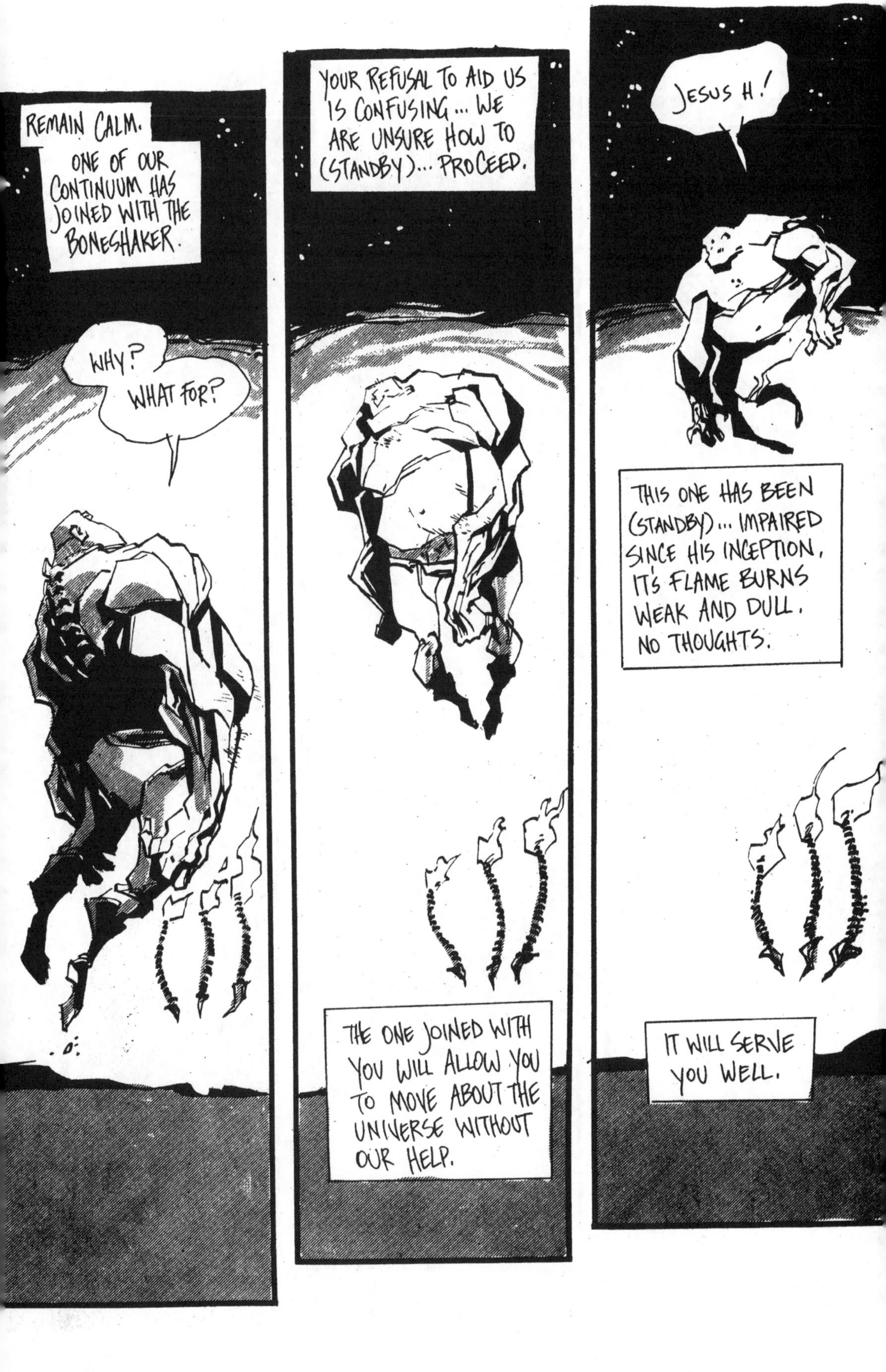
REMAIN CALM.
ONE OF OUR CONTINUUM HAS JOINED WITH THE BONESHAKER.
WHY? WHAT FOR?
YOUR REFUSAL TO AID US IS CONFUSING... WE ARE UNSURE HOW TO (STANDBY)... PROCEED.
THE ONE JOINED WITH YOU WILL ALLOW YOU TO MOVE ABOUT THE UNIVERSE WITHOUT OUR HELP.
JESUS H!
THIS ONE HAS BEEN (STANDBY)... IMPAIRED SINCE HIS INCEPTION, IT'S FLAME BURNS WEAK AND DULL. NO THOUGHTS.
IT WILL SERVE YOU WELL.

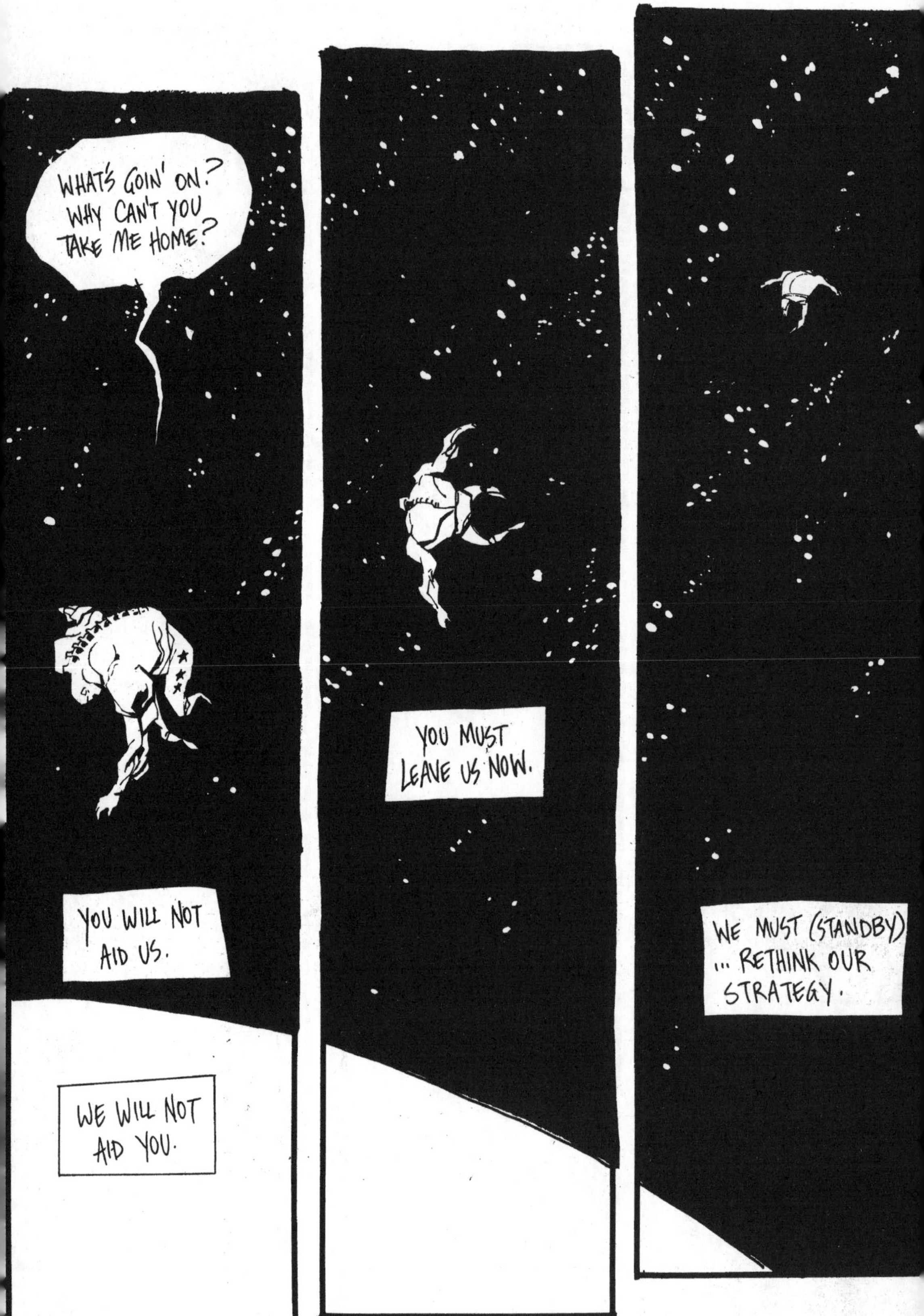
WHAT'S GOIN' ON? WHY CAN'T YOU TAKE ME HOME?
YOU WILL NOT AID US.
WE WILL NOT AID YOU.
YOU MUST LEAVE US NOW.
WE MUST (STANDBY) ... RETHINK OUR STRATEGY.

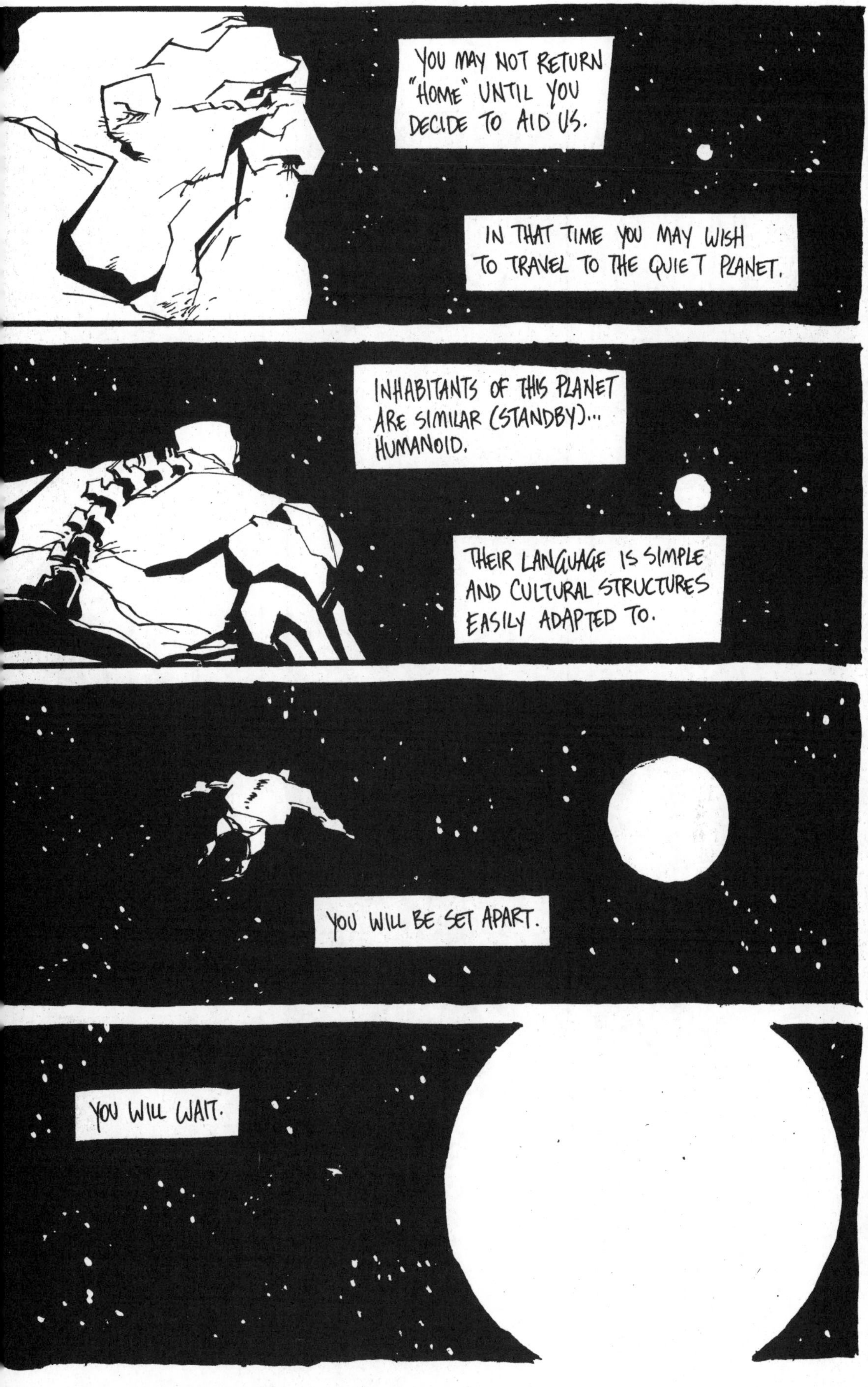
YOU MAY NOT RETURN "HOME" UNTIL YOU DECIDE TO AID US.
IN THAT TIME YOU MAY WISH TO TRAVEL TO THE QUIET PLANET.
INHABITANTS OF THIS PLANET ARE SIMILAR (STANDBY)... HUMANOID.
THEIR LANGUAGE IS SIMPLE AND CULTURAL STRUCTURES EASILY ADAPTED TO.
YOU WILL BE SET APART.
YOU WILL WAIT.

BONESHAKER PART IV - PHILLIP HESTER

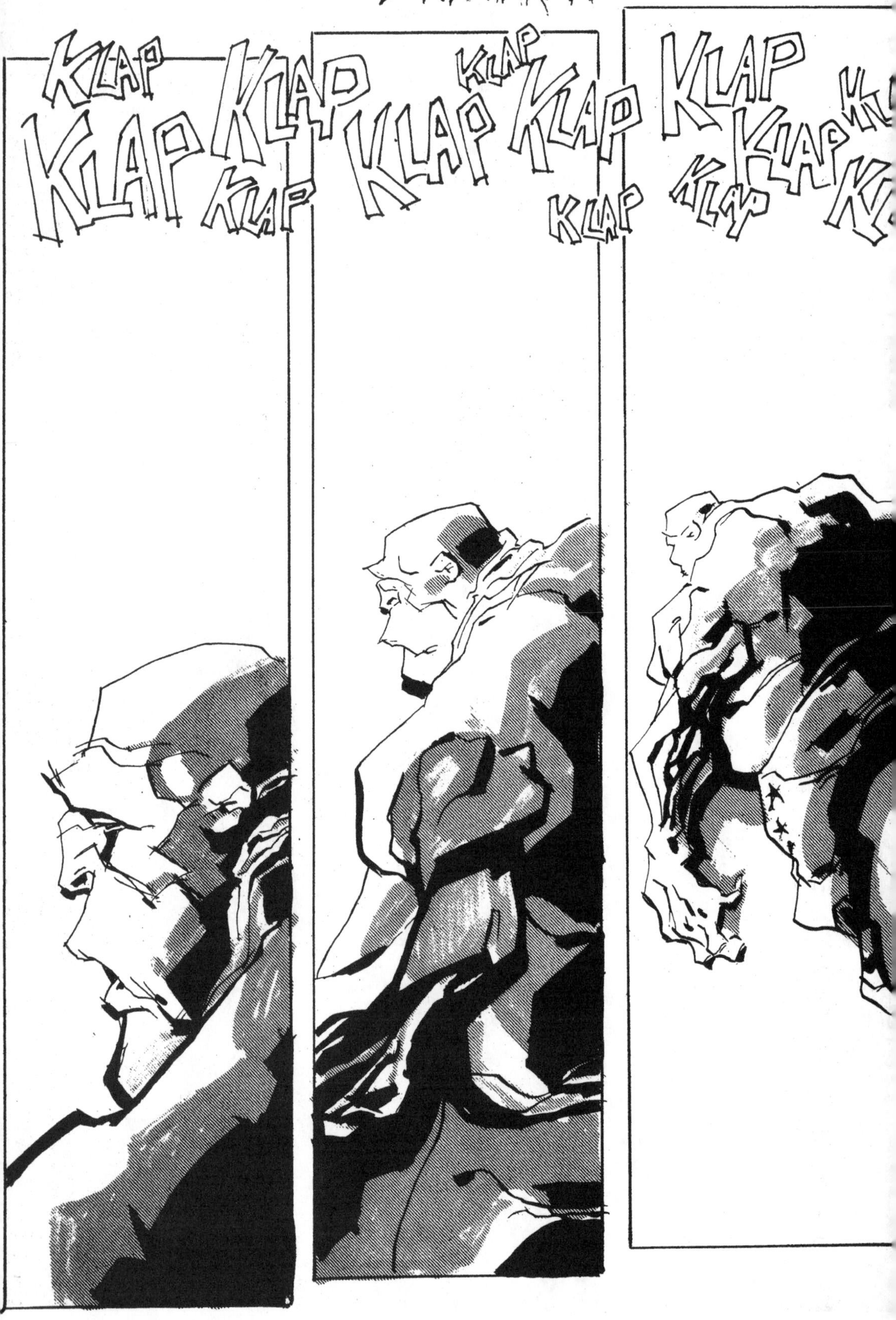
KLAP
KLAP
KLAP
KLAP
KLAP
KLAP
KLAP
KLAP
KLAP
KLAP
KLAP

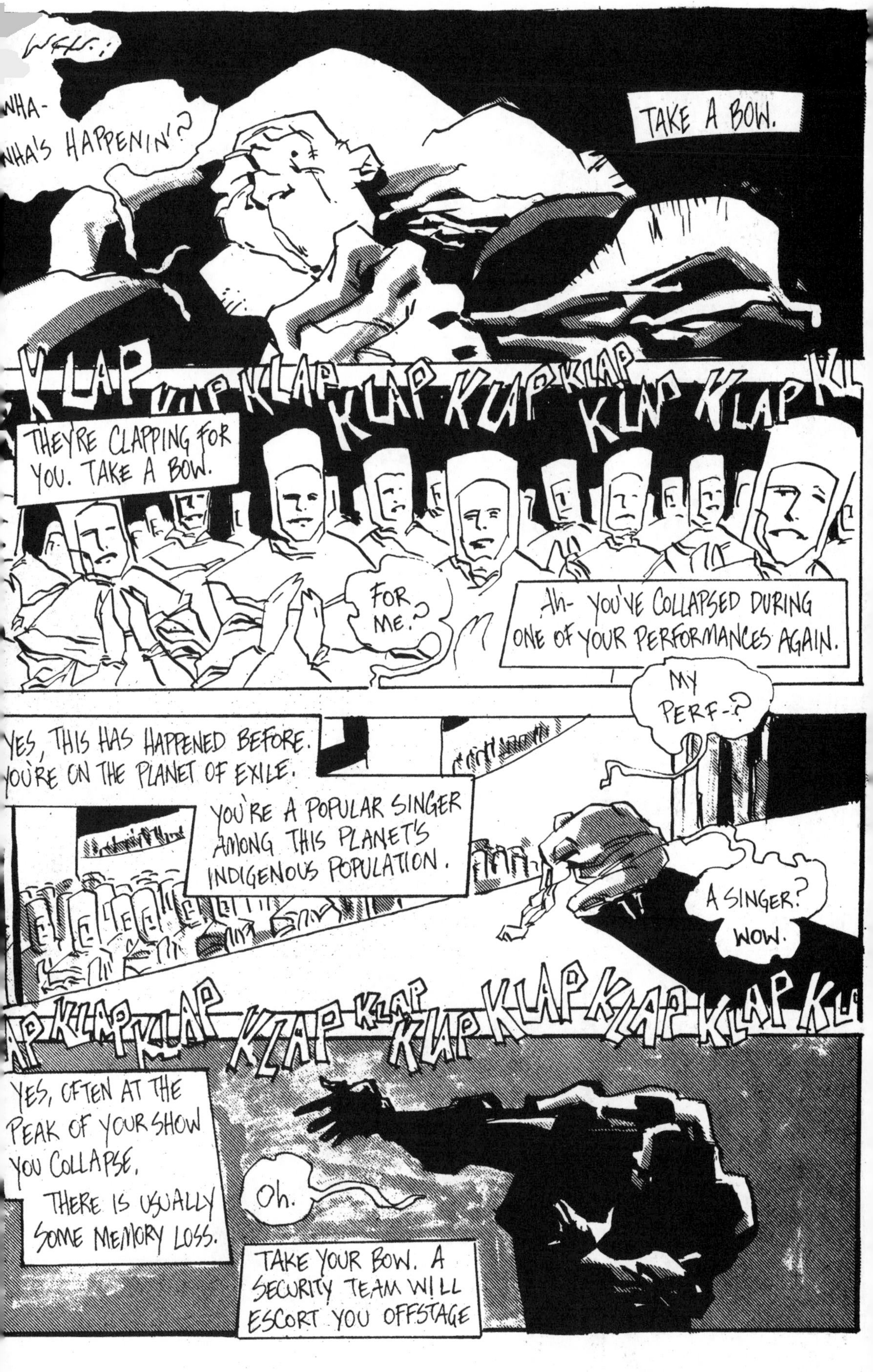
WAK-:
WHA-
WHA'S HAPPENIN'?
TAKE A BOW.
KLAP KLAP KLAP KLAP KLAP KLAP KLAP KLAP KLAP KL
THEY'RE CLAPPING FOR YOU. TAKE A BOW.
FOR ME.?
Ah- YOU'VE COLLAPSED DURING ONE OF YOUR PERFORMANCES AGAIN.
MY PERF-?
YES, THIS HAS HAPPENED BEFORE. YOU'RE ON THE PLANET OF EXILE.
YOU'RE A POPULAR SINGER AMONG THIS PLANET'S INDIGENOUS POPULATION.
A SINGER? WOW.
AP KLAP KLAP KLAP KLAP KLAP KLAP KLAP KLAP KL
YES, OFTEN AT THE PEAK OF YOUR SHOW YOU COLLAPSE.
THERE IS USUALLY SOME MEMORY LOSS.
Oh.
TAKE YOUR BOW. A SECURITY TEAM WILL ESCORT YOU OFFSTAGE

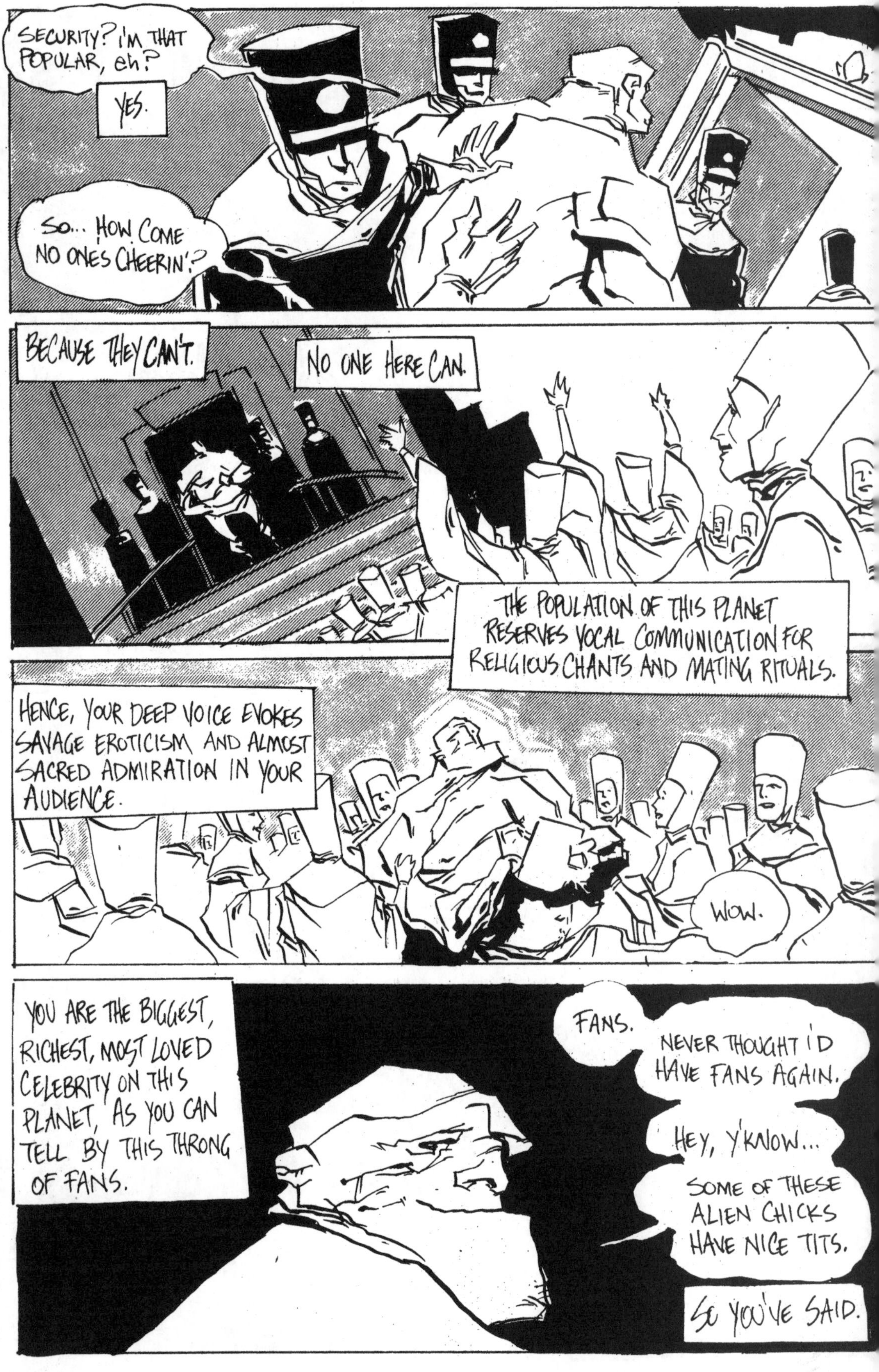
SECURITY? I'M THAT POPULAR, eh?
YES.
SO... HOW COME NO ONE'S CHEERIN'?
BECAUSE THEY CAN'T.
NO ONE HERE CAN.
THE POPULATION OF THIS PLANET RESERVES VOCAL COMMUNICATION FOR RELIGIOUS CHANTS AND MATING RITUALS.
HENCE, YOUR DEEP VOICE EVOKES SAVAGE EROTICISM AND ALMOST SACRED ADMIRATION IN YOUR AUDIENCE.
WOW.
YOU ARE THE BIGGEST, RICHEST, MOST LOVED CELEBRITY ON THIS PLANET, AS YOU CAN TELL BY THIS THRONG OF FANS.
FANS.
NEVER THOUGHT I'D HAVE FANS AGAIN.
HEY, Y'KNOW...
SOME OF THESE ALIEN CHICKS HAVE NICE TITS.
SO YOU'VE SAID.

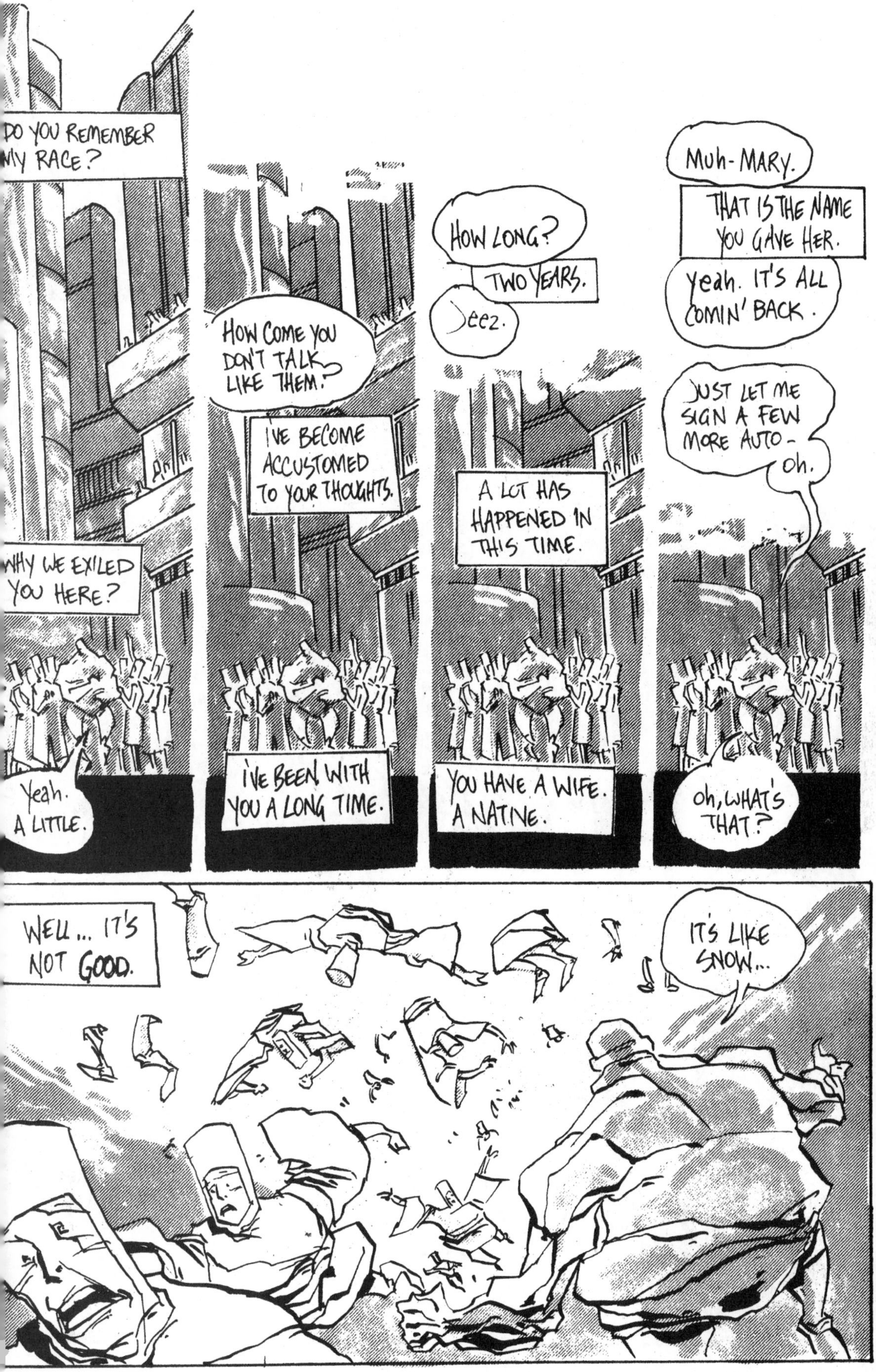
DO YOU REMEMBER MY RACE?
WHY WE EXILED YOU HERE?
Yeah. A LITTLE.
HOW COME YOU DON'T TALK LIKE THEM?
I'VE BECOME ACCUSTOMED TO YOUR THOUGHTS.
I'VE BEEN WITH YOU A LONG TIME.
HOW LONG?
TWO YEARS.
Jeez.
A LOT HAS HAPPENED IN THIS TIME.
YOU HAVE A WIFE. A NATIVE.
Muh-MARY.
THAT IS THE NAME YOU GAVE HER.
yeah. IT'S ALL COMIN' BACK.
JUST LET ME SIGN A FEW MORE AUTO- oh.
oh, WHAT'S THAT?
WELL... IT'S NOT GOOD.
IT'S LIKE SNOW...

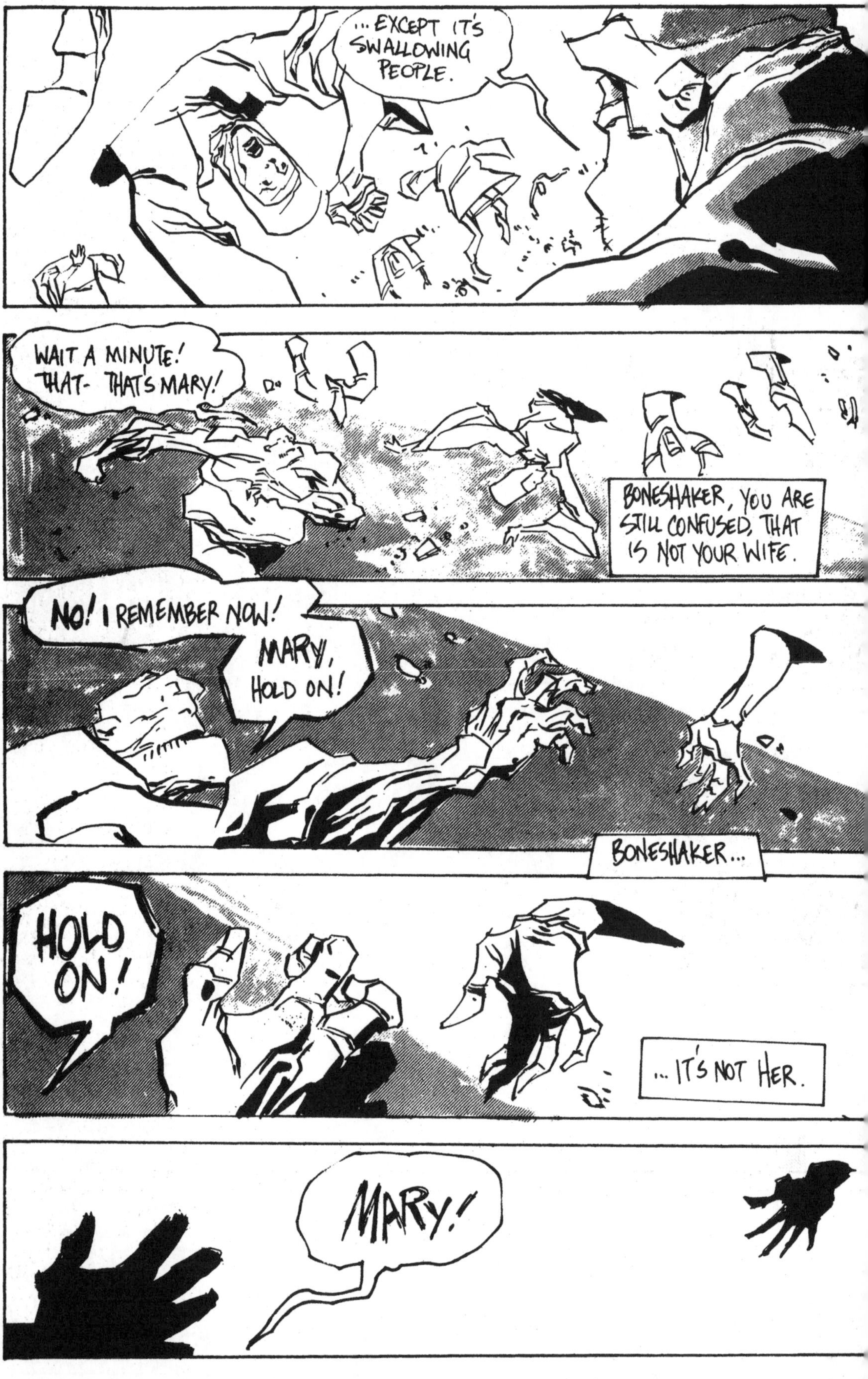
...EXCEPT IT'S SWALLOWING PEOPLE.
WAIT A MINUTE! THAT- THAT'S MARY!
BONESHAKER, YOU ARE STILL CONFUSED, THAT IS NOT YOUR WIFE.
NO! I REMEMBER NOW!
MARY, HOLD ON!
BONESHAKER...
HOLD ON!
...IT'S NOT HER.
MARY!

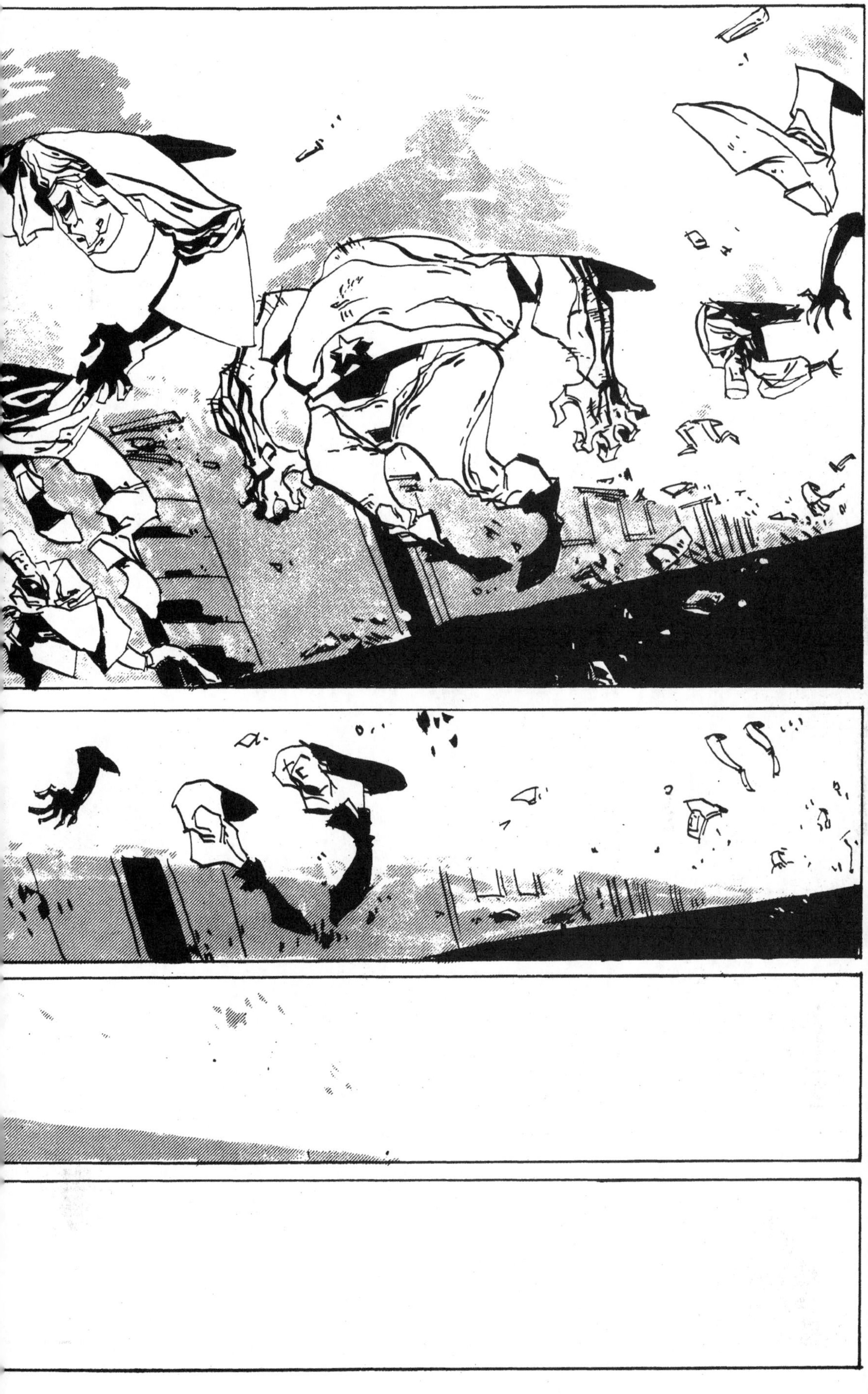

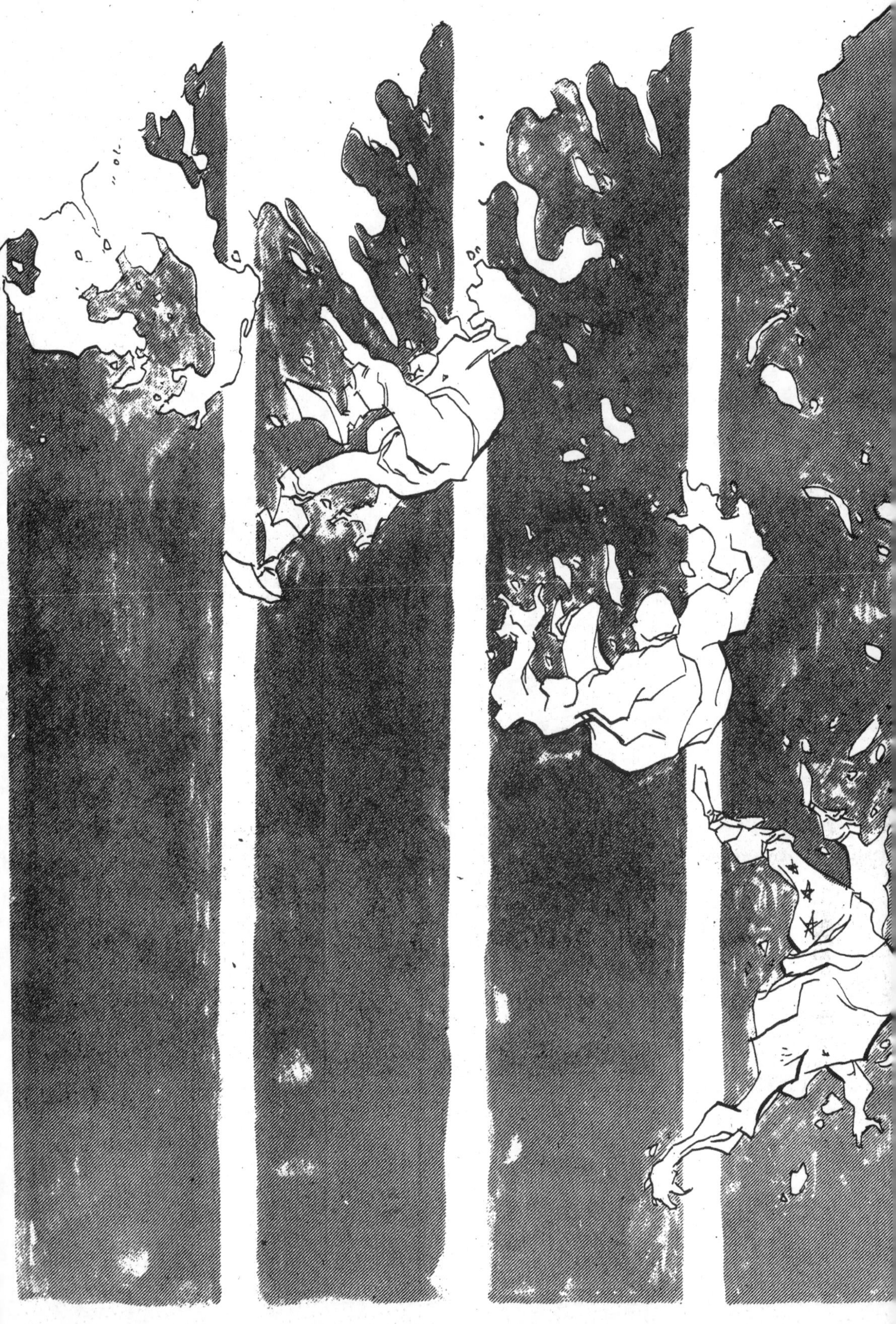

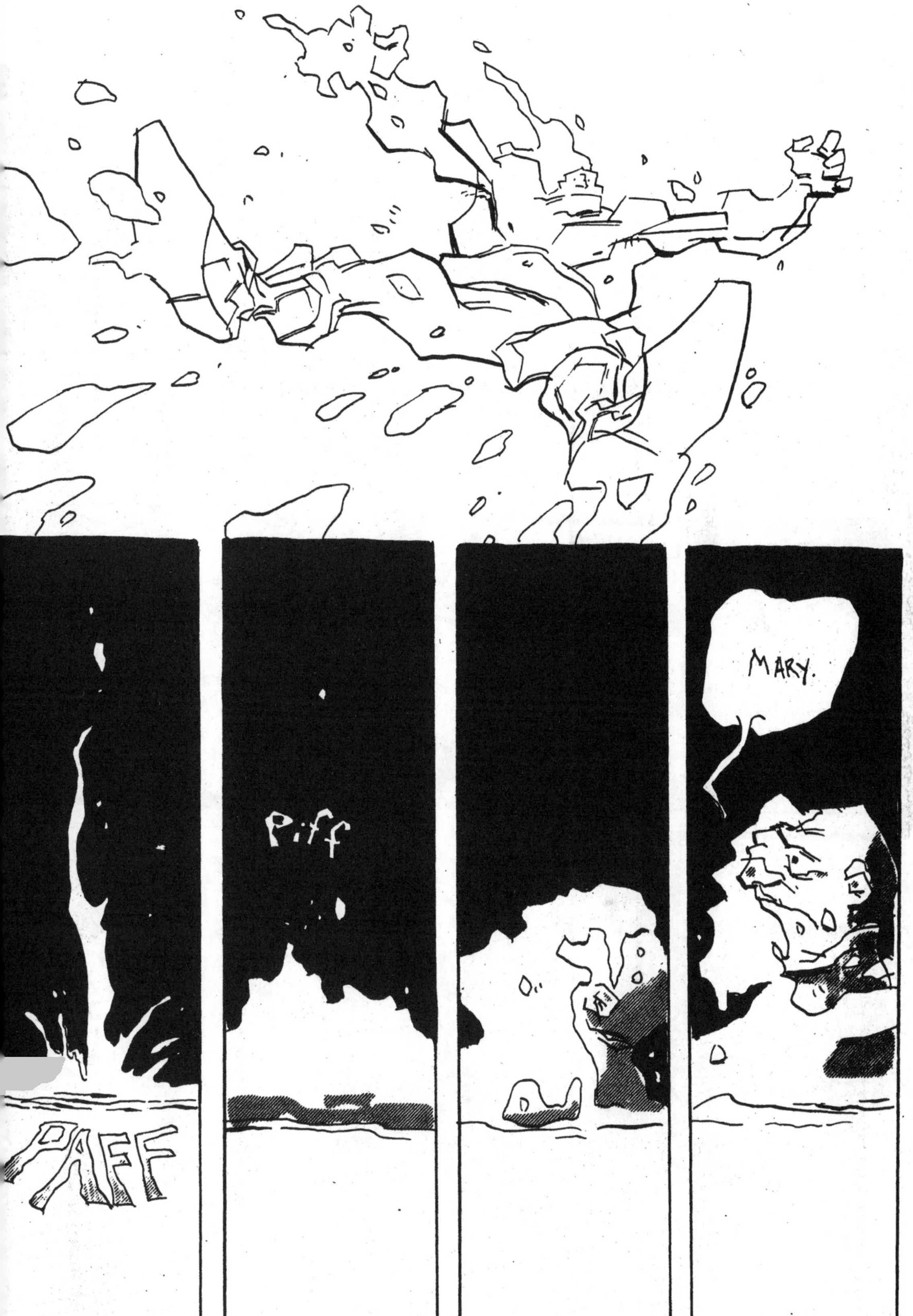
PAFF
Piff
MARY.

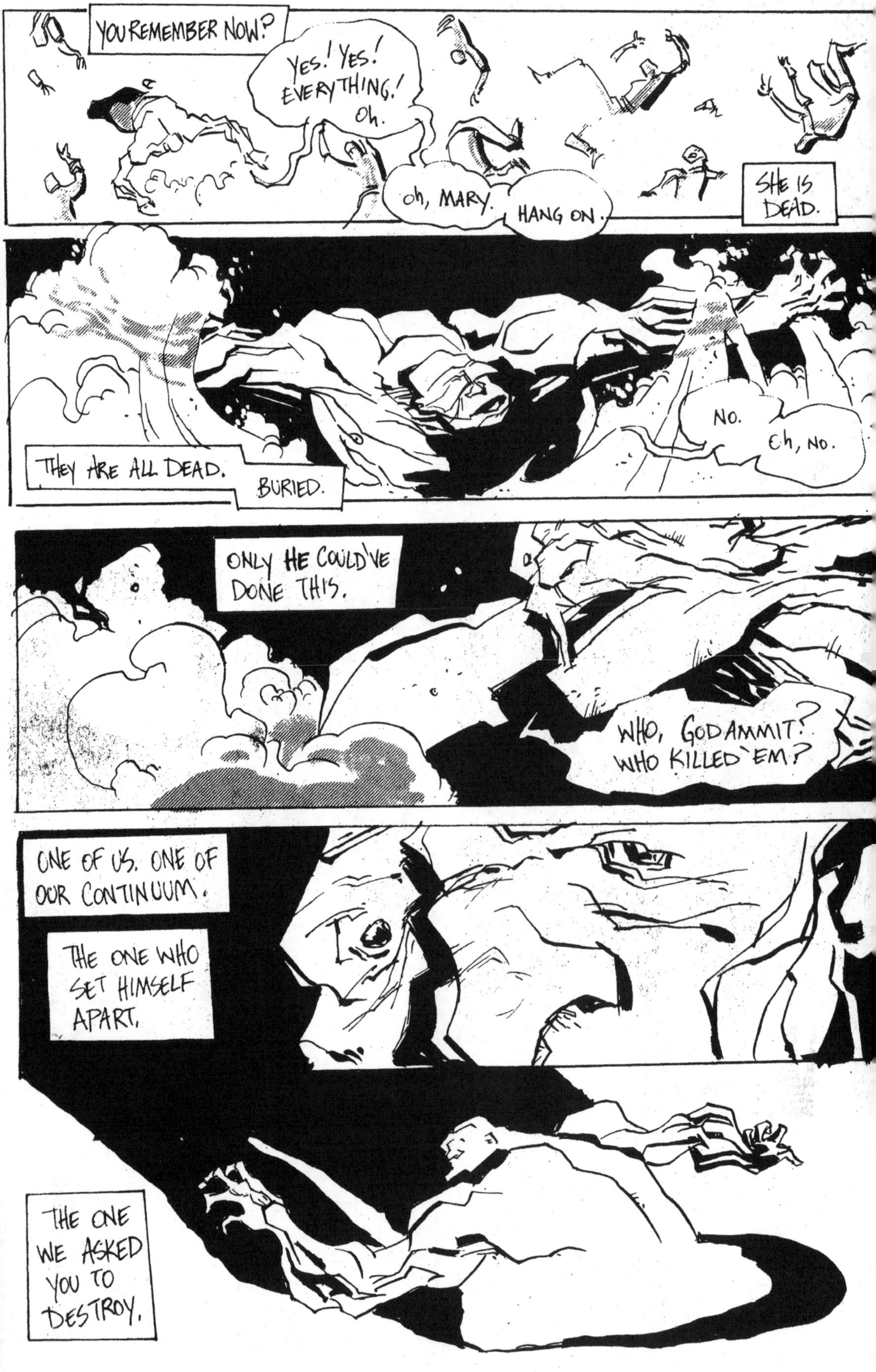

YOU REMEMBER NOW?
YES! YES! EVERYTHING! Oh.
Oh, MARY.
HANG ON.
SHE IS DEAD.
THEY ARE ALL DEAD.
BURIED.
NO. Oh, NO.
ONLY HE COULD'VE DONE THIS.
WHO, GODAMMIT? WHO KILLED 'EM?
ONE OF US. ONE OF OUR CONTINUUM.
THE ONE WHO SET HIMSELF APART.
THE ONE WE ASKED YOU TO DESTROY.

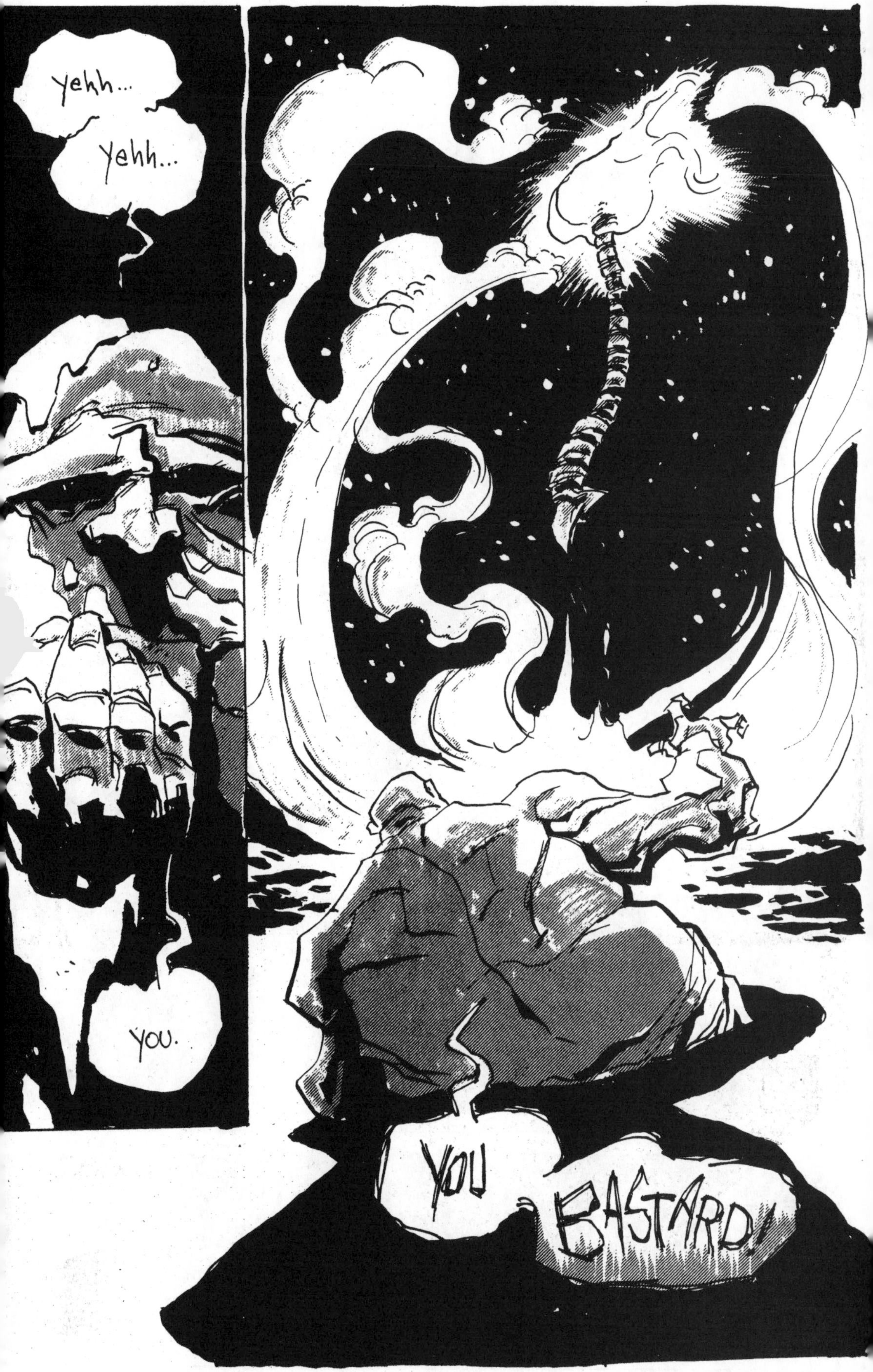
yehh...
yehh...
YOU.
YOU
BASTARD!

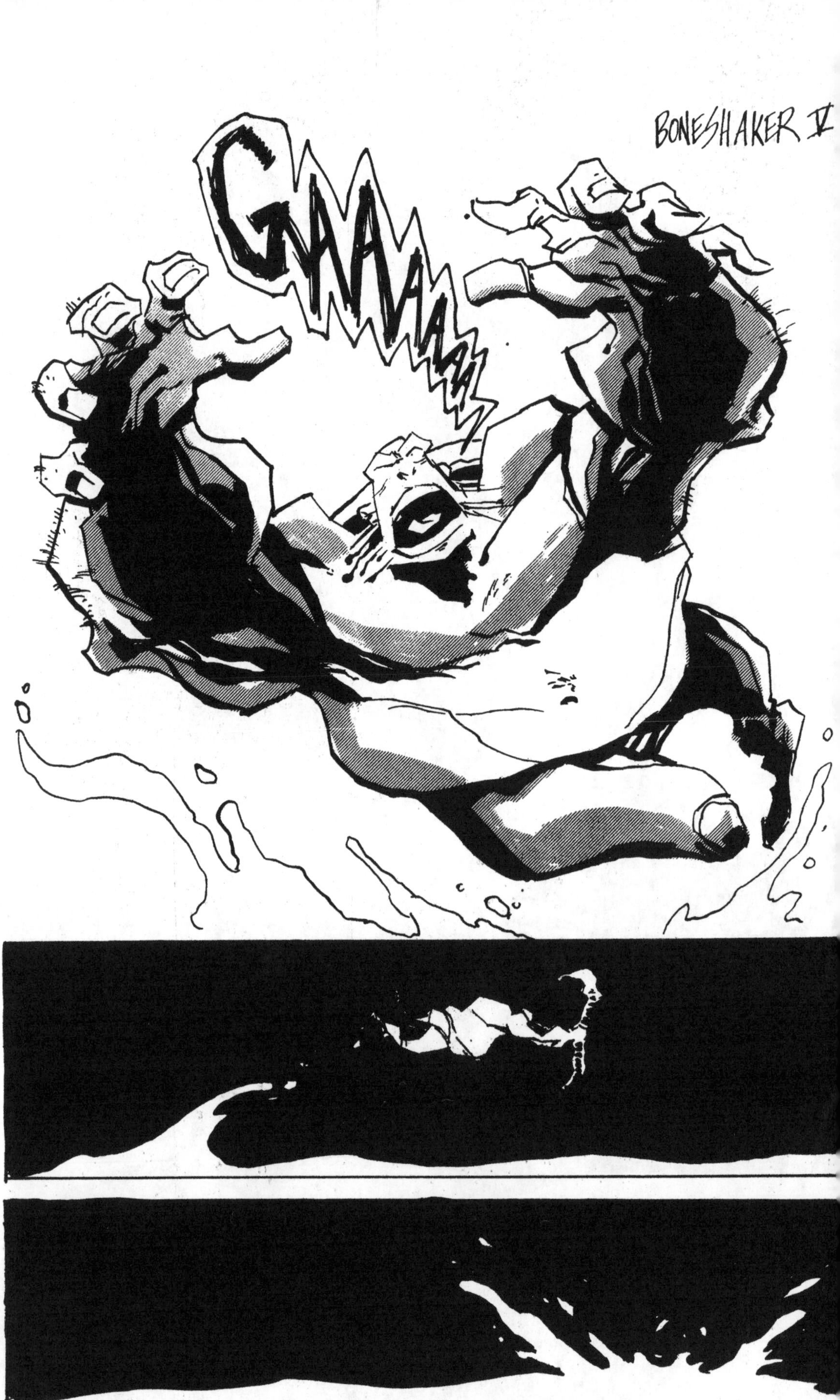
GAAAAAAAA

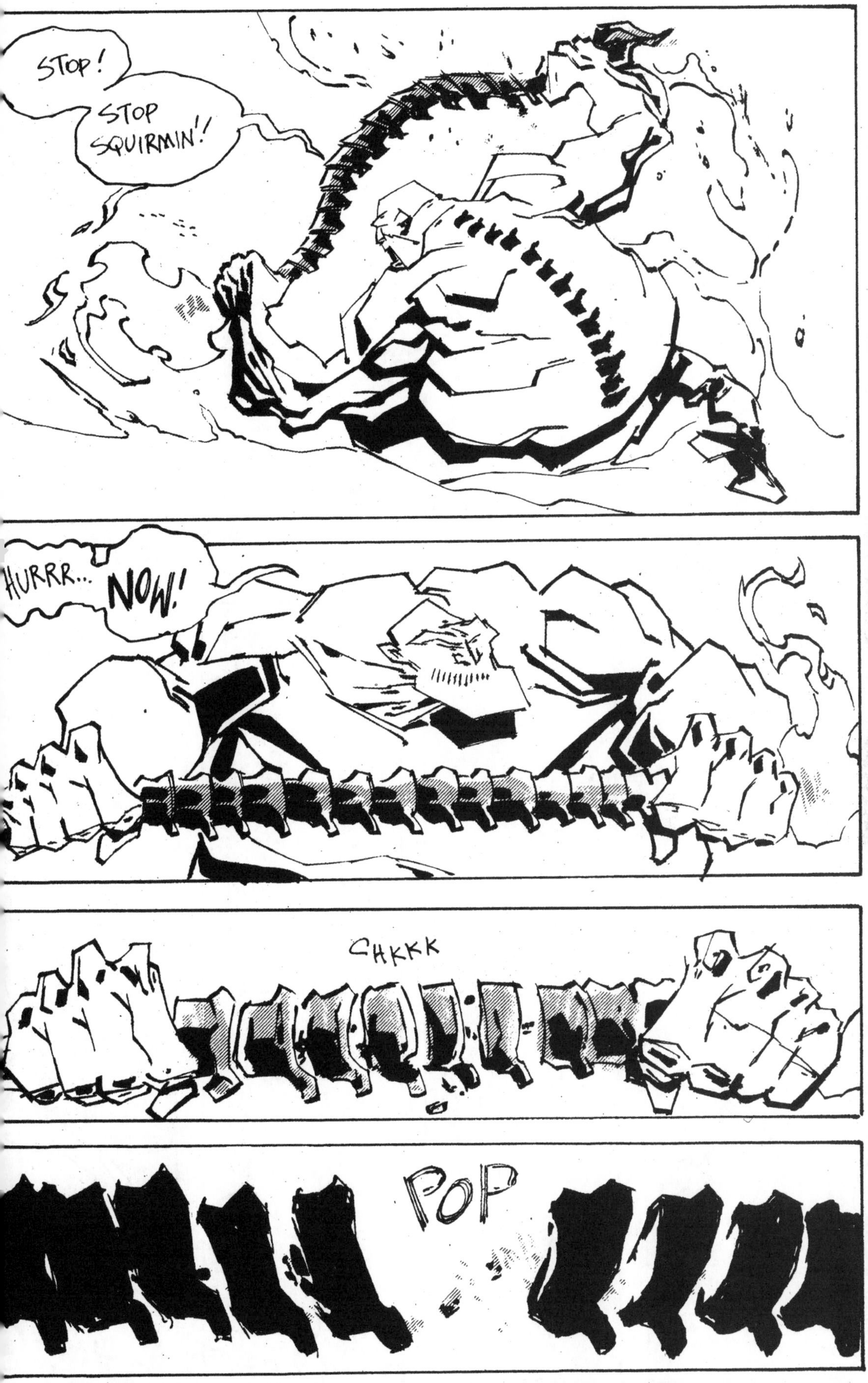

STOP!
STOP SQUIRMIN'!!
HURRR... NOW!
CHKKK
POP

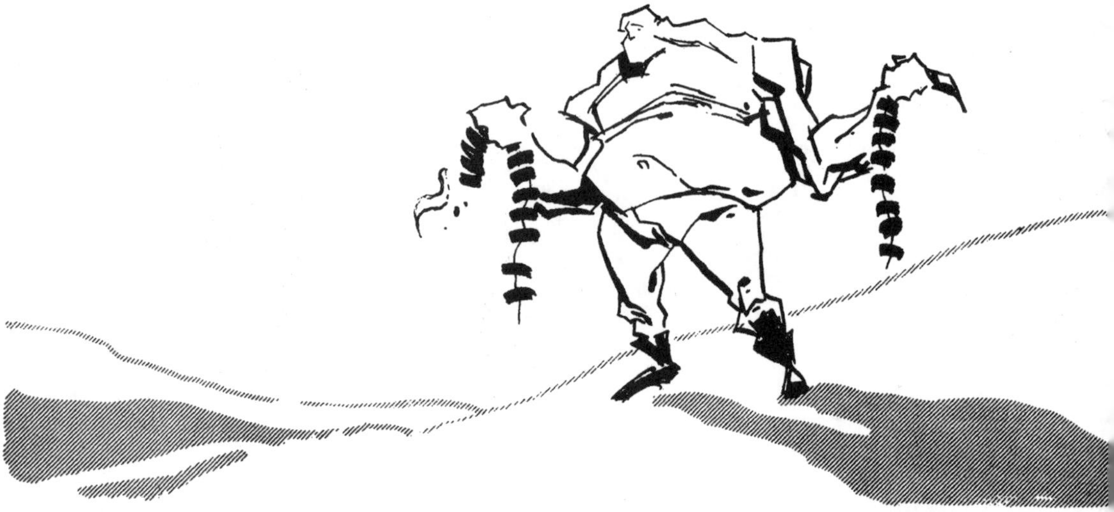

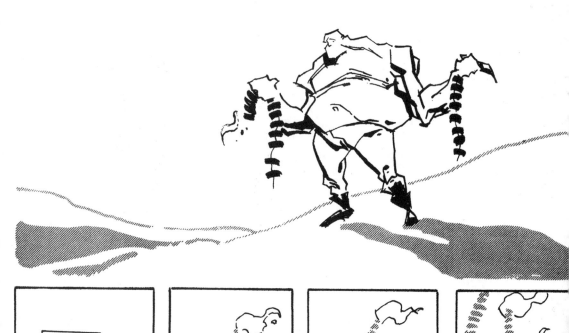

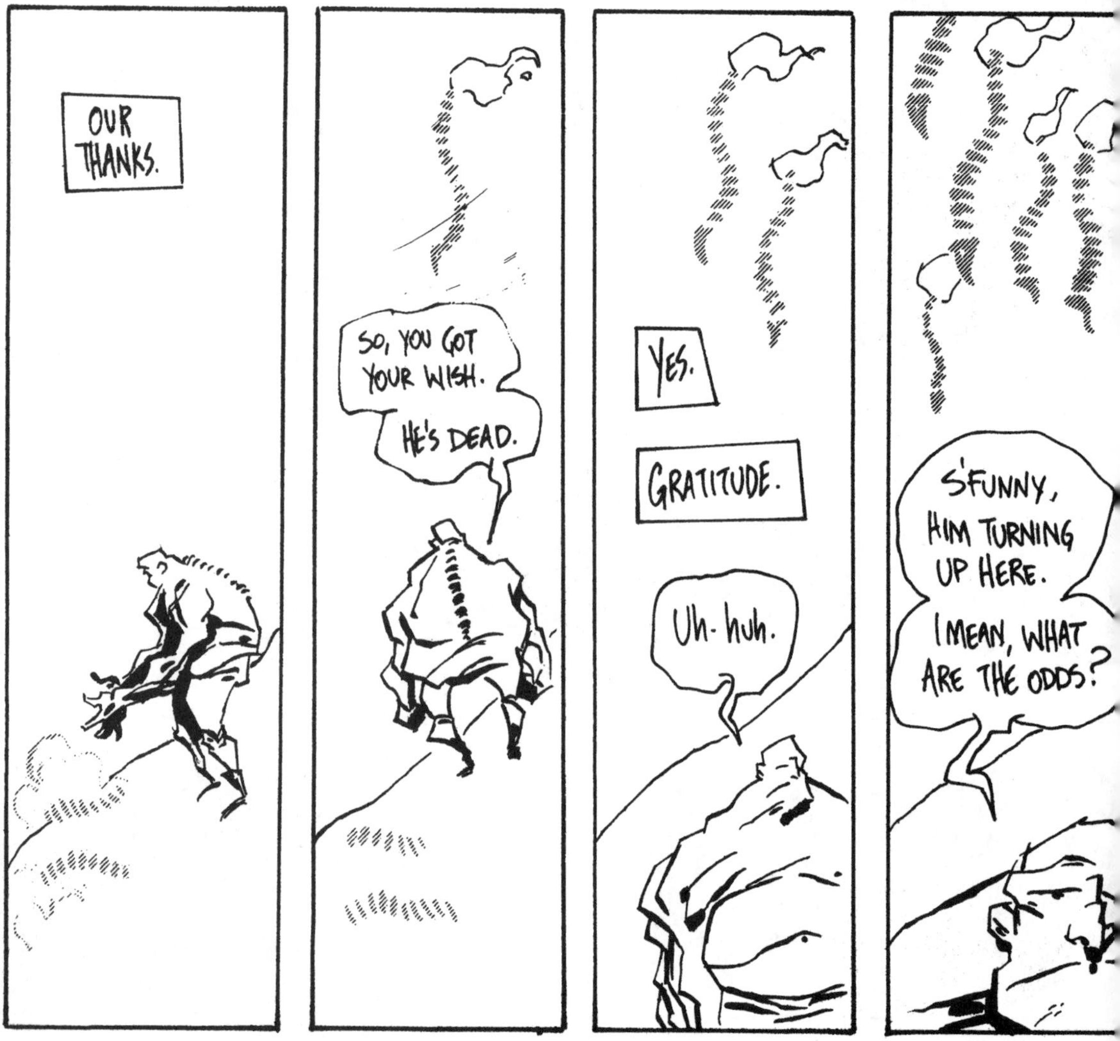
OUR THANKS.
SO, YOU GOT YOUR WISH.
HE'S DEAD.
YES.
GRATITUDE.
Uh-huh.
S'FUNNY, HIM TURNING UP HERE.
I MEAN, WHAT ARE THE ODDS?

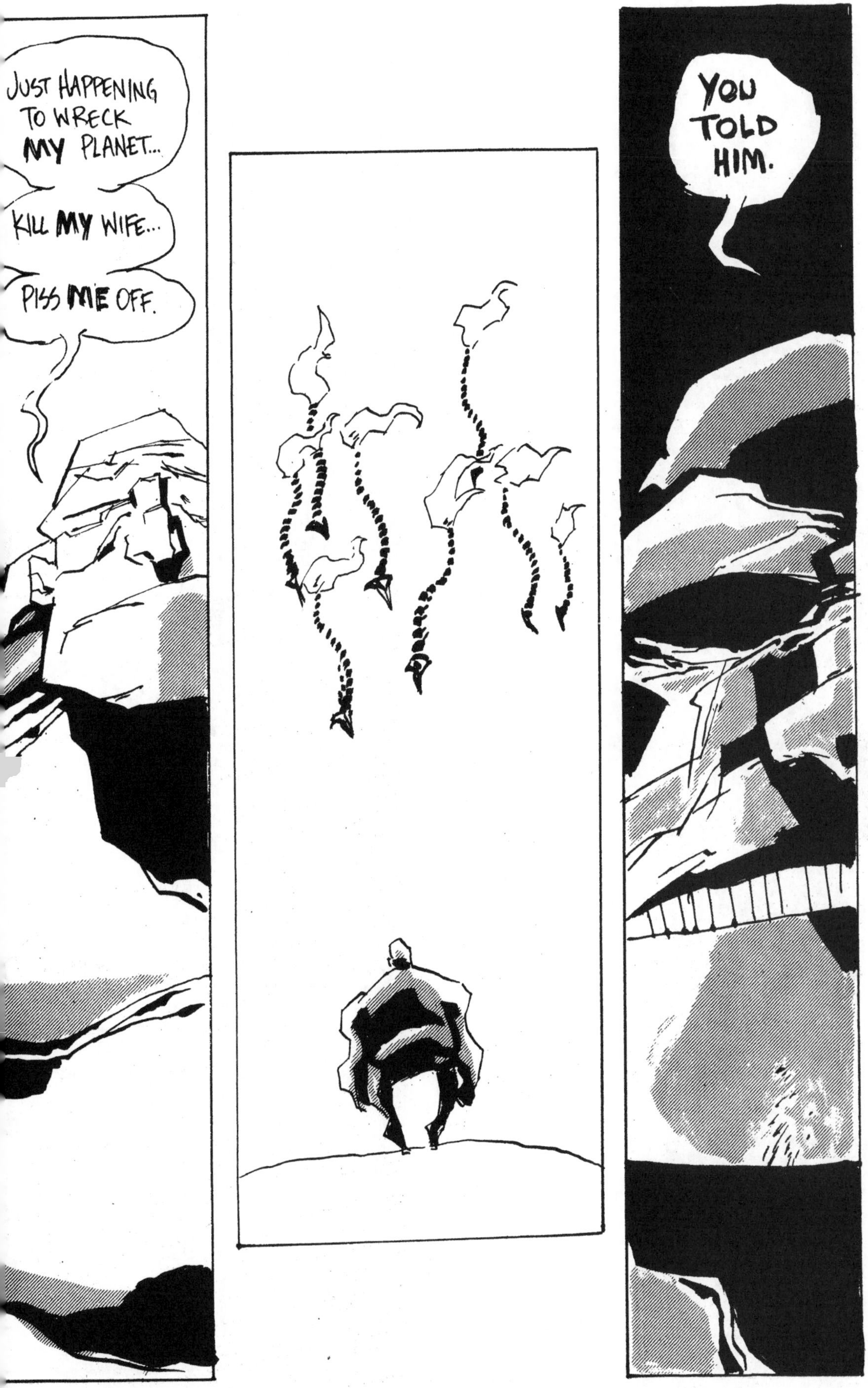
JUST HAPPENING TO WRECK MY PLANET...
KILL MY WIFE...
PISS ME OFF.
YOU TOLD HIM.

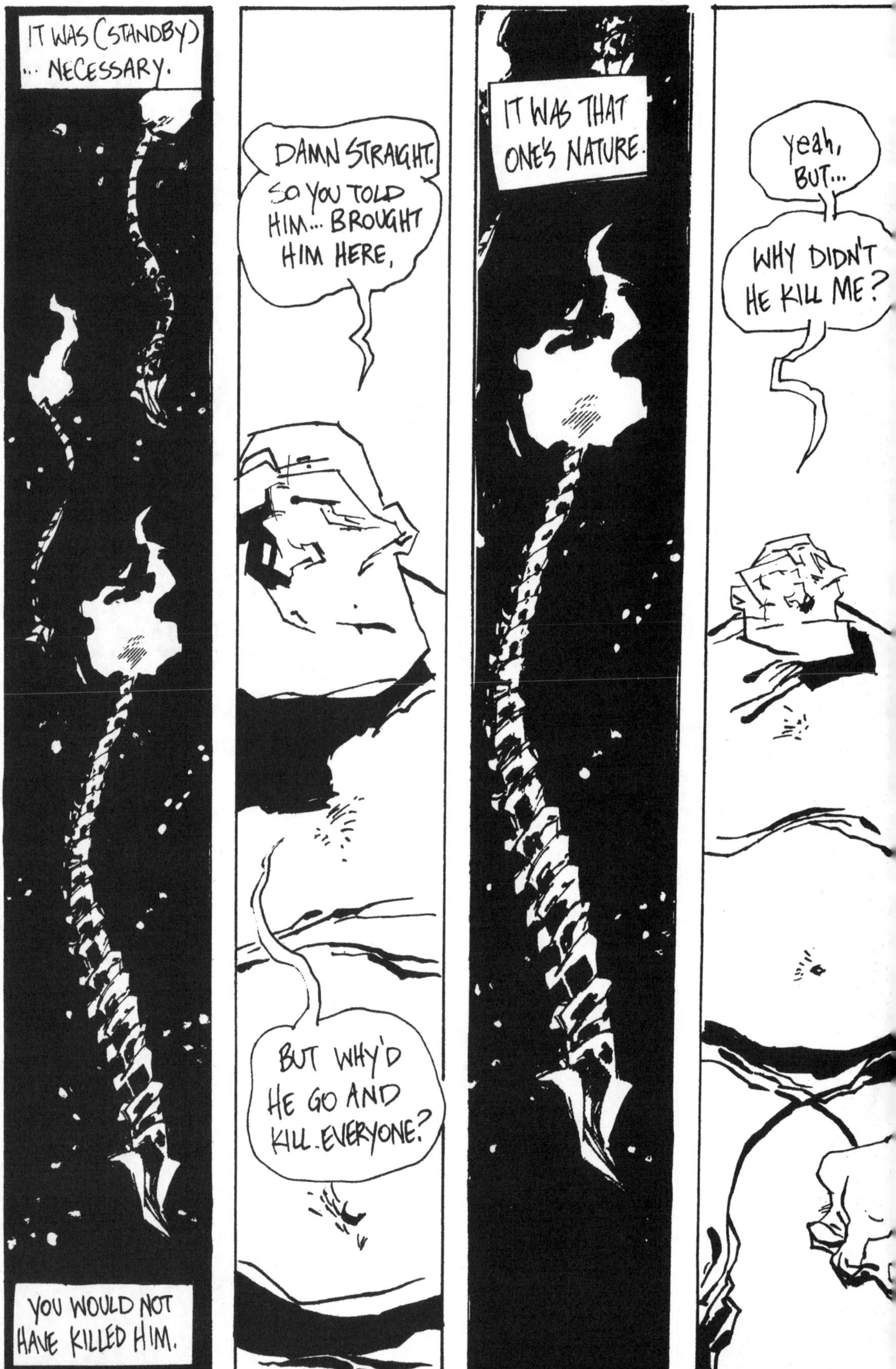
IT WAS (STANDBY) ... NECESSARY.
YOU WOULD NOT HAVE KILLED HIM.
DAMN STRAIGHT.
SO YOU TOLD HIM... BROUGHT HIM HERE,
BUT WHY'D HE GO AND KILL EVERYONE?
IT WAS THAT ONE'S NATURE.
Yeah, BUT...
WHY DIDN'T HE KILL ME?

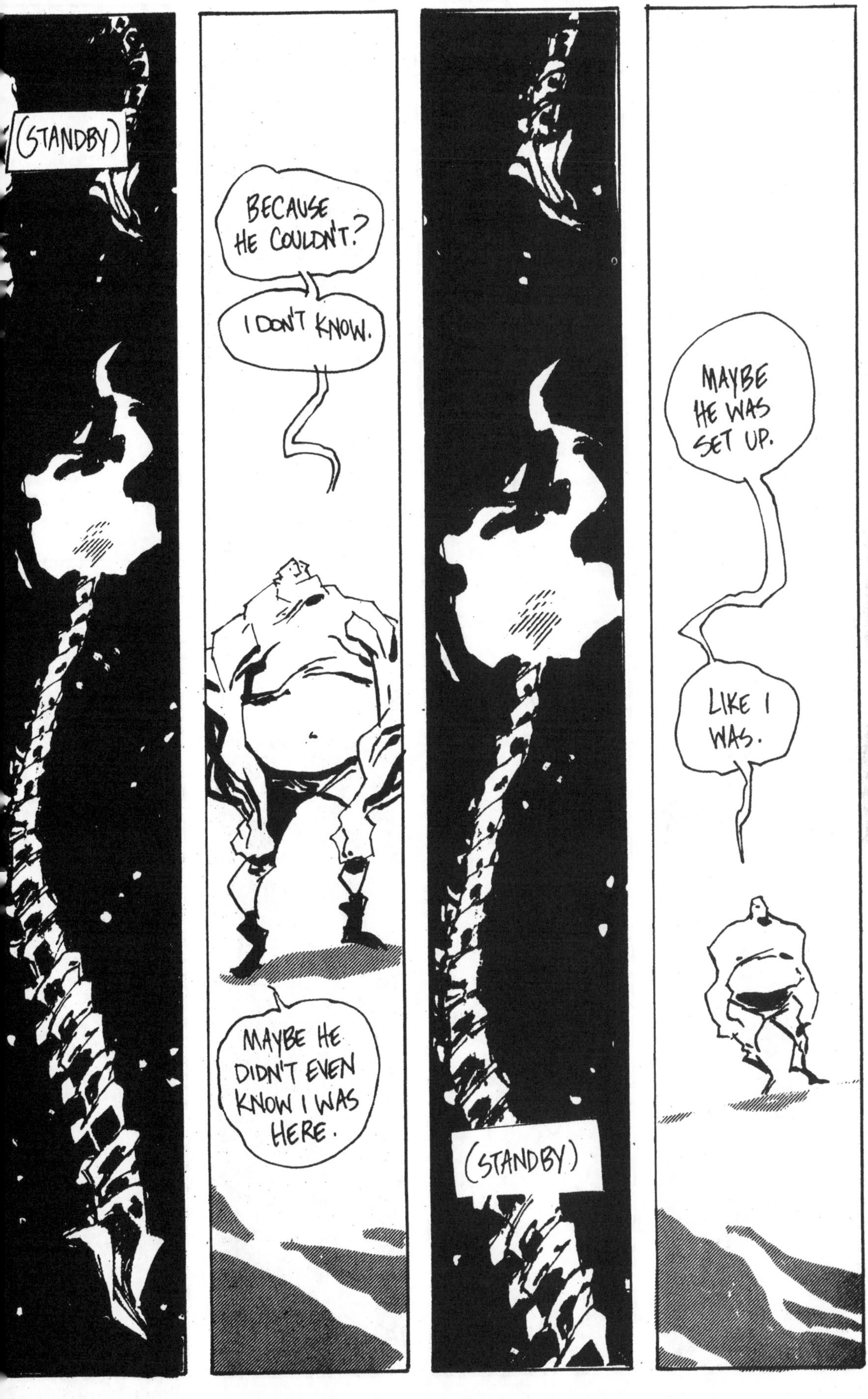
(STANDBY)
BECAUSE HE COULDN'T?
I DON'T KNOW.
MAYBE HE DIDN'T EVEN KNOW I WAS HERE.
(STANDBY)
MAYBE HE WAS SET UP.
LIKE I WAS.

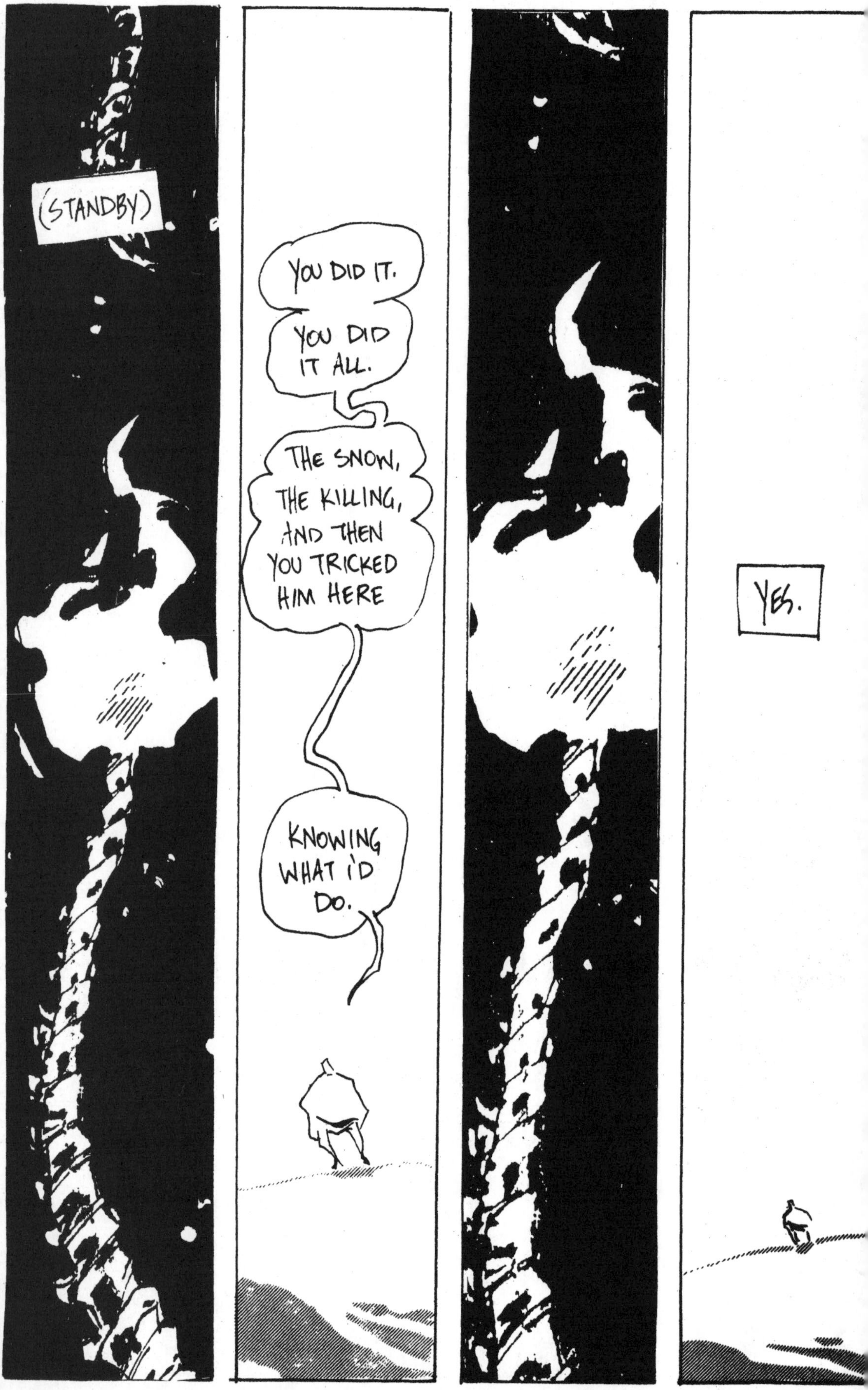
(STANDBY)
YOU DID IT.
YOU DID IT ALL.
THE SNOW, THE KILLING, AND THEN YOU TRICKED HIM HERE
KNOWING WHAT I'D DO.
YES.

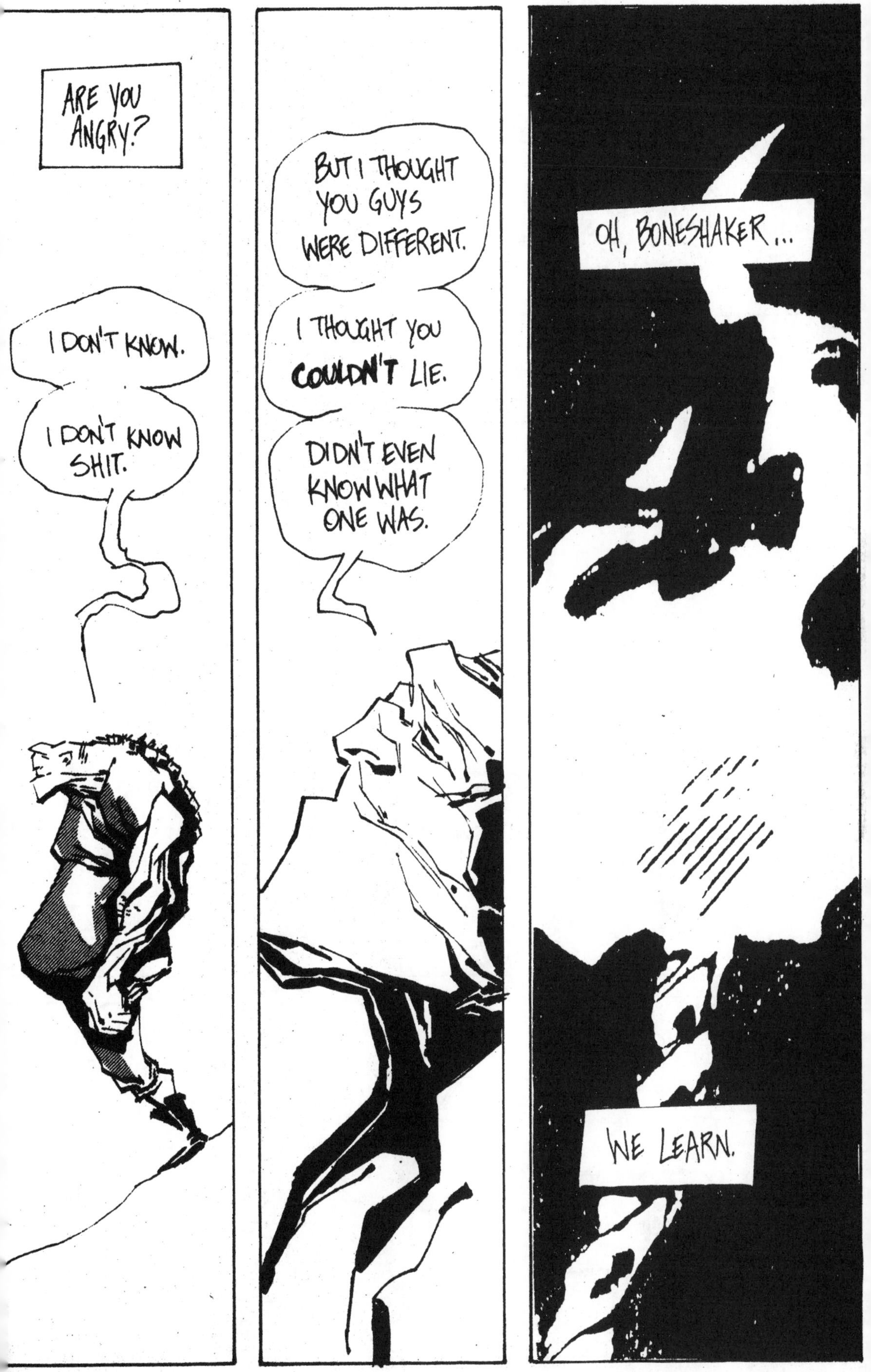
ARE YOU ANGRY?
I DON'T KNOW.
I DON'T KNOW SHIT.
BUT I THOUGHT YOU GUYS WERE DIFFERENT.
I THOUGHT YOU COULDN'T LIE.
DIDN'T EVEN KNOW WHAT ONE WAS.
OH, BONESHAKER...
WE LEARN.

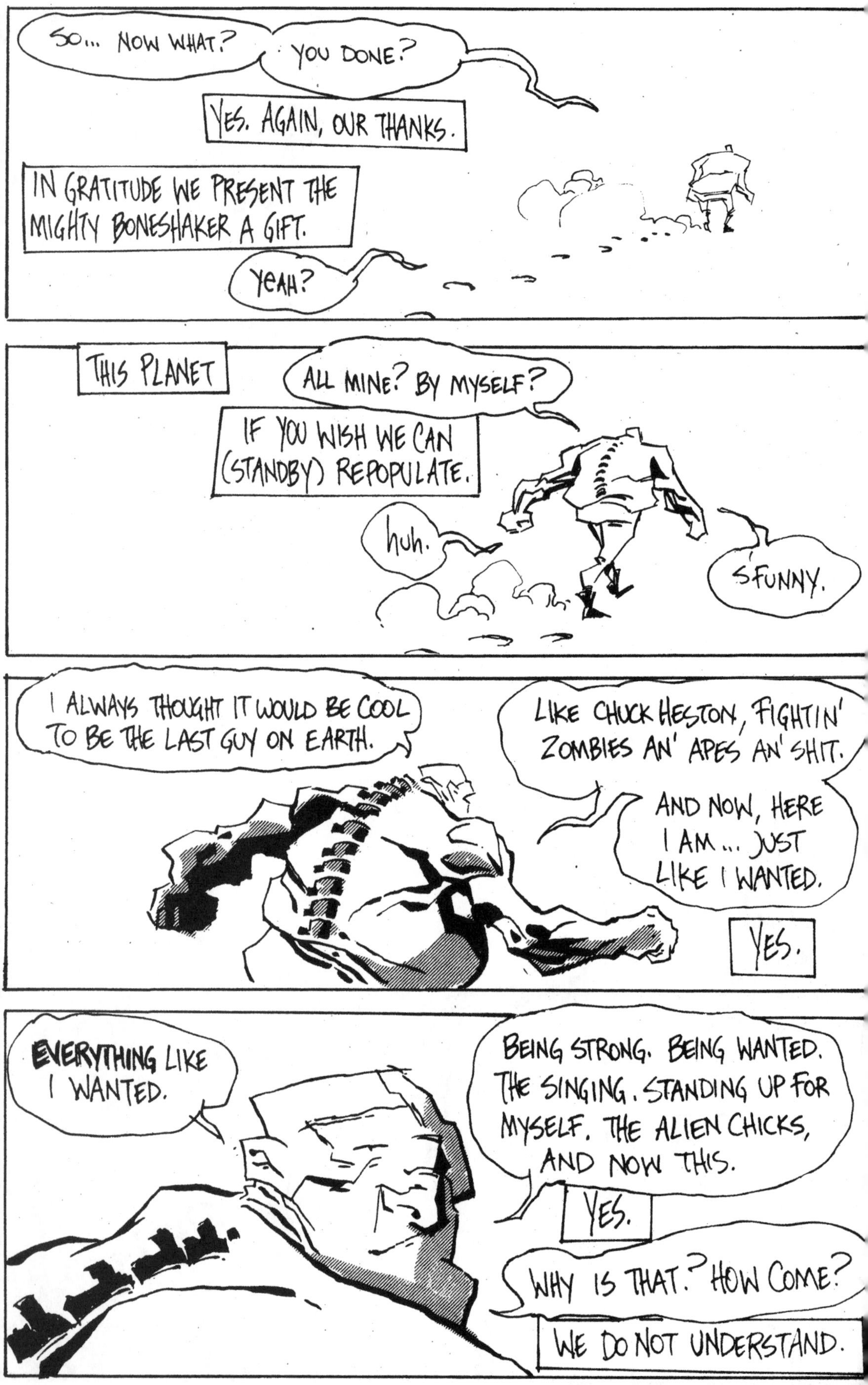
SO... NOW WHAT?
YOU DONE?
YES. AGAIN, OUR THANKS.
IN GRATITUDE WE PRESENT THE MIGHTY BONESHAKER A GIFT.
YEAH?
THIS PLANET
ALL MINE? BY MYSELF?
IF YOU WISH WE CAN (STANDBY) REPOPULATE.
huh.
S'FUNNY.
I ALWAYS THOUGHT IT WOULD BE COOL TO BE THE LAST GUY ON EARTH.
LIKE CHUCK HESTON, FIGHTIN' ZOMBIES AN' APES AN' SHIT.
AND NOW, HERE I AM... JUST LIKE I WANTED.
YES.
EVERYTHING LIKE I WANTED.
BEING STRONG. BEING WANTED. THE SINGING. STANDING UP FOR MYSELF. THE ALIEN CHICKS, AND NOW THIS.
YES.
WHY IS THAT? HOW COME?
WE DO NOT UNDERSTAND.

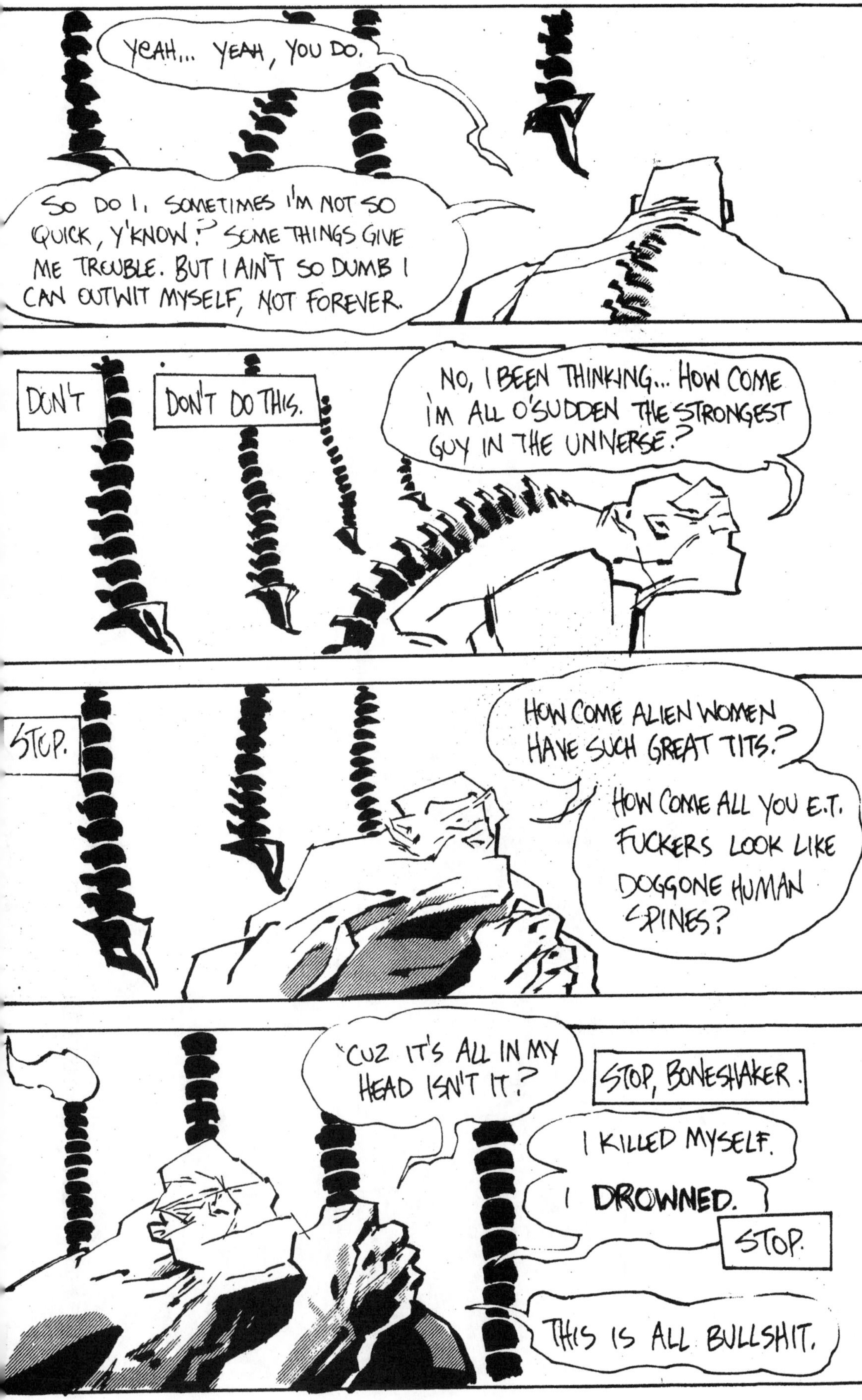
YEAH... YEAH, YOU DO.
SO DO I. SOMETIMES I'M NOT SO QUICK, Y'KNOW? SOME THINGS GIVE ME TROUBLE. BUT I AIN'T SO DUMB I CAN OUTWIT MYSELF, NOT FOREVER.
DON'T
DON'T DO THIS.
NO, I BEEN THINKING... HOW COME I'M ALL O'SUDDEN THE STRONGEST GUY IN THE UNIVERSE?
STOP.
HOW COME ALIEN WOMEN HAVE SUCH GREAT TITS?
HOW COME ALL YOU E.T. FUCKERS LOOK LIKE DOGGONE HUMAN SPINES?
'CUZ IT'S ALL IN MY HEAD ISN'T IT?
STOP, BONESHAKER.
I KILLED MYSELF.
I DROWNED.
STOP.
THIS IS ALL BULLSHIT.

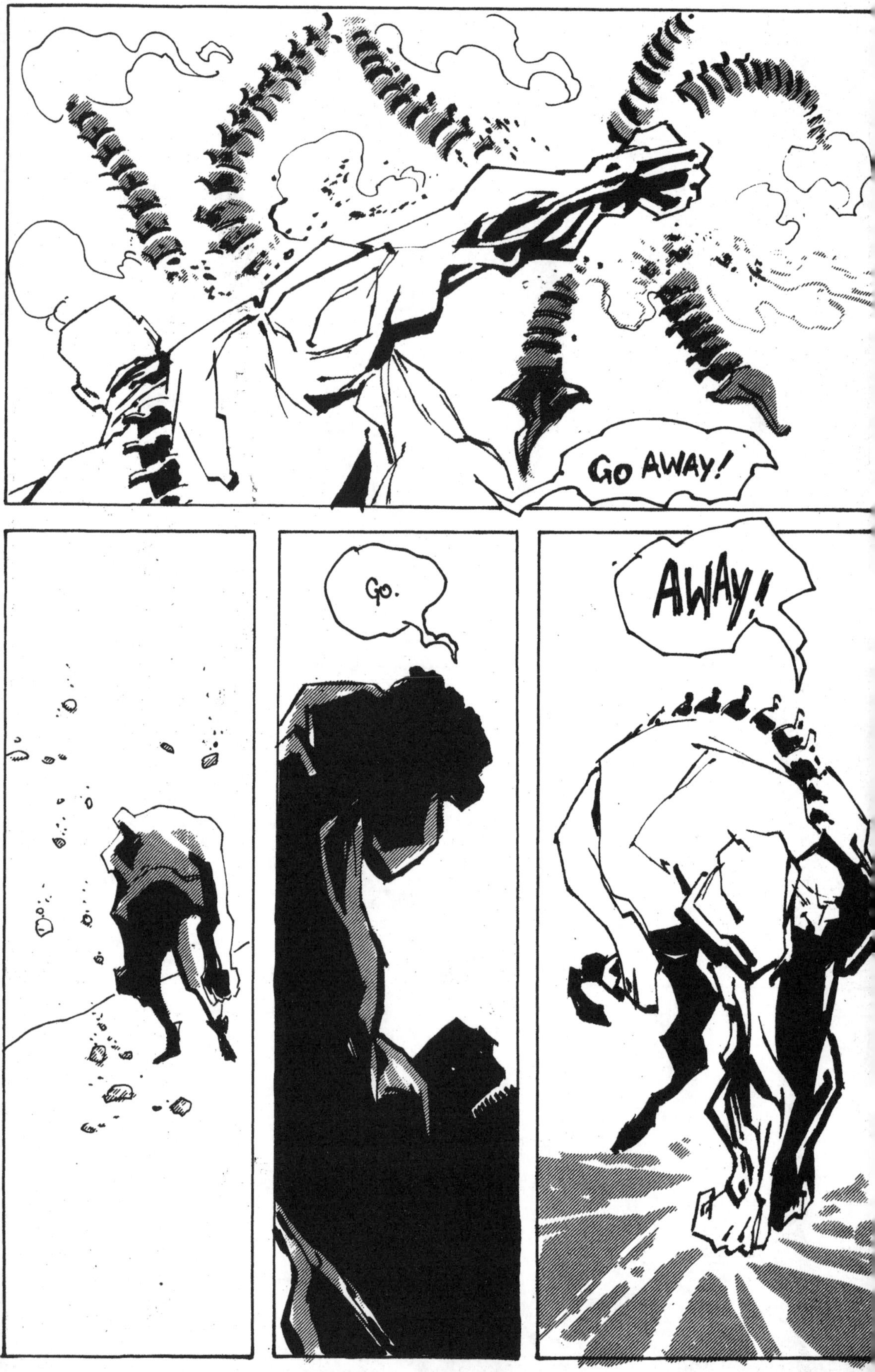
GO AWAY!
GO.
AWAY!

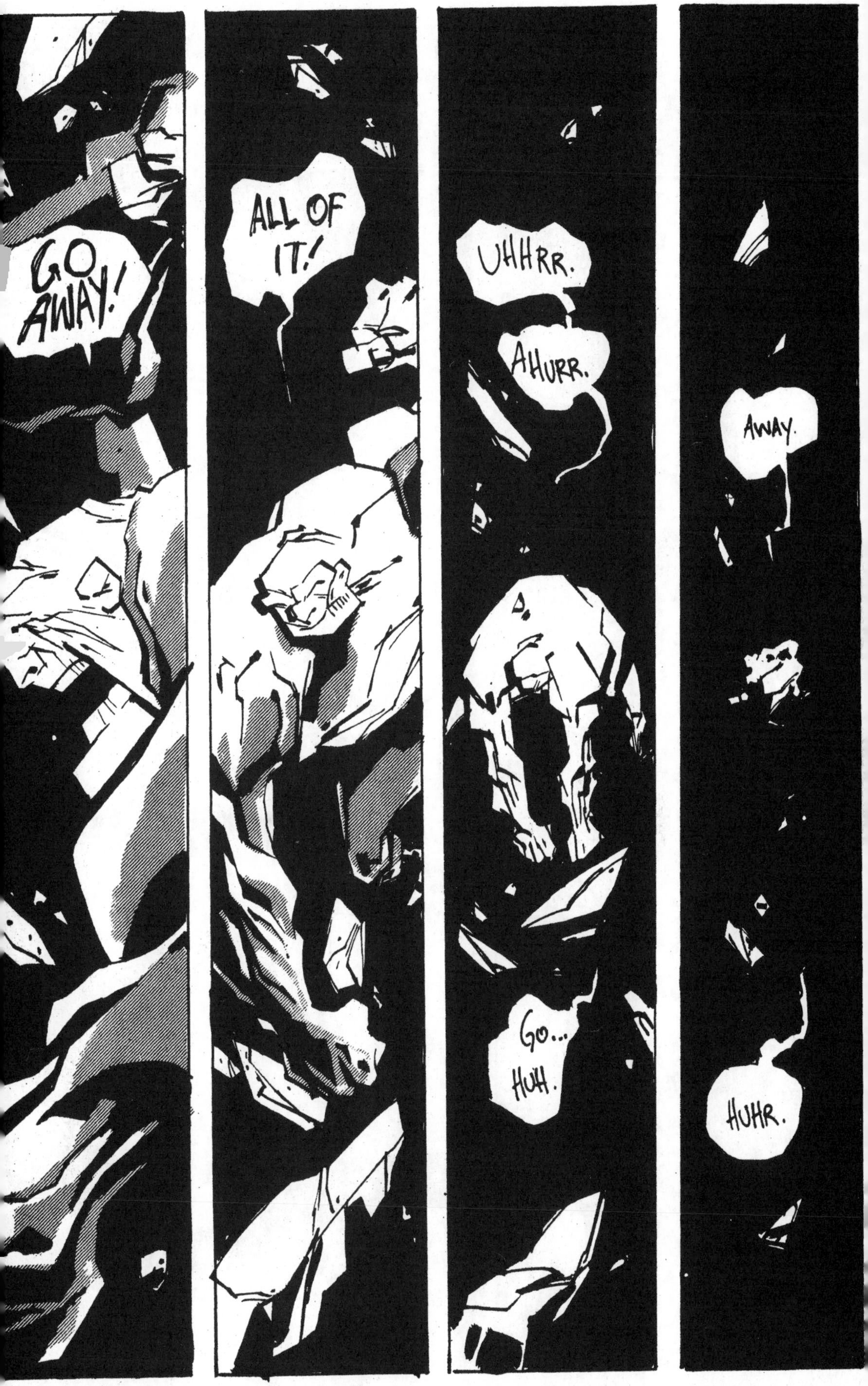
GO AWAY!
ALL OF IT!
UHHRR.
AHURR.
GO... HUH.
AWAY.
HUHR.

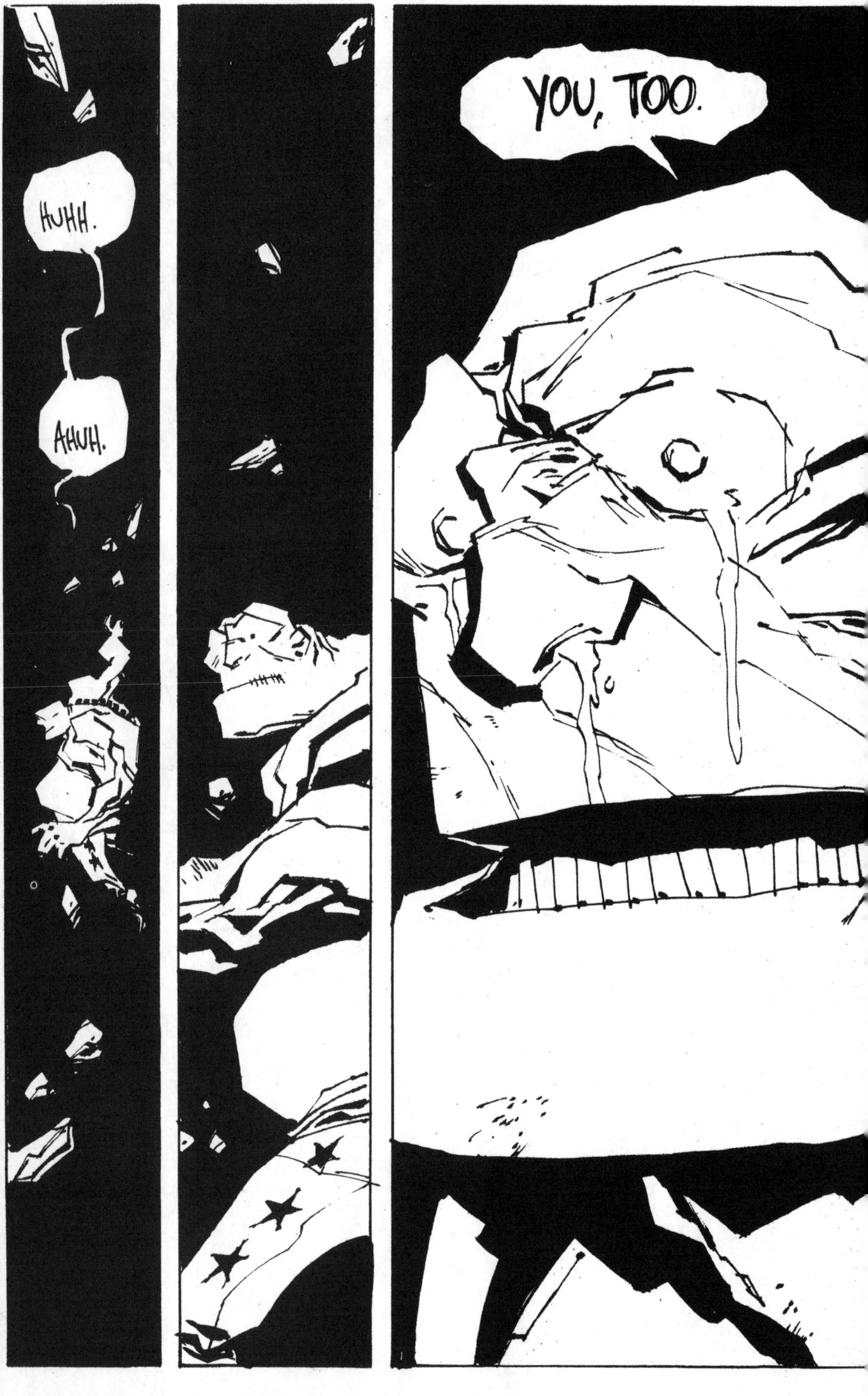
HUHH.
AHUH.
YOU, TOO.

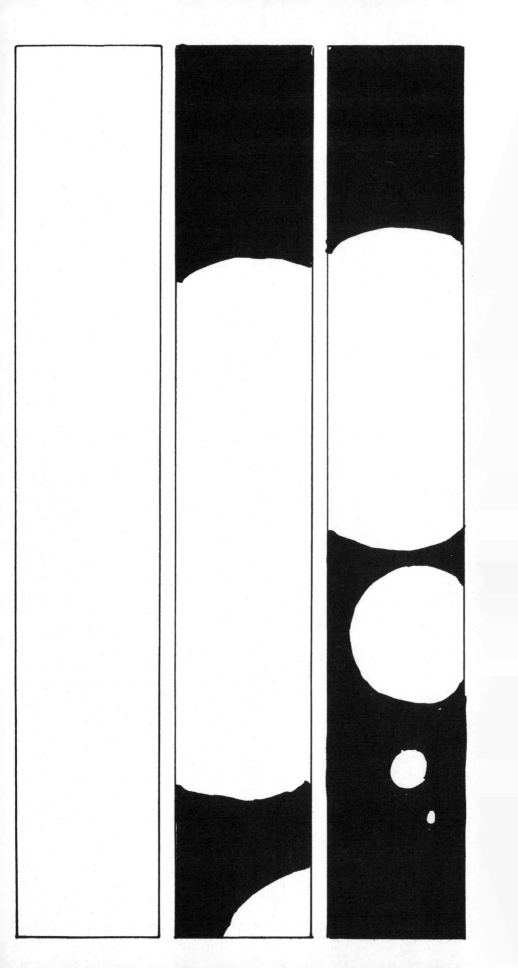

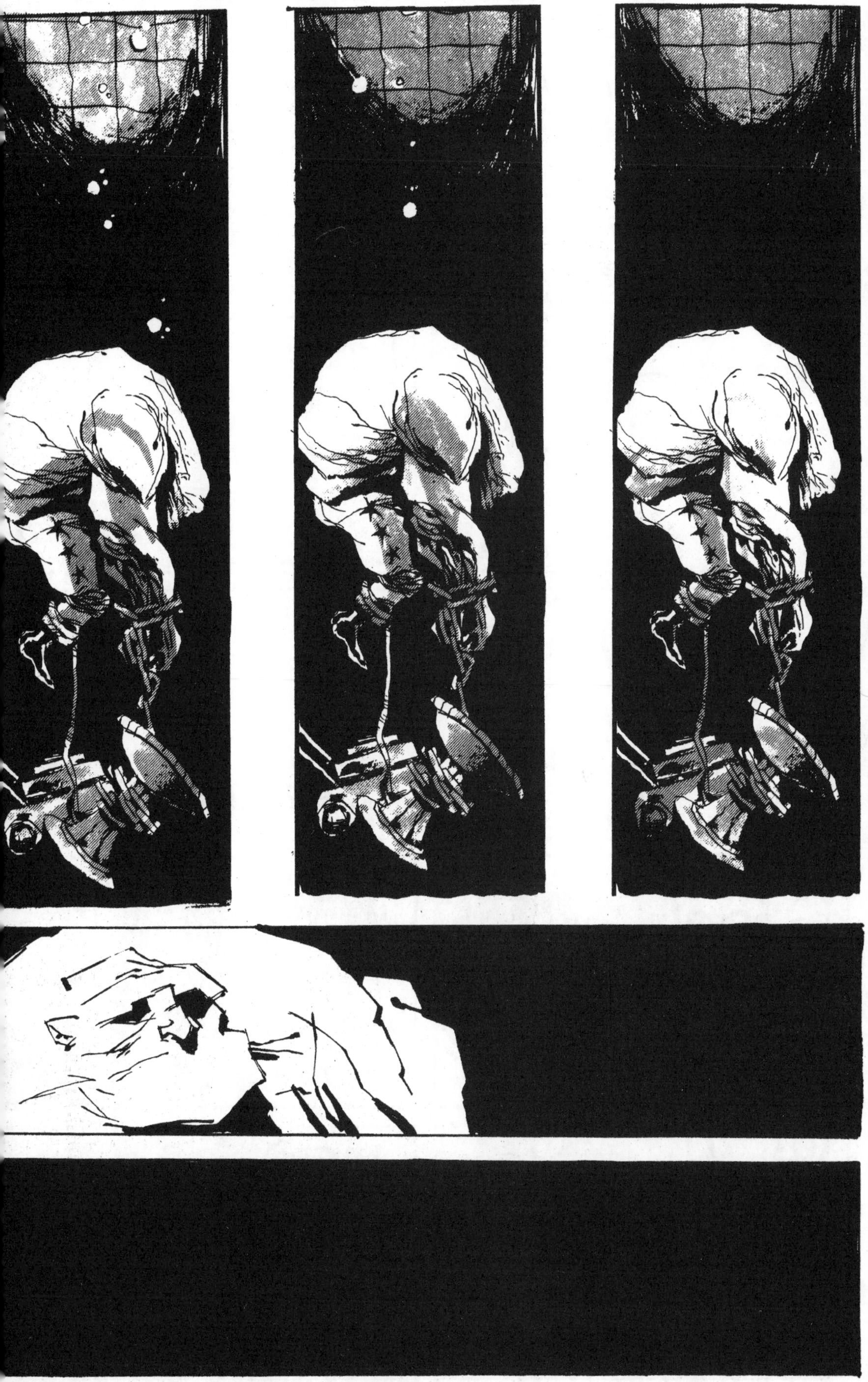

END

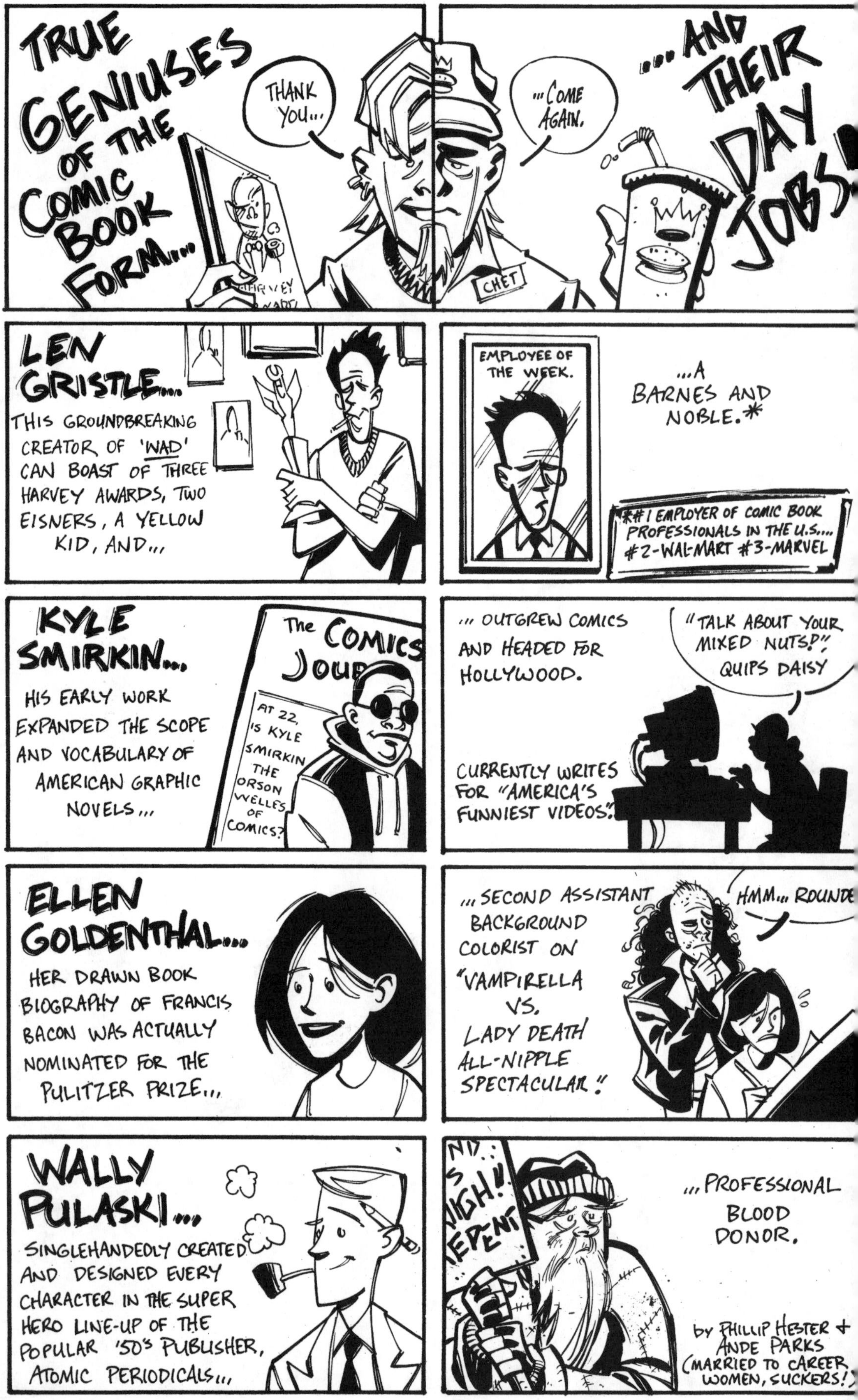
TRUE GENIUSES OF THE COMIC BOOK FORM...
THANK YOU...
...COME AGAIN.
CHET
...AND THEIR DAY JOBS!
LEN GRISTLE...
THIS GROUNDBREAKING CREATOR OF 'WAD' CAN BOAST OF THREE HARVEY AWARDS, TWO EISNERS, A YELLOW KID, AND...
EMPLOYEE OF THE WEEK.
...A BARNES AND NOBLE.*
*#1 EMPLOYER OF COMIC BOOK PROFESSIONALS IN THE U.S.... #2-WAL-MART #3-MARVEL
KYLE SMIRKIN...
HIS EARLY WORK EXPANDED THE SCOPE AND VOCABULARY OF AMERICAN GRAPHIC NOVELS...
The COMICS JOU
AT 22, IS KYLE SMIRKIN THE ORSON WELLES OF COMICS?
...OUTGREW COMICS AND HEADED FOR HOLLYWOOD.
"TALK ABOUT YOUR MIXED NUTS!" QUIPS DAISY
CURRENTLY WRITES FOR "AMERICA'S FUNNIEST VIDEOS."
ELLEN GOLDENTHAL...
HER DRAWN BOOK BIOGRAPHY OF FRANCIS BACON WAS ACTUALLY NOMINATED FOR THE PULITZER PRIZE...
...SECOND ASSISTANT BACKGROUND COLORIST ON "VAMPIRELLA VS. LADY DEATH ALL-NIPPLE SPECTACULAR!"
HMM... ROUNDE
WALLY PULASKI...
SINGLEHANDEDLY CREATED AND DESIGNED EVERY CHARACTER IN THE SUPER HERO LINE-UP OF THE POPULAR '50'S PUBLISHER, ATOMIC PERIODICALS...
...PROFESSIONAL BLOOD DONOR.
by PHILLIP HESTER + ANDE PARKS (MARRIED TO CAREER WOMEN, SUCKERS!)